Climbing in North America

Climbing
in
North
America

Chris Jones

Published for the American Alpine Club by the
University of California Press
Berkeley • Los Angeles • London

iv

University of California Press
Berkeley and Los Angeles, California

University of California Press, Ltd.
London, England

Copyright © 1976, by
The Regents of the University of California

ISBN 0–520–02976-3
Library of Congress Catalog Card Number: 75-3771
Printed in the United States of America

Designed by Geri Davis

Contents

Foreword

The sport of mountain climbing was invented in the Alps over two hundred years ago, and more histories of alpinism have been written than anyone can remember. Chris Jones, however, has written the *first* complete history of mountaineering in North America. It is a remarkable saga of exploration, discovery and high adventure—the evolution of a new sport to fit the mountains of a new continent. It is equally remarkable for a book on mountaineering to be at once popular, authentic, serious and entertaining. You are about to read such a book.

For all its intrinsic excitement, mountaineering is a subtle and difficult subject. The wild inaccuracies and antic confusions of popular books and films are legendary among climbers. The climber's reality is so different (and so much more fascinating) than the false heroics that have been sold for mass consumption that we would be suspicious indeed if a non-climbing author were to attempt to write such a history. But Chris Jones is himself a climber of great accomplishment, and so has been able to approach his task with an insider's awareness of what climbing is really about.

An authentic history of American mountaineering must deal sensitively not only with an evolutionary past but with a revolutionary present. Like so many other microcosmic activities, mountaineering today is suffering from its own form of future shock, or accelerated change. Techniques, standards, values and codes of ethics of five years back are adamantly rejected by many modern mountaineers: clean climbing with nuts and artificial chockstones has replaced pitons and hammers, just as nylon ropes replaced hemp after World War II. But unlike earlier technical (and technological) advances, recent changes are largely the product of esthetic and environmental concerns, ushered in with intense debate among the climbing community. In a time like this, of changing values and strongly voiced opinions, it has become harder than ever to evaluate objectively the past and present of climbing on this continent.

Yet few are so well qualified as Chris Jones to undertake the task. For Chris is a foreigner, an expatriate English climber, and, as such, seems to have the detachment and perspective needed to form a broad, objective view of the American climbing scene—even though today Chris is very much a part of that scene, in the front rank of those doing alpine-style ascents of major North (and South) American walls.

Chris found that, unlike the story of the Alps and alpinism, North American mountaineering had not yet received much interpretive, integrative study. True, records of most significant ascents did exist, and the periodical literature is substantial. But considerably more history has never been written down. Much of this survives today only in the memories of pioneer climbers, and in the twice-told tales that climbers still trade around campfires.

The job of source gathering for this book was monumental but a long convalescence from a ski accident gave Chris the free time to begin the research for his book. Later he drove back and forth across the country several times to interview many of those who made the climbing history of this century.

What emerges is a singularly fascinating story of the independent development of American climbing. For with some notable exceptions, American climbers have often been isolated from their European counterparts, forcing them to "re-invent" techniques they were unaware of, and leading at times to the development of truly native climbing styles, which today have been adopted throughout the alpine world.

People climb mountains, and this history is ultimately a story of people, as well as their deeds. Chris has included the folklore, the mythology and the actual social history of American climbing and of many regional climbing areas. It's all here—the campfire pranks, the ribald stories, the occasional tragedy, the petty jealousies and the struggle for meaning, as well as the great peaks, the great routes, the great adventures.

The American climber has always been a maverick, often an eccentric, at times virtually a social outcast. Perhaps it is the ultimate merit of Jones' history that these characters don't merely pass through the pages in chronological sequence. They are understood and known, we meet them and won't soon forget them; they come alive.

LITO TEJADA-FLORES

Preface

As a young climber in Europe I was fascinated by the history of the sport. My pals and I swapped legends and stories for hours on end. One time when we recounted one of the preposterous Joe Brown stories, Brown was quietly sitting next to us in the bar. To gaze up at a crag was exciting, but to know something of those who had been before added another dimension. When I came to North America, it seemed that climbing had little tradition; it seemed to have begun just a few years ago. The mountains were superb, but they seemed strangely empty. Who had preceded me?

In this book I have attempted to trace the development of North American climbing. My intent has been to follow the key personalities and events that carried forward the sport. It is not an exhaustive treatise on every climbing area on the continent; rather, it highlights the areas that were at the forefront.

Mexico has been excluded from this treatment of North American climbing because, apart from the unprecedented ascent of Popocatepetl in 1519, it has never been a leader. In this respect Mexico is much like Alaska's Brooks Range, Canada's Monashees, the Sawtooth Range of Idaho, and countless other areas; they are omitted because they have contributed little to the development of climbing. On the subject of boulder climbing I have said nothing and must admit to personal bias: I once broke a leg while bouldering.

During convalesence from a ski accident, I had the opportunity to delve into American climbing. It is my hope that this work will give mountain lovers a sense of the roots of the sport and that it will add to their appreciation of our mountains and crags. The mountains are not just masses of rock and ice. They are places where people have struggled, laughed, dreamed, and sometimes died.

I am indebted to many persons who helped me during the preparation of this book. Whether through interview, correspondence, the loan of pictures, or their friendly attitude, they all contributed much. If I do not single out those who helped me in special ways, it is because the acknowledgments would fill several pages. I ask their indulgence if I thus appear ungrateful; believe me, I could have done nothing without their support. The persons and organizations listed below contributed to the work; I alone am responsible for its shortcomings.

Pat Ament; American Alpine Club Library, New York; Lloyd Anderson; Burt Angrist; Archives of the Canadian Rockies, Maryalice Stewart, Director; Archives of Western History, University of Wyoming, Laramie; Wally Ballenger; Bancroft Library, University of California; Henry Barber; Bob Bates; Wolf Bauer; Scott Baxter; Eric Beck; Fred Beckey; Raffi Bedayn; Charles Bell; Gus Benner; Alex Bertulis; Phil Bettler; Eric Bjornstad; T. S. Blakeney; Carl Blaurock; Glen Boles; Orrin Bonney; Jim Bridwell; Dave Brower; Mrs. Belmore Browne; Bill Buckingham; William Bueler; Dean Caldwell; Pat Callis; H. Adams Carter; Yvon Chouinard; Lewis Clark; Gary Colliver; Colorado Mountain Club Library, Denver; Ed Cooper; Bud Couch; Henry Coulter; Lawrence Coveney; Mike Covington; Jim Crooks; Dick Culbert; Bob Culp; Ome Daiber; Larry Dalke; Scott Davis; Glen Dawson; Frank de la Vega; Al DeMaria; Glen Denny; Denver Public Library, Western History Department; Gregg Donaldson; Dick Dorling; Dave Dornan; Jeff Dozier; Dick Dumais; Jack Durrance; Dennis Eberl; Jules Eichorn; Marjory Bridge Farquhar; Harvey Firestone; Bill Forrest; Jack Fralick; Chris Fredericks; Walt Fricke; Tom Frost; Fritiof Fryxell; Tom Gerughty; Bradley Gilman; Bob Godfrey; Art Gran; Brian Greenwood; Mel Griffiths; Andrew Gruft; Barry Hagen; Henry Hall; Robin Hansen; Warren Harding; John Hart; Kenneth Henderson; TM Herbert; Tom Higgins; Frank Hoover; Jack Hossack; Bill House; Dick Houston; Huntley Ingalls; Dick Irvin; Ray Jacquot; Cliff Jennings; Don Jensen; Jim Jones; Bob Kamps; Joe Kelsey; Steve Komito; Hans Kraus; Roman Laba; Don Lauria; Chong Lee; Dick Leonard; Pete Lev; Jiggs Lewis; Charles Locke; Dick Long; George Lowe; Les MacDonald; Jim McCarthy; Cleve McCarty; Lloyd MacKay; Merrill McLane; Dave Mahre; Harry Majors; John Mendenhall; Imre Michalik; Helmut Microys; Rick Millikan; Yukio Mita; Dee Molenaar; Mike Moore; Terris Moore; Alf Muhlbauer; Phyllis Munday; Ax Nelson; Ray Northcutt; John Oberlin; Lincoln O'Brien; Robert Ormes; Leigh Ortenburger; Marion Peterson, Colorado Mountain Club; Bernard Poisson; Mark Powell; Chuck Pratt; Jerry Pryor; Bill Putnam; Norman Read; Dave Rearick; Royal Robbins; Dave Roberts; Bestor Robinson; Homer Robinson, Devils Tower National Monument; Steve Roper; Galen Rowell; Al Rubin; Leo Scheiblhener; Kim Schmitz; Betsy Shaw; Mike Sherrick; Christie Hakim and Janet Stake, librarians, Sierra Club Library, San Francisco; Pete Sinclair; Phil Smith; John Stannard; Howard Stansbury; Al Steck; Joseph Stettner; Jim Stuart; Claude Suhl; Herb Swedlund; Bob Swift; Frank Tarver; Lito Tejada-Flores; Gray Thompson; Monroe Thorington; John Thune; Doug Tompkins; Otto Trott; John Turner; Hermann Ulrichs; Robert Underhill; Willi Unsoeld; Hervey Voge; Bradford Washburn; Gene White; Jim Wickwire; Fritz Wiessner; Harry Wills, Mount Rainier National Park; Ken Wilson; Jim Wilson; Chuck Wilts; Walter Wood; Elizabeth Woolsey.

Finally, I must thank Grant Barnes, who saw a glimmer of hope in a draft manuscript, and Mike Loughman, who helped me grasp the essence of the subject matter, organize my thoughts, and produce a book from a mass of data.

Publications Cited

AAJ: American Alpine Journal, American Alpine Club, New York, N.Y.

AJ: Alpine Journal, Alpine Club, London, England.

Alpinismus, Munich, Germany.

Appalachia, Appalachian Mountain Club, Boston, Mass.

Ascent, Sierra Club, San Francisco, Calif.

Der Bergsteiger, Osterreichischen Alpenvereins, Munich, Germany.

CAJ: Canadian Alpine Journal, Alpine Club of Canada, Banff, Alberta.

Climbing, Aspen, Colo.

Dartmouth Mountaineering, Dartmouth Mountaineering Club, Hanover, N.H.

The Eastern Trade, Silver Spring, Md.

Harvard Mountaineering, Harvard Mountaineering Club, Cambridge, Mass.

Mazama, The Mazamas, Portland, Ore.

La Montagne, Club Alpin Français, Paris, France.

Mountain, London, England.

The Mountaineer, The Mountaineers, Seattle, Wash.

Mountaineering Journal, Wallasey, Cheshire, England.

Off Belay, Renton, Wash.

SCB: Sierra Club Bulletin, Sierra Club, San Francisco, Calif.

Summit, Big Bear, Calif.

T & T: Trail and Timberline, Colorado Mountain Club, Denver, Colo.

Rugged Individualists

The exploration of a continent is an experience given only a few peoples, but in the early nineteenth century this unique experience awaited the European settlers of the New World. The persons caught up in the excitement of western exploration were a diverse band of opportunists, adventurers, soldiers, and scientists. Their motives ranged from economic gain to humanitarianism to empire building. The mandates given the expedition leaders were wide-ranging in their scope although particular attention was paid to the discovery of trade routes; it was well known that a mountain barrier blocked the way to the Pacific.

The explorers' home was the eastern portion of the continent, a lush landscape of woods, meadows, and low-lying hills. The Great Plains presented no real obstacle to the explorers, but when the parties reached the Rocky Mountains, they were confronted by a totally new landscape: a desolate land of canyons and mountainsides, swift-flowing torrents and stately conifers. At first appearance the mountains were both repellent and commercially worthless; the only interest lay in discovering ways to get through them. A few men, however, whether to spy out the land or from natural curiosity, were drawn toward the summits shimmering in the distance. Who knew what discovery and adventure the unknown upper regions of the land might hold?

The first exploring party to attempt the ascent of a high peak was led by Lt. Zebulon Pike.* An ambitious man, Pike was well aware of the fame of his predecessors, Lewis and Clark. He hoped that his own explorations would result in a meteoric rise through the ranks. The ostensible purposes of Pike's expedition were the return of a group of captured Osage Indians to their lands, the securing of friendly relations with the Comanches, and

*Although outside the scope of this book, the Spanish conquistadores' ascent of Mexico's 17,888-foot Popocatepetl in 1519 must be mentioned. The conquistadores were amazed at the sight of the erupting volcano, and Diego de Ordaz asked Cortés' permission to investigate. Ordaz and his men set off for the snow-covered peak and, in spite of smoke and ashes, carried on toward the top. Although it is unlikely that they reached the actual summit, their courage was remarkable. The first definite ascent came in 1522. Cortés was short of gunpowder and offered a reward for sulphur brought back from the crater. In the face of freezing temperatures and eruptions, Francisco Montaño and three companions reached the rim. Here, first Montaño and then a companion were lowered some ninety feet into the crater. They filled their sacks with 300 pounds of sulphur and returned to a hero's welcome.

1

the exploration of the Red and Arkansas rivers. However, Pike's expedition was not an official government undertaking but the idea of Gen. James Wilkinson, governor of the Louisiana Territory. Knee-deep in intrigue, Wilkinson was both a double agent of the Spanish and a confidant of former Vice President Aaron Burr. The real objective of the expedition was espionage: information on a possible invasion route into Santa Fe and Spanish territory.

Pike began his journey near St. Louis in July 1806. Early in November he headed toward the western mountains and Spanish land. By now the first winter snow had fallen on the plains, and prospects for the journey must have looked bleak. But Pike persisted. Near the site of present-day Lamar, Colorado, he caught sight of a mountain "which appeared like a small blue cloud" in the distance. Shortly afterward a range of mountains came in sight, and the whole party gave "three *cheers* to the *Mexican mountains*." Pike was intrigued by this glimpse of the unknown and determined to climb the "blue mountain" in order to map out the surrounding country.

In the manner of those unfamiliar with the mountains, he severely underestimated the task. He imagined the ascent would take just one day. On the morning of the third day his men cached their food and blankets, fully expecting to get to the summit and back that day. When night fell, they huddled in a cave still short of their goal. The following day they struggled on through waist-

deep snow. Arriving on top of a minor summit, Pike discovered to his dismay that the "Grand Peak" now appeared "at the distance of 15 or 16 miles from us, and as high as what we had ascended, and would have taken a whole day's march to have arrived at its base, when I believe no human being could have ascended to its pinical [*sic*]. This with the condition of my soldiers, who had only light overalls on, and no stockings, and every way ill provided to endure the inclemency of the region . . . determined us to return."

In the early winter conditions the ascent was hopeless and perhaps foolish, considering the thin reserves of the party. Nonetheless, whether in the pursuit of glory or his alleged purpose of mapping out the country, Pike made a strong attempt. He was the first of the western explorers intent on climbing a mountain.

Over the years Pike's "Grand Peak" was not forgotten. One of the objectives of the subsequent Yellowstone expedition, under the command of Maj. Stephen Long of the U.S. Topographical Engineers, was to measure the height of the peak. In the early summer of 1820 the expedition members, traveling westward up the gentle slope of the plains, "were cheered by a distant view of the Rocky Mountains." At first they believed that the most prominent summit was Pike's "Grand Peak." However, they soon realized that this mountain (subsequently named Longs Peak) was not the one mentioned by Pike. They headed south and identified the real Pikes Peak. Twenty-three-year-

Edwin James as a young man. Courtesy Denver Public Library, Western History Department.

old Edwin James, the botanist of the expedition, led the climbing party. A contemporary described him as "tall, erect, with a benevolent expression of countenance, and a piercing black eye." James and his companions each carried buffalo meat, corn meal, a blanket, and a gun.

After the first day's climb they spent a miserable night camped in a clump of firs. The ground was so steep they had to place poles against the trees to prevent themselves rolling downhill. The next day, as they climbed higher, James noted a drop in temperature and the gradual disappearance of trees. From the plains he had noticed that the treeline carried up to near the summit; but when he arrived at treeline, it appeared that the major part of the climb was still ahead. He was not the last mountaineer to find that the stretch to the top is the longest.

High on the 14,110-foot peak, the climbers began to pant for breath, and at two o'clock they took a half-hour rest as James took stock of the situation. Farquhar records in "Colorado Rockies" how James faced a dilemma that has perpetually confronted mountaineers, "We now found it would be impossible to reach the summit of the mountain, and return to our camp of the preceding night, during the part of the day which remained; but as we could not persuade ourselves to turn back, after having so nearly accomplished the ascent, we resolved to take our chances of spending the night on whatever part of the mountain it might overtake us."

Boldness won the day. At four o'clock they arrived on the summit. The summit plateau was level and without vegetation, and James was surprised to see grasshoppers in such a bleak location. After a brief halt they headed down, camped once more in the timber, and arrived at their equipment cache at noon on the following day. James had thus completed the first known high mountain ascent in North America. Yet his ascent involved no more than rough hiking. From a technical

4

David Douglas, the Scottish gardener who rose to fame as a botanical collector. Courtesy Bancroft Library, University of California.

standpoint it was nowhere in the same class as the ascent of glacier-hung Mont Blanc. Today a highway goes to the top of Pikes Peak, and although Mont Blanc has been tunneled under and its satellite peaks traversed by cable cars, it seems safe to say that no highway will ever be forced to its summit. Perhaps the key difference between Pikes Peak and Mont Blanc is that the latter involves a new dimension in negotiating glaciers.

However, the difficulties of Pikes Peak were not confined to the actual climb. There was also the problem of the approach. James and his men had to find a feasible route to the base of the peak (a problem that had foiled Pike); they had to traverse unknown country, where a confrontation with Indians was always possible; and they were surrounded by hundreds of miles of wilderness. On the first ascent of Mont Blanc the adventurers set out from the village of Chamonix; they spied out the proposed route through a telescope; and they were familiar with the game trails of the region. Although the ascent of Pikes Peak was technically simple, the overall difficulties were comparable with those on Mont Blanc. In both cases the climbers had to have an overriding belief in their own abilities.

The Rocky Mountains of the United States generally lack extensive glaciers and snowfields. However, in the more northerly, cooler latitudes of the Canadian Rockies, glaciers descend to around 7,000 feet. It is here that the first climb of a glacier-hung peak in North America took place.

The mountain barrier of the Canadian Rockies began to assume economic importance at the beginning of the nineteenth century. It held the key that would unlock fabulous wealth: a trade route to the Pacific. Two trading companies, the Hudson's Bay Company and the Northwest Company of Merchants, were locked in battle for supremacy in the lucrative fur trade. The discovery of a pass through the mountains would enable them to exploit the sea otter and additional beaver grounds. Perhaps, it would enable the successful company to squeeze out its rival. The search for a suitable pass was a long one, but in 1811 geographer and Northwesterner David Thompson opened up Athabasca Pass. This pass subsequently became the key link between Fort Vancouver, near the mouth of the Columbia River, and the forts to the east of the Rockies. Early each spring, before the rivers were charged with meltwater, a brigade of boats left Fort Vancouver and worked up the Columbia to the Big Bend. There they met traders who had traveled by boat and packtrain across the rivers and plains of central Canada and through the Rockies.

In 1827 one of the party from Fort Vancouver was David Douglas, a Scottish horticultural collector in his midtwenties. He had begun his career as a gardener on the estate of a Scottish nobleman. His diligence and curiosity led him to employment

at the botanical garden of Glasgow University, where he came under the patronage of the renowned botanist William Hooker. When the Horticultural Society of London needed a collector to go to North America, Hooker recommended his protégé.

Douglas spent two years ranging over the Columbia River basin. In April 1827 he was on his way home. As his party neared Athabasca Pass, their way frequently led over snow, for the land was still in the grip of winter. At the pass Douglas was seized with the idea of climbing one of the nearby mountains. His plan was a novel one. He was confronted by an ice-covered peak far different from the gentle slopes of Pikes Peak. Even in Europe climbing was largely unknown at this date, and ice-covered mountains instilled fear in men's hearts. When contemporary writers spoke of "awful precipices," they were describing terrain and dangers quite outside their normal experience.

Why then did Douglas want to climb such a peak? Did he, like Pike, want to look for a way to travel? Or like James to determine the height of the mountain? Or was it his own scientific curiosity, perhaps the thought of a yet unknown specimen? Thorington notes that in Douglas's journal, which is written in large part for his employers and in which he is careful to explain his actions, he says simply, "After breakfast at one o'clock, being as I conceive on the highest part of the route, I became desirous of ascending one of the peaks, and accordingly I set out alone on snowshoes to that on the left hand or West side, being to all appearances the highest." He does not give us science, botany, or geography, but he has stated what makes a mountaineer: a person who, without qualification, *desires* to climb peaks. We see in him the archetypal mountaineer. If we understand what it was about those wintry peaks at Athabasca Pass that drew him to them, we have a grasp of mountaineering.

Douglas made his solitary way up the peak and recorded,

The labor of ascending the lower part, which is covered with pines, is great beyond description, sinking on many occasions to the middle. Half-way up vegetation ceases entirely, not so much as a vestige of Moss or Lichen on the stones. One-third from the summit it becomes a mountain of pure ice, sealed far over by

Nature's hand, a momentous work of Nature's God. The height from its base may be about 5,500 feet; timber, 2,750 feet; a few mosses and lichens, 500 more; 1,000 feet of perpetual snow; the remainder, toward the top 1,250, as I have said, glacier with a thin covering of snow on it.

Douglas was a tough customer, accustomed to fifty-mile hikes, and made the ascent in a fast five hours. On top he looked out over mile upon mile of unmeasured distance. Lost in contemplation, he remained on top for some twenty minutes. "The sensation I felt is beyond what I can give utterance to. Nothing as far as the eye could perceive, but Mountains such as I was on, and many higher, some rugged beyond description, striking the mind with horror blended with a sense of the wondrous works of the Almighty." But with night closing fast he had to descend. He shot down in little more than an hour. "Places where the descent was gradual, I tied my [snow]shoes together, making them carry me in turn as a sledge. Sometimes I came down at one spell 500 to 700 feet in a space of one minute and a half."

Back home in Britain, Douglas found that his collections of the past two years had made him a celebrity in scientific circles. The former gardener of humble birth was introduced to several of the most eminent scientists in Europe. He hoped for their acceptance. Morwood records that a contemporary said, "Unfortunately for his peace of mind he could not withstand the temptation (so

natural to the human heart) of appearing as one of the *Lions* among the learned and scientific men of London." But he never received the recognition he felt was his due. The Horticultural Society of London had promised to publish his journal, and perhaps he believed that it would give him a place beside the foremost scientific explorers of the day. He spruced up his field notes, and he made a few interesting changes. For the first time he named the peak he had climbed and recorded its height. He now wrote,

This peak, the highest yet known in the Northern Continent of America, I felt sincere pleasure in naming Mount Brown, in honor of R. Brown Esq., the Illustrious Botanist, no less distinguished by the amiable qualities of refined mind. A little to the South is one nearly of the same height rising more into a sharp point I named Mount Hooker, in honor of my early patron the enlightened and learned Professor of Botany in the University of Glasgow, Dr. Hooker, to whose kindness I in great measure owe my success hitherto in life.

And referring to the peak he climbed, Mount Brown, he stated that "the height from its apparent base exceeds 6,000 feet, 17,000 feet above the level of the sea."

Thus, where Douglas formerly wrote that there were many higher mountains in the vicinity of Mount Brown, he now claimed the peak as the highest known in North America and gave it the astounding height of 17,000 feet, considerably higher than 15,771-foot Mont Blanc, the highest peak known to have been climbed up to that time. In 1829 he collaborated in the preparation of a map of North America under his patron, Professor Hooker. On this map Mounts Hooker and Brown were marked, although Mount Brown had strangely lost 1,000 feet and appeared as 16,000 feet. The reason for this exaggerated height was no doubt the then current misconception that Athabasca Pass was at 11,000 feet (its real height is 5,740 feet), so we should not censure Douglas too harshly. However, his claim to have ascended the highest known peak on the continent was plain deception. The mapmakers of the time took Douglas at his word. Mounts Brown and Hooker appeared as massive peaks on North American maps until the twentieth century, and speculation about the peaks continued for seventy years.

Douglas is best remembered today as a botanical collector, his name immortalized in the Douglas fir. Yet his climb of Mount Brown has its own significance. Some 150 years ago a young Scot set out alone to climb an ice-covered mountain. He did this at a time when no others on the continent had ever conceived of such a feat, and he did it because he "became desirous." He was our first mountaineer.

Although Athabasca Pass was used regularly for many years after Douglas's journey, no other travelers ventured up the nearby peaks, or, if they did, their climbs went unrecorded. The next record of climbing on the continent comes from one of the friendlier regions of the Rockies: Wyoming's Wind River Mountains. In their northern portion the granitic Wind Rivers are marked by active glaciers although nowhere as extensive as those in the Canadian Rockies. A range of sharply defined summits, the Wind Rivers were a familiar mountain barrier to the trappers of the early nineteenth century.

Life at the frontier garrisons of the day was dull and routine. To the imaginative Capt. Benjamin Bonneville the future lay elsewhere. He had observed the expansion of the fur trade and sensed that the course of empire lay westward. He took a leave of absence from the military and obtained the backing of a group of Eastern businessmen for a fur-trapping venture. In September 1833 with over a year of exploration already behind him, he was on his way to a cache on the west side of the Wind Rivers. Rather than detour clear round to the south, he determined to look for a more direct route through the range, but he found the going rougher than he had anticipated. On the second day of the journey among the peaks, he and his companions faced the backbone of the range, and he decided to climb one of the peaks to look for a way through. His biographer, Washington Irving, reported that Bonneville soon found that he had "undertaken a tremendous task"; and Irving observed, "But the pride of man is never more obstinate than when climbing mountains."

Although Irving's knowledge of mountain

climbing was probably confined to an account of the ascent of Mont Blanc, if that, his intuitive feel for the forces that drive climbers was correct. In his short phrase lies much of the story of mountaineering.

Irving continued:

The ascent was so steep and rugged that [Bonneville] and his companions were frequently obliged to clamber on hands and knees, with their guns slung over their backs. . . . At one place, they even stripped off their coats and hung them upon bushes, and thus lightly clad, proceeded to scramble over these eternal snows. As they ascended still higher, there were cool breezes that refreshed and braced them, and springing with new ardour to their task, they at length attained the summit.

In the account that has come down to us by Irving, Bonneville carefully described the view from the summit and noted that the peak he climbed was not only the highest in the range, but the highest in North America, a delusion that afflicted many early explorers. However, nothing in the account enables us to determine just which peak he climbed. A recent case has been made for 13,875-foot Gannett Peak, the highest of the Wind Rivers, but this is unlikely for two reasons. First, there is mention of bushes on which the men placed their coats, which they "soon regained" after they left the summit. There are no bushes large enough to act as coat racks within hours of the summit of snow-girt Gannett Peak. Second,

the account makes no mention of any technical climbing difficulties. On even the simplest route on Gannett Peak, inexperienced persons would probably want a rope. Thus, unless new documents are discovered, Bonneville's peak will remain a mystery as will the next recorded Wind River climb.

In 1842 dashing Lt. John Frémont led an expedition to map the Oregon Trail and to report on its suitability as an emigration route. The young lieutenant had recently married the daughter of influential Senator Benton and was embarked on a heady rise to power (he later became the first U.S. senator from California and a presidential candidate). Senator Benton was an advocate of western expansion, and his son-in-law's ambition to become a famous explorer made them ideal collaborators.

Frémont rounded South Pass and headed up to the sources of the Green River. He planned to locate and climb the highest peak in the Wind Rivers. In part, he wanted to determine if these were, as then supposed, the highest of the Rocky Mountains; in part, he was attracted by the spectacular nature of the feat, for it could not fail to add to his renown. His guide, Kit Carson, pointed out the peak that the frontiersmen reckoned the highest, and the party set out to make the ascent. The peak appeared so close that they left behind their blankets and provisions, as they expected to make the summit and return that night, a mistake still made by climbers today. They crossed ridges and canyons, and always the peak remained in the dis-

Frémont's party approaches the Wind Rivers. Is the snowy peak Mount Woodrow Wilson? Is it the one Frémont climbed? Courtesy Bancroft Library, University of California.

tance. When they reached a favorable campsite late in the afternoon, the exhausted party was happy to stop for the night. There was no food for supper, nor any for breakfast. The next day Frémont carried on unperturbed.

The hardships of the undertaking did not sit well with the German mapmaker, Charles Preuss. He detested the uncouth frontier life and belittled Frémont's desire to reach the peaks, which he compared unfavorably with the Swiss Alps. When the party reached the snowfields that surround the peak, each man chose his own route. Preuss slipped and fell down a snow slope but felt duty-bound to continue. However, the demoralized and undisciplined party was now scattered over the mountainside, and before long the attempt was abandoned.

Back at their meager camp of the previous night, the men viewed the situation in a brighter light; a few of them had gone back and brought up fresh supplies. Frémont had heeded Preuss's pointed observation that a little organization was helpful in mountain climbing. The following morning Preuss fervently hoped that Frémont would be satisfied with the height determinations made the day before. But he was not. They were going up, in Frémont's words, "deliberately resolved to accomplish our object if it were within the compass of human means." They had learned a lesson from their erratic attempt the day before and now climbed steadily and deliberately upward. Frémont worked up the snow, climbed around a rock

wall, and shortly "sprang upon the summit." Amid shouts of hurrah and wild pistol shooting, they unfurled the stars and stripes and consumed a well-earned victory bottle of brandy. Frémont was delighted. He had climbed what he took for the highest peak in the Rocky Mountains, and he declared, "We had accomplished an object of laudable ambition, and beyond the strict order of our instructions." Unfortunately, the identity of Frémont's peak is not certain. Extensive arguments have been advanced for both Fremont Peak and Mount Woodrow Wilson.

The North American mountain ranges in which the earliest climbs occurred were remote from population centers. The scientists and soldiers who climbed the peaks were enroute through the mountains. But with the settlement of the coastal areas of the Pacific Northwest in the 1840s, Americans lived in sight of snow-capped peaks. The well-known dormant volcanoes of the region were different from the peaks climbed up to that time. They stood out dramatically above the surrounding country, for they were not part of a range of roughly equivalent peaks. The Cascade volcanoes formed a constant backdrop to the daily lives of the settlers, and a few of the more adventurous of the new inhabitants set out to master the heights. First to succeed was Thomas Dryer, owner and editor of the *Weekly Oregonian*.

Accompanied by three companions, Dryer climbed the classically shaped Mount Saint Helens in 1853. Encouraged by this success, he launched

an attack the following year on Mount Hood, the peak that rises near the Columbia River and the city of Portland. David Douglas had approached this peak some thirty years earlier, but he declared it insurmountable. According to McNeil, the equipment used by Dryer and his men consisted of "well made creepers, iron socket staffs, with hooks, ropes, etc. etc. the same kind that we used in ascending Mt. St. Helens." A few of the party were forced to drop out when they became dizzy in the rarified air, and one was turned back by a passage of "70.5 degrees by the theodolite." On his triumphant return to Portland, Dryer claimed that Mount Hood was 18,361 feet high, a figure obtained by the dubious technique of measuring the thickness of the snow. For a long time afterward, he was needled by rival newspaper editors who considered this claim ridiculous. Worse yet for Dryer, because of inconsistencies in his account, it was later determined that he had not reached the summit. This honor later fell to a party that included one of his employees, Henry Pittock. When Pittock had the cheek to suggest that his employer's ascent was incomplete, he was roundly scolded by the embarrassed Dryer.

Although Mount Hood and the other Cascade

Mount Rainier from the south. Kautz made his attempt up the slender Kautz Glacier that descends left from the summit. Nisqually Glacier is at the center; the successful 1870 party climbed up snowfields and rock ribs to the right of the Nisqually. *Austin Post*.

volcanoes are notable landmarks, pride of place among them must go to 14,410-foot Mount Rainier. Both by reason of its noble proportions and the image it creates from the vicinity of Seattle, Mount Rainier is the preeminent peak of the Northwest. Even today climbers are entranced by Rainier, as I discovered for myself.

In the fall of 1972 I set off across the country, a fledgling historian hell-bent on discovery. In Tacoma, Washington, I visited the U.S. Geological Survey, where I pored over the photographic collection. I had been in the Seattle-Tacoma area twice before. Both times it rained. I was assured that Mount Rainier was visible from the city, but I had yet to see it. That morning the weather was cloudy, but when I left the building at midday the sky had cleared. Suddenly, unexpectedly, there it was. A dream mountain floated over city and plain. I was spellbound.

My lunch companion, Dee Molenaar, was delighted that his favorite peak had jolted the blasé British alpinist. Although he had seen the peak hundreds of times, I could tell that he, too, was moved by the spectacle. He also knew the mountain's inner secrets from days spent on its icy flanks.

As I gazed at the peak, I felt the urge to know it from within: the crunch of snow underfoot, the sting of the wind, the slow upward toil. I *must* come to grips with it. When Molenaar and I drove through town, we caught glimpses of the mountain. It was almost too much to bear. And what of

the townspeople? Did they feel as we did? Did their pulses quicken? For the majority the answer was no. They were content to view Mount Rainier from a distance. Perhaps I had stumbled on the definition of a mountaineer. Is it a person who is not content to view the mountains from a distance, who is compelled up into them? Molenaar and I were simply the modern-day counterparts of the unknown early climbers on Mount Rainier. Like us they were bugged by the peak. They had to go for it, as we shall see.

The early climbs on Mount Rainier are shrouded in doubt. In 1852 and again three years later parties are supposed to have reached the crater rim, but the surviving accounts do not tell whether they reached the summit. Better documented by Meany is the attempt led by German-born Lt. August Kautz in 1857. Kautz was stationed at Fort Steilacoom on Puget Sound, and he often gazed toward Mount Rainier from the barracks. With a self-confessed "passion for going to the tops of high places," he frequently told his fellow officers of his plan to climb the distant peak. But as he never put his plan into practice, they began to rib him about it. Thus stirred into action, Kautz studied an account of the ascent of Mont Blanc and equipped his four-man party with iron-tipped alpenstocks and ice creepers.* The creepers were made by

---

*A wooden staff, the alpenstock, had been employed by Alpine travelers at least as far back as the Renaissance. Used to give a footing on ice, ice creepers, or climbing irons, have been found and dated back to the fifth century B.C.

driving four-penny nails through an extra boot sole, which was then sewed onto their boots. They rounded out their gear with a fifty-foot rope, a hatchet, a thermometer, hard biscuits, and dried beef.

The would-be climbers first had to slog through 140 miles of forest and brush. Near the mountain they engaged an Indian guide and set off up the gleaming snowfields. In ten hours three of the party climbed to the vicinity of the upper plateau. The summit was within their grasp, but it was already five o'clock, a strong wind was blowing, and clouds swept the heights. From below him Kautz heard one of his companions urge retreat. Kautz's hands and feet were chilled, and he knew that a night spent out on the snow was a grim prospect. Reluctantly, he began to retrace his steps.

From the account it is apparent that Kautz was over the steepest part of the climb, with only a tiring walk remaining to the summit. One might feel that he had cracked the mystery of the peak, established the route, and therefore deserved the honor of the first ascent. Unfortunately for Kautz and many others, mountaineers insist that a party go to the highest point in order to claim a first ascent. Were this not the case, the arguments over who made a particular first ascent would be even more hotly contested than now. If the summit is no longer necessary, just what are the criteria?

Of the next attempt on Mount Rainier in 1870, there is an accurate description of the climb and the summit area itself, leaving no doubt that the principals accomplished the ascent. The climbers were Hazard Stevens, the twenty-eight-year-old surveyor general of Washington, Philemon Van Trump, a former prospector, and Edmund Coleman, an English mountaineer and artist who had climbed the northernmost of the volcanic peaks of the Cascades, Mount Baker, in 1868. All three had fallen under the spell of Mount Rainier. Van Trump recalled that the mountain "impressed me so indescribably, enthused me so thoroughly, that I there and then vowed, almost with fervency, that I would some day stand upon its glorious summit, if that feat were possible to human effort and endurance."

By this time mountaineering was well established in the European Alps, and Coleman gave his fellow members of England's august Alpine

Philemon Van Trump.
Courtesy National Park Service

session. Stevens writes that the floor was "literally covered with his traps," which ranged from a ground sheet, a strong rope, ice creepers, and an ice axe,* to a

spirit-lamp for making tea on the mountains, green goggles for snow-blindness, deer's fat for the face, Alpine staffs, needles and thread, twine, tacks, screws, screwdriver, gimlet, file, several medical prescriptions, two boards for pressing flowers, sketching materials, and in fact every article that Mr. Coleman in his extensive reading had found used or recommended by travelers. Every one of these he regarded as indispensable.

When they reached the vicinity of the mountain, the three climbers engaged a Yakima Indian, Sluiskin, to guide them to timberline. Unfortunately for the forty-seven-year-old Coleman, his pack full of gear began to slow him down. He took it off in order to negotiate a tricky cliff, and when he attempted to drop it to a lower ledge, it hurtled down and disappeared in the brush. While he went to look for it, the others pressed on without him, Stevens remarking that Coleman "had been a dog on our march from the outset."

The Indian led them on a roundabout course, probably trying to tire them out and discourage them from going any higher on the mountain. By the evening campfire Stevens and Van Trump

Club what he took to be the reason for the relative lack of climbing in the United States,

The absorbing pursuit of money, the strangely practical character of the American mind, so averse to anything merely visionary, are quite sufficient to account for the absence of that *passion des montagnes* which is so often to be met with in older communities. . . . those who come out to the Western States do so either to make money, or to build up a home for themselves and families; consequently, they have neither the time nor the money to spend in what is generally considered to be a visionary, if not a foolhardy, pursuit.

With his knowledge of European climbing conditions, Coleman assembled an impressive array of equipment for the Mount Rainier attempt. Meany records Stevens's impressions when he and Van Trump came to Coleman's quarters for a planning

*The early climbers used a woodsman's axe for step cutting in snow and ice. The ice axe itself resulted from an 1864 discussion among members of Britain's Alpine Club as to the ideal tool for the job.

enthusiastically discussed their plans, but Sluiskin warned them against the dangers, but to no avail. They pressed on to timberline, and the two climbers scouted out their intended route and settled down for a final night in camp.

Stevens and Van Trump anticipated a quick roundtrip. They left their blankets and coats behind and set out early for the summit. Full of optimism, they carried a brass plate inscribed with their names. Their route lay along an unstable rock ridge until they reached today's Gibraltar Rock. Here they crept along a narrow ledge, constantly on the lookout for rockfall, and so gained the snowfields that lead up to the summit plateau. The ice axe and rope now came into play. In order to overcome one of the crevasses that barred their way, they lassoed an ice block on the far side and shinnied up the rope. As they climbed higher, their breathing became labored, and they were forced to stop and catch their breath every few steps. At five o'clock they reached a high, wind-swept promontory (Point Success); the real summit was still ahead. Although they realized that to go on meant a night on the snow, they continued and eventually arrived at a circular crater 200 yards across. The air was thick with a pungent sulphur smell. The pair eagerly pressed forward and discovered steaming fumaroles. They were overjoyed, Stevens reported: "Never was a discovery more welcome! Hastening forward, we both exclaimed, as we warmed our chilled and benumbed extremities over one of Pluto's fires, that here we would pass the night, secure against freezing to death, at least." They found a cavern in the ice and huddled inside. Here they spent a miserable night: One side of their bodies froze while the other side was doused in hot steam.

Several things contributed to Stevens's and Van Trump's success. They did not make the mistake of starting from low in the valley. They made a high camp close to the final difficulties and scouted out the route the evening before the summit climb. But the real key to the ascent was their determination to continue when night approached. It is this willingness to go all out that has marked the mountaineers who have achieved the hardest goals.

Fifty years before the ascent of Mount Rainier, Edwin James had climbed Pike's "Grand Peak," a high but unexciting peak tucked away miles from civilization, and the feat went unrepeated for years. The ascent of Mount Rainier was different. Perhaps the single most impressive isolated peak in the conterminous United States, it immediately appealed to the adventurer. Although the ascent was not difficult, it had the authentic mountain air. Moreover, Mount Rainier did not hide its charms; it was readily viewed from the new communities of Tacoma and Seattle. In the years that followed the first ascent, Mount Rainier became an almost popular outing. More than thirty parties reached the summit before the turn of the century. Mountaineering had progressed from an isolated event to an embryo sport.

REFERENCES

Bent, Allen H. "Early American Mountaineers." *Appalachia* 13 (May 1913): 45.

Bonney, Orrin H. "New Facts About Early Wyoming Ascents" *AAJ* 12 (1960): 73.

Coleman, E. T. "Mountains and Mountaineering in the Far West." *AJ* 8 (Aug. 1877): 232.

Douglas, David. *Journal Kept by David Douglas During His Travels in North America, 1823–1827.* London: Royal Horticultural Society, 1914.

Ewan, Joseph. *Rocky Mountain Naturalists.* Denver: University of Denver, 1950.

Farquhar, Francis P. *First Ascents in the United States, 1642–1900.* San Francisco: Grabhorn Press, 1948.

———. "Naming America's Mountains: The Cascades." *AAJ* 12 (1960): 49.

———. "Naming America's Mountains: The Colorado Rockies." *AAJ* 12 (1961): 319.

Frémont, J. C. *Report of the Exploring Expedition to the Rocky Mountains in the Year 1842.* Washington, D.C.: Gales & Seaton, 1845.

Hooker, William. "A Brief Memoir of the Life of David Douglas." *Companion to the Botanical Magazine.* London, 1836.

Irving, Washington. *The Adventures of Captain Bonneville, U.S.A.,* ed. Edgeley W. Todd. Norman: University of Oklahoma, 1961.

McNeil, Fred H. *Wy'East the Mountain.* Portland, Ore.: Metropolitan Press, 1937.

Meany, Edmond S. *Mount Rainier: A Record of Exploration.* New York: Macmillan, 1916.

Molenaar, Dee. *The Challenge of Rainier.* Seattle: The Mountaineers, 1971.

Morwood, William. *Traveler in a Vanished Landscape: The Life and Times of David Douglas, Botanical Explorer.* New York: Potter, 1973.

Pike, Z. M. *The Journals of Zebulon Montgomery Pike,* ed. Donald Jackson. Norman: University of Oklahoma, 1966.

Preuss, Charles. *Exploring with Frémont,* trans. Erwin Gudde and Elizabeth Gudde. Norman: University of Oklahoma, 1958.

Terrell, John Upton. *Zebulon Pike: The Life and Times of an Adventurer.* New York: Weybright and Talley, 1968.

Thorington, J. Monroe. "A Note on the Original Journals of David Douglas." *AJ* 37 (Nov. 1925): 327.

———. *The Glittering Mountains of Canada.* Philadelphia: John Lea, 1925.

———. "The Centenary of David Douglas' Ascent of Mount Brown." *CAJ* 16 (1928): 185.

Toll, Roger W. "Major Long's Expedition to Colorado." *T & T,* no. 64 (Jan. 1924), 2.

Van Trump, P. B. "Mount Rainier." *Mazama* 2(1) (Oct. 1970): 1.

Wheeler, A. O., and J. M. Thorington. "Mounts Brown and Hooker." *CAJ* 17 (1929): 66.

Wood, Richard G. *Stephen Harriman Long, 1784–1864.* Glendale, Calif.: Arthur Clark, 1966.

Scientists and Surveyors

The climbers of the early 1800s were moved by a sense of adventure and bravado. Although they made desultory observations, their purpose was not primarily scientific. By the 1860s a new breed of men were in the mountains: the government surveyors. They were charged with mapping the new lands of the West, and mountain summits made ideal observation posts.

In 1860 the California legislature established the Geological Survey. This was not a case of enlightened public servants recognizing a need. Rather, a scientist had a bold plan that needed funding. The Yale-trained geologist Josiah Dwight Whitney lobbied for the creation of the Survey and then had himself named its chief. His plan was ambitious: a complete survey of California. Like Frémont before him, Whitney took the German scientist Alexander von Humboldt for his model. He wanted to make important scientific discoveries, and the California survey was a perfect vehicle for his purpose.

Snow-covered Mount Shasta, a volcanic mountain in the north of the state, enjoyed a local reputation as the highest in the United States.

Whitney was anxious to determine the highest peak in the state, perhaps the country. In 1862 he and his principal assistant William Brewer set out for Mount Shasta with specially made barometers to make the first accurate measurement of a high peak in the United States. Along the way they heard conflicting stories about the mountain. Some claimed it was impossible and that many climbers had failed from lack of breath or bleeding from the nostrils. Others said five hundred persons had been up that very year. In the Shasta vicinity, Whitney and Brewer found a man who had actually climbed the peak and lost no time hiring him as guide. When the small party clambered onto the summit cone, they made a convincing discovery, as Brewer noted in his "Remarks," "There was a liberal distribution of 'California conglomerate,' a mixture of tin cans and broken bottles, a newspaper, a Methodist hymn-book, a pack of playing cards, an empty bottle, and various other evidence of a bygone civilization."

A keen wind whipped over the summit. While the rest of the party retreated, Whitney and Brewer resolutely set up the barometers and made their observations. Then the dedicated pair hurried to catch their companions. They glissaded down the snow, sliding on their feet and sometimes on their backsides. Brewer had the worst of it; his pants ripped apart and filled with snow.

Back in the Survey office, Whitney made his calculations: Mount Shasta was 14,442 feet.* Of the known peaks in the United States, only Mount Hood was reckoned higher, and Whitney disbelieved its reputed 18,000 feet. He was convinced he had found the highest peak in the land.

Brewer wrote about the Mount Shasta climb to a colleague at the Yale Scientific School. This stirring letter helped Yale student Clarence King decide to travel west in 1863 and make geology his life's work. King was enthusiastic and bore letters of introduction from the Yale professors. He obtained an unpaid position with the Survey (money was a perpetual problem throughout the life of the Survey) and went with a field party to the mines in the Sierra foothills near Yosemite Valley. One clear winter day he climbed an oak-covered ridge and saw from it a range of high peaks far to the south. He insisted to his chief that these peaks rivaled Mount Shasta. Whitney was skeptical, but eventually his curiosity won him over. He authorized Brewer to lead a party in search of King's high peaks.

Whitney's desire to find the highest mountain was a natural one, but his dispatch of the field party to the High Sierra in 1864 came at an inauspicious time. The previous winter the California legislature had rewritten the Survey charter suppressing the emphasis on pure science and directing the Survey to concentrate instead on the gold-, silver-, and copper-producing regions. While

California State Geological Survey party that discovered Mount Whitney, 1864. Left to right: Charles Hoffman, Dick Cotter, William Brewer, Clarence King. Courtesy Bancroft Library, University of California.

*The official U.S. Geological Survey height is 14,162 feet.

Whitney himself went to the Mother Lode, Brewer and most of the Survey's small staff journeyed to the granitic High Sierra, an unlikely place to find mineral deposits.

Brewer's party traveled up the timbered western slope, visited the already famous giant sequoia trees, and camped at the foot of a towering conical peak. Brewer and topographer Charles Hoffman climbed the peak (Mount Brewer) and from its summit got a staggering view. Mountains stretched into the distance. Sharp ridges and deep canyons led the eye southward to a massive peak. Surely *it* was the highest in the Sierra. Perhaps it was the highest in the United States.

When the pair returned to camp, their vivid portrayal of the new region and the dominant peak stirred Clarence King's imagination. He enlisted the packer Dick Cotter and asked Brewer for permission to attempt the peak, which the party named Mount Whitney. Brewer reluctantly agreed and noted, "King is wonderfully tough, has the greatest endurance I have ever seen, and is withall very muscular."

King recorded that when he and Cotter left their friends, "there was not a dry eye in the party." This melodramatic parting seemed justified when the two climbers came to grips with the mountain. King recalled, "We climbed alternately up smooth faces of granite, clinging simply by the cracks and protruding crystals of feldspar, and then hewed steps up fearfully steep slopes of ice [with Cotter's bowie knife], zigzagging to the right and left to avoid the flying boulders." Once past these difficulties and many more, they came to a smooth wall, "absolutely impregnable" except where a great icicle column leaned against it. King embraced the ice as if it were a tree trunk and cut toe holds for his feet. When they arrived on the

A barometer case slung over his shoulder, Clarence King hams it up for the photographer. Courtesy Bancroft Library, University of California.

summit, it was immediately apparent that they had climbed the wrong mountain. A higher peak was visible to the south. Not lost for a dramatic gesture, King rang his hammer "upon the topmost rock; we grasped hands, and I reverently named the grand peak *Mount Tyndall*."*

Reading King's vivid account, we can picture a life and death struggle as the protagonists fought it out with the mountain. But it should be stated that King's narrative bears little relationship to the actual events. A parallel account of the ascent of Mount Tyndall, "nearly in King's own words," is given in Whitney's official Survey report, "The summit was reached, without serious difficulty, after some risky climbing." Furthermore, later climbers experienced few of the troubles that always seemed to attend King's climbs. However, the colorful dressing up of events makes a fine story, and King has left us an adventure classic in his *Mountaineering in the Sierra Nevada*. He was neither the first nor the last mountaineer to embellish his story; he was just uncommonly good at it.

King, whom we left on top of the wrong mountain, had set out to climb Mount Whitney. Some days later he made a lone attempt and apparently got within four hundred feet of the top. Where his route lay or why he turned back is not clear.

*King admired the British scientist and mountaineer John Tyndall. In large measure he was inspired to climb by Tyndall's *Hours of Exercise in the Alps*. This book may have provided the model for King's own climbing tale.

Suffice to say that he missed the simple routes most commonly used today, and he had no further opportunities to climb Mount Whitney while he worked for the California Survey. In 1867 he left to head up his own survey of the fortieth parallel.

A charming, debonair man in his midtwenties, King was not only the head of an important government survey. He soon drew attention as a rising literary star. His stories appeared in the *Atlantic Monthly*. In the light of his new fame, Mount Whitney exerted a strong appeal. Under a flimsy pretext to his superior, King journeyed to the Owens Valley in 1871 to have another crack at the mountain, this time from the east. For once a climb of King's was relatively straightforward, although he did have to crawl on his hands and knees. On the cloud-covered summit for which he had fought so hard, he made a dramatic discovery: a rock cairn with an arrowshaft stuck in it. Did King really see the cairn and arrowshaft, or were they a literary touch? If he did see them, what did they mean? Had white men or Indians, or even both, preceded him?

Indians on the Peaks

King's cairn and arrowshaft have a distinctly Western ring to them. Maybe white men found the arrowshaft on the mountainside and carried it to the top, where they built their triumphant cairn because summit cairns do not seem to be part of the Indian tradition.

On the other hand, arrowheads have been found all over the Sierra, including the summit of Mount Whitney. Although these findings are no proof that Indians climbed the peaks, they are strong supporting evidence. (A popular event on Sierra Club trips was the discovery of Indian artifacts. Occasionally, an enterprising trip leader would carry a pocketful of obsidian chips into the Sierra and unobtrusively plant them.)

If definite proof of Indian ascents has yet to be found in the Sierra, it does exist for other ranges. John Muir saw hunting blinds on the slopes and summits of the nearby White Mountains of Nevada. The Indians drove mountain sheep toward the blinds, where hidden accomplices lay in wait. Other definite reports of Indian structures on mountaintops came from the "first ascent" parties on Colorado's 14,345-foot Blanca Peak and Wyoming's 13,165-foot Cloud Peak.

A firsthand account of Indian ascents of Longs Peak, Colorado, is undoubtedly authentic. In 1914 an elderly Arapahoe told how his father, Old Man Gun, used to trap eagles on top of the peak. Gun laid out a dead coyote as bait and hid in a narrow hole. When an eagle landed, he grabbed it by the feet. The son became curious about the trap and with a group of friends went up to see it for himself. It was partly filled in. When John Wesley Powell and party made their "first ascent" in 1868,

they made no mention of this trap, but it would have been hard to spot on the four-acre summit plateau even had they known about it.

From the evidence it is reasonable to suppose that Indians climbed numerous peaks throughout the West. The pursuit of game gave them a definite purpose. They were intimately familiar with the mountain passes, and the peaks themselves would hardly have stopped them. Several of the summits for which the white men struggled were undoubtedly commonplace to the Indians. They lived in harmony with nature and felt no compulsion to build summit cairns as evidence of their visits. The white men looked upon the mountains as hostile, and they recorded their triumphs with a flourish.*

Although Clarence King apparently was not the first up his peak, he was content to have finally downed his old adversary. Not yet thirty years old, he was known as the conqueror of Mount Whitney. His *Mountaineering in the Sierra Nevada* was a huge success, and his geological work was also gaining recognition. In the midst of all this pleasantry he received a rude shock. In a communication to the California Academy of Sciences a Mr. Goodyear pointedly stated that he and a compan-

---

*It was recently established that fifteenth-century Chilean Indians built stone structures on the summits of the 22,000-foot peaks that border the Atacama Desert, peaks that were tied in with their religious beliefs. They thus nullified many of the height records so dear to white men.

The southern High Sierra from the Owens Valley. Mount Langley, King's "highest peak," is at the left, Lone Pine Peak is nearest the camera, and the east faces of the Whitney group are in the right background. *Chris Jones*.

ion rode their mules up King's highest peak. Worse yet, they plainly saw the real Mount Whitney a few miles to the north. Poor King! He had climbed the peak in cloudy conditions and was hardly helped by his own rudimentary map. There was no time to lose. He hurried back to California from the East Coast and climbed the real Mount Whitney, only to find that three other parties had preceded him that very year.

Which of these parties was first was not clear, and a spirited debate started. The evidence favored three local men: Charley Begole, Al Johnson, and John Lucas. These three had enjoyed a roaring good time at a camp in the Sierra, where they escaped the summer heat of the lowland and indulged in bouts of eating, drinking, and fishing.

The year before, Professor Whitney was in the Owens Valley to investigate the great 1872 earthquake. The outspoken Whitney had antagonized the locals. Now it was clear his name had been used for the wrong peak for several years, and they saw a great opportunity. The locals would name the highest mountain Fishermans Peak and retain Whitney's name on the lesser summit. The local newspaper editorialized, "Wonder who the old earthquake sharp thinks is running the country, anyhow?"

The renaming effort fizzled out temporarily, but in 1881 an Owens Valley assemblyman introduced a bill in the California legislature to redesignate the mountain Fishermans Peak. After passing the Assembly, the bill came before the Senate on April 1. In the spirit of the day one member suggested that since the peak was in Senator Fowler's district, it should be named Fowlers Peak. The amendment carried but was vetoed by the governor because he considered the affair undignified.

In 1869 a young Scotsman eagerly accepted a job as a part-time sheepherder in the Sierra Nevada. John Muir was to find his spiritual home. He lacked the scientific training of a King or a Whitney, yet he was to make notable scientific observations. During his first summer in the Sierra he took every chance to get away from the sheep. His eyes and mind were open. He had no dogmas to guide or hinder him, and he built up his theories from observation. His interest in the formation of mountains led him up many summits, including Yosemite's Cathedral Peak. Even though this peak is as difficult as King's climbs, Muir's *First Summer* description was matter of fact, "I made my way . . . up to its topmost spire, which I reached at noon, having loitered by the way to study the fine trees." Muir had little to say about his climbing, and from his accounts it is difficult to know even which peaks he climbed. As he pointed out, "I never left my name on any mountain, rock, or tree."*

*Muir's modest approach was largely lost, for in the years that followed mountaineers generally made a considerable song and dance over their achievements. A trend back to Muir's ethos is evident today among a few.

Muir and King both relished the mountains, but they viewed them in different ways. King spoke on occasion of barrenness and gloom in the high places, and we get the impression that he was relieved when he was back in the valley. He was the adversary of nature. Muir was at home among the peaks, forever extolling their beauty. The reactions of the two men to storms are indicative of their make-up. Muir would climb into the branches of a swaying tree to feel the full impact of the wind. King was afraid the trees might crash down on him.

Their views carried through to their climbing experience. King clung to the rock and faced life-and-death decisions; Muir climbed carefully and indulged in no heroics. King built up difficulties in his mind and was threatened by forces of his own making. Muir dealt with the mountains as friends; he wrote, "I am forever and hopelessly a mountaineer."

Muir's geological observations led him to the conclusion that the spectacular Yosemite Valley had evolved through glacial action. This theory, now regarded as substantially correct, was at odds with Whitney's opinion that the bottom had dropped out of the valley in a cataclysmic disturbance. Muir's challenge drew scorn from the professor. He labeled Muir "a mere sheepherder, an ignoramus."

Whitney had a penchant for definitive statements. He considered Yosemite's Half Dome "perfectly inaccessible, being probably the only one of all the prominent points about the Yosemite which never has been, and never will be, trodden by human foot."

The problem presented by Half Dome was unique in North American climbing up to that time. The bare granite had a smoothness matched

John Muir as a young man.
Courtesy Bancroft Library, University of California.

by no mountain then climbed. Nonetheless, Whitney was soon proved wrong. In 1871 Yosemite resident John Conway and a "flock of small boys who climb smooth rocks like lizards" attempted the monolith. Conway sent up one of the boys with a rope, in the hope that he could drive a spike into a crack. However, it was quickly apparent that even spikes would not do the job. Drilling was required, and Conway gave up the attempt.

Just four years later the Scottish trail builder George Anderson made use of the rope left by Conway; then employing the skills of his life's work, he drilled holes for eyebolts in the flawless granite. He stood on one bolt, attached to it by a safety line, while he drilled the hole for the next higher bolt. The climb was a bold feat. It also marks the first appearance of the nefarious bolt on the climbing scene, but this in no way detracts from Anderson's achievement.

The Rocky Mountains

The California survey was disbanded before its members had mapped the Sierra. However, the skills learned were not lost but passed on to other surveys. Methods were refined until it was possible accurately to map mountainous country. Whitney's topographer, Terry Gardner, worked under King on the survey of the fortieth parallel, then, much to King's disappointment, left to join yet another survey led by Dr. Ferdinand Vandiveer Hayden.

Hayden was a shrewd man. He wrote glowing reports on the regions he studied—the very stuff that legislators liked to hear—and year by year his survey grew. In 1871 and 1872 he explored an almost legendary area: the Yellowstone and the

Phimister Proctor making the second ascent of Half Dome. He stood on Anderson's iron spikes and lassoed the next above. From *History of the Sierra Nevada.*

The Grand Teton from the west as photographed by Hayden Survey member William Jackson. The Exum Ridge forms the right skyline; the final section of the North Ridge is seen on the left. Spalding's route lay up ledges to the left of the Exum Ridge. Courtesy Bancroft Library, University of California.

"Stevenson in Peril." A typical artist's impression of the day. Courtesy Bancroft Library, University of California.

Tetons. In 1873 he was caught up in the popular quest of the day, the search for riches in Colorado. This fabled state was the source of endless rumors: of gold and silver, of Aztec ruins, of a mountain emblazoned with a holy cross.

By the time the Hayden survey began to map Colorado, their technique was polished. A base line was laid out and accurately measured, its location precisely determined by star sightings. From the base line nearby peaks were sighted, and these peaks in turn were used as triangulation points to tie in other summits. The surveyors hefted their forty-pound transits, plane tables, and mercurial barometers to the 14,000-foot summits. While a couple of men made sightings, another drew a careful panoramic sketch. In this way they covered all the mountain ranges of the state, making innumerable first ascents on the way. After four summers in the mountains, the field work was complete. Back in the Survey office, Gardner and his associates worked on a masterful series of maps, the first in North America accurately to depict mountain topography.

Before we leave the Hayden survey, we must trace certain events during the 1872 trip to the Tetons. A range of jagged peaks that burst upon the traveler from the plains of Idaho, the Tetons were a familiar landmark to the early voyageurs and trappers. Their dramatic uplift out of the plains gave the Tetons a look of impregnability; as far as was known, no one had reached the summits. Boldest of all was the Grand Teton, and

Nathaniel Langford and survey member James
Stevenson determined to try for the summit. They
returned triumphant and named the peak Mount
Hayden after their chief, but whether they reached
the summit is not clear. They certainly climbed to
the top of the West Spur, some 400 feet below the
summit, where they discovered a man-made stone
structure, the Enclosure. (The Enclosure may have
been built by Indians, or perhaps by the trapper
Michaud, who is reported to have attempted the
ascent in 1843.) However, the Enclosure is located
below the difficult climbing, and Langford's account is unconvincing.

Several attempts were made on the Grand Teton
over the years, but it was not until 1898 that the
peak was conclusively climbed. The successful
party was organized by Wyoming state auditor
William Owen, led by Rev. Franklin Spalding, a
man with wide experience climbing in Colorado,
and completed by Frank Petersen and John Shive.
Owen had made numerous tries at the peak, and
successful at last when guided up by Spalding,
intensified his bitter campaign to discredit the
Langford-Stevenson climb. There is no space here
to probe the various aspects of this unfortunate
dispute. Perhaps Spalding made the most clear-
headed statement about it in a letter to Langford.
Wilson records that Spalding could see no reason
to doubt Langford's word, only regretting that
both Owen and Langford had exaggerated the difficulties of the climb. As far as he was concerned,

"If you did not reach the top when you started out
to do it, you are a mighty poor mountaineer in my
humble judgement, and I cannot understand why
Mr. Owen failed so many times before he
succeeded."

An interesting sidelight on the Owen-Langford
affair is the recent discovery in Owen's personal
papers of a letter that he never revealed publicly.
This letter and an accompanying sketch suggest
that a Captain Kieffer and two other soldiers

Rev. Franklin Spalding, leader of the first proven ascent of the Grand Teton. From *American Alpine Journal* (1939).

climbed the Grand Teton five years before Owen. Whatever the merits of this claim by Kieffer, it is pertinent that Owen kept it under his hat.

By 1900 many of the more prominent mountains in the contiguous United States had been climbed. Mount Ranier, Mount Whitney, and Longs Peak were almost popular excursions; enterprising local men regularly guided parties up these summits. Mountain climbing was under way. But was it mountaineering? If we follow the *Oxford English Dictionary* and define a mountaineer as "one skilled or occupied in mountain climbing," we must conclude that mountaineering hardly existed. The majority of climbers were content to follow the easiest routes, where fitness and determination were the only prerequisites.

There were two major obstacles to the emergence of mountaineering. The first was topographical; the peaks then climbed were simply too easy. Getting to the top of a 14,000-foot peak was no real challenge. The second reason was sociological; everyday life in the new territories was a continual challenge. The pioneers might enjoy a good scramble up Pikes Peak, but they had no need to risk their necks to get a feeling of accomplishment. Life itself was accomplishment enough.

The advance of mountaineering in North America required a class of men with the leisure and the desire to indulge in an adventurous pastime. Ideally, it needed an area where the peaks were challenging from every side. While Owen argued the toss with Langford, a group of sportsmen were busily at work in the Canadian mountains.

REFERENCES

Bartlett, Richard A. *Great Surveys of the American West*. Norman: University of Oklahoma, 1966.

Beuler, William M. *Roof of the Rockies*. Boulder: Pruett, 1974.

Bonney, Orrin H., and Lorraine Bonney. *Guide to the Wyoming Mountains and Wilderness Areas*. Denver: Sage, 1960.

———. "New Facts About Early Wyoming Ascents." *AAJ* 12 (1960): 73.

Brewer, William H. *Up and Down California in 1860–1864*, ed. Francis P. Farquhar. New Haven: Yale University Press, 1930.

Echevarría, Evilio C. "The South American Indian as a Pioneer Alpinist." *AJ* 73 (May 1968): 81.

Farquhar, Francis P. "The Story of Mt. Whitney." *SCB* 14 (1) (Feb. 1929): 39.

———. "Franklin Spencer Spalding and the Ascent of the Grand Teton in 1898." *AAJ* 3 (1939): 304.

———. *First Ascents in the United States, 1642–1900*. San Francisco: Grabhorn Press, 1948.

———. "Naming America's Mountains: The Sierra Nevada of California." *AAJ* 14 (1964): 131.

———. *History of the Sierra Nevada*. Berkeley: University of California Press, 1966.

Hall, Ansel F. "Mount Shasta." *SCB* 12 (3) (1926): 252.

Hart, John L. J. *Fourteen Thousand Feet*. Denver: Colorado Mountain Club, 1972.

King, Clarence. *Mountaineering in the Sierra Nevada*. New York: Norton, 1935.

Langford, Nathaniel. "The Ascent of Mount Hayden." *Scribner's Monthly* 6 (2) (June 1873): 129.

Muir, John. *My First Summer in the Sierra*. Boston and New York: Houghton Mifflin, 1911.

———. *John of the Mountains*. ed. Linnie Marsh Wolfe. Boston: Houghton Mifflin, 1930.

Mumey, Nolie. *The Teton Mountains: Their History and Tradition*. Denver: Artcraft, 1947.

Ortenburger, Leigh. *A Climber's Guide to the Teton Range*. San Francisco: Sierra Club, 1965.

Owen, William O. "The Ascent of the Grand Teton." *AJ* 19 (Aug. 1899): 536.

"Remarks of Professor Brewer." *Appalachia* 4 (4) (Dec. 1886): 367.

Stewart, Charles L. "Early Ascents of Mount Shasta." *SCB* 19 (3) (1934): 58.

Whitney, J. D. *Geology. Vol. 1*. Sacramento: Geological Survey of California, 1865.

———. *The Yosemite Guide-Book*. Sacramento: Geological Survey of California, 1869.

Wilkins, Thurman. *Clarence King*. New York: Macmillan, 1958.

Wilson, Neil C. "Climbing the Grand Teton." *SCB* 12 (4) (1934): 359.

The Heroic Age

There is a marked difference between the men we met in the previous chapters, in what might be termed the predawn era in North American mountaineering, and the men we are to meet now—the first real mountaineers on the continent. To the scientists and adventurers of the mid-nineteenth century, the climbing experience was often a one-time thing. With few exceptions these men were not dedicated mountaineers, and in general the climbs they made required little mountaineering skill. However, several of the climbers who emerged in North America during the last years of the nineteenth century were technically accomplished, climbed extensively, and made ascents that are difficult even by today's standards.

Most important to the establishment of a community of mountaineers in North America were the developments then taking place in the European Alps. Although mountaineering in Europe began slowly in the late eighteenth century, by the mid-1850s a corps of predominantly British amateurs, accompanied by their guides, were zeroing in on the remaining unclimbed summits. The formation of the Alpine Club in London in 1857 helped to focus the efforts of these men, who eagerly recorded their climbs in the pages of the prestigious *Alpine Journal*. At this time the scientific motive for climbing was still much in vogue. The title page of the *Alpine Journal* was inscribed, "A record of mountain adventure and scientific observation." However, as time progressed, science assumed less and less importance.

A noteworthy date in the history of mountaineering is 1865, the year when the combined parties of Edward Whymper and Rev. Charles Hudson first climbed the "impossible" Matterhorn. Within another fifteen years few major European peaks remained unclimbed. This circumstance, far from signaling the decline of the sport, represented its coming of age. Having climbed the European summits, the innovators began two new lines of advance: first, the search for new routes on previously climbed peaks; and, second, the exploration of the other mountain ranges of the world. By the late nineteenth century, European mountaineers were active in the South American Andes, the Caucasus of Russia, the Himalayas, and, inevitably, the mountains of North America.

The European Alps, birthplace of mountaineering, are striking for their active glaciers and extensive snowfields. Thus, when the Europeans turned to North America, they looked for snow-covered ranges. Interest centered on the Alaskan, Canadian, and Cascade ranges since the peaks of the Sierra Nevada and the Rocky Mountain chain in the United States lack extensive permanent snowfields. Due in part to the railroad that crossed the ranges and in part to the fact that the majority of the visiting Europeans were British, the Canadian mountains were the first to be attempted in a systematic way by competent climbers.

One of the first Europeans to look at the Canadian mountains with a climber's eye was the Rev. Henry Swanzy, who crossed the Selkirk Range on horseback in 1884, following the route of the partially completed transcontinental railroad. Back in England, Swanzy fired the imagination of his cousin, Rev. William Green, with descriptions of this new field of alpine climbing. The Selkirk peaks themselves certainly resembled the Alps with that combination of rock and snow that is the essence of alpine climbing. The valleys, however, were markedly different. The high mountain valleys of the Alps had been settled for centuries before the first climbers arrived, and the peaks were relatively accessible. But in the Canadian mountains there were no permanent settlements. Lush primeval forests filled the valleys.

Green and Swanzy journeyed to Canada in 1888 and headed west on the recently completed Canadian Pacific Railway (C.P.R.). They left the train at Glacier House, a stopping-off place in the heart of the Selkirks (below today's Rogers Pass) where the weary passengers got meals and gazed in wonder at the Illecillewaet or "Great Glacier" that descended almost to the railroad line. (Some of the passengers were cynical about the glacier, openly wondering whether the all-powerful C.P.R. had not manufactured it as a publicity stunt.) After resting up from their journey halfway around the world, Green and Swanzy left the comforts of Glacier House and headed into the trackless wilderness with an ambitious climbing and mapping program. Their first important ascent was Mount Bonney, a 10,000-foot peak visible from Glacier House. This was the first technical climb in Canada and one which they found so tricky that they resorted to the rope on the way down. "Taking off the rope and making a bowline hitch on one end, we descended, trusting to the rope for handhold, then, jerking it clear of the rock it was fixed to, we hitched it on to one lower down and thus reached safe footing." Green's enthusiastic descriptions in his subsequent book *Among the Selkirk Glaciers* stimulated interest in the region and gave the concept of mountaineering in Canada the approval of a distinguished member of Britain's illustrious Alpine Club.*

*Green may also be regarded as the originator of mountaineering in New Zealand. He was the first person to attempt serious climbing in the Mount Cook region in 1882, only just failing by some 200 feet to climb Mount Cook itself.

William Green, seated, during his New Zealand campaign with Swiss companions Ulrich Kaufmann, left, and Emil Boss. From *A Land Apart*.

In connection with Green's descent and his use of the rope as a primitive rappel, it should be noted that the original conception of rope management differed from today's practice. On rock as well as snow the entire party moved simultaneously with the rope taut between each person. If a slip occurred, the hope was that the falling climber would be pulled up by the tightening rope. Apart from the "alpine rope," of highly dubious strength, the only other climbing tools then in general use

were stout boots, preferably nailed, and a massive shoulder-high ice axe.

Two years after the ascent of Mount Bonney, Swiss Alpine Club members Carl Sulzer and Emil Huber boldly climbed Mount Sir Donald, the finest peak in the vicinity of Glacier House. On their way home, the Swiss mountaineers addressed a meeting of the Boston-based Appalachian Mountain Club. Despite its name, the A.M.C. was not then a mountaineering club but an organization primarily devoted to the study and enjoyment of the New England hills. One of the most attentive listeners at this gathering was the professor of modern languages at Tufts College, Charles Fay, who had himself scrambled up to the foot of Mount Sir Donald that same year. Fay was already in his 44th year when thus introduced to the Canadian mountains, yet his spirit and his enthusiasm for this new passion were boundless. He would play a key role in turning the attention of his fellow club members to the sport of mountaineering and, more importantly, toward the Canadian mountains.

At this time it was simpler for a climber from Boston to climb in the Alps than the Canadian mountains. Largely through Fay's advocacy, the Canadian Alps, as they were then called, attracted a small but increasing band of climbers during the last years of the nineteenth century. Their base was the genial Glacier House, where the regulars met year after year for the climbing season. After a hard day on the peaks these pioneers joined to-

Glacier House, August 1893. Left to right: Demster, Stables, Charles Thompson, Harry Nichols, Samuel Allen. Note the huge ice axes. From *American Alpine Journal* (1941).

gether for a hearty supper and then gathered round the log fire to swap experiences and study their "bible," William Green's *Among the Selkirk Glaciers.*

Although Glacier House continued to be an important climbing center for many years, the focus of innovative climbing shifted eastward to the Canadian Rockies. These somber peaks, rising above lakes of an almost surrealistic range of colors and flanked by forests and turbulent rivers, had one important advantage over the Selkirks: The forests were more open, which made it possible to travel through the range on horseback instead of on foot. Thanks to the patronage of hunters and other sportsmen, a horse-packing business flourished at Banff, principal township in the newly created Banff National Park. The men who led the packtrains were a colorful bunch who fought and cussed their way through the fearsome swamp and brush and across the swift-flowing rivers. Their role in the exploration of the Rockies was second only to that of the climbers themselves.

Samuel Allen and Walter Wilcox, both just graduated from Yale, were the first climbers of consequence in the Rockies. In 1893 they were defeated by a bitterly cold wind, ice-glazed rock, and a snowstorm on that majestic symbol of the Lake Louise area, Mount Temple. Undeterred, they returned the next year to master it; climbing in the Canadian Rockies was under way in earnest. The following year Charles Fay brought a large party to the Rockies, among whom was Phillip Abbot, a dashing young lawyer and climber with wide experience in Switzerland. After some preliminary climbs, they settled on the massive and brooding Mount Lefroy as their principal objective, but they were unsuccessful. Abbot badly wanted to take this prize and urged Fay to keep details of the climb secret for fear a hotshot team from Britain's Alpine Club would be drawn across the Atlantic. The climb was kept quiet, and one year later an Appalachian Mountain Club party again set out for Mount Lefroy. Abbot, unquestionably the strongest climber in his party, was soon probing the route high above his rope mates. As he was still not sure whether his was the right way, he told his friends to untie and remain where they were while he went ahead with the rope. Minutes went by. They wondered what was taking him so long. Then, suddenly a stifled cry, the sound of falling rock, and Abbot fell past them and rolled down the slope. His companions were aghast. Just seconds before they had all been full of life, confident of Abbot's ability. Now he lay motionless below them.

This fatality, the first known in North American mountaineering, was a severe blow at a time when it was considered unacceptable for educated young men to risk their lives in such aimless pursuits. A heavy pall hung over the new sport. There was talk that this foolishness would have to cease. Yet Fay persuasively argued the case for the new

Phillip Abbot, the first climber to lose his life in North America. From *Appalachia* (1896).

climbing of which Abbot himself had been such an enthusiast, and happily Fay's views prevailed.

He immediately arranged for a strong Anglo-American party to attempt Mount Lefroy and lay its tragic past to rest. As was then common, members of the party gathered at Glacier House in the neighboring Selkirks for warm-up climbs. According to a rumor among the thronging tourists, a party of Swiss guides was expected in the vicinity. When a tall and distinguished-looking man left the train wearing puttees and nailed boots and carrying an ice axe, he found himself the center of attention. Despite his apparent indifference, he could not escape the curiosity of the lady travelers, who got him seated in a chair and marveled at his strange clothing, especially his boots, on which they "tested with dainty fingers his Mummery screws." Norman Collie, British scientist,* art connoisseur, and mountaineer had arrived in the Canadian mountains! An early advocate of climbing without guides (then almost a heresy among fellow members of the Alpine Club), he was an outstanding mountaineer. With his friend Albert Mummery, inventor of the screws designed to replace boot nails, and without guides, he had made first ascents of some of the hardest climbs in the Alps. Apart from being an early pioneer of rock climbing in the British Isles, he had joined Mummery in an audacious, even today almost incredible, 1895 attempt on Nanga Parbat, the isolated Himalayan peak that became the last resting place for Mummery and so many others during the following years.

The party assembled by Fay and Collie was a strong one and included the Swiss, Peter Sarbach, the first professional guide to climb in Canada. The Thorington Archive contains Abbot's prophecy, "Lefroy is bound to be captured by the most obvious way the first time any first-class climber from the Alpine Club gets his eye on it," and now a powerful team was intent on the ascent. Shortly after 2 A.M. the group rowed across the still waters of Lake Louise by starlight and began the climb. They chose a different line to Abbot and passed the danger zone without difficulty. From there, steep snow climbing led them to the summit one year to the day after Abbot's death. Following this success, a smaller party accounted for the other

*Collie was the discoverer of neon, and one of the first persons to take x-ray photographs for medical purposes.

"The Canadian Alps" as photographed by Walter Wilcox. Mount Lefroy, at left, is connected to the many summited Mount Victoria by Abbot Pass. The first ascent routes on both peaks were via Abbot Pass. From *Camping in the Canadian Rockies*.

outstanding peak overlooking Lake Louise, which a patriotic Britisher had named Mount Victoria.

Collie and his companions then decided to push into the unmapped country north of the railroad. One particularly clear day Collie gazed into the distance and made out two peaks that dominated all others. Could these mountains be David Douglas's 17,000-foot giants, Brown and Hooker, reported some seventy years before but never sighted again? Back in England Collie looked into the question of those almost mythical mountains. The Canadian scientist Arthur Coleman had devoted

parts of three summers to tracking them down and was convinced that their great height was a fraud, but Collie's researches persuaded him that the matter deserved further investigation. If the peaks he had seen did not turn out to be the missing ones, that was perhaps even better; in that case they were new and unknown mountains.

For the following year's Canadian campaign Collie talked two "crack Alpine Club men" into joining him, Hugh Stutfield and Hermann Woolley, the latter a well-known amateur boxer. Hopkinson records that on one occasion Woolley was

Swiss guide Peter Sarbach, left, and British Alpine Club members George Baker and Norman Collie outside the C.P.R.'s Banff Springs Hotel. Courtesy Archives of the Canadian Rockies, Banff, Alberta.

The 1897 first ascent party on Mount Lefroy. Norman Collie, far left, Charles Fay holding a cup and Peter Sarbach, right front. The other members were Harold Dixon, A. Michel, Charles Noyes, Herschel Parker, Charles Thompson and J. R. Vanderlip. Courtesy Archives of the Canadian Rockies, Banff, Alberta.

riding a bus in Manchester, his hometown, when the conductor asked his help in removing a "noisy ruffian." Woolley suggested that the man step off the bus, but the man wouldn't budge. However, a broad-accented spectator chimed in, "Tha'd better, it's Woolley." The suddenly attentive man jumped for his life.

In the Canadian mountains Collie, Stutfield, and Woolley were described by their packer as perfect gentlemen. Nonetheless, these trips into the wilds gave them a chance to throw off the conventions of formalized Victorian society, the tall hats and frock coats that went with them, and to live the carefree wandering life.

After more than two weeks of hard going through trackless forest and swamp, Collie and his friends viewed an unknown range of magnificent snow peaks and glaciers. Around their campfire they determined to climb the nearest and boldest peak, which they named Mount Athabasca. Between them they had climbed in the Alps, the Caucasus, and the Himalayas; however, they had never had to spend two weeks getting to their chosen peaks, and by now they were almost out of food. The following day, while his companions slowly disappeared from sight on their way to Mount Athabasca, Stutfield went off in search of game. If he did not succeed, they would all have to head home. Before long he spotted a band of bighorn sheep and stalked up to them; within moments three of them lay dead, and the exploration could continue. Yet at a time when most men shot anything that moved, Stutfield was genuinely sorry that he had to kill such magnificent animals.

While Stutfield was hunting, his friends scrambled up the last few feet to the top of Mount Athabasca. "The view that lay before us in the evening light was one that does not fall often to the lot of modern mountaineers. A new world spread at our feet: to the westward stretched a vast icefield probably never before seen by human eye, and surrounded by entirely unknown, unnamed and unclimbed peaks." Yet close to them was the most exciting discovery of all, for here were two magnificent peaks. Could these be Mounts Brown and Hooker? Collie felt that they were and as rapidly as possible set up his plane table and mercury barometer to make the necessary measurements. (Collie had burdened himself with this bulky equipment because mapping and scientific observations were still part of the total mountaineering experience.) He came to the conclusion that the mountains were indeed Brown and Hooker.

After a day of rest the whole party set out for the snow peak that Collie took to be Mount Hooker, but it was farther away than they imagined, and they had to settle for a lesser climb, the Snow Dome. The revealing view from this peak threw Collie's earlier conclusions on Brown and Hooker into disarray, and he was as mystified as ever. Hoping to shed fresh light on the problem, they next climbed Diadem Peak and obtained a clear view of the forbidding black cliffs of the supposed Mount Brown, which they later named Mount Alberta. It was "a superb peak," Stutfield wrote, "like a gigantic castle in shape," that inspired the greatest respect, having an air of "grim inaccessibility about it." By now the campaign was almost over for that year; Mount Alberta's time would not come for many years.

That winter Collie again pored over early references to the elusive Brown and Hooker. Coming across Douglas's journal, he finally concluded, as Coleman had before him, that far from being 17,000-foot giants, they were inconsequential minor peaks of around 10,000 feet. But to David Douglas we must give the credit for causing so much intensive exploration in search of them.

In 1900 Collie and Stutfield and their packers were in the Rockies once more, slowly fighting their way toward the Mount Alberta region from the west by way of the Bush River. It was a hopeless task. On the west side of the Rockies the dense brush and forest, fed by moist Pacific winds, are virtually impassable. The area is the home for swarms of malignant insects, as the mountaineers learned to their sorrow. Their packer, Fred Stephens, a good-natured Michigan lumberman, showed them his arm, "which was quite swollen with the bites of black flies—a new form of insect plague which, together with the clouds of midges, now began to form quite an agreeable variation to the incessant attacks of the mosquitoes." All was

not lost that year. On their return from the abortive Bush River trip, Collie and Stephens climbed Mount Edith, a rock peak near Banff. On top, the bon vivant Collie opened a bottle of his favorite champagne and inquired of the rough-and-ready Stephens what he thought of the vintage. "Well, Collie," came the reply, "I've tasted cider back in old Michigan that beats this stuff all to hell."

The transcontinental railroad greatly facilitated systematic climbing of a high caliber in the Canadian Rockies and Selkirks. Although the mountain section of the C.P.R. was an engineering triumph and a boon to climbers, it was an economic disaster. William Van Horne, the energetic and far-seeing general manager, realized that a profit might be made by promoting the mountains as a second Switzerland. He imported the Swiss guides Christian Hasler and Edouard Feuz to Glacier House for the 1899 climbing season. In a similar vein, a 1901 C.P.R. brochure, "Mountaineering in the Canadian Alps," announced that "British Columbia, in many respects, is an improvement on Switzerland." However, the chief supporting evidence offered for this claim was the presence in the area of magnificent and highly touted hotels managed, of course, by the C.P.R. The brochure continues,

The man who has won his spurs in the Alps, Caucasus, Himalayas or Andes needs no hint, but, for the benefit of the tyro, it may be worth while to point out that, as a general thing, snow is safer than rock; that couloirs are less dangerous then arêtes; that if the rope is to be of any use it must always be taut; that twelve feet should be the minimum distance between men when they are roped; that crampons* are snares, and that boots should be well nailed.

As for the rest of the equipment, Alpine Club ropes, strong tweed suits, and ice axes are recommended, with particular emphasis on the latter. "The ice axe preferred by most old climbers weighs four pounds, the head being modeled on that of the pick-axe." What the significance of "old climber" is, we cannot be sure.

The brochure ends by mentioning the mountaineer's indispensable barometer and the opinion of a "Mr. Whymper" as to the best type of barometer to use. For their publicity campaign the C.P.R. had engaged the services of the most famous English-speaking climber of the day, Edward Whymper, to give the new alpine playground his solicited approval.

Meanwhile, from England, Collie anxiously informed Appalachian Mountain Club member Charles Thompson of the forthcoming onslaught on "their" mountains by Whymper and a team of Swiss guides. Thorington preserves for posterity his angry words, "Why the devil he won't leave them alone I don't know . . . all I can say is *damn*

the man! Why I am so mad about it is that it is not done for sport at all, or because Whymper has any real liking for the hills. From beginning to end it is all *dollars.*"

Whymper, now in his sixties, was no longer the fiercely determined climber who had mastered the Matterhorn in 1865. He was a lonely, haunted man, who still lived in the shadow of the Matterhorn tragedy, where he had watched four of his ropemates slide to their deaths in the most notorious accident in climbing history. The tragedy marked the man. The most brilliant climber of his day increasingly withdrew from life and in his later years was known to be fond of the bottle. Although Whymper was out of serious contention for the major peaks, a young British clergyman, James Outram, was very much interested. Outram, a "delightful fellow and excellent climber," according to Whymper's Swiss guide, Christian Klucker, was much like the young Whymper of yesteryear: ambitious and determined, as the author learned from first-hand experience.

In July 1967 Yvon Chouinard, Joe Faint, and I set out for Mount Assiniboine. We knew nothing of the peak save that it was popularly known as the "Matterhorn of the Rockies" and that its north face was unclimbed. I was impressed when I saw a picture of the face some weeks before, impressed and intimidated. Although I had climbed in Europe and South America, I had never tried such a difficult-looking new route.

---

*Derived from the earlier ice creepers, crampons are spiked metal frames that are strapped to the soles of climbing boots to give a better grip on snow and ice. At their stage of development in 1901 they were often more trouble than help.

Mount Assiniboine as photographed by Walter Wilcox, who attempted the peak with Henry Bryant and Edouard Feuz in 1901. Outram's party climbed the far side and descended the north ridge, facing camera. From *Camping in the Canadian Rockies*.

It was late afternoon when we got to our campsite near the peak. Shadows fell across the valley. There was a chill in the air, and a wind ruffled the water of Lake Magog. We gazed at the face—and the face gazed back. How hard was the climbing? Would the weather hold? What about rockfall? We made supper and went to bed early. On the surface I was calm. Deep inside I was scared; scared of the unknown.

In that summer of 1967 I knew nothing of the story of North American climbing. It was only later that I learned about the Canadian pioneers and the struggle to climb Mount Assiniboine. If I was that scared, how much worse must the peak have looked through the eyes of the early mountaineers?

At the turn of the century several mountaineers vied for the honor of first climbing Mount Assiniboine. Three determined attempts had been beaten back, and Outram hints at the strong current of competition, "Who should be the next to storm the citadel and what the outcome? This question was uppermost in many minds when the disappointing news of the last failure became known, and the pros and cons were most exhaustively debated around Mr. Whymper's campfire." Christian Klucker was anxious to try this alluring peak, but as the days went by, it dawned on him that Whymper was in the Rockies merely as propaganda for the C.P.R. The party stuck to areas near the railroad, and Klucker's eager wish to try Mount Assiniboine was not even considered, Whymper replying, "I have no orders to do that."

However, Outram was under no such restraints and set off hotfoot for the "Matterhorn of the Rockies" accompanied by two of Whymper's guides, Christian Bohren and Christian Hasler. Their first attempt was frustrated by worsening weather. On their second try, after bouts of arduous stepcutting up steep ice and problems with the loose and brittle rock, Outram excitedly clambered onto the top of the highest peak then climbed in Canada. From there he could see the possibility of descending, not by the route they had come up, but by the north ridge, the route that had defeated all previous comers. His guides wanted none of this and nervously pleaded to go back the way they had come, but Outram's mind was made up. With his reluctant guides in tow, he descended the north ridge. Bold tactics, but the leading amateurs of the day were often better climbers than the average guide. Outram's triumph was complete. According to his own estimate, it was "perhaps the most sensational mountaineering feat then achieved in North America."

They descended over much unstable rock and ice, but Outram felt that with a rope "a careful party of experienced mountaineers is absolutely free from danger." This is arguable since the only belays then known (the climber stood firmly and braced himself or hitched the rope around a rock projection) would not hold a serious fall. The many instances, particularly in the Alps, of whole parties falling roped together were a tragic consequence of the rudimentary knowledge of rope handling. Nevertheless, the rope helped those behind the leader who, in contemporary accounts, frequently were thankful for a tight rope from above.

Collie had been away from the front for a year (or three, if we count the season he spent fighting his way through the bush), but he and his friends, Stutfield and Woolley, were determined to return to the fray. They particularly wanted to keep as many "scalps" away from Outram as possible.

The successful party on Mount Assiniboine. Left to right: Christian Hasler, James Outram and Christian Bohren. Courtesy American Alpine Club.

Collie and the Appalachian Mountain Club climbers had painstakingly discovered the ways to the peaks. Now it looked as if "the interloper Outram" was going to muscle in and grab the best of the unclimbed summits.

Now that Mount Assiniboine was climbed, Collie considered Mount Forbes the finest and probably the most difficult of the major unclimbed peaks in the Rockies. More to prevent the rival party from taking the prize than from friendship, the Collie and Outram forces formed an uneasy alliance for the expected hard struggle. The most forceful climbers of the day united to attack this striking peak. We may picture the scene at their camp on the evening before the advance: the men smoking their pipes and rechecking their equipment, the horses corralled nearby, and the packers preparing the evening meal over a smoking fire. The quiet conversation touched on many subjects, for these were educated men. Woolley perhaps recounted his travels in the Caucasus while Collie explained his pioneering work on x-rays, and the brothers Hans and Christian Kaufmann spun tall stories about climbing back home in the Alps.

The guides began preparing breakfast at 3 A.M., and the entire team left their bivouac at sunrise. By late morning they had arrived at a false peak; the crucial section of the climb lay ahead. The route went up a narrow ridge which dropped away for several thousand feet on either side; they felt vulnerable and exposed. Outram relates that the climb was a continual test of skill made more difficult by the poor rock. At one point Hans Kaufmann fell when a rock gave way under his feet. Only his instinctive clutch for the ridge avoided a disaster. Finally, they climbed the last snow slope, and the coveted Mount Forbes was won. Yet after this triumph the two groups went their separate ways. Outram, hot for glory, headed north to the alluring Mount Bryce. Collie and his friends, hoping to forestall Outram elsewhere, turned to the south. With unclimbed peaks stretching from horizon to horizon, this furtive and competitive dashing about may seem hard to understand. However, the competition paid off, for each team amassed an impressive list of firsts.

The ascent of the magnificent triple-summited Mount Bryce by Outram demanded skill on both rock and ice and required a level of mountaineering far above that achieved by the earliest climbers on the continent. Climbing a steep, smooth sixty-foot rock wall, Outram's guide, Christian Kaufmann, was near his limit. Pondering Kaufmann's position, Outram summed up the near worthlessness of the rope for protecting the leader in those days. This statement stands in marked contrast to his earlier remarks on the Mount Assiniboine climb, "The rope is practically of no advantage to the leader. . . . Though his companions may be firmly planted at the cliff base, the rope clutched in an iron grasp or anchored round a solid mass of rock, yet should the first man fall, a drop of twice the length of the rope paid out must follow."

Following this momentous 1902 season, Outram seldom climbed again. But Collie's love of the hills was deeply ingrained and never faded. The distinguished British climber Geoffrey Young said of Collie, "He was all but the last survivor of a group of great mountaineers. . . . Freshfield, Conway, Slingsby, Bruce, Collie, Mummery, each found his own new territory and wrote his own prophetic books of adventure. And of them all, perhaps, Norman Collie was the man of the greatest natural endowment and the man most exclusively devoted to mountains."

Collie spent his last years on the hauntingly beautiful Isle of Skye off Scotland's west coast, scene of his early climbing experiences. During the Second World War three Royal Air Force pilots were enjoying a brief leave at Skye's Sligachan Hotel. Young preserves an enduring portrait of the elderly Collie. The pilot and his companions were alone at the almost deserted hotel, "save for one old man, who had returned there to die. His hair was white, but his face and bearing were still those of a mountaineer, though he must have been of a great age. He never spoke, but appeared regularly at meals to take his place at a table tight-pressed against the window, alone with his wine and his memories. We thought him rather fine."

After a day out on the peaks, the three young men enthusiastically told the landlord of their adventures. He was indifferent to them, but to the old man sitting by the window their adventures rang true. As he turned and smiled at them, perhaps he saw those peaks and times of long ago. In his later years he had written about the pioneering days. He noted all that the mountains had meant to him and the changes that were taking place. However, he was not one to glorify the past

Mount Bryce from the Columbia Icefield. Outram and Kaufmann's route started at the col on the left and traversed the ridge to the highest summit. *Max Dehamel.*

and bemoan the present. What he said is as relevant today as when he wrote it half a century ago, "Civilization has stretched out its hand and changed it all, and though those who know the old days are somewhat sad that the old order has changed, yielding place to new, yet the new order is good, and the land of the great woods, lakes, mountains and rushing rivers is still mysterious enough to please anyone who has eyes to see, and can understand."

The contributions of Collie, Outram, and their guides and friends were exceptional in laying the foundation of the sport in North America. But if it is true that these men accepted and overcame the major challenges of the day, there were others who were hard on their heels. The Appalachian Mountain Club members were the most important secondary group. Although they failed to make first ascents of the most spectacular peaks, it should be pointed out that they seldom employed professional guides. Every year a hardy band of A.M.C. members gathered at the traditional climbing centers, such as Lake Louise and Glacier House, for another season. In order to move around in those days, they often hitched a ride on the freight cars of the C.P.R. or energetically sped a handcar along the rails in the grey light of dawn to start another tussle with the frozen peaks. The sport had all the ingredients they wanted. It was just the sort of glorious conspiracy of excitement and derring-do that appealed to a certain type of educated man in the Victorian era. To give the United States an organization equivalent to the Alpine Club and to encourage "expert climbing of a distinctly alpine character," these climbers in 1902 formed the American Alpine Club. Many of its founding members played significant parts in opening up the mountains of the continent.

When William Green and Henry Swanzy journeyed from England to the Selkirks in 1888 there were no first-class climbers in North America and no difficult mountain climbs. Yet, within the short span of fifteen years, members of Britain's Alpine Club and Boston's Appalachian Mountain Club accounted for an impressive number of genuinely difficult climbs. Even today several climbs accomplished by the pioneers with their antiquated equipment and primitive techniques are by no means easy. The men have died, but their legacy remains in the ever-growing sport of climbing they brought to North America and in the lonely, storm-swept summits that bear their names.

REFERENCES

Allen, Samuel E. S. "Ascent of Mount Temple, Canadian Rockies." *Appalachia* 7 (June 1895): 281.

Coleman, A. P. *The Canadian Rockies, New and Old Trails.* London: Fisher Unwin, 1911.

Collie, J. Norman. "Climbing in the Canadian Rocky Mountains," *AJ* 19 (May 1899): 441.

———. "The Canadian Rocky Mountains a Quarter of a Century Ago." *CAJ* 14 (1924): 82.

Dixon, Harold B. "The Ascent of Mount Lefroy and Other Climbs in the Rocky Mountains." *AJ* 19 (May 1898): 97.

Fay, Charles E. "Up to the Crags of Sir Donald." *Appalachia* 7 (Dec. 1893): 157.

———. "The Casualty on Mount Lefroy." *Appalachia* 8 (Nov. 1896): 133.

———. "The Canadian Rocky Mountains." *Alpina Americana.* Philadelphia: American Alpine Club, 1911.

———. "Old Times in the Canadian Alps." *CAJ* 12 (1933): 91.

Green, William. *Among the Selkirk Glaciers.* London: Macmillan, 1890.

Henderson, Yandell. "The Summer of 1894 Around Lake Louise." *CAJ* 12 (1933): 133.

Hickson, J. W. A. "Mountaineering in the Canadian Alps, 1906–1925." *Appalachia* 16 (Feb. 1926): 230.

Hopkinson, Charles. "Hermann Woolley." *AJ* 33 (Nov. 1920): 260.

Klucker, Christian. *Adventures of an Alpine Guide.* London: Murray, 1932.

Longstaff, F. V. "The Story of the Swiss Guides in Canada." *CAJ* 28 (1943): 189.

———. "Historical Notes on Glacier House." *CAJ* 31 (1948): 195.

Lukan, Karl. *The Alps and Alpinism.* New York: Coward-McCann, 1968.

Mountaineering in the Canadian Alps. Canadian Pacific Railway, 1901.

Outram, James. *In the Heart of the Canadian Rockies.* New York: Macmillan, 1905.

Scattergood, J. Henry. "After Forty Years." *AAJ* 4 (1941): 190.

Stutfield, H. E. M., and J. Norman Collie. *Climbs and Explorations in the Canadian Rockies.* London: Longmans, Green, 1903.

Thorington, J. Monroe. "Artificial Aids in Early Mountaineering." *Appalachia* 23 (Dec. 1940): 181.

———. "As It Was in the Beginning." *AJ* 62 (1957): 4.

Thorington Archive, Princeton University.

Wilcox, Walter D. *Camping in the Canadian Rockies.* New York: Putnam, 1896.

———. "Early Days in the Canadian Rockies." *AAJ* 4 (1941): 177.

Young, G. Winthrop. "John Norman Collie." *AJ* 55 (May 1943): 62.

To the Top
of the Continent

While mountaineering slowly came into prominence in Canada, other climbers were drawn to the coast of Alaska. There huge, cloud-draped mountains rose above unending glaciers. These Alaskan mountains were larger and more remote than the Alps and the Canadian peaks. They required an expeditionary approach, an unappreciated fact which helped to defeat several early parties. The tallest of these coastal peaks, Mount Saint Elias, had been estimated at around 19,500 feet and briefly enjoyed the reputation as the "highest on the continent." In 1886 a party sponsored by the *New York Times* set out for Mount Saint Elias. Much impressed by the grandeur of the surroundings, they declared the summit utterly inaccessible. Two years later the skilled English climber Harold Topham and his brother Edwin were also turned back by the steep and complex southern side of the mountain.

The better approach appeared to be from the north, and it was from the north that the next attempt on Mount Saint Elias was made. In 1890 Israel Russell led a party sent out by the U.S. Geological Survey. When Russell and his companion Mark Kerr were in position for their final push,

they discovered that their cooking fuel was almost finished. Kerr went back for fresh supplies. As Russell waited, a snowstorm covered and finally crushed his tent, forcing him to abandon it in favor of a narrow snow hole. Here he huddled with his meager possessions, trying to cook what little food he had over a wick dipped in bacon grease. Kerr was hardly better off. Stranded by the same storm, he lay on the snow with nothing but a rubberized ground cloth for shelter and nothing but raw flour to eat. Only good fortune prevented a disaster. When the two were reunited six days later, they were in no condition to carry on.

In reviewing the results of this expedition, Russell sensibly concluded that to climb the peak the highest camp should be placed at the saddle or col below the final ridge. It is a pity that he did not put his own advice into practice when he returned the following year. His highest camp was more than two miles below this col. Even so, Russell and two companions struggled up to the col and, after a welcome lunch, continued through a strange and lonely world toward the summit. Late that afternoon they held a hurried conference. Ahead of them was the summit, now because of the hour,

Mount Saint Elias from the east. Israel Russell discovered the route up the wide glacial basin to Russell Col, and attempted the summit up the north flank. *Bradford Washburn.*

Geologist Israel Russell. Courtesy Bancroft Library, University of California.

slowly slipping from their grasp. If only they had placed their camp at the col! But the game was up. Russell had found the route, and had he been a more experienced mountaineer, he would undoubtedly have climbed it. As it was, his failure opened the way for an expedition led by His Royal Highness, Prince Luigi Amedeo of Savoy, Duke of the Abruzzi.

The duke was the third son of the king of Spain, but the king was deposed soon after his son's birth. It might be supposed that the young man would become a dilettante and pass his life in idle pursuits. However, by the age of twenty he commanded a ship in the Italian navy. A year later he climbed the demanding Zmutt Ridge on the Matterhorn. After visiting the Himalayas, he determined to climb there, but outbreaks of food rioting in India caused him to turn instead to Mount Saint Elias in 1897.

Thorough preparation characterized all his undertakings, and his large party moved steadily toward the mountain. However, all was not harmonious. A burly packer threw his weight around and picked on his companions. Only one man stood up to him, and the bully refused to fight unless there was a wager on the match. On hearing of this, the young duke, so the story goes, came up to the braggart, handed over the wager and soundly beat him.

Once the team was established at Russell Col, the climb to the summit was almost a formality and ended in a "hearty shout for Italy and the king" as they planted a flag on top. On the duke's return to the coast, the American mountaineer Henry Bryant, who had also tried Mount Saint Elias that year, came on board the duke's yacht to offer his congratulations. The duke was in a miserable state, savagely bitten by the fearsome Alaskan

Luigi Amedeo, Duke of the Abruzzi.
From *Les Alpinistes Célèbres*.

The same year that the Duke of the Abruzzi climbed Mount Saint Elias, an even higher peak in the Alaskan interior was reported in the *New York Sun*. A party of prospectors named this peak after William McKinley, who would shortly take office as president of the United States, and correctly claimed that *it* was the highest in North America. Although it had been known to the Russians in the 1830s, and to American prospectors as early as 1875, this massive, 20,320-foot ice mountain escaped the notice of the world at large until gold fever and patriotism fastened attention on it.

Before detailing the first efforts to reach and climb Mount McKinley, it is worthwhile considering the problems that this mountain presented to the pioneers. First, there was the arduous journey into the McKinley range, which took from one to three months. Most of the explorers chose to leave civilization in the spring, travel upriver by boat, and pack their loads over tundra and glacier to the peak itself. Others elected to leave in the winter and employ dogsled teams to haul the loads. Conditions were harsh, and it was essential to be self-sufficient as there were no villages where supplies could be obtained. Lightweight, special-purpose gear was not yet available; the food and equipment carried were cumbersome, to say the least.

The next problem facing the pioneers was the selection of a line of attack on the mountain. Mount McKinley has such a complex network of

mosquitoes and barely recognizable. He exclaimed in his broken English, "Mr. Bryant, I have conquaired ze Mt. St. Elias, but ze mosquitoes, zay have conquaired me!"

In later years the Duke of the Abruzzi organized expeditions which approached closer than anyone before to the North Pole, explored the mysterious Mountains of the Moon in Africa, and climbed higher than any previous group in the Himalayas. He belonged to an almost vanished race of explorers who had the private means to organize their own adventures and, more important, the drive to carry them off.

surrounding peaks that finding a feasible overland approach is a difficult problem even with today's maps. Then, switching from one side of the massif to another line of attack was a major undertaking compounded by the relaying of loads; an error in the choice of route was not easily corrected. Finally, there was the climb itself, perhaps not technically demanding, but made difficult by the poor weather, the high altitude, and the scale of the climb—a height gain of over two miles. Mount McKinley is a formidable adversary.

In 1902 a U.S. Geological Survey party led by Harvard graduate Alfred Brooks surveyed the McKinley region. Although unable to attempt the peak, Brooks foresaw that the northern approach was the best. The first climbing attempt was organized the following year by Judge James Wickersham of Fairbanks. Wickersham's group took the northern approach favored by Brooks but hardly probed the mountain's defenses before retreating in the face of avalanche danger. While this party was still in the field, another expedition set out from New York led by Dr. Frederick Cook, who had served with distinction on four expeditions to the polar regions. Among other honors paid Cook, Roald Amundsen (who later led the first party to reach the South Pole) highly praised his outstanding medical services during the 1897 Antarctic expedition, when Amundsen's ship was trapped by the winter ice.

Dr. Cook's party was put ashore at Cook Inlet (named not for Dr. Cook but for the English navigator Capt. James Cook) and headed northwest. They took nine weeks to penetrate the forest and tundra, round the McKinley massif, and come to the Peters Glacier, the route suggested by Brooks. Time was running out. They were not prepared to winter over, so the long journey home had to start within a few days. Before leaving, they pushed up the glacier and boldly attempted the west buttress of the north peak, reaching about 11,000 feet. On their return journey, they completed the first circuit of the McKinley range by coming back to the east, eventually abandoning their horses and rafting downstream to Cook Inlet.

On his return to New York, Cook published his observations on the McKinley region and was subsequently elected president of the Explorers Club. When he announced that he intended to make another attempt on Mount McKinley in 1906, he was able to choose a strong party. Two of his companions were Herschel Parker, who had climbed extensively in the Canadian Rockies, and Belmore Browne, who had spent three rugged seasons in the Alaskan bush.

These two had met by chance. Browne explained the circumstances,

More than seven years have passed since I sat down in a smoking car on the Canadian Pacific Railway to enjoy a morning pipe. . . .

Sitting opposite to me was a man whose eyes never left the rugged mountainsides as they flew by the window. As I studied my companion I knew that his interest in the mountains came from a deeper feeling than the casual curiosity of a tourist, and while the train sped on we talked of mountains and mountaincraft. From the Canadian Rockies our talk drifted back to other ranges we had known, and then I told of how, from high mountains in distant Alaska, I had looked longingly northward to where the great cloud-like dome of Mount McKinley—America's highest mountain—hung above the Alaskan wilderness.

And then I found that my companion was planning an attempt on Mount McKinley's summit the following year, and when I left the smoking-car I had cast my lot with his.

A fateful meeting indeed.

Cook's expedition outfitted in Seattle, which was gripped in an infectious excitement over a new gold rush in the McKinley region. He remarks in his book that when the ship steamed northward out of Puget Sound, it carried a cargo of Alaskan dreamers: prospectors, nimrods, and mountaineers. Intrigued by the power that gold had over the prospectors, the climbers remarked that when the men returned from the gold diggings empty handed, as they usually did, they were "depressed, melancholy, and cursing their fate." However, within a year, these same prospectors had forgotten their disappointments and were back once more on the same often hopeless search for gold. How different, we might say, from our small band of mountaineers, motivated not by gain, but by their ideals. But the similarities between the climb-

ers and prospectors are more striking than the differences: the intense struggle against raw nature and the way that the unknown, be it gold fever or mountain fever, lured the visitors back again and again.

The boat stopped at the new boom town of Cordova, whose main street consisted of a few shanties and tents filled with men in various states of intoxication, all intent on pushing real estate and whiskey. Browne and Parker entered the best-looking saloon, and Browne asked the bartender to play a sentimental favorite on the cylindrical record player: *Absence Makes the Heart Grow Fonder.* The bartender replied, "We ain't got it, but we have what makes the jag grow longer."

From Cook Inlet the party made an extensive but fruitless investigation of the rivers and glaciers on McKinley's southern side. They returned to Cook Inlet by mid-August, after two and a half months in the field, discouraged by the apparent impossibility of climbing Mount McKinley from that side. Parker returned to New York, Browne went off to collect botanical specimens for Cook, and Cook himself did some further exploring. He had told Browne that additional climbing attempts were out of the question for that year, so we can imagine Browne's surprise when Cook cabled a backer in New York, "Am preparing for a last desperate attack on Mount McKinley."

When the party reunited a few weeks later, Browne was amazed to hear that Cook and his

were alone I turned to him and asked him what he knew about Mount McKinley, and after a moment's hesitation he answered, "I can tell you all about the big peaks south of the mountain, but if you want to know about Mount McKinley go and ask Cook." I felt all along that Barrill would tell me the truth.

Back in New York, Cook lectured on his climb, while the doubts of Browne and Parker soon became known among mountaineers. Without proof on either side, no conclusions could be reached, but the tradition of respecting a man's honor, coupled with the thought that perhaps Browne and Parker were disappointed at having missed the climb, kept Cook's claim alive.

In May 1907 Cook published an article in *Harper's Monthly Magazine* entitled "The Conquest of Mount McKinley." It included a photograph of Barrill triumphantly holding the stars and stripes on the summit of North America. Browne and Parker felt the article had inconsistencies, but they were unable to refute it. Shortly after the article appeared, Cook quietly left New York with the object of reaching the North Pole, the exploratory quest of the decade.

When Cook's book *To the Top of the Continent* appeared in 1908, Browne and Parker went to work again. They subjected the narrative and pictures to minute scrutiny. In the summit picture itself there was a small but significant discrepancy. In the book version an indistinct rock-ribbed peak was just visible in the right-hand margin; in the

lone packer, Ed Barrill, had come back triumphant. Browne had traveled in the country guarding the southern side of the peak and felt that it was impossible even to reach the mountain in so short a time, let alone the summit. While Cook and Barrill basked in the glory of their feat, Browne decided to investigate.

After a word with Dr. Cook I called Barrill aside, and we walked up the Seldovia Beach. Barrill and I had been through some hard times together. I liked Barrill and I knew that he was fond of me for we were tied by the strong bond of having suffered together. As soon as we

58

"The Top of Our Continent" (original caption). The telltale peak that gave Cook away is just visible at the right margin. From *To the Top of the Continent*.

magazine version the right-hand margin had been adjusted to cut the distant peak out of the picture. They then went back to the other photographs in the book. By careful comparison, it appeared that this same rock-ribbed peak was also visible in a picture obviously not taken anywhere near McKinley's summit. Browne and Parker had a case with which to confront Cook on his return from the Arctic.

But in September 1909 a cablegram announced that Cook had reached the North Pole. It was the sensation of the day. Before the triumphant Cook arrived in New York, the veteran polar explorer Robert Peary also claimed to have reached the North Pole and cast doubt on Cook's polar journey. However, Peary himself was too involved in the race for the pole for his doubts to seriously weaken Cook's claim. Cook was given a tumultuous reception and the freedom of the city.

Within a few weeks various geographical societies called for the supporting evidence. Cook was in trouble. His only companions had been two Eskimos, who were not available to corroborate him. Moreover, his vital field notes were apparently entrusted to one of Peary's associates. They were cached and never again found. Cook's claim began to look less and less substantial whereas Peary's grew stronger. The public, however, was unaware of these developments. When Congress honored Peary by appointing him rear admiral, while ignoring Cook, there was a groundswell of popular opinion in Cook's favor.

In connection with his Mount McKinley climb, Cook appeared before a special committee of the Explorers Club to answer the charges of Browne and Parker. The hardships of the polar journey had affected his memory, he said, and he asked for two weeks to collect his facts. Before the two weeks were up the enigmatic Cook disappeared from public view. Late in 1909 the Explorers Club decided to organize another expedition to Mount McKinley to study Cook's account on the spot. Unknown to them two other parties had Mount McKinley and Cook in their sights for the following summer.

While the controversy over the North Pole and Mount McKinley raged outside Alaska, Cook was openly disbelieved in Fairbanks. According to Hudson Stuck, Episcopal Archdeacon of the Yukon,

The men . . . who lived and worked in the placer-mining regions about the base of the mountain were openly incredulous. Upon the publication of Doctor Cook's book *To the Top of the Continent,* in 1908, the writer well remembers the eagerness with which his copy (the only one in Fairbanks) was perused by man after man from the Kantishna diggings, and the acute way in which they detected the place where vague "fine writing" began to be substituted for definite description.

Some of these men, convinced that the ascent had never been made, conceived the purpose of proving it in the only way in which it could be proved—by making the ascent themselves. They were confident that an enterprise that had baffled several parties of "scientists," equipped with all sorts of special apparatus, could be accomplished by Alaskan "sourdoughs" with no special equipment at all.

They were right. Tom Lloyd, a Fairbanks miner who knew of a practical route to the summit, organized a climbing party known ever since as "The Sourdoughs." It comprised fellow miners Pete Anderson, Charley McGonagall, and Billy Taylor, whose experience in the Alaskan wilderness better suited them for this arduous climb than the despised "outside doctors and expeditions." Local confidence was running high when they set out for the mountain in December.

On April 12, 1910, the *Fairbanks Daily Times* proudly announced, "McKinley is Conquered. Stars and Stripes Placed on Top of Continent and the Hitherto Unscaled Heights of America's Highest Peak Mastered, Is Proud Boast of Tom Lloyd, Who Returned Last Night." Tom Lloyd had returned alone. His unassuming companions had remained in the back country to work their mining claims. According to Lloyd, the whole party climbed both the true summit, the South Peak, and also the somewhat lower North Peak, where they left a flagpole as proof of their feat. Unfortunately, Lloyd had no convincing photographs. His companions were not around to substantiate his story, and he himself was widely regarded as too old and unfit to make the summit. By the time his partners arrived in Fairbanks, nothing they could say altered the fact that Lloyd's claim was widely disbelieved.

Mount McKinley. The North Peak is at right; the higher South Peak is enveloped in cloud. The route pioneered by the Sourdoughs was up Karstens Ridge, center, then onto the Harper Glacier above the icefall. *Bradford Washburn*.

The Sourdoughs in their Sunday best. Tom Lloyd seated, and standing, left to right, Charley McGonagall, Pete Anderson and Billy Taylor. From *Mount McKinley, the Pioneer Climbs*.

loads of more than seventy pounds per person, and they worked even through the long twilight of the subarctic summer night.

We can imagine Browne's excitement, then, when he noticed the surrounding peaks bore a striking resemblance to those in Cook's photographs, "reproductions of which I carried with me." Cook had not bargained for sleuths of the caliber of Browne and Parker to follow him so relentlessly.

Browne stated,

Our mountain detective work was based on the fact that no man can lie topographically. In all the mountain ranges of the world there are no two hillocks exactly alike. We knew that if we could find one of the peaks shown in his photographs we could trace him peak by peak and snow-field by snow-field, to within a foot of the spot where he exposed his negatives. And now, without going out of our way, we had [not only] found the peaks he had photographed, but we had found as well . . . he was not going towards Mount McKinley but that he was high up among the peaks at the head of glacier No. 2—*at least a day's travel out of his course!*

Cook's failure to mention this detour up a side glacier indicated that it might be the site of his deception. Browne and Parker were closing in for the kill as they climbed up to a minor peak. As they turned to follow a saddle, Professor Parker shouted, "We've got it!" They had found Cook's fake peak! They excitedly matched the cracks in a rock outcrop with those in Cook's summit picture. Then, looking across a glacial basin, they saw the rock-ribbed peak that had given Cook away.

Meanwhile, the Explorers Club expedition under Browne and Parker headed upriver and unexpectedly met yet another group of McKinley aspirants, this one led by attorney Claude Rusk of the Mazamas Climbing Club of Oregon. Browne and company took an early lead in the race for the summit, and they intended to stay in front. Relaying equipment up the glaciers to the site of Cook's camp took one month. It was crushing work under

Belmore Browne packing in Alaska.
From *The Conquest of Mt. McKinley*.

Herschel Parker enveloped in a wolf-fur suit.
From *Hearst's Magazine* (Dec. 1912).

Although there were many flaws in Cook's account, his notorious summit photograph, "probably the most controversial picture in the entire history of exploration," was decisive. Had the telltale rock-ribbed peak not been visible, as it had not been in the *Harper's* piece, Cook's claim might have held up much longer.

With the evidence they sought now gathered, Browne and Parker pursued their other goal, the ascent of Mount McKinley. Despite repeated attempts, they found themselves hemmed in by icefalls and ridges. They returned to civilization defeated, but not demoralized.

The Mazama expedition also made startling discoveries, independently locating Cook's peak (which Rusk went so far as to name "Mazama"). Rusk concluded, "That is all for Dr. Cook. He had many admirers who would have rejoiced to see his claims vindicated, and I, too, would have been glad to add my mite to clear his name. But it could not be. As he has sowed so has he reaped. If he is mentally unbalanced, he is entitled to the pity of mankind. If he is not there is no corner of the earth where he can hide from his past."

These opinions by both the Explorers Club and the Mazama expeditions helped discredit Cook's other and more ambitious claim to have reached the North Pole. Browne's book, *The Conquest of Mount McKinley,* included a chapter titled "The End of the Polar Controversy." However, Browne was overoptimistic; it was the end of neither the polar nor the McKinley controversy, which both raged for years and occasionally surface even today.*

*Although the majority of Arctic specialists support Peary as the discoverer of the North Pole, not a few believe Cook. Had Cook not invented the Mount McKinley climb, his word might have been sufficient to sway the majority to his view. What irony if the Mount McKinley fiction denied permanent recognition to the first man to reach the North Pole!

Belmore Browne photographs Cook's fake peak. Note similarity of right skyline in Cook's picture, page 58. In this photograph the telltale Peak 8450 is the middle of the background peaks. From *The Conquest of Mount McKinley.*

Browne and Parker were not finished with Mount McKinley. The combination of their two defeats, the Cook business, and the commonly dismissed Sourdough expedition made them keener than ever to climb the peak. They were now convinced that the route tried by the Sourdoughs, the northeast ridge, was the best. Although an approach from Fairbanks was more straightforward, they could not resist an opportunity to explore the east side of McKinley. Toward the end of January 1912, their party left the port of Seward and began the 200-mile dogsled journey to the mountain. By mid-April they and an old ally from their previous expedition, Merl La Voy, had rounded McKinley and were waiting for summer conditions. Ahead of them the immense northeast slopes reached two miles into the arctic sky. They left their base camp early in June and two weeks later were at grips with the northeast ridge (Karstens Ridge), an airy succession of dips and rises which fall away steeply to either side.

Conditions on the ridge were tough. Sometimes they had to wade through deep snow; other times they had to chop their way up steep ice. Always there was the cold. To combat it, Browne carried a wolf-fur sleeping bag weighing seventeen pounds. Inside the bag, he wore three pairs of wool socks, two suits of wool underwear, wool trousers, outer trousers, two wool shirts, a sweater, and a scarf wrapped around his waist. With such back-breaking loads, they established a high camp some 3,500 feet below the summit and prepared for the day of reckoning. Early in the morning they reached the last rocks on the ridge, where they had a clear view of the longed-for summit. It seemed deceptively close. Browne recalled, "It rose as innocently as a tilted snow-covered tennis-court and as we looked it over we grinned with relief—we *knew* the peak was ours!"

But, as so often happens in mountaineering, the weather played the decisive role. Within minutes the sky darkened, and they faced a furious storm.

What had looked like a simple walk to the top became a bitter struggle. The wind cut through their clothing, and ice dust swirled about them. The cold was so intense that Browne was afraid to get his spare mittens out of his pack for fear his hands would freeze in the process. It was dangerous to carry on, but they knew the summit was close at hand. Browne continued,

> The last period of our climb on McKinley is like the memory of an evil dream. . . . As I brushed the frost from my glasses and squinted upward through the stinging snow I saw a sight that will haunt me to my dying day. *The snow above me was no longer steep!* That was all I could see. What it meant I will never know for certain—all I can say is that we were close to the top!
>
> As the blood congealed in my fingers I went back to La Voy. He was getting the end of the gale's whiplash and when I yelled to him that we couldn't stand the wind he agreed that it was suicide to try. With one accord we fell to chopping a seat in the ice in an attempt to shelter ourselves from the storm, but after sitting in a huddled group for an instant we all arose—we were beginning to freeze!
>
> I turned to Professor Parker and yelled, "The game's up; we've got to go down!"
>
> And he answered, "Can't we go on? I'll chop if I can!"
>
> The memory of those words will always send a wave of admiration through my mind, but I had to answer that it was not a question of chopping and La Voy pointed out our back steps—or the place where our steps ought to be, for below us everything was wiped out by the hissing snow.

The retreat to their 17,000-foot camp was a grim affair in the storm, but made worse by the knowledge of their narrow defeat. Their food was now low; they had enough for just one more attempt. After a day of rest they set out again, and again the storm closed in around them and drove them back.

We can imagine their disappointment. They had come three times to McKinley; they had almost stood on the summit. Parker concluded, "Perhaps I wanted it too much, but at least I had the privilege of trying." However, the trying had culminated in what was essentially the ascent of McKinley's highest summit. The story of their "failure" is one of the true epics of mountainerring, remembered long after countless successes have faded away.

By the end of 1912, the McKinley situation was unresolved. While few people still had any faith in Cook, the Sourdoughs' claim was equally disbelieved, and Browne, Parker, and La Voy freely admitted they had not made the summit.

In this uncertain atmosphere Archdeacon Hudson Stuck and Alaska pioneer Harry Karstens embarked upon a new attempt. Stuck was one of the few who never doubted that the Sourdoughs reached the lower North Peak. He knew them and had talked to them about their route. The climbing team was completed by Alaskan Indian Walter Harper, who had been Stuck's dog driver during the winter, and young Robert Tatum, who was training for the ministry.

Parker and LaVoy descend Karstens Ridge.
From *The Conquest of Mount McKinley.*

Karstens, often singlehandedly, moved the equipment up the Kantishna River during the fall of 1912 and cached it. The following spring the party attacked the ridge climbed by both the Sourdoughs and Browne and Parker. Methodically, they built a series of well-stocked camps, taking a month to position themselves for a summit bid. The night before the final climb, Karstens cooked flour dumplings that left all except Harper lying awake most of the night with indigestion. Sleep or not, the party was astir at 3 A.M. and set out under a clear sky. Walt Harper remained in front all day. Stuck described the last few triumphant moments,

At last the crest of the ridge was reached. . . . With keen excitement we pushed on. Walter, who had been in the lead all day, was the first to scramble up: a native Alaskan, he is the first human to set foot upon the top of Alaska's great mountain, and he had well earned the lifelong distinction. Karstens and Tatum were hard on his heels, but the last man on the rope, in his enthusiasm and excitement somewhat overpassing his narrow wind margin, had almost to be hauled up the last few feet, and fell unconscious for a moment upon the floor of the little snow basin that occupies the top of the mountain. . . . So soon as wind was recovered we shook hands all round and a brief prayer of thanksgiving to Almighty God was said.

Not only did the Karstens-Stuck party climb to the true summit of McKinley, the South Peak, they also saw the flagpole the Sourdoughs had planted on the lower North Peak. At least part of the Sour-

Hudson Stuck's companions: Robert Tatum, Esais,
Harry Karstens, Johnny Fred, and Walter Harper.
From *The Ascent of Denali*.

dough story was true, but it was still not clear who
of that gallant band raised the pole. Doubts about
the climb lingered on.

One summer evening in 1937 a young climber,
Norman Bright, was reading in the roadhouse of
the McKinley Park railroad station. A massively
built, genial man of about fifty put up his dogs outside. The old-timers greeted him warmly as he
entered the roadhouse. When the big man gave his
name as Billy Taylor, Bright excitedly realized that
he was face to face with a living legend, a member
of Tom Lloyd's Sourdough party. They talked late
into the night. Of Lloyd, Taylor said, "I imagine he
was damn close to sixty. . . . He was awful fat.
Had kind of a nervous breakdown and just keeled
over. . . . He was fine in his way, but he was
lookin' for too much fame." And of his partner,
Pete Anderson, Taylor recalled, "Big husky
Swede. Hell of a good fellow on the trail. Him and
I'd go along and never have no trouble at all. He

was a husky sonofagun. We done all the work but
we never got credit for nothin'."

As Taylor reported, the Sourdoughs had no
mountaineering background, which was perhaps
an advantage, for they had no preconceptions nor
fears. Instead of laboriously setting up a series of
camps and stocking them with provisions in the
approved fashion, they climbed to the summit and
back from their highest camp at 11,000 feet in one
day. For them it was just another long mush.

According to Bright, Taylor reported, "On the
first trip—April 1st—we had to stop four hours
from the top. Had to turn back—saw a storm
coming. Stormed all that day and all the next day."
They waited out the storm at their 11,000-foot
camp and set off for the top once more on April 3.
Bright was absorbed by the unfolding narrative
and asked Taylor a series of searching questions.

"Did you have any special high altitude rations?"
"No. Just bacon and beans. Had doughnuts on the
highest. That's all we took up with us—and hot chocolate—a thermos bottle apiece. Just took a half dozen
doughnuts in a sack and started out. I had three left
when I got back."
"Did you, like Stuck, make pemmican?"
"No, we just had steaks and stews. They took two
weeks on the trip we made in eighteen hours. No, a
month, I think. Well we made it all in one day, by God!
Just breaking day, a little after three, when we started,
and I know it was dark—getting dusk—when we got
back. I know it was an even eighteen hours. I don't

know the exact time. We never paid no attention to that."

"What kind of mountaineering and personal equipment did you take along?"

"Gumshoes. We put on moccasins when we put on our creepers. We had pole-axes and double-bitted axes for chopping wood. We started out cutting [steps] with the pole-axe but finally quit it, and took our climbing poles and creepers and walked right over everything and forgot about steps."

"Why didn't you use climbing ropes?"

"Didn't need 'em."

"What did you leave at the top?"

"A fourteen foot pole . . . dry spruce. We packed and pulled it up. Where we couldn't pack it we pulled it up on a line."

One curious fact about the Sourdoughs was their decision to climb the slightly lower North Peak instead of the true summit. Taylor's explanation was straightforward: The north summit was more prominent from Fairbanks, and they hoped the flagpole would be spotted from town.

The whistle of the train sounded, and the rest of the interview took place on the run as Taylor went to fetch his dogs.

"What stands out most strongly in your mind concerning the climb?"

"I can see the whole route all the way up. It was grand!"

"Would you consider climbing the mountain again if you had a chance?"

"Yes, if there was enough money in it. But not just for sport."

Taylor loaded his dogs into a boxcar and climbed on the freight. Bright shouted to him to take good care of the dogs. "Oh, I will," came the reply, and with that Billy Taylor disappeared into the night, little realizing that this chance meeting would help ensure him and his friends a permanent place in history for one of the remarkable achievements in American climbing.

But for the flagpole they carried to the summit, it is almost certain that the Sourdough climb would never have been generally accepted. However, the story of the early climbs and attempts on Mount McKinley finally assumed its true perspective. As with other great mountains, for example, Mont Blanc and Mount Everest, the people who were drawn to make the first ascent of this "highest on the continent" were a diverse and colorful group: the carefree Sourdoughs, mushing to the top; the stoic Browne and Parker, beaten at last; Stuck, Karstens, Harper, and Tatum, the final victors; and, finally, the tragic Dr. Cook, whose fictitious ascent haunted him to his death.

The early efforts on Mount McKinley were exploratory mountaineering of the first order. The country was unknown, the conditions extreme, the equipment archaic. The pioneers relied entirely on their own resources for months on end. They played the game for keeps.

REFERENCES

Balch, Edwin Swift. *Mount McKinley and Mountain Climbers Proofs*. Philadelphia: Campion, 1914.

Bright, Norman. "Billy Taylor, Sourdough." *AAJ* 3 (1939): 274.

Brooks, Alfred H. "Plans for Climbing Mt. McKinley." *National Geographic* 14 (Jan. 1903): 30.

———. "Mountain Exploration in Alaska." Philadelphia: *Alpina Americana*, American Alpine Club, 1914.

Browne, Belmore. *The Conquest of Mt. McKinley*. New York: Putnam, 1913.

———. "Herschel Clifford Parker." *AAJ* 6 (1947): 408.

Cook, Frederick A. "The Conquest of Mount McKinley," *Harper's Monthly Magazine* 114 (May 1907): 821.

———. *To the Top of the Continent*. London: Hodder & Stoughton, 1908.

———. *My Attainment of the Pole*. Chicago: Polar, 1913.

DeFilippi, Filippo. *The Ascent of Mount St. Elias*. New York: Stokes, 1900.

Dunn, Robert. *The Shameless Diary of an Explorer*. New York: Outing, 1907.

Eames, Hugh. *Winner Lose All, Dr. Cook and the Theft of the North Pole*. Boston: Little, Brown, 1973.

Farquhar, Francis P. "The Exploration and First Ascents of Mount McKinley." *SCB* 34 and 35 (June 1949, June 1950): 95 and 20.

———. "Henry P. Karstens, 1878–1955." *AAJ* 10 (1956): 112.

Ladd, William S. "The Duke of the Abruzzi." *AAJ* 2 (1933): 113.

Moore, Terris. *Mt. McKinley, The Pioneer Climbs*. College: University of Alaska, 1967.

Palmer, Howard. "Early History of the American Alpine Club." *AAJ* 5 (1944): 163.

Parker, H. C. "Conquering Mt. McKinley." *Appalachia* 13 (June 1913): 32.

Russel, Israel. *Second Expedition to Mount St. Elias, in 1891*. Thirteenth Annual Report, U.S. Geological Survey.

———. "An Expedition to Mount St. Elias, Alaska." *National Geographic* 3 (May 29, 1891): 53.

Rusk, C. E. "On the Trail of Dr. Cook." *Pacific Monthly* (Portland) (Oct. 1910, Nov. 1910, Jan. 1911).

Schwatka, Frederick. "Mountaineering in Alaska." *New York Times*, Sept. 20, 1886.

Stuck, Hudson. *The Ascent of Denali*. New York: Scribner's, 1914.

Thorington, J. Monroe. "Frederick Albert Cook (1865–1940)." *AAJ* 6 (1946): 86.

Topham, Harold. "An Expedition to Mount St. Elias, Alaska." *AJ* 14 (1889): 345.

Victor, Paul-Emile. *Man and the Conquest of the Poles*, New York: Simon and Schuster, 1963.

Washburn, Bradford. *Mount McKinley and the Alaska Range in Literature, A Descriptive Bibliography*. Boston: Museum of Science, 1951.

———. "Doctor Cook and Mount McKinley." *AAJ* 11 (1958): 1.

Williams, William. "Reminiscences of Mt. St. Elias." *AAJ* 4 (1942): 355.

Conrad Kain
and Albert MacCarthy

Once Mount McKinley was conclusively climbed, interest in the area waned. It was not until the 1930s that another expedition set out for the summit of North America. In contrast to the remote and inhospitable McKinley region, the Canadian mountains began to assume the role of the European Alps: *the* area on the continent where mountaineers would go for the climbing season. With guides available at the luxurious C.P.R. hotels, mountaineering became an acceptable pastime for professional people. In response to the growth of the sport, a group of Canadians formed their own club in 1906, the Alpine Club of Canada (A.C.C.), modeled after Britain's Alpine Club.

A major objective of the A.C.C. was to provide its members with an economical means to reach and climb the nation's peaks. The club instituted an annual climbing camp at which professional guides were available. The accommodations at these camps were, of course, segregated by sex, but the club's acceptance of women members was enlightened. (Until 1974 Britain's austere Alpine Club was strictly for men.) Nonetheless, Arthur Wheeler, the A.C.C.'s first director, demanded a

certain decorum. Only when the women were well away from camp did he permit them to unhitch their voluminous skirts and reveal the racy climbing knickerbockers underneath.

To promote the idea of women climbing, an article appeared in the *Canadian Alpine Journal* of 1909. The author, Mary Crawford, wrote,

There is no recreation which, in all its aspects of surrounding and exercise, will bring about a quicker rejuvenation of worn out nerves, tired brains and flabby muscles than mountaineering. It is for women one of the new things under the sun and every fresh mountain is a new delight. . . . She spends a night under canvas and feels the first pangs of healthful hunger to which she had long been a stranger. And now—suitably dressed, and with feelings of excitement and wonder—she waits with her party of guides and companions the word which starts her off on her first mountain ascent. Nervous about the experiences to come? Perhaps . . . But there are guides, men of experience, whom she has only to obey, and who will show her the right thing to do.

The great majority of men as well as women relied on professional guides. With few exceptions, the guides in Canada appeared uninterested

Arthur Wheeler, Director of the Alpine Club of
Canada, and two suitably dressed women climbers
at the 1907 annual camp. Courtesy Archives of the
Canadian Rockies, Banff, Alberta.

in advancing the standards, causing one observer
to remark that they preferred walking to climbing.
They did little to pass on skills to their clients, and
they preferred to work from their comfortable
bases at Glacier House and Lake Louise rather
than break paths into new areas. After the first
ascents of the more obvious Canadian peaks,
mountaineers concentrated on the established
routes and thus built up a repertoire of "classic"
climbs.

Among forward-looking mountaineers, the
repetition of classic routes was not enough; the
search for new ground continued. Typical of the
peaks now under attack was Pinnacle Mountain. It
was only on the fourth attempt that a team headed

by Prof. Joseph Hickson of McGill University won
the summit. Hickson wrote about this and his
next ascent, the often-attempted Mount Saint
Bride, in 1911. Approaching Saint Bride with his
guides, he found the campsite of an unknown
predecessor and made an interesting discovery, "a
couple of suspicious *pitons,* quite suitable (though
not employed by us) for mountaineering purposes."*

Although they disdained pitons as unsporting,
the early climbers did have a few cunning ploys.
One of these was the "three-man trick," an unstable and, in nailed boots, painful shoulder stand
where the lower man had to bear the weight of
first one and then both of his companions. Having
put the three-man trick to good use on Mount
Saint Bride, Hickson and his guides then came to a
tough chimney where there was no room for this
maneuver. The resourceful guides had another
trick; they had dragged a pole up behind them.
The plan was to pass this section by clambering up
the pole. This circus act proved too precarious. It
was neither poles nor shoulders that overcame the
narrow chimney but just plain good climbing.

Despite the tricks, Hickson and his contemporaries were hampered by equipment and technique little different from that employed by William Green twenty-five years earlier. The main-
stays were nailed boots, the ice axe, and manila
rope. Crampons were not widely accepted. They
were cumbersome, and the leather straps were
always breaking. The ice axe remained the tool of
the accomplished "ice man." He wielded it with

*This reference to "pitons" (specially constructed metal
spikes for driving into cracks in the rock)—and the implication
that, though some scurrilous knave might use them, *we* would
not—is one of the first times that we get a hint of the dilemma
that the introduction of pitons caused in some quarters.

telling effect as he hewed a line of steps up precarious ice slopes, slopes that today's climber might not want to tackle with such primitive gear. The pioneers also invariably carried their axes on rock climbs. There was a vague feeling that a climb made without an axe was not a real climb. It was used as a walking stick and sometimes served as a temporary hold when wedged into a crack. (Despite popular opinion, it was not used for chopping holds in rock.) Although the early climbers were especially cunning in using the ice axe, it was more hindrance than help on a rock climb.

The use of the manila rope had not improved since Outram's day (and would not improve until the 1930s). At difficult passages, one climber moved at a time. The stationary climbers looped the leader's rope over a rock nub and stood firmly. In 1910 Forde cautioned, "Do not attempt a difficult place where at least one good anchorage cannot be obtained within the length of the rope.

From *Canadian Alpine Journal* (1911).

A slip on such a place will mean disaster for the whole party, and if such a place is met with, a party is not justified in attempting it."

The lack of innovation in equipment and technique had a dampening effect in the years to come. For the sport to progress, it was essential that a method be found to safeguard the lead climber. However, the pioneers saw no way to accomplish this; perhaps, they did not consider it too desirable. There was a strong tradition that "the leader never falls."

Although Hickson and most others favored the Rockies, Canadian climbing had begun in the Selkirks. After the initial explorations around Glacier House, little new climbing was done. The almost impassible forest prevented extensive use of horses, and the Swiss guides were therefore obliged to pack loads and hack trails for days on end. They were not enthusiastic. However, a few climbers were prepared to dispense with guides and attack the undergrowth, especially if an unknown mountain waited at the end of the trail.

In 1908 the robust Howard Palmer sighted remote, glacier-hung Mount Sir Sandford and noted, "Even a far-off view of Mount Sandford is sufficient to arouse enthusiasm in any one with a proclivity for alpine scrambling." At 11,580 feet it is the highest peak in the Selkirks. Even today it requires three days to reach on foot. Palmer, Frederick Butters, and Edward Holway, "that hard-bitten trio," went after Mount Sir Sandford year after year. They failed during three successive summers for want of good weather and technical skill. Then in 1912 Palmer and Holway, joined by guides Rudolf Aemmer and Edward Feuz, Jr., stood on the summit.

Palmer still felt the need to justify climbing as a scientific enterprise, "There is a sentiment current. . . . that mountaineering is an aimless daredevil kind of sport. . . . Whatever modicum of truth this charge may contain with respect to some varieties of mountain climbing, unquestionably it cannot be supported when alpinism is practiced in the interests of exploration and geographical work." Palmer and his contemporaries were hindered by their failure to realize, or admit, that climbing *is* an aimless daredevil kind of sport. They regarded it as a gentlemen's pursuit and had little interest in innovation. They were the powers in the mountaineering clubs, and their views carried weight. The institutions and customs became ever more rigid. In this constrictive atmosphere, strong individuals alone were able to make decisive contributions. Who, then, would master a peak that even today is considered a major challenge?

Mount Robson. A name familiar to every climber in North America. Ever since I began to climb here I knew something of Mount Robson's history and legends: the early climbers, the attempts and failures, the big routes of the present day, the unclimbed "last problems." I heard about the size of the peak, about the violent storms, about the years when avalanche conditions made it almost impossible.

In July 1973 George Lowe and I drove down from northern British Columbia. The weather was perfect, and as we swung up toward Yellowhead Pass, I realised I would get my first close look at Mount Robson. It was a staggering sight. I had never seen a mountain that so dominated its surroundings; it filled the sky. The forested lower slopes rose up to meet the rock and ice, where three steep ridges led the eye upward. The summit was two miles above us, yet we could see clearly the monstrous ice encrustations on the final ridge. We looked at Mount Robson with the eyes of practiced mountaineers. We measured up the difficulties, picked out the routes, and weighed the problems. It looked hard. Yet there was an additional factor: the awe we felt as we gazed at the peak. We knew that Mount Robson could demand everything a climber had to give and then hold out for more. Here was a mountain without compromise.

Although the bulk of the prominent peaks in the Canadian Rockies were climbed by the early 1900s, the highest peak, 12,972-foot Mount Robson was not even approached until University of Toronto geologist Arthur Coleman, his brother L. Q. Coleman, and the Rev. George Kinney set out from Lake Louise in 1907. They were more than a month on the trail. Once in the Robson area, they lost precious time hacking their way through dense undergrowth. In mid-September, with worsening weather and little food, they had to turn for home.

The next year they were on the trail once again for more than a month just to reach Mount Robson. As luck would have it, the clear days seemed to fall on Sundays, and in deference to the minister they did not climb. After days of miserable waiting in the rain, clear weather arrived. Each man set out with "a grouse and a bannock and a bottle of tea" in his pack. They climbed a small forepeak near Robson's east face before nightfall forced a retreat. Then Kinney decided to make a solo bid on the untried northwestern flank. It was a bold stroke. He was confronted by a peak that was both psychologically and technically demanding. It was a far cry from Mount McKinley. The latter had a definite weakness, and the untrained Sourdoughs soon spied out a route that would "go." Mount Robson reared up into the sky. It was steeper and more dramatic; the Sourdoughs would have dismissed it as "impossible." Kinney bivouacked, and, in the words of his 1909 article, "by the first light of dawn I was storming the heights." He reached about 10,500 feet before turning back, an inconclusive attempt, but it demonstrated his determination.

The following day dawned so clear that they decided to make one last effort, which Kinney described, "For four hours and a half we literally hung on the face of that wall of ice, by finger and toe-holes only; and in all that time we gained not

Mount Robson; the Fuhrer ridge (1938) forms the right skyline. Kinney and the Colemans climbed The Dome in the center foreground but stopped at the bergschrund on Robson. Kain climbed to the left of the hanging icefall above The Dome to gain the ridge facing the camera. *Ed Cooper*.

more than five hundred feet. . . . We followed the steep winding valleys of snow, up almost inaccessable grades . . . till at last our rough boots ploughed the white, dry snow of the crest of the highest cliff, and but a narrow field separated us from the peak of the mountain itself." Their progress was blocked by a gaping bergschrund. From Kinney's stirring account, we might suppose they were near the summit. In fact, they had been involved with the complex approach and had not even set foot on Mount Robson!

During the winter Kinney heard that a team from England's Alpine Club had an eye on his peak for the following year. As soon as spring arrived, he set out alone with three packhorses and three months' provisions. On the trail he was joined by Donald Phillips, a young adventurer who had never climbed before. But this detail did not bother Kinney.

He decided to abandon the eastern side in favor of the western slopes, the scene of his solo attempt. According to their account, the two climbers reached an altitude of 12,000 feet. However, they believed that Robson was 13,700 feet high; their actual high point is unclear. Undeterred by this defeat, they tried again and again. Phillips had no ice axe but used instead a sturdy wooden pole. "On all that upper climb we did nearly the whole work on our toes and hands only . . . we finally floundered through these treacherous masses and stood, at last, on the very summit of Mt. Robson. . . . Baring my head I [Kinney] said 'In the name of Almighty God, by whose strength I have climbed here, I capture this peak, Mt. Robson, for my country, and for the Alpine Club of Canada.' "

If anyone deserved the honor of first climbing Mount Robson, it was George Kinney. However, at the annual A.C.C. camp a number of well-known mountaineers found his descriptions of the climb vague. It was soon rumored that he had "instructed" Phillips to support his summit claim. Phillips is later reported to have said that they reached an ice dome some fifty feet high, which they took for the summit, but did not climb because of the danger. A contemporary tells us this admission "nearly broke Kinney's heart." Whether the plucky pair really were close to the summit or just on the long final ridge will never be known. Although no one has retraced Kinney's avalanche-prone route for its entire length, several climbers have finished on the Emperor Ridge, where Kinney's route would have ended up. His case is hurt by his failure to mention the unique "ice gargoyles" on the ridge. The climb remains an enigma.

In 1911 A.C.C. director Arthur Wheeler led the first survey party into the Robson area. A crusty character and a keen disciplinarian, he rode his subordinates hard. The story goes that one afternoon while Wheeler was ahead of the outfit looking for a suitable campsite, Fred Stephens decided to make camp where he was. As Thorington preserves the story, the following morning, after Wheeler had spent an unpleasant night separated from the outfit, he confronted the packer, "Stephens, I always heard you were a damn good man, but you're not." Which earned the reply, "Wheeler, I always heard you were an S.O.B., and you are." The incident dissolved their relationship on the spot.

Wheeler was accompanied by both Kinney and Phillips and by a young Austrian guide, who was to play a leading role in Canadian climbing, Conrad Kain. Kain's origins were not those of the well-known European guides of the day. He was born in an impoverished village tucked away in the Austrian foothills, not a famous alpine center. His

Members of the 1911 Alpine Club of Canada-Smithsonian survey party to Mount Robson. Arthur Wheeler is at the far left, Donald (Curly) Phillips is beside him and Reverend George Kinney is seated in front. Courtesy Archives of the Canadian Rockies, Banff, Alberta.

early life was hard. Long periods of unemployment were interspersed with occasional jobs in a quarry and spells as a poacher. His hand-to-mouth existence continued after he earned a guide's diploma, especially when guiding tailed off in the winter. He had a restless urge to travel, and he left his home for North America with the thought that a guide might make a better living there.

During the 1911 Robson survey, Kain badly wanted to attempt the peak, and Kinney was anxious to return for photographs (and perhaps because his conscience bothered him). However, Wheeler managed to keep the young enthusiasts busy with survey tasks. One day Kain's impetuosity got the better of him. He could not bear to be among such striking peaks without climbing. He quietly stole away from camp and made the first ascent of Mount Whitehorn, a feat generally disbelieved until his summit record was found some years later.

In the summer of 1912 Kain guided a botanical collecting expedition in Russia, then traveled to New Zealand for the southern summer. He found no work as a guide but worked instead at a lumber camp. One day an unexpected letter arrived from Arthur Wheeler. There would be a Mount Robson camp in 1913, and the director of the A.C.C. wrote, "How does the prospect strike you, old boy?" He knew the answer; Kain eagerly returned to Canada.

Wheeler was determined that his club decisively master Mount Robson. He had picked the best available guide, and from the strong group of climbers in camp he selected two staunch friends, C.P.R. engineer William Foster and ex-U.S. Navy captain Albert MacCarthy. Kain had already picked out a route: the northeastern face that had defeated both Coleman and Kinney and the climbers from England's Alpine Club. It was avalanche-prone, but Kain reasoned that with an early start they would be above the danger before the sun loosened the snow.

The three climbers left their bivouac at dawn. By eight o'clock Kain had found a way over the bergschrund and was at work on the lower face. His fears were confirmed; avalanche tracks scoured the snow above them. A fellow guide, who had almost been swept away on this slope, had confided to Kain, "I never saw death so near." Kain cut steps hurriedly and took to the rocks wherever possible. After four tense hours they reached the shoulder of the mountain. Along the final ridge the snow conditions constantly changed. One moment they waded through waist-deep snow; another they climbed terraced ice walls so steep that Kain had to balance with one hand and cut steps with the other. A keen wind whipped across the ridge, and Foster and MacCarthy huddled against the slope while they waited for Kain to finish the leads. When the slopes eased off, Kain quickened his pace. Then he turned around and called back, "Gentlemen, that's as far as I can take you."

Not content with just one success, Wheeler delegated another team to attempt Mount Robson from the west. The intended route was the mile-long Wishbone Arête. Due to its length and the sustained difficulties on steep rock and ice, it was an undertaking ahead of its time. The team was guided by Walter Schauffelberger, a Swiss tea importer who had turned away from his middle class position in order to climb full time. The two home members were Vancouver climber Basil Darling and Harley Prouty, a businessman who had retired early in order to travel.

The three climbers reached the arête shortly after daybreak. The rock was dry, and Schauffelberger was in top form. They were used to climbing limestone and made rapid time up exposed walls and across rubble-strewn ledges. Even so, twelve hours were required to reach the upper ice slopes. There was just 1,000 feet to go! Soon they came to the ice gargoyles. There was no way over the tops, and Schauffelberger furiously cut steps as he led the way around and between them. They could see the summit slope, and their daring bid seemed assured.

On Mount Robson one can never be sure. A storm was gathering in the west. Soon black clouds boiled around the ridges below them, and the first snowflakes fell. Darling and Prouty urged Schauffelberger to go faster, but the wind and cold

Conrad Kain, William Foster and Albert MacCarthy just back from Mount Robson. Courtesy Archives of the Canadian Rockies, Banff, Alberta.

Walter Schauffelberger at the bivouac on the Wishbone Arête. From *Canadian Alpine Journal* (1914).

intensified, mocking their efforts. It was six o'clock. Below them, the rocks they had climbed so quickly in the morning were becoming coated with rime and snow. Ahead was victory, but at what cost? They would have to sleep out on the summit in a raging storm. There was only one reasonable course. Bitterly disappointed, they headed down and spent an awful night huddled on the ridge while the wind and snow hammered into their clothing. High above them thunder and lightning crashed about the summit that might have been their last.

Schauffelberger keenly wanted to return to the Wishbone Arête, but it was not to be. He perished in an avalanche while skiing in Europe the following winter. Despite numerous tries over the following years, his route was not climbed until 1955. The successful team included two of the strongest climbers of the day. They spent two and a half days on the climb, made liberal use of pitons, which Schauffelberger did not have, and referred to it as their hardest mountain climb.

The A.C.C. climbers had discovered one route and probed another on Mount Robson, but neither could be regarded safe or straightforward. Wheeler formed another team and urged them to discover a route usable by average parties. This third team, MacCarthy and Kain, Darling and Schauffelberger, elected to probe the southern flank, the side on which Kain's party had descended. Dogged by bad weather, they were unable to complete this climb. They did reach the summit slopes and thus established the route most commonly used today.

The Mount Robson camp was an outstanding success. The highest, most awesome peak in the Canadian Rockies had been climbed, and two other strong attempts had been made. The patriotic Wheeler was delighted that Canadians were among those who had so convincingly carried off the climbs. Even today none of them is simple. They require mature judgment and have repeatedly turned back fine climbers. Lesser mountains come and go in climbers' esteem, but Mount Robson remains a test of a mountaineer. Many contemporary climbers realize a lifetime's ambition when they climb it.

Conrad Kain's reputation was firmly established, and he began to guide year round: the northern summers in Canada, the southern summers in New Zealand. In Canada he frequently teamed up with MacCarthy, who now ranched in sight of British Columbia's Interior Ranges. In 1916 he accompanied MacCarthy and several companions into the virgin Bugaboo group. These granite spires were strikingly dissimilar to the Canadian peaks then climbed. Instead of the classical snow and ice of the early days, there were stark rock towers; instead of the abundance of holds characteristic of sedimentary rock, there was uncompromising smoothness. Even the simplest route promised a struggle. Kain was forcibly reminded of the famous Chamonix Aiguilles.

Mealtime at an ACC camp. Charles Fay is at the extreme right; Conrad Kain is wearing a dark shirt. Courtesy Archives of the Canadian Rockies, Banff, Alberta.

Climbing Naiset Peak in 1920. Leader Albert MacCarthy belays William Stone, President of Purdue University, who died the next year on the first ascent of nearby Mount Eon. Note the primitive belaying methods. Courtesy Archives of the Canadian Rockies, Banff, Alberta.

For their first climb Kain led a group to 11,150-foot Howser Spire, the highest in the area. He was soon at work on a typical granite problem, a six-inch crack in a blank wall. There were no obvious hand- or footholds. He jammed his side into the crack, twisted his knee against the rock, and wormed his way up. The smooth granite demanded a new technique, where hands, boots, knees, and even the whole body were wedged inside cracks.

After Howser Spire the most appealing summit was Snowpatch. However, even to Kain and MacCarthy it seemed "clearly impossible." They turned instead to Bugaboo Spire. Here the team included Mrs. MacCarthy. She was probably among the dozen top amateurs in North America and a forerunner of high standard mountaineering by women. The climbing went rapidly on Bugaboo until Kain came to a smooth wall. The ridge had narrowed, and there was no way around the wall. The only hope was a direct attack. He worked up a tricky slab and then squirmed into a chimney-like crack. The situation reminded him of a similar problem he had solved some years earlier by wedging an ice axe in a crack, an old standby of the early guides. But when the axe was in place, it proved no use at all. He had to struggle up and remove it. Kain was far above his friends, and his rope arched down to them without any intermediate belays. He experienced the full meaning of his lonely position as leader: If he slipped, there was nothing to stop him, and the jerk would probably wrench MacCarthy from his stance. After several all-out attempts, Kain poked his head out of the crux chimney and called down, "I make it."

This key passage was probably the hardest rock pitch in North America. Kain later said that Bugaboo Spire was his most difficult Canadian ascent, fully comparable with the best climbs he had made in the Alps. In Kain's opinion, Bugaboo Spire was more difficult than Mount Robson. Today the estimate is just the reverse. Bugaboo Spire is no more than an enjoyable rock scramble whereas Mount Robson will test the best climbers. The explanation of this anomaly lies in the difference in the kinds of problems posed by the two mountains. Mount Robson is classic alpinism: a big mountain, steep ice, avalanche danger, loose rock, exposure, a sense of isolation, sustained effort—all the elements that make mountain climbs a psychological problem. The early climbers could deal with these elements. From years of experience they had the "feel" of big mountains. But when Kain and MacCarthy came to steep granite, they were on new ground. They had to improvise their technique. A fall was a distinct possibility, and they knew of no adequate safety measures.

Today, climbers learn the "moves" and belaying techniques on practice cliffs. But no amount of cliff climbing will prepare them for a Mount Robson. When they confront such a peak, they have to overcome again the problems of an earlier age.

Why did Kain achieve more than his fellow guides? The answer lies in his own drive and his good fortune in guiding MacCarthy, one of the best amateurs of the day. Their collaboration was fruitful; without it, neither would have made so many fine climbs. Unlike some guides who were content to take their clients up the "milk run," Kain was interested in difficult climbs. For him mountaineering meant technical climbing; otherwise, as he once put it, "Why not go for a stroll in the park?"

In the traditional guide-client relationship of the day, MacCarthy let Kain take the brunt of the leading. However, MacCarthy's expertise is brought out by their first ascent of the spectacular rock spire, Mount Louis, which they daringly climbed unroped. For several years it had a reputation as the toughest rock climb in the Canadian Rockies.

Mount Logan

Although a few North Americans were active in the Alps in the early 1900s, climbing here proceeded independent of the European mainstream. One British effort, however, captured the imagination of American climbers and brought the sport to the attention of the public: the struggle to climb Mount Everest in the 1920s. Something about this confrontation between the phlegmatic gentlemen climbers of Britain and the world's highest mountain inspired people. The climbers in tweed suits and puttees seemed so vulnerable to the whims of the elements; the dice were loaded against them.

George Mallory and Andrew Irvine set out for the summit on June 8, 1924, but never returned. Many people in the western hemisphere were deeply moved. It was a tragedy that contained within it the essence of man's aspirations to greatness. The *New York Times* editorialized, "But other attempts will be made to scale and stand on the peak of Everest, 'because,' as the gallant Mallory has explained, in terms that mountaineers can understand, 'it is there,' a challenge to come and conquer. The casualties may be many, but there will be a victor at last."

The Everest saga inspired the Alpine Club of Canada to attempt Canada's highest peak, 19,850-foot Mount Logan. Situated twenty-five miles inland from Mount Saint Elias, its great height was unappreciated until the 1913 International Boundary Survey. Although Mount Logan is no match for Everest in altitude, several factors made it a tough proposition. The best starting point was 140 miles from the peak, the last half of the distance over icefields. Mount Logan lies among the most extensive glaciers on the continent, a land of "utter desolation" the Survey had termed it. The peak itself has a base circumference of some ninety miles. But more telling is the eleven-mile long summit plateau, which the climbers would have to cross.

When plans for a Mount Logan expedition were drawn up in 1924, Albert MacCarthy was named leader. At age forty-nine he was still a forceful climber. (In 1926 in the Alps he made 101 ascents in sixty-three days and reputedly exhausted several guides in the process.) He weighed the problem of Mount Logan and decided to delay the climb by one year in order to scout its defences. From this reconnaissance he concluded that for the climbers to reach the mountain in good condition, it would be necessary to take in the equipment in advance. This involved hauling ten tons of supplies the 140 miles, and *MacCarthy proposed to do it in winter*.

MacCarthy and five companions set out with two horse-drawn sleds and three dog teams. The February temperatures plunged to −45° F. The horse harnesses froze solid and could not be removed for two weeks. It was often midmorning before men and equipment were sufficiently thawed to get moving. After more than two months of grueling work under atrocious conditions, the equipment was cached. This feat was a testament to MacCarthy's spirit. And still there was no rest. Two weeks after his return, he met the rest of the climbing team and set out for Mount Logan once more.

Deputy leader Fred Lambart had been through the Mount Logan region with the International Boundary Survey, and William Foster was a tried companion from the Mount Robson climb. Research engineer Allen Carpé represented the American Alpine Club. The team was rounded out by Henry Hall, Norman Read, and twenty-three-year-old Bob Morgan, a former president of the Dartmouth Outing Club. Andy Taylor, who played a key role in the winter freighting, was also a member of the party.

The climbers left McCarthy, Alaska, in the middle of May and picked up caches on the way. Although they used the best equipment then available, they had a staggering load. Their sleeping bags weighed eighteen pounds and their air mattresses eight pounds. Four weeks were required to backpack loads and haul the sleds to King Col, which gave access to the summit. They were now 6,000 feet below Logan's summit, but over eight miles from it along the backbone of the mountain.

When men under stress live in close proximity, personal relationships often become strained. The younger team members, Morgan and Read, began to chafe at MacCarthy's leadership. They felt he treated them like underlings, and they disliked the trivial tasks he assigned to them. They also saw little reason for the slow pace and frequent delays. Could it be that these were efforts to prolong the climb, to make it appear a long and arduous undertaking?

Of MacCarthy's personal example on the mountain there could be little criticism. Despite bad weather, he insisted the party press forward. On one occasion climbers were ferrying loads up to a higher camp when they were caught in a furious storm that hurled them back in their tracks. Retreat seemed the best course. As they veered back, MacCarthy arrived at the head of the second rope. He would not even consider retreat. He struck out into the teeth of the storm and led the way to the

Expedition members sledge-hauling toward Mount Logan. Courtesy Archives of the Canadian Rockies, Banff, Alberta.

Mount Logan on the left, King Col and King Peak from the north. The expedition gained the summit plateau from King Col. *Bradford Washburn.*

higher camp. Possibly as a consequence of this bitter day, Morgan's toes were frostbitten, and he was accompanied off the mountain by Hall.

On June 22, 1925, the six remaining members pitched their last camp on Mount Logan's summit plateau. Ahead lay the long trek to the top; behind them the way home was a stiff climb back to a ridge camp at 18,500 feet. The following day broke cloudy. It was uncertain which of the peaks protruding from the plateau was the summit. When they reached the nearest peak at 4:30 P.M., they saw the true summit still two miles away across an intervening saddle. Wearily, they descended into the depression, cached their snowshoes, and by eight o'clock were on top.

Lambart was weakening fast and had to be assisted. There was little alternative but to scrape holes in the snow and settle down for a night in the open at 19,000 feet. Snow was falling, the thermometer registered twelve below zero, and the climbers had little more than their clothes for warmth.

It was imperative that they escape from the summit plateau and reach their lower camps. But the party was not underway until 2 P.M. the next day. Groping along in the clouds, they found it almost impossible to make out what lay ahead. Eventually, they located the willow wands which marked their route. Lambart, Read, and Taylor reached the plateau camp at 8:30 P.M. However, MacCarthy's rope stopped to fix a pack and be-

came separated from the others. When they set out again faithfully following the willow markers, *they were headed back toward the summit!* The snow slopes did not look right, but there was nothing to tell them the correct direction, for falling snow had covered their tracks. The decision they faced was crucial. If they continued toward the summit, they were lost. But which way was the summit? After many minutes of uncertainty, they turned around. When they rejoined the others early in the morning, they had been without shelter for forty-two hours. The team rested all that day.

The next day dawned fine, and prospects looked good for making the crucial 18,500-foot crossing to the lower slopes of the mountain. Telltale clouds indicated a storm, and Read pushed ahead to locate the crossing. A fierce gale was already blowing when he reached it. Looking back, he saw that the others were contouring around the slopes in the wrong direction. He shouted and waved his arms; if they spent another night out, they would probably perish. For some reason Carpé looked up and spotted Read. The two ropes veered up toward the ridge. It was as much as the stronger members could do to make the ridge. Lambart had fallen in the snow and had to be assisted. They struggled on through the night and reached the King Col camp after 1 A.M.*

*The second ascent of Mount Logan did not take place until 1950. The two-man team consisted of the Swiss mountaineer André Roch and the veteran of the first ascent Norman Read, then aged sixty!

Sheltering from a storm on the descent from Mount Logan. From *Canadian Alpine Journal* (1925).

The mountaineering establishment viewed the climb as a daring success. England's *Alpine Journal* commented, "Greater hardships have probably never been experienced in any mountaineering expedition." However, the official accounts played down or omitted obvious questions about the *reasons* for the hardships. Should Lambart have continued to the summit, thus making the first bivouac inevitable? Why did the ropes become separated in the storm? Why did they almost miss the 18,500-foot ridge crossing? Perhaps the suffering was as much due to the slow pace and the party's state of mind as to the intrinsic difficulties of the mountain. The nub of the problem may be that the climbers approached Mount Logan as if it were a Mount Everest. Difficulties are sometimes as much a creation of man's imagination as a creation of nature.

REFERENCES

Carpé, Allen. "The Mt. Logan Adventure." *AAJ* 2 (1933): 69.

Coleman, A. P. *The Canadian Rockies, New and Old Trails.* London: Fisher Unwin, 1911.

Crawford, Mary E. "Mountain Climbing for Women." *CAJ* 2 (1909): 85.

Darling, B. S. "First Attempt on Robson by the West Arête (1913)." *CAJ* 6 (1914): 29.

"The Everest Tragedy," editorial. *New York Times,* June 22, 1924, p. 4.

Forde, J. P. "Hints on the Use of the Rope in Mountain Climbing." *CAJ* 2 (1910): 191.

Foster, W. W. "Mount Robson (1913)." *CAJ* 6 (1914): 11.

Fynn, Val. A. "On Equipment." *CAJ* 2 (1910): 187.

Hall, Henry S. "Mount Logan." *Appalachia* 16 (Feb. 1926): 205.

Hickson, J. W. A. "Two First Ascents in the Rockies." *CAJ* 3 (1911): 40.

———. "Mountaineering in the Canadian Alps, 1906–1925." *Appalachia* 16 (Feb. 1926): 230.

Kain, Conrad. *Where the Clouds Can Go,* ed. J. Monroe Thorington. New York: American Alpine Club, 1935.

Kinney, G. B. "Mount Robson." *CAJ* 2 (1) (1909): 1.

Kinney, G. B., and D. Phillips. "To the Top of Mount Robson." *CAJ* 2(2) (1910): 21.

Lambart, H. F. "The Conquest of Mount Logan." *National Geographic* 49(6) (June 1926): 597.

MacCarthy, A. H. "The Howser and Bugaboo Spires, Purcell Range." *CAJ* 8 (1917): 17.

———. "The First Ascent of Mt. Louis." *CAJ* 8 (1917): 79.

——— et al. "The Mount Logan Expedition." *CAJ* 15 (1925): 1.

"The Mount Logan Expedition." *AJ* 37 (Nov. 1925): 334.

Palmer, Howard. *Mountaineering and Exploration in the Selkirks.* New York: Putnam, 1914.

Thorington, J. Monroe. *The Glittering Mountains of Canada.* Philadelphia: John Lea, 1925.

———. *The Purcell Range of British Columbia.* New York: American Alpine Club, 1946.

Thorington Archive, Princeton University.

Underhill, R. L. M. "An Attempt on Mt. Robson by the N. W. Ridge." *CAJ* 19 (1931): 73.

Mount Alberta

While Kain and MacCarthy were in the Bugaboos, a large number of their younger fellow climbers fought a more serious battle; the First World War raged in Europe. Many North American climbers served in what they had been led to believe was the "war to end all war." When the conflict ended, several outstanding performers did not return.

It was not until the 1920s that mountaineering in Canada again picked up and continued its slow growth. Hitherto unknown areas were visited, but the actual difficulty of the climbs increased marginally, if at all. As the easiest ways on the new peaks were usually chosen, the problems were not much different from those overcome by MacCarthy and Kain, or Outram and Kaufmann before them. The pace of advance in Canada had never been brisk, and by the midtwenties it all but ceased. The vital creative spark was missing.

In the Alps, on the other hand, no new peaks beckoned. Climbers had to look for new routes up old peaks. This requirement combined with the far greater number of climbers in Europe raised the standards.

One mountaineer in Canada who appreciated the difference between climbing a new peak by its easiest side and putting up a hard route on a previously climbed peak was British engineer Val Fynn. Before he came to live in the United States, he completed several of the most demanding climbs in Europe. He made the second ascent of the awe-inspiring northeast face of the Finsteraarhorn, where he spent the second of two nights on the route sitting in rope slings. Regarded by English alpinist Percy Farrar as the finest guideless climber of his generation, Fynn was as good as the best guides of the day. The guides paid him the rare compliment of referring to him as "one of us." Moreover, he was not put off by the apparent difficulty of a route viewed from a distance. He was able to overcome the psychological problem of a forbidding-looking peak and deal with the actual difficulties encountered.

Fynn was interested in sterner stuff than that usually found in Canada. The Canadian climbs of the day sought out the lines of weakness on a peak, typically ridge routes. Progressing upward in a series of tiers or steps, the ridges alternated hard sections with good resting places. Difficulties tended to be concentrated in a few areas. The contemporary movement in the Alps was out onto

Guides Edward Feuz, Rudolf Aemmer and clients at a
1912 camp. Courtesy Archives of the Canadian
Rockies, Banff, Alberta.

Val Fynn in the Alps. Courtesy American Alpine Club.

the faces that lay between the ridges, routes of more sustained steepness and difficulty. Fynn had firsthand experience of this type of climb and brought the concept to Canada. In 1922 he and guide Rudolf Aemmer climbed the north face of Mount Victoria, a route which pointed to the concept of deliberately seeking out difficulties. On this and other routes Fynn and Aemmer climbed as equals; they formed as strong a team as the MacCarthy-Kain rope. Had Fynn not spent his best years in the Alps, his contributions to Canadian climbing would probably have been far greater. He might well have provided the shot in the arm that was needed to get the sport moving once again.

Mount Alberta

The two notable climbs of 1925, Mount Logan and Mount Alberta, illustrate the situation in Canada. Mount Logan summarized the achievements of the past: stoic heroism in the face of brute nature. Mount Alberta looked to the future: New skills learned in Europe were applied to a technically demanding route. The turn-of-the-century mountaineers would have had an excellent chance on Logan; they would have had no chance on Alberta.

Hidden away in the remote Columbia Icefields, 11,874-foot Mount Alberta was the last peak of its stature left unclimbed in the Rockies. There were no climbers then active in Canada who were unaware of its significance. This significance was underlined by the publication in 1921 of a climbing guide to the Rockies by Howard Palmer and alpine historian Monroe Thorington. The frontispiece in this guide was unclimbed Mount Alberta. It was a challenge, an insult almost, to the climbing fraternity.

Palmer and Joseph Hickson went into Alberta with Conrad Kain. However, Palmer was past his prime. The packer Jim Simpson gave them little chance of success, though he allowed that with Kain's help "even" Palmer might make it. As it happened, bad weather kept them pinned down in their camp. Val Fynn was also interested in the mountain, but he was unable to get up a sufficiently strong team. Mount Alberta remained inviolate.

Unknown to the Canadian regulars, a party was organizing in Japan to attempt Mount Alberta. The leader of the Japanese effort, Yuko Maki, like Fynn was a good climber by European standards. In 1921 he made the first ascent of one of the landmark alpine climbs of the era, the Mittellegi Ridge of the Eiger. He was aide-de-camp to Japanese Crown Prince Chichibu. While on a skiing trip, Maki and Prince Chichibu studied the climber's guide to the Rockies and its frontispiece. They were surprised that such a fine peak as Mount Alberta remained unclimbed.

When the Japanese party arrived in Jasper National Park, they met Fynn, who had just been turned back from an attempt on Alberta by forest fires. They urged him to join forces with them, but his leave was over. In search of the strongest possible party, Maki engaged two Swiss guides from Jasper, Heinrich Fuhrer and Hans Kohler, and another Swiss, Jean Weber, who was an experienced amateur. We are in debt to Weber for his vivid account of this historic climb.

The mountain writing that survives from this era is formal and restrained. There are no revelations of the inner self. The mountaineers appear as splendid fellows incapable of error or malice. Harsh words are never spoken, and the climbs progress in orderly fashion from base to summit. Weber cut across these conventions with a lively pen. He wrote for his own interest, not for the pages of some stuffy journal, and his sometimes distorted English adds flavor to his account.

Even the mere fact of one's nationality may be in the hands of chance a sort of clay to create with a new sphere of adventure and thrills not even dared to dream of. The circumstances of my birth made me a subject of Swiss nationality and this was the main reason that my Canadian environment attributed me with the legendary Swiss qualities of being an expert climber, yodeler, cheese and watchmaker, not to speak of the sweet craftmanship as chocolate candy artist!

Contrary to my insisting claims to be inossent of all these venerable attributes except that of a climber was I called at times to the deathbed of a watch of American birth or to produce on different occasion the marvelous acustic phenomena of yodel echos with the effect that by and by people looked with obvious glances of discredit at my alleged Swiss origin.

But, when in the summer of 1925, a distinguished Japanese party of climbers arrived at Jasper to get a crack at the unconquered Mt. Alberta in the Columbia Icefields, was I given a chance to save the honour of my nationality with my climbing virtues.

Weber then described his fellow travelers.

Yuko Maki's party left Jasper on the 11th of July, 14 men and 39 horses and an outfit that would stir up any conaisseurs envy. . . .

To give a clearer idea of these men in their different function I pass them in a short review. Mr. Yuko Maki, leader, organisator and arbiter in any case of misunderstanding a man of small phisical size but of the highest intellect and charming character and not supposed muscular strength, with a smile he was able to disperse clouds of annoying circumstances which allways will appear on parties of some weeks duration and many different minds.

Mr. Hashimoto the leaders secretary and dramatic agency, knowing enough of the English language to acquire a terrible fluency in the cursing horsewrangler language and giving the whole party a good laugh at his expenses when it helped to animate a somewhat dreary or even dangerous position.

Mr. Hatano, if I remember right was well versed in matters of geology and gegraphy and a connaisseur of horses being a match for any horse wrangler. I asked him how it came that he could make a colt go under his guidance like a good broken saddlehorse and he replied very modestly that he owns at home a stable with imported racehorses from England. Mr. Mita, was fond of botanic, always eager to gather some new flower specimens or to sketch with artistic skill a landscape in a few strokes, besides he was never too tired to read off

Weber's "Sons of the Rising Sun" in Jasper, 1925. From left: N. Okabe, with movie camera, M. Hatano, Yukio Mita, T. Hayakawa, S. Hashimoto, Yuko Maki, Fred Brewster, Heinrich Fuhrer, Jean Weber, Hans Kohler. Courtesy Yukio Mita.

the different scientific instruments or to engage in a interesting conversation.

Attending specially to the photographic part, including everything from picture taking to the finished print was Mr. Okabe's task. For this purpose was excellent established darkroom tent at his disposition. Knowing only a fragmentary English, some amusing misunderstandings were its results doing nobody harm. The last man was the biggest of them in size and strength a very suspicious appearance full of jokes and enjoying every minute of the trip, Mr. Haiakawa the medical man. He enjoyed to be called rather for assistance to carry some very heavy log than for medical aid.

The party entered the magnificent valley leading to the headwaters of the Athabasca River only to find that the forest fires still raged out of control. They picked their way along the river flats, past the smouldering hulks of fallen trees. However,

the way to the mountain was clear, and spirits soared.

At the head of the valley stood the pyramidal Mount Columbia, to the left the Twins, and to the left again Mount Alberta.

Rising from the shadowy darkness of the valleys depth in one almost unbroken flight, first a stand of timber clinging to the steep sides, then a short green slope of a more gentle grade with rock bolders merging with the last almost perpendicular rise of darkgrey cliffs weatherworn and forbiding to the sublime silver glittering top, a difference in altitude of about 7500 feet.

The first view was demoralizing.

Six days after they left Jasper, the party pitched their base camp at the foot of the peak. The north and west sides appeared impregnable, and the face above their base camp, the south face, looked

no better. Spirits sagged and were only partially restored by Fuhrer's remark that they had yet to see the east side. There was a keen anticipation in the air when Maki and Fuhrer returned from scouting it.

Only fragmentary came the information which collected gave vivid picture of the difficulties we probably would encounter on the way to victory. We were told about some narrow ledges, of almost by blue air only suspended ice or snowpatches, of loose gravelslides which ended above vertical cliffs which cooled off their feet in cracked and torn glaciers. And that there was possibly no other path then by these infernal sounding contrivance just mentioned.

The nine members of the climbing team filed out of base camp and made their way to a timberline bivouac. Then,

Nine men tried to sleep, to accumulate in few hours left until the early hour of the morning, which would be the signal for the battle, as much as possible of the benefits of rest, but the mind was in advance occupied with difficult problems of climbing and when we staggered about half past two in the morning of July the 21st from the tents into the darkness had anyone seen the sleepy expression on the faces he would not have been convinced by everybodys ascertion of having had a wonderful rest. . . .

We made good progress the first hour where no difficulties slowed down the pace, darkness gave away

Mount Alberta. The Japanese party went up the broken ground to the left then climbed the steep black band to gain the summit ridge near the prominent gap, *Glen Boles*.

95

to soft dawn embrassing the mountains and valleys like a mother presses the sweet fruit of love to her breast, a miraculous one-ness. But soon day hammered his iron-fist cruelsome between the feast of passions lust and there they emerged to light: distinct formes, peak and valley, river and glacier, and life. For a moment stood we facinated in the sun, let his reys of golden aboundance rins the hair and cling caressing to the neck. God—how wonderful, and to be alive, to experience it oneself! . . .

Like a fragment of a gigantic bowl opened a semi circus to our right, overtowered by frail spires of dark material conected with the main-arrête of Mt. Alberta by perpendicular sheets of almost black rock. Patches of snow on underlying ice were dazzling ornaments in the upper part of the circus for which we headed in rising spiral-line. Those glittering patches had to be tackled with delicate understanding, since the ice was of a very brittle quality and a hit with the iceaxt not given in exactly the right angle and well chosen strength would have spoiled many a good step which after a short time lead the whole party comfortably over these otherwise unpleasant intersections to a much broken ridge or buttress. . . .

Beyond the buttress was the eye surprised by an impressive and instructive sight upon the east face of the Mountain in a close-up. Sheer walls upon sheer walls laced together with silverlined mouldings rose from unseen depth overtook us on the buttress and disappeared to our eager glances high up in the brownish smocky mist which again advanced from the forest fire devastated lower valley.

Ahead lay a key passage, a narrow band of rock giving access to the steep headwall itself.

We climbed now with utmost care from bench to bench over lose gravel on icy ground to the dark rockformation of the final erection. Until now everybody was convinced that this rock of smocked shade would be of a solid construction and allow a most enjoyable climb with plenty of trustworthy grips. Too bad, the first acquaintancy busted the last glamour of hope; every gripp had the tendency to remain in the hand. . . .

It released a quaint feeling to creep along the band with about no holds for the hands to keep the body from overbalancing where excrescences in the wall almost forced one out into the empty space. One after one moved at the time so far the rope allowed and the fact that the rope was not extensible was the reason to ackward positions if one had to stick on a place where wings had better taken the place of arms. The Japanese tourists of lesser bodily proportions then we three Swiss had on this particular traverse some advantage as regarding the space at our disposal, yet we Europeans were used to similar positions and aided by climbing qualifications not to be had a priori.

At the end of the traverse they climbed a series of tough rock pinnacles, only to be stopped by a fifteen-foot overhanging wall.

The prospects were rather discouraging, the ledge we stood on was narrow and led around a sharp cliff to the abys on the righthand, to the left it run out into a few grips of loose rock after a short distance. Right underneath were the gendarmes a doutful comparison of restfulness for the eye that was searching for some substantial means from where to give aid to Fuhrer in his attempt to reach the upper part of the balcony and to be able to choke an eventual fall with the aid of the rope

A rest stop on the descent. *Yukio Mita.*

from a safe standpoint. The determination to succeed was great enough to convince us that both points under question were on hand, well later on we agreed they were only of problematical value, but anyhow they had not to stand the extreme test and that was just the lucky thing. After a short counsel of war, were the forces distributed to their places. Mr. Hayakawa and Hans Kohler unroped to be used as a human ladder. Fuhrer was to climb first and put on for this keen test his special rock climbing shoes to make use in the best way of any unevenness and plenty of rope ready to not to hamper him in the advancement. On the very edge of the bottomless abyss Mr. Hayakawa stood facing the wall on the narrow ledge, then Kohler mounted him and ankered his legs around his horses shoulders and tried to catch with his hand a firm gripp on a not too solid hold; after this Fuhrer climbed with the push of some-one over both and could just reach the borde of the exposed balcony. Fortunately was he sceptical to gripps he was feeling and he begann a thoroughly cleaning anxiously watched by the rest who gave rope a little by little as he proceeded and ankering ourselves to imagi-nary holds in case that terrible thing should happen none dare to think of.

At least gave the tension away to joy when Fuhrer disappeared above the precipice and he declared from unseen spaces better conditions ahead. The progress of the rest to get up was rather slow since each one hung for an instance in the air until he was able to grasp some rocks which mostly just yielded with the result of experiencing a choking sensation connectet with the dropping back into airy spaces. Although it was neither easy nor harmless what followed after this performance of alpinistic accrobatic, the grade was quite agreeable to

the body's craving to be at intervalls at ease in a straight up human like position. . . .

The sun was in spite of smocky mist quite effectiv, snow and ice melted and loosened more and more rocks taking all attention to avoid their kicking power. Just in attempting to ridge the top of the arrete on the right side of the ravine, bombarded a volley of different sized gravel the middle party choosing Mr. Hashimoto as victim, hitting his face. He used to wear white gloves for the climb and when he passed one hand over his face holding still with the other to a gripp. He turned his face to the followers and with a dramatical geste showing the blood soiled around declared solemnly "The first blood" and forgetting the ernest of the situation every-body burst into a hearty laugh.

By four o'clock they climbed the last pitches of steep rock and gained the narrow summit ridge. The guides led the way, probing the snow cornice with their axes and cutting steps in the ice.

All of a sudden oppened a big gap before us an elegantly lined ice-edge steeply leading to the bottom and on the other side unmistakably the arrete rising without any further nasty caprices to the top. The spare silk ropes once more had to do their duty, taking them doubled, puting above the ice around a big rock for suspension, Fuhrer let himself down to the bottom and cut quickly the steps for descent of the rest, coming uphills as being far easier than the contrary. . . .

A not to be named emotion held us in its gripp so near the destination, the aim of a careful arranged expedition by these determined lovers of nature from the isle of the rising sun, and so from the gap up . . . we continued

despite the almost sixteen hours of hard work, up the broad and gentlesloped rest of the way in enthusiasme showing speed to arrive literally together on the Top of Mt. Alberta, 11,874 ft. at half past seven p.m. 16 hours after we left the highcamp on timberline about 6800 ft above sea-level.

Mutual we shaked hands and Mr. Yuko Maki extended his sincere appreciation to Fuhrer for the excellent leadership and his thanks to all of us Swiss for the aid to which he said the party owes this wonderful achievement of alpinism.

The job was only half done. They had now to descend their long and intricate route. They built a rock cairn, triumphantly stuck an extra ice axe into it, and began the descent. Night overtook them on the summit ridge, and they set up a makeshift bivouac. The next day they had to rope down from pitons at several places. They did not reach their high camp until late evening.

This first visit by Japanese climbers was remarkable. They took the finest unclimbed peak in the

Alpine Club of Canada camp, 1925. Left to right, back row: Malcolm Geddes, Joseph Hickson, T. B. Moffat, B. F. Seaver. Front row: Arthur Wheeler, Henry Hall, Albert MacCarthy, Stanley Mitchell, Charles Fay, Julia Henshaw. These people were among the powers in the club; they were responsible for both its rise and its period of stagnation. Courtesy American Alpine Club.

Canadian Rockies and established the most demanding climb in North America. Over the following years the story of this bold climb, and of the ice axe left on top, assumed ever greater proportions. It was widely believed that the axe was made of silver, a gift from the emperor himself. A number of noted climbers responded to the romance of Mount Alberta; British climber Frank Smythe remarked of his rebuff, "I can only say of Alberta that I know of no Alpine peak so difficult by its easiest route, and but one or two Alpine routes to compare with the pitiless limestone slabs with no belays and few resting places."

It was not until 1948 that Fred Ayres and John Oberlin, two of the strongest American climbers of the postwar period, retraced Maki's steps and found the legendary axe. Although not made of silver, they took it with them and also retrieved Maki's summit record. Written twenty-three years before, the record ends with a statement that captures the lure of high peaks, "We came from Japan so far called by this charming great mountain."

REFERENCES

Finch, G. I. "Valere Alfred Fynn." *AJ* 41 (Nov. 1929): 397.

Fynn, V. A. "Northeast Face of Mount Victoria." *CAJ* 13 (1923): 257.

Oberlin, John C. "Alberta and the Silver Ice Axe." *AAJ* 7 (1949): 124.

Palmer, Howard. "The First Ascent of Mt. King Edward, Canadian Rockies, with a Note on Mt. Alberta." *AJ* 37 (Nov. 1925): 306.

———. "A Note on Mt. Alberta." *Appalachia* 16 (Feb. 1926): 408.

Palmer, Howard, and J. Monroe Thorington. *A Climber's Guide to the Rocky Mountains of Canada.* New York: Knickerbocker Press, 1921.

Segogne, Henry de, and Jean Couzy. *Les Alpinistes Célèbres.* Paris: Mazenod, 1956.

Smythe, Frank. *Rocky Mountains,* Adam and Charles Black: London, 1948.

Thorington Archive. Princeton University.

Weber, Jean. "Conquering Mt. Alberta, 1925." *AAJ* 8 (1953): 446.

A Piece of Bent Iron

The Colorado Rockies were the best known part of the Rocky Mountain chain within the United States. With more than fifty summits in excess of 14,000 feet, we might suppose that climbing would have come on apace, but from the early mountaineers' standpoint these summits suffered from a fatal flaw. Few of the Colorado peaks required more than a strenuous hike. The ideal peak was one that was difficult on all sides like Robson or Alberta. Although one side of a Colorado peak might be steep and difficult, this was outweighed by the obvious simplicity of another side. The summits lacked challenge in themselves. Furthermore, the Colorado mountains lacked snow and ice; the emphasis in early twentieth-century North American mountaineering was on alpine climbing. The potential of the Colorado Rockies went unregarded.

In 1916 twenty-eight-year-old Albert Ellingwood, a professor of political science at Colorado College, vacationed in the rugged Sangre de Cristo Range of southern Colorado. A few years before as a Rhodes Scholar from Colorado, he had studied at Oxford University. While at Oxford he became interested in rock climbing and visited the English Lake District, one of the key areas in the evolution of the sport. Ellingwood's orientation to the mountains was influenced by his experiences on the hillsides of Britain. He appreciated a tough rock climb for its own sake, even though it might be on the steep flank of an otherwise uninteresting peak.

Ellingwood and his companions made three first ascents in the Sangre de Cristo Range, occasionally using a rope as a safeguard. Although Ellingwood's rope handling was rudimentary, these were probably the first rock climbs in the United States where a conscious effort was made to belay. He returned to the area eight years later to make a classic rock climb, the airy east ridge of Crestone Needle.

Although most of Colorado's high peaks may be climbed by a strong hiker, 13,113-foot Lizard Head is capped by a 350-foot volcanic plug, sheer on all sides. This final tower was considered unclimbable, but in 1920 Ellingwood and Barton Hoag left Colorado Springs hellbent for Lizard Head. Ellingwood examined every side of the tower for a weakness and concluded that all sides save the

Albert Ellingwood, right, with Colorado Mountain Club members, left to right, Herman Buhl, Mrs. Buhl and Carl Blaurock. *Carl Blaurock.*

west were out of the question. On this face the barely adequate handholds forced him to remove the thick leather gloves he preferred to wear when climbing. He had with him a handful of primitive pitons: iron spikes similar to those used for steps on telegraph poles. On the second pitch he hammered in two of these spikes and, standing at full length on top of them, gained a few precious feet. However, he had no way of securing his rope to the spikes; in North America the carabiner was an innovation that still lay in the future.* Fortunately, the climbing eased, and the happy pair were soon piling up rocks to make the time-honored summit cairn.

They roped down the climbing route, but after one of the rappels the rope stuck fast. Vigorously trying to free it, they dislodged a rock. Ellingwood's heavy hat absorbed the worst of the blow, but he was nearly knocked from his stance. The rope had to be abandoned. Without it for a safeguard, Hoag slipped near the bottom of the first pitch and slithered over a fifteen-foot cliff.

The climb was a fine effort by Ellingwood, probably the hardest rock climb in the United States and one that approached the standard of such Canadian climbs as Mount Louis and Bugaboo Spire. In view of this success we might antici-

*Carabiners are metal snap-links used to attach the rope to a belay point. They evolved from the pear-shaped *karabiner* used by German firefighters. They were introduced in the Eastern Alps around 1910.

pate that technical climbing would come forward strongly in Colorado during the 1920s. However, the majority of climbers were more interested in scrambling up the "14,000-ers." In 1922 a plan was put forward in the Colorado Mountain Club to award medals for climbing certain peaks. James Grafton Rogers, the club's first president, considered the awards ridiculous since Lizard Head was the only mountain he knew of in Colorado that would attract even "a second-rate Alpine guide."

The early initiatives toward technical climbing were almost plaintive cries in the wilderness. In

1923 Colorado Mountain Club correspondent Rudolph Johnson was moved to wonder "if I am different from other mountain enthusiasts in that I enjoy difficult rock climbs." Johnson and his fellow "thrill seekers in Boulder" were pioneering on the spectacular sandstone Flatirons, but he did not recommend the Flatirons to any "except the most foolhardy rockclimbers."

The showpiece of Rocky Mountain National Park, Longs Peak, was the one Colorado peak where a guide service was available. However, the guiding was up a nontechnical route safeguarded by cables. In 1922 a relative neophyte arrived at Longs Peak. Princeton mathematics professor James Alexander had almost no climbing experience, but he had plenty of talent. Climbing for the most part with just tennis shoes and an ice axe, he systematically explored Longs Peak; in two summers he climbed it some nineteen times. He is credited with three new routes, his best the solo ascent of Alexander's Chimney.* This route was the first breach in the impressive east face, but it was in the traditional vein; it took a line of weakness that avoided the main challenge. The climbing team first attracted by the inner mysteries of the east face was altogether stronger than any previously in the area; a case can be made that the

*Alexander's solo effort is notable. However, rope handling was then so inadequate that the leader was little safer than a solo climber in an exposed situation. After his Colorado introduction to climbing, Alexander concentrated on the Alps.

Stettner brothers formed the most powerful rope in the United States.

Coppersmith Joe Stettner and his photoengraver brother Paul were bitten by the climbing bug while apprentices in Munich, Germany. Inspired by innovators like Hans Dülfer and Louis Trenker, they climbed and skied in the Kaisergebirge at every opportunity. They were poor, but poverty is no obstacle when men are moved by a great passion. They had no money for the train fare, so they walked to the mountains.

The brothers emigrated to the United States in the mid-1920s and settled in Chicago. It was perhaps an odd choice of home for mountaineers. They missed the mountains, which had been at their doorstep in Munich and determined to take their annual vacation in Colorado. In September 1927 they set off on their heavily laden Indian motor bikes. On the sixth day of rattling and bouncing over dirt roads, they reached Denver. After warm-up climbs in the Garden of the Gods near Colorado Springs, they headed for the east face of Longs Peak. A supply of pitons had arrived from Munich just before the pair left Chicago, and they planned to buy a rope in Colorado. At Longs Peak Inn they learned about the existing routes on the peak and were pleased to find a climbing rope. However, the innkeepers not only refused to sell or lend the rope but discouraged the Stettners from attempting any climbs, saying that September was too late in the year, and recently there had been several accidents. All the brothers' arguments over the rope were in vain. Finally, they unearthed a stiff, one-half inch sisal rope in a general store in Estes Park. It was not the best, but it looked strong enough. They were in business.

At Chasm Lake the Stettners studied the east face through binoculars. They knew the lines taken by the previous climbs, but they were interested in something else. About 200 feet to the right of Alexander's Chimney they discovered a promising line. They cramponed up a snowfield to the rock and changed into felt-soled shoes. Paul eagerly went into the lead while Joe took the job of shouldering the pack. Several pitches were difficult, in particular, the one now known as the Piton

Ladder. Paul placed several pitons, but he made this lead without standing in rope stirrups—as some later climbers have had to do. Snow fell while they were on the upper reaches of the face, but the Stettners completed the climb in less than seven hours and hurried down in the gathering dusk.

This route on the east face of Longs Peak, Stettners Ledges, was the most demanding climb in the United States up to that time. It was not surpassed in Colorado until the 1940s. The Stettner brothers continued climbing in Colorado and in the Tetons in later years. In 1936 Joe made the first ascent of Joe's Solo on the east face of Longs Peak. In September 1937 the two made the fourth

Working class climbers: Joe and Paul Stettner arrive back from the east face of Longs Peak, 1927. Courtesy Joe Stettner.

Joe Stettner on the east face of Longs Peak.
Courtesy Joe Stettner.

ascent of the north ridge of the Grand Teton, against the advice of Jack Durrance, who considered the season too late and the rock likely to be iced up. Durrance was right. The poor conditions caused the Stettners to bivouac just under the summit. The following day, unfamiliar with the normal descent route, they headed straight down the south face, forging a new line that they later returned to climb. As with the rest of their early climbs, this new route on the Grand Teton went unrecorded. Recognition of their achievements had to wait the researches of later climbers. If this talented pair had enjoyed the leisure time of other climbers of the day, who were mostly well to do, their contribution undoubtedly would have been even more significant.

The Stettner brothers were not Colorado locals. Their historic Stettners Ledges climb, which went unrepeated for nine years, did nothing to advance the cause of technical climbing among Coloradans. Although Ellingwood had introduced the use of the rope eleven years earlier, a viable rock climbing movement had yet to be established. Certainly Ellingwood had the skills to impart, but evidently he was not the sort of person to gather a group of friends and carry them along with his enthusiasm. Writing on technical climbing in 1930, Ellingwood advised that the true mountaineer had to develop his skills. "He is not content to march up the same hill repeatedly, and then march down again." For the great majority of Colorado mountaineers, marching up and down the peaks was still the order of the day. A contemporary noted that home climbers bowed to the "fetish of the 14,000 peak," a fetish that was conspicuous also in California and the Pacific Northwest. Another climber lamented that the proper use of the rope was almost unknown. However, the days when marching *was* mountaineering were about to end. In the early 1930s technical climbing got a start among both the San Juan Mountaineers and the Colorado Mountain Club.

The San Juan Mountaineers were a few friends brought together by Dwight Lavender, a geology student whose family owned a ranch near the San Juan Mountains. Lavender and his fellow enthusiasts rummaged through libraries and secondhand bookstores for European climbing manuals and learned from them the theory of rope handling and pitons. Pitons were not then made in America, so Lavender made up a batch of his own design in the engineering workshop at Stanford University. These pitons had an open eye which admitted the rope. The opening was closed by hammering the eye flush with the rock.

In the Colorado Mountain Club, the state's premier mountain organization, interest in technical climbing was inspired by a joint meeting with the Appalachian Mountain Club in 1931. On this meet, Lizard Head was climbed for the fourth and fifth times. The Coloradans became keenly aware that a new level of skill was growing in the East. When Lizard Head was first climbed, there were no

San Juan Mountaineers on Kismet Peak, 1932. Dwight Lavender, left, Gordon Williams and Mel Griffiths. *Mel Griffiths*.

routes on the East Coast to equal it. Now the Eastern climbers were more skilled than the locals.

In the fall of 1933 the University of Colorado at Boulder held a series of rock climbing classes, about which Carleton Long wrote, "At first, competent instruction made the meetings successful. Later, attention veered toward plain and fancy rope-descents, until finally the activities consisted almost entirely of scampering up a rock the easy way and making 100 ft. rappels down the steep face." It was a relief to learn that a further course would focus on the "real fundamentals of rock climbing."

If the students were busy descending the Flatirons, other Boulder residents were belatedly following the example of Rudolph Johnson in ascending the self-same peaks. By 1934 the Flatirons were sufficiently well explored to have a climber's guidebook of their own. Authors Long and McCrumm believed in detail,

"Go straight up center of depression 7' to good R handhold. Then 8' further up is handhold for both hands. 2½' further is good L handhold and 2½' above that is one for R hand, and also one for L hand. Pull body up to a double foothold." One climb carried the warning, "Be extremely careful not to fall, especially on the first part of the pitch where the route leads out over empty space."

Another popular practice area was Colorado Springs' Garden of the Gods. Here Robert Ormes learned the fundamentals of rock climbing from Ellingwood and went on to make the third ascent of Lizard Head. In 1935 Ormes teamed with San Juan Mountaineer Mel Griffiths on fortress-like Chimney Peak, where a 400-foot crack gave a tough climb. However, the peak that appealed most lay just across the state line in New Mexico. This was Shiprock, a volcanic plug that abruptly rises 1,800 feet above a bleak desert landscape.

Shiprock was just gaining prominence as "America's toughest climbing problem." Griffiths and Ormes feared that outsiders would snatch this prize away from them. They made two preliminary skirmishes, then returned in 1937 with Gordon Williams and Easterner Bill House. The way led up over increasing difficulties to a basalt rib, the key to the upper wall. Belayed by House, Ormes snapped the rope into a couple of pitons and edged upward. Just a little higher, he thought, and things may ease. Suddenly his foothold crumbled, and he hurtled downward. Grimly holding the rope, House was jerked into the air and slammed against the rock face, but he stopped Ormes after a thirty-foot fall. They laughed nervously over their luck. House was not anchored to the rock; they had just two pitons between them and eternity. After a few more futile efforts, they retrieved the piton that held Ormes's fall; the shaft was almost bent double.

House and Ormes returned two days later for another try. With the level of climbing skills then developed, it was essential that they use pitons to climb the pitch that had turned them back, the Ormes Rib. However, Ormes was unfamiliar with the use of pitons as a direct aid. Although House and the East Coast climbers used an occasional safety piton, they were philosophically opposed to piton-assisted climbing, and they made no progress. They were stopped cold. Shiprock demanded a new level of expertise.

Ormes summarized their attempts and his dramatic fall in "A Piece of Bent Iron," which appeared in the *Saturday Evening Post*. If Shiprock ever tempted him again, he concluded, he would take the bent piton in his hand and ponder the fate of climbers who push their luck.

Shiprock, New Mexico.
The early attempts
were on the far side.
Ed Cooper.

Bob Ormes' fall on Shiprock. Gordon Williams looks
anxiously upward as Bill House holds onto the rope.
Mel Griffiths.

REFERENCES

Blaurock, Carl. "A Trip up the Northeast Face of Longs Peak." *T & T*, no. 63 (Dec. 1923):2.

"Climbing Notes." *T & T*, no. 144 (Oct. 1930):9.

Ellingwood, Albert R. "First to Climb Lizard Head." *Outing Magazine* 79(2) (Nov. 1921): 51.

———. "Climbing in the Sangre de Cristo." *T & T* no. 81 (June 1925):1.

———. "The Eastern Arête of the Crestone Needle." *T & T*, no. 86 (Nov. 1925):6.

———. "Technical Climbing in the Mountains of Colorado and Wyoming." *AAJ* 1 (1930): 140.

Fricke, Walter W., Jr. *A Climber's Guide to Rocky Mountain National Park*. Boulder: Paddock, 1971.

Griffiths, Melvin T. "Rock Climbing." *T & T*, no. 166 (Aug. 1932):115.

Johnson, Rudolph. "Scaling the Flatirons." *T & T*, no. 54 (March 1923):4.

Long, Carleton C. "Present-Day Rockclimbing in Colorado." *Appalachia* 20 (June 1934): 132.

Long, Carleton C., and John D. McCrumm. "Boulder Rock Climbs." *T & T*, no. 187 (May 1934):55.

Means, Winthrop. "Colorado Climbs, 1931." *Appalachia* 18 (Dec. 1931): 357.

Ormes, Robert. "Attempt on Shiprock." *T & T*, no. 229 (Dec. 1937) 133.

———. "A Piece of Bent Iron." *Saturday Evening Post*, July 22, 1939.

———. *Guide to the Colorado Mountains*. Denver: Colorado Mountain Club, 1970.

Rogers, James Grafton. "Editorial." *T & T*, no. 41 (Feb 1922):2.

Thorington, J. Monroe. "James Waddell Alexander 3d." *AAJ* 18 (1972): 241.

Wilm, Harold G. "The Second Ascent of Lizard Head." *T & T*, no. 130 (Aug. 1929):10.

Zumwalt, Clerin. "Is Rock Climbing Dangerous?" *T & T*, no. 174 (April 1933):50.

Robert Underhill and Jack Durrance

Throughout the early years of climbing in North America, the majority of the accomplished climbers came from the East. The East first witnessed industrialization, the growth of large cities, and the rise of a well-educated professional class. These people had the time and money to travel and to indulge in leisure pursuits. It was customary for educated Easterners to make the several-months-long European grand tour, and the Alps were definitely part of the itinerary. In Europe many Americans first got a taste of climbing. Several of those who took to the sport devoted the majority of their climbing careers to the Alps.

Although it may appear strange that these climbers traveled to Europe year after year when there were mountains at home, it must be remembered that Europe had a cultural heritage singularly lacking in the boorish West; many educated Easterners felt more at ease in Paris than rubbing shoulders with loggers and ranchers. The Alps were in their heyday, and every season wellknown amateurs and guides carried off brilliant climbs. The Alps were simply more exciting than the Rocky Mountains. An additional factor was the alpine ambience: picturesque villages, rustic hotels, and colorful mountain guides. The American West was largely devoid of amenities; climbers had to rough it.

The American club with the strongest tradition of alpine climbing was Boston's Appalachian Mountain Club. This interest in the Alps predated the club's long-standing explorations in the Canadian mountains. (It was the similarity of the regions that led Charles Fay to initiate the club's expeditions to Canada in the 1880s.) With their frequent visits to the Alps, the A.M.C. climbers kept abreast of developments in Europe.

One such development was crag climbing. The crags were readily accessible from large cities, were out of the weather pattern of the high mountains, and lacked the awe of the Alps. The attention given to local rock outcrops was a major break with the past. There was little thought of reaching the top of a peak, the sine qua non of earlier days. This was climbing for climbing's sake, summits be damned.

Rock scrambling was a popular activity on Appalachian Mountain Club outings in the early

111

1920s. However, the majority of mountaineers still looked upon it merely as training for "the greater ranges." They resolutely carried their ice axes, their badge of office, up the cliffs, either dangling from a wrist loop or thrust into a waist holster.

The A.M.C. evidently regarded the beginnings of rock climbing as unworthy of comment. While alpine deeds were written up in their journal *Appalachia*, little was said about the local crags until 1928. Then the journal gave wide coverage to the emerging sport. The journal's sudden interest in rock climbing was no chance occurrence. Harvard philosopher and mathematician Robert Underhill had just taken over as editor.

Tall, donnish, and bespectacled, young Underhill was already one of the country's best mountaineers. Like many of his contemporaries, he had learned to climb with alpine guides. During his 1928 alpine season, he climbed the Peuterey and Brenva ridges on Mont Blanc, descended the Innominata Ridge, and attempted the Brouillard Ridge, all considerable undertakings. Then with his wife-to-be, Miriam O'Brien, and guide Armand Charlet, he made the first complete ascent of the Aiguilles du Diable, one of the hardest climbs accomplished at that time in the Chamonix area. Underhill was well prepared to take a leading part in opening the New England hills to climbing.

In 1928 he and his companions tackled the most obvious break in the 1,000-foot granite face of New Hampshire's Cannon Mountain, but they were stopped short of a sinuous twenty-foot crack. Later in the year Underhill returned with his future brother-in-law, Lincoln O'Brien. After delicate slab climbing, they reached a point several feet to the left of the key crack. There was no apparent connection to it, but they were prepared. In "Cannon Mountain" he writes how they produced a wood stake "brought along for some such purpose," hammered it into a fissure, and looped the rope over it. Then Underhill held the rope tight while O'Brien leaned across and struggled into the crack. The resulting climb, Old Cannon, became a favorite. The stake succumbed some five years later when a Harvard party made the traverse. After they were across, they gave a tug on the rope, and the stake rattled down to the valley.

Underhill said of the climb, "This appears, from all examination to date, to be the only possible route up the cliff." This assertion has been repeated about countless cliffs by generations of climbers, and it is always wrong. It invariably appears that a cliff is "worked out," and then someone comes along who sees it in a fresh light. In the case of Cannon Mountain the fresh perspective arrived the following year.

Harvard lawyer Bradley Gilman and his Yale cousin Hassler Whitney made a series of excellent guideless climbs in the Alps in 1928. Back home the following year, they heard about the explorations on Cannon Mountain and went to investigate. As they walked in to the base of the cliff, a

deeply shadowed break caught their attention. However, it was not the break that they attacked but the intimidating ridge on its left side. Both climbers were in top form and alternated leads as they worked their way up. They were so enthusiastic about the climb that they scrambled down to the foot of the cliff and did it again, making sure that each of them had led every pitch. A bold line up a difficult cliff, the Whitney-Gilman Route was a remarkable achievement for its time. It remained one of the hardest climbs in New England until the 1940s.

Another key figure in the emergence of technical climbing was Boston banker Kenneth Henderson. He and other experienced Easterners encouraged newcomers, organized club climbs, taught the fundamentals, and led ropes. They even took pains to prepare a route for later parties. On Mount Willard, Henderson explained in "Some Rock Climbs," Gilman took the lead while his teammates worked on the route. "One or two others wielded mighty hammers, driving in pitons where these were needed, while behind came that self-sacrificing soul with the paint-pot and brush to leave a mark that others might follow where we had been."

During these years there was a continual search for new climbing areas, the nearer the city the better. Boston's Quincy Quarries was a popular hangout for Harvard mountaineers. Lincoln O'Brien exhorted them to climb at night with a candle lantern gripped between their teeth in preparation for early morning alpine starts. With the discovery of new areas, encouragement of beginners, and

Kenneth Henderson on Mt. Willard, 1936.
Note the necktie. Courtesy Kenneth Henderson.

Betty Woolsey rock climbing in Connecticut.
Bill House.

dissemination of ideas, abilities improved rapidly. The unthinkable came to be openly considered, and last year's horror climbs became commonplace. Routes pioneered on Maine's Mount Katahdin in 1928 were dismissed by Underhill two years later as scarcely worth bothering with. The foundations were laid for a new generation of rock climbers.

Parallel with the advent of rock climbing was the discovery that in the winter the New England hills provided excellent snow and ice climbing. Winter climbing was done in the very places shunned by the summer rock climbers, the brushy and loose gullies between the ridges and faces. These gullies are natural drainage paths and glisten with hard water-ice (frozen water) during the winter. This water-ice is harder and tougher to climb than the typical snow-ice (compacted and recrystallized snow) of alpine ranges.

Huntington Ravine on New Hampshire's Mount Washington was the most popular area. Winter climbing began here largely on the initiative of British Everest climber Noel Odell. In 1928 he and members of the recently formed Harvard Mountaineering Club climbed the relatively simple central gully.* In 1929 the nearby 1,000-foot Pinnacle Gully came under attack. Underhill and O'Brien cut hand- and footholds up the initial ice bulges, but after two hours of effort and only 100 feet of progress they retreated. The next year a Yale team took up the challenge. Julian Whittlesey fell twice trying to pass a bulge, but each time he managed to jab in his axe and stop himself. He and his partner carried on in poor weather to the top. (Not

*The Harvard Mountaineering Club and the corresponding clubs at Yale and Dartmouth played a major role. They produced many strong climbers and provided a framework for the organization of climbs and expeditions.

all later climbers have been so fortunate, as there have been several fatalities in Pinnacle Gully.)

The year after the Yale team's ascent, Frank Truslow led three Harvard companions on an attempt. He noted, "There was more than a little vanity in our attack." However, their belaying technique was primitive, if not unique. While the leader and second worked up the gully, the other pair stretched a taut rope across it below the climbers. The idea was that the rope would snag a

Harvard Mountaineering Club in the Selkirks, 1930. At the left of the back row are Arthur Emmons, Francis Farquhar and Noel Odell. At the left of the front row Guy Crawford and Lincoln O'Brien. It was on this trip that Farquhar learned rope management from Underhill and asked for an article for the *Sierra Club Bulletin*. *Francis Farquhar*.

Bill House leads Alan Willcox on the second ascent of Pinnacle Gully, 1934. *Betty Woolsey.*

fall, which it apparently did. "It saved a nasty spill when one of us fell backwards from a cold hand-hold, slid down the slope, and caught the horizontal rope in passing." Truslow and his companions ran out of time before they ran out of luck. The second ascent eventually fell to Yale climber Bill House. A major force in the Yale club and a devotee of climbing on the college buildings (where the thrill of illegality heightened the experience), House used more orthodox protection methods, including ice pitons.

Interest in winter climbing never equaled that in rock climbing. In contrast to the pleasures of sun-warmed rock, ice climbing was a bleak affair that appealed mainly to the ascetic. Perhaps more important was the rise of another winter sport, downhill skiing. This was skiing's heroic age; techniques such as the *telemark, gelaendesprung,* and new-fangled *christiania* swing held untold mystery. A.M.C. members played a key role in the evolution of the new sport. In fact, they skied down Mount Washington while fellow members struggled up nearby. Lying immediately to the left of Huntington Ravine is an improbable ski hill: the steep, rocky, 1000-foot headwall of Tuckerman Ravine. The first race was held on the headwall in 1933. With good reason it was named the American Inferno. It was a downhill; there was no pussyfooting about with slalom poles. The skiers chose a line that bordered between the improbable and the suicidal. Wrote Rockwell Stephens, "Livermore, halfway down the headwall, found himself trapped in a comparatively narrow lane between two long slides of tumbled snow. Disdaining further turns, he pointed his skis straight down the slope and shot for the bottom while the whole mountain seemed to hold its breath. His luck was out, however, for he struck an avalanche cone at terrific speed. . . ." But that is another story.

The Tetons

The 1898 ascent of the Grand Teton and the acrimonious debate over Langford's prior claim brought wide publicity to the Tetons. However, despite the publicity no more climbers came for another twenty years. The Alps and the Canadian mountains more than absorbed the interest of the few technical climbers on the continent.

An initiative for subsequent Teton climbing came from the superintendent of nearby Yellowstone National Park, Horace Albright. He wanted to draw attention to the Tetons in order to have them made a national park. In 1919 he invited New York librarian LeRoy Jeffers to visit the range. Jeffers solo-climbed to the lower (north) summit of Mount Moran. Following his climb, he wrote widely about the Tetons. As secretary of an organization he had formed, the Bureau of Associated Mountaineering Clubs of North America, he was well known to mountaineers.* However, no further climbs were recorded in the Tetons for the next two summers.

Undaunted, Albright invited Colorado mountaineers Eleanor Davis and Albert Ellingwood to the region in 1923. They climbed the Grand Teton and made the straightforward first ascents of Middle and South Tetons.

The following year a strapping seventeen-year-old arrived in the area. The Grand Teton was a prized goal among local Jackson people, and young Paul Petzoldt saw that he could make a few dollars guiding parties up it. He had negligible mountain experience, but made up for this with his brash entrepreneurial front. That summer he led four parties to the summit. Over the following years he built up a solid guiding business.

In 1925 Fritiof Fryxell came to the range to work on his doctoral dissertation on the Teton glaciers. He met Coloradan Phil Smith, who was in Wyoming to climb the Grand Teton and to homestead. Together they embarked on a program of exploration, placing registers on the summits, and keeping a record of the emerging sport. Under their methodical attack, the majority of the principal summits were climbed. By 1928 Mount Owen, second highest peak in the range, remained the outstanding unclimbed summit.

*The Bureau, whose objectives were conservation and the dissemination of mountain-related information, died with Jeffers, who perished in an airplane crash in 1926.

Summit of Mount Owen. From left: Phil Smith, Robert Underhill, Fritiof Fryxell. *Kenneth Henderson.*

Albright's dream of a Grand Teton National Park came true in 1929, and mountaineers Fryxell and Smith were among the first rangers appointed. The year also marked the first visit by Appalachian Mountain Club members Kenneth Henderson and Robert Underhill. At this time the only route on the Grand Teton was the 1898 route. Although Ellingwood and others had attempted the bristling east ridge, no one had passed the "first gendarme." The previous attempts foundered when they tried to take this gendarme directly. Henderson and Underhill scouted this possibility, then traversed around the gendarme. The discovery of a simpler way was not cheating but the stroke of superior mountaineers. After ten hard hours they were on the summit.

When they got down to the valley, they met Fryxell and Smith. Eastern visitors were no novelty to the two rangers, for most of the patrons of the local dude ranches were from the East. But Henderson and Underhill did not fit the pattern of the dudes. They had come to the Tetons expressly to climb, and they brought with them the knowledge and skills evolved through several generations in the Alps. When they heard of the four failures on Mount Owen, they agreed to join Fryxell and Smith for a concerted effort the following year.

The agreement was kept. Late one July evening Fryxell and Smith hiked up to the Easterners' base camp at Amphitheater Lake. They were impressed. Henderson and Underhill camped in style; a packer brought up supplies, and a cook prepared the meals. The next morning Underhill quietly cursed the tedious hike to Mount Owen while Henderson shared the rangers' keen enthusiasm for the natural scene and their interest in the human influences now shaping the future of the park. Underhill interjected the comment that scenery and scientific observations were all very well in their place, but they were a distraction on a climb.

Once they were on the rock, Underhill was a changed man. Apparent boredom was replaced by restless energy. The party rapidly gained the base of the summit block, where Fryxell, Gilman, and Smith were defeated two years before. They stopped for lunch, but Underhill was too keyed up to rest. He disappeared around to the unexplored north side and within moments found the key to the ascent.

This same summer Underhill was in the Canadian Rockies with Lincoln O'Brien for an attempt on the northwest ridge of Mount Robson, the Emperor Ridge. They reached the summit ridge in five hours, but there the real problems begin. The rock gendarmes are plastered with unstable snow, and the two climbers had no security as they fought their way past these "gargoyles." They were close to the summit, but the continual danger wore them down. Finally, O'Brien turned to Underhill, "Robert, if our objective in life is making first ascents, I believe we will make more of them if we avoid making this one." They descended.

In 1931 Underhill made his finest Teton climbs. On July 15 three parties climbed the Grand Teton, two by new routes. First on top was Idaho student Glenn Exum, who had left a party guided by Petzoldt and soloed the upper part of the ridge that now carries his name. Petzoldt and his clients arrived soon after, followed by Underhill, Smith, and Frank Truslow, who climbed the easterly of two south ridges, now known as the Underhill Ridge. The latter climb was particularly satisfying because Underhill had twice been stormed off it. With the success of these ascents, there were routes on all the more obvious sides of the Grand Teton save one.

Underhill was keenly aware of the peculiar fascination that attached to the great north faces of

Paul Petzoldt on the first ascent of East Prong, 1927. The Grand Teton is in the background, the east ridge is on the left and the north ridge to the right. The north face climb follows the snowfields. *Fritiof Fryxell.*

Willi Unsoeld on ice-glazed rock on the north ridge of the Grand Teton during an early ascent. *Leigh Ortenburger.*

the Alps. The North Face of the Matterhorn was climbed that very year, and the north side of the Grand Teton similarly exerted a strong appeal. Dark and shadowed, seldom catching the sun, it was both attractive and repellent. There were not only the obvious difficulty of the climbing, the steepness, the loose rock, and the ice-covered ledges but also the fears associated with an attempt on an awesome north wall. According to Underhill it was dismissed as unclimbable by all who examined it, "and our avowed opinion had always been the same. Secretly, however, we had for long thought that the matter would bear closer inspection. It is futile to judge such a mountain face from any distance."

He had made a solo reconnaissance in 1930, and now he returned with Fryxell for an attempt. Fryxell's boots had not arrived at camp, so he made do with smooth-soled work shoes. Underhill took the lead on snow, but they switched leads on the rock. The climbing went well until they came to an evil-looking chimney capped by a chockstone, the now-famous "Chockstone Chimney." There were no holds in reach. Fryxell clambered onto Underhill's shoulders, grasped the chockstone, and searched for the vital holds. But he found nothing and was soon back at Underhill's side.

They were high on the face essentially unbelayed in a difficult, exposed situation. They had to force the pitch or retreat down the wall. Therefore, they considered it legitimate to use pitons, and Underhill hammered two into the rock. Fryxell tied into them and took up the rope while Underhill climbed onto his shoulders. After three all-out attempts, Underhill managed to hook his boot onto a key hold. Almost overbalancing, he was feeling anxiously for something to stand on when Fryxell whispered hoarsely, "Stand on the piton!" Underhill stretched up from the piton and, after a few more tense moments, got to a resting place. Higher up the face, Fryxell climbed a chimney and called down excitedly, "Do you see what I see!" They were level with the Upper Saddle and certain of making the summit. As Underhill said later, moments like that put life into a man.

The climb was a great achievement. They had overcome the considerable technical difficulties and cracked the aura of impregnability that surrounded the somber wall. Underhill considered the north face climb the culmination of his mountain career and wrote that he was content. It was then the hardest climb in the United States.

Underhill was a major figure in the development of technical climbing in North America both by virtue of his fine climbs and his influential articles on climbing. Together with Henderson, he introduced many North Americans to rope management and advocated the restrained use of pitons and carabiners. However, the old guard still regarded pitons unfavorably. Underhill and his contemporaries used this new equipment sparingly, partly from the feeling that it was unethical and partly because it was scarce. In writing of it, Underhill attempted to correct the impression that it simplified climbing. He pointed out that the reverse was often the case; pitons place new demands on climbers' skill and daring.

Turning to ice climbing, Underhill did not exaggerate the dangers before the introduction of ice pitons when he wrote, "They provide, for the first time, the chance for real securing methods in ice-climbing (whereas the best that could be done heretofore was to hew a large step, belay over the shoulder, and hope fervently one could retain one's footing and balance under a pull)."

In 1933, sensing that his own best days were behind him, Underhill suggested that Fryxell look at the direct west face of the Grand Teton, and added wistfully, "I won't ask you to hold it for another year." But the west face would have to wait. Underhill had done his last major routes in the Tetons, and there was a pause in climbing at the highest standards. His contemporaries were unable to break any new barriers. It was a time of consolidation, and the number of climbers increased gradually. By 1934 more than one hundred ascents were recorded throughout the park, hardly a flood, but a tenfold increase since Ellingwood's 1923 visit. Fryxell and Smith continued their pioneering. Petzoldt guided hard as well as simple climbs and sometimes took clients on new routes. Mention should be made of his solo climb of the

Jack Durrance. Courtesy Jack Durrance.

northeast face of Mount Owen and the first winter ascent of the Grand Teton, the latter climb in the company of his brother Eldon and noted Jackson skier Fred Brown.

In 1936 a carefree young man in tattered clothes arrived in the Tetons to work as a guide for Petzoldt. More at home speaking German than English, Jack Durrance had spent the past eight years in Germany. He attended high school near Garmisch and worked in a Munich machine factory. On frequent trips to the Wetterstein and the local Munich rocks, he became a first-class climber. The 1930s were a time of momentous achievements in the Alps, and Durrance met several of the best German climbers, among them the Schmid brothers, who made the sensational ascent of the North Face of the Matterhorn. He was attuned to the best alpine standards.

When Durrance reached the Tetons, Underhill's climbs were the touchstone. Yet Underhill's alpine experience was in the Alps of the 1920s; Durrance and his Munich friends were of a new generation of climbers. In the Tetons the finest climb was Fryxell and Underhill's still unrepeated north face of the Grand Teton. However, their route lies on the corner that bounds the face on the right. Today it is referred to as the north ridge. For the new generation the problem of the forbidding north face had to be solved anew.

As early at 1933 Petzoldt descended some distance on the north side of the mountain with the express purpose of checking out the possibilities.

He was keen to take this much-prized climb. One afternoon in August 1936, Durrance returned to camp with a client from the first descent of the Exum Ridge. He was greeted by Petzoldt and his brother Eldon. The Petzoldt brothers were eager to attempt the second ascent of Underhill's north ridge without delay. At 7 A.M. the next morning the three climbers were under the 3,000-foot north side of the Grand Teton. They held a hurried conference and changed their objective from the north ridge to the North Face. No doubt the presence just then in the Tetons of the brilliant Eastern climber Fritz Wiessner had much to do with this switch.

Durrance on the first ascent of the complete Exum Ridge. *Kenneth Henderson.*

There was fresh rockfall on the snow beneath the face, and the air was tainted with the smell of rock dust. Durrance took the majority of the leads, and they hurried up the face, sheltering under projections where they could. They used pitons freely as an additional safety factor. Late in the afternoon, taking advantage of a rightward traverse (the Second Ledge), they exited from the face to the upper reaches of the north ridge. The North Face of the Grand Teton had been climbed.

Durrance considered this a particularly arduous climb. However, he never felt it was a good one; his passion was for high standard climbing on sound rock. Far more typical of this concept was his ascent of the entire Exum Ridge, which Exum had gained at midheight. The ridge gave Durrance and Kenneth Henderson a demanding rock climb; they used some twenty pitons for safety.

Durrance was the first climber in the Tetons to seek out bare ridges and smooth walls, routes which often lacked ledges and natural belays. Thus, his use of pitons went beyond Underhill's, although he still used them primarily for security, not for progress.

At the time, the majority of American climbers were not yet mentally prepared to tackle multiday climbs. They made high camps, but they would not undertake a climb where a bivouac was inevitable because it was considered too debilitating, and the problems of storms on a multiday route were not to be taken lightly. Durrance knew that mountain bivouacs could be survived, and he was ready to pull his rubberized cotton bivouac sack over his head and sit out bad weather. In 1938 he and fellow Dartmouth student Michael Davis climbed the complete northwest ridge of the Grand Teton. They made two bivouacs on the route, one of the longest in the range.

In 1940 Durrance made a series of outstanding climbs. There were new routes on Middle Teton and Nez Perce and two on the Grand Teton. The first of the Grand Teton climbs was the southwest ridge, where he was joined by brother-in-law Henry Coulter and research chemist Fred Ayres. Durrance then decided that the time was ripe to attempt the west face of the Grand Teton, the face that Underhill considered the last major problem on the mountain.

The morning of the climb the sky was threatening. Plagued by falling ice, Durrance and Coulter climbed the lower section of the wall quickly. Then a snow squall pinned them down, but they waited it out under the bivouac sack. By midday only 1,000 feet remained. Three hard pitches in a chimney blocked by ice-covered chockstones brought them to a ledge below a smooth wall. The combination of heavy pack and hot sun exhausted Coulter. When Durrance turned to check the belay, his second was asleep. Not for long; Durrance cussed Coulter out and paced back and forth on the ledge. Finally, he moved to the left side of the ledge, up a steep crack, and then back right, almost slipping on a "bastard of a traverse." It was his closest call. Overcoming complicated route finding and a variety of problems on ice and steep rock, he put up one of the finest climb in the Tetons. It was then the most demanding alpine climb in North America.

Durrance and his Dartmouth companions were a light-hearted bunch. They whiled away many hours in the local Jackson bars, where Durrance roared forth with the beer-drinking songs of his Munich days. After one memorable night on the town, they drove back toward camp, with the driver nodding asleep at the wheel. They never made it back that night. When they awoke the car was in the middle of the sagebrush flats, its engine still running.

Durrance was a keen boulder climber when few others indulged in such an extreme form of the art. He worked out regularly at the Teton's Jenny Lake boulders. Nonchalantly smoking a cigarette while leading a difficult pitch—he led almost all of his climbs—he displayed the self-confidence of a master climber. Although he pursued a successful medical career, he stands apart from his contemporaries. Most of them treated climbing as just one facet of their lives; Durrance was both more dedicated and more skillful. He is a transitional figure between the gentlemen climbers of the prewar era and the totally committed climbers who emerged in America during the late 1950s. Much of his attitude toward the mountains came from his experiences in Europe, but his drive had to come from within. It was a drive shared by his brother, Dick Durrance. While Jack set a new standard for

American climbing, his brother was the best ski racer in America.

In the early 1920s Teton climbing was nonexistent. Technical climbing arrived with Henderson and Underhill in 1929; yet within ten years the most difficult climbs on the continent were in the Tetons. The standards of Canada were surpassed. What produced this rapid turn of events? A key element was the limited size of the Tetons. A climber could see the bulk of the range from the valley. There was no opportunity to fritter away time looking for untrod summits. If you wanted to do something new, it had to be a route shunned by earlier climbers. Another element was the superb Teton rock. Here was a medium where a good technician could exploit his skills. But the key element was the introduction of new talent and ideas. Drawing from their alpine experience and their crag climbing, the newcomers made advances unthinkable to an earlier generation. American climbing was on the move.

REFERENCES

Coulter, Henry. "The West Face of the Grand Teton." *AAJ* 4 (1941): 235.

Coulter, Henry, and Merril McLane. *Mountain Climbing Guide to the Grand Tetons.* Hanover, N.H.: Dartmouth Mountaineering Club, 1947.

Davis, Eleanor S. "The Tetons." *T & T,* no. 71 (Aug. 1924):9.

Davis, Michael. "First Ascent of the W. Ridge of the Grand Teton." *AAJ* 3 (1939): 364.

Durrance, Jack. "Ascent of the North Face of the Grand Teton." *Appalachia* 21 (June 1937): 425.

F. M. Fryxell Collection, Archives of Western History. Laramie: University of Wyoming.

Fryxell, Fritiof. "The Grand Teton by the North Face." *AAJ* 1 (1932): 465.

———. "The 1931 Mountaineering Season in Grand Teton National Park." *AAJ* 1 (1932): 535.

———. *The Teton Peaks and Their Ascents,* Grand Teton National Park: Crandall Studios, 1932.

Henderson, Kenneth A. "Some Rock Climbs in the White Mountains." *Appalachia* 17 (Dec. 1929): 343.

———. "The East Face of the Grand Teton." *T & T,* no. 141 (July 1930):5.

———. "Southwest Ridge of the Grand Teton." *Appalachia* 21 (Dec. 1936): 271.

House, William P. "An Ascent of the Pinnacle Gully, Huntington Ravine." *Appalachia* 20 (June 1934): 113.

Jeffers, LeRoy. *The Call of the Mountains.* New York: Dodd, Mead, 1922.

O'Brien, Lincoln. "Local Rock Climbing." *Harvard Mountaineering* 1 (2) (1928): 78.

Ortenburger, Leigh. *A Climber's Guide to the Teton Range.* San Francisco: Sierra Club, 1965.

Petzoldt, Paul. "A Winter Ascent of the Grand Teton." *T & T,* no. 211 (May 1936):43.

Rotch, William B. "Introducing the Dartmouth Mountaineering Club." *Appalachia* 21 (Dec. 1937): 531.

Stephens, Rockwell, "The American Inferno." *Appalachia* 20 (June 1934): 121.

Truslow, Francis Adams. "Mount Washington for the Weekend." *Appalachia* 19 (June 1932): 66.

Underhill, Miriam. *Give Me the Hills*. London: Metheun, 1956.

Underhill, Robert L. M. "Three Ridges of Mont Blanc." *Appalachia* 17 (Dec. 1928): 93.

———. "Cannon Mountain by the East Cliff." *Appalachia* 17 (Dec. 1928): 170.

———. "Spring Snow and Ice Climbing." *Appalachia* 17 (June 1929): 286.

———. "On Artificial Aids in Climbing." *Appalachia* 18 (June 1930): 79.

———. "The Grand Teton by the East Ridge." *AJ* 42 (Nov. 1930): 267.

———. "Rock Climbing." *Appalachia* 18 (Dec. 1930): 188.

———. "An Attempt on Mt. Robson by the N.W. Ridge." *CAJ* 19 (1931): 73.

———. "Two New Routes up the Grand Teton." *CAJ* 20 (1932): 72.

———. "Winter Climbing: In the Heroic Age." *Appalachia* 19 (June 1932): 136.

———. "Competitive Mountaineering." *Appalachia* 19 (Dec. 1932): 288.

———. "Modern Rock Climbing Equipment." *CAJ* 21 (1933): 165.

———. "The Technique of Rock Climbing." *Appalachia* 19 (Dec. 1933): 565.

Whitney, Hassler. "Cliff of Mt. Cannon, New Route." *Appalachia* 17 (Dec. 1929): 395.

Whittlesey, Julian H. "Pinnacle Gully of Huntington Ravine." *Appalachia* 18 (June 1930): 83.

The Sierrans

Hotfoot from his brilliant 1931 season in the Tetons, Robert Underhill joined a group of Sierra Club climbers in the High Sierra. After the initial exploration of the range, climbing had been carried out largely on Sierra Club "High Trips." It focused on repetition of the early ascent routes and on first ascents of less prominent peaks. As these invariably had an easy side, no real progress was made in climbing technique. The proper use of the rope was unknown, and there was a limit to a person's ambition when a slip might be fatal.

A few Sierra Club climbers learned about rope handling on outings to the Canadian Rockies in the late 1920s. However, they felt that the rope was more applicable to snow climbing, which is almost nonexistent in the Sierra, and that the Swiss guides used it to keep their clients in line and haul them up when necessary. When the Sierrans took a rope, it was either a quarter-inch "hay rope" used to give the second confidence in a tight spot, or a half-inch manila, which could be anchored at one end and used as a handrail. Formal belays were unknown. The hay rope was sometimes employed in continuous roped climbing, such as traversing narrow ridges. The theory was that if a climber fell from one side of a ridge, his partner would jump off the other!

Francis Farquhar, editor of the *Sierra Club Bulletin* and historian of the Sierra, requested an article from Underhill, which he titled "On the Use and Management of the Rope in Rock Work." He also invited Underhill to the Sierra to give firsthand instruction. After the Sierra Club's 1931 outing, Underhill joined a select group of mountaineers. They made several climbs, but their most ambitious project was the longest and steepest face on Mount Whitney, highest peak in the conterminous United States. For this climb Underhill was joined by Norman Clyde, Glen Dawson, and Jules Eichorn.

Clyde was the dean of the Sierra Club climbers. A large, powerfully built man dressed in patched-up clothes with a battered campaign hat crammed on his head, he had been a schoolmaster at one of the small towns that abut the eastern escarpment of the Sierra. But he ran afoul of the school board and took to the Sierra, roaming the range summer and winter, making more than a hundred first ascents, and guiding for the Sierra Club High Trips. The packs he carried are legendary: pots, pans, a cast-iron skillet,

Just down from the east face of Mount Whitney, from the left: Jules Eichorn, Norman Clyde, Robert Underhill and Glen Dawson. *Francis Farquhar*.

several pairs of boots, boot lasts, an axe, a few pistols, a rifle, a couple of fishing rods, up to five cameras, and a small library of classics in the original German, French, Spanish, and Greek. (He particularly favored the Greek, because he was a bit rusty in it, and the books lasted longer.) He climbed alone for the most part, but a rope is usually used on several of his fine routes today.

Dawson was a student at UCLA, and Eichorn studied piano with Ansel Adams, later internationally known for his photography. According to Underhill, they were "young natural-born rock-climbers of the first water." They had never seen Mount Whitney, "but neither had they seen any [peak] up and down the Sierra that they could not climb, and they were all enthusiasm." Although they acknowledged Underhill's greater experience, inwardly they felt they were his equals when it came to the rock.

In mid-August the party started up the trail to Mount Whitney. Underhill rode a mule for the first part of the journey. Clyde shouldered an enormous pack when they left the mule train behind, and they worked up to a base camp under the 2,000-foot east face. Examining the mountain in the evening light, they concluded they might be in for a hard time. But when they approached the face the following morning, they saw an encouraging series of cracks and ledges. Roped in teams of two, they climbed rapidly upward and after only three hours were congratulating each other on the summit.

Underhill later referred to the climb as "a mere bluff, but great fun." It was no match for many of the already established Canadian or Teton climbs. Its significance lay not in its difficulty but in its symbolism. The most impressive face on the Sierra's highest peak had fallen; the way was open. From this small beginning modern rock climbing evolved in California. Dawson noted prophetically, "Last summer Sierra climbing took a stride forward. . . . More and more we are becoming interested in new routes and traverses rather than in the ascents of peaks by easy routes."

Independent of these Sierra Club climbers, a young San Francisco Bay Area law student, Dick Leonard, embarked on a get-fit program. He had scrambled about in the Sierra as a Boy Scout, and now he explored the thirty-foot-high rock outcrops in the Berkeley hills. He interested some of his friends, and the group called themselves the Cragmont Climbing Club. Set in a residential neighborhood, the Berkeley rocks were nevertheless steeper than the typical Sierra peak. A fall was a distinct possibility. Soloing was foolish, so the Cragmont climbers studied the available European mountaineering literature. These books described a rudimentary belay but invariably contained the golden rule, the leader must not fall. The rope was used to assure the weaker members of the party. Should the leader fall, he violated his solemn duty. His rope was belayed rigidly over an edge of rock. Better it break than drag the whole party down the mountain.*

Leonard considered this attitude illogical and inhuman, and his group began a methodical study of belaying techniques. Practice sessions in belaying

*In fact German-speaking and Italian climbers were already using advanced piton and belay techniques. However, Leonard and other American researchers were unaware of these developments. First, there was a time lag between actual practice and written description. Second, the most accessible books were by British authors out of touch with the European mainstream.

might seem an obvious idea, yet the Cragmont climbers were the first group in America to do this and were ahead of the Europeans in this regard.

The European books emphasized the shoulder belay, where the rope lies across the belayer's back and over his shoulder. Leonard and his comrades quickly found its inherent weakness; a sharp pull doubled the belayer over, and there was a good chance the rope would slip from his grasp. Experience convinced them that a belay around the back of the hips was far superior. They also discovered the tremendous wrench on the rope from even a short fall. To reduce this force, they developed a sliding or *dynamic* belay, where the rope is checked less suddenly by allowing it to slip slightly through the belayer's hands. The dynamic belay put less strain on climber, belayer, and rope alike. It was a real improvement on the Europeans' static belay.

The Cragmont climbers' first victim using the new methods was a heavy sack. As their confidence grew, they worked up to impressive drops with live bodies. The brave volunteer climbed thirty feet above the ground, tied into the rope, gathered up to eighteen feet of slack in his hand, and jumped. In his article on local rock climbing, Leonard observed, "It is then up to the belayer to hold him." This no-nonsense approach to climbing paid off. It laid the groundwork for the advances that the Sierrans were to make in the years ahead.

With the practice sessions, abilities and confidence improved, and they were eager to see what they could do on full-sized rock faces. From their

Belay practice at Berkeley's Indian Rock in the 1930s. Peter Grubb has just stopped Jack Riegelhuth, who jumped from above the anchor point. *Dick Leonard*.

trips into the High Sierra, they knew there was plenty of unclimbed rock, but closer at hand and more spectacular was famed Yosemite Valley. At that time it was virtually untouched as a climbing center. Many of the summits are no more than minor bumps on the rim of the valley. Of greater interest to the early climbers were the rock spires, but these appeared to be impregnable. Unlike the High Sierra, where the rock has been fissured and broken by frost, the granite in Yosemite is monolithic and smooth. The most successful early Yosemite climber was the local postmaster, Charles Michael. But without equipment, he soon reached the limits of pioneering, and he told his young friend Eichorn that he considered the needle-like Cathedral Spires unclimbable. Eichorn was intrigued.

The Cragmont group reorganized as the Rock Climbing Section of the Sierra Club (though not without opposition from the faint-hearted within the club). Over the 1933 Labor Day holiday the R.C.S. set off on their first climbing trip to Yosemite Valley. The strongest climbers, Eichorn, Leonard, and San Francisco attorney Bestor Robinson, gathered up their makeshift gear and naïvely hiked to the base of the awesome Higher Cathedral Spire. On the north side it drops sheer for some 1,000 feet. The three climbers turned to the 400-foot southern flank. Their previous experience on near-vertical rock, on the local Bay Area outcrops, was invariably with an upper belay. They now faced the problem of leading up steep rock. Before long they placed their pitons, ten-inch nails bought at a hardware store.

They made a primitive leader belay by running the rope through slings attached to the nails, but they knew this method was basically unsafe. The climbing rope would burn through the rope loops in any but the shortest fall. The nails were also inadequate; they bent when the leader stood on them. After seven hours they gave up, defeated by the difficulties and the limitations of their equipment.

They would have to obtain real pitons and carabiners from Sporthaus Schuster in Munich, Germany. In those depression days this gear was fabulously expensive. Eichorn saved what he could from the twenty-five-cent piano lessons he gave. When the gear arrived, they practiced piton technique at the local rocks. They studied pictures of the Cathedral Spires under hand lens and protractor, and in November they were back in Yosemite.

On the southwest face of the Higher Spire they ran into a new problem: The carabiners generated so much friction as the rope zigzagged through them that the leader could barely move. They thought out a solution. Eichorn set out with *two* ropes. At first he clipped just one of them into the carabiners and left the other hanging from his waist. When the friction built up, he untied the first rope and used the second for the remainder of the lead. With the aid of pitons and rope stirrups, he led across a difficult traverse (the Bathtub Pitch) to an easy jamcrack. They reached midheight before darkness, and lack of equipment forced a retreat.

In April 1934 they set out once again. With the thorough preparation that typified all their endeav-ors, they had had their manila yachting rope tested at MIT. In 1934 Robinson proudly recorded their equipment, the most advanced then used in North America, "Two half-inch ropes (120 feet long, tensile strength 2,650 pounds); 200 feet of roping-down line (tensile strength 1,000 pounds); 60 feet of extra rope, for slings; 55 pitons, assorted; 13 carabiners; two piton-hammers, with slings attached; three piton step-slings; extra clothing; first-aid kit; two small cameras; one motion-picture camera; and lunch."

Yet it was not equipment alone that would make the difference, but also their determination. They were extending themselves. If they got into trouble, no one would be able to get them out of it.

With a cheering party that included Sierra Club president Farquhar, they hiked up to the base of the spire. Using the pitons already in place, they quickly gained the previous high point. Above loomed a steep thirty-foot wall, on which they used a new two-rope technique they had learned from a German writer. As Leonard stood up in a rope stirrup, Robinson energetically hauled on the first rope and held him into the rock by tension. Leonard then placed a higher piton and snapped his second rope and a stirrup into it. When he stood up on this next piton, Robinson hauled on the second rope and let the first one go slack. The double-rope technique freed the leader from grimly hanging on while he snapped his rope into each piton. (Tension climbing is nonetheless exhausting for belayer and leader alike. It has been superseded by more sophisticated methods.)

Jules Eichorn triumphantly signals from near the summit of Higher Cathedral Spire. The route lies close to the left skyline. *Marjory Bridge Farquhar*.

Worn out by the strenuous methods and the mental strain, Eichorn and Leonard swapped the lead five times on the thirty-foot wall. Finally, they were blocked by an overhang. Leonard hammered in a piton and instructed Robinson to lower him twenty feet and hold tight. Suspended from the rope Leonard scrambled back and forth over the face until he managed to clutch onto a crack. The new crack was too narrow for his fingers and too wide for the pitons. Back in the lead, Eichorn solved the problem. He hammered the pitons in crossways, their greatest width spanning the crack.* Displaying the innovative spirit essential to advances in climbing, the three companions arrived on top at sunset. Modern climbing had come to Yosemite.

Robinson summarized the adventure as follows,

Looking back upon the climb, we find that our greatest satisfaction is in having demonstrated, at least to ourselves, that by the proper application of climbing technique extremely difficult ascents can be made in safety. We had practiced belays and anchorages; we had tested pitons and ropes by direct falls; we had tried together the various maneuvers which we used on the peak, until three rock-scramblers had been coordinated into a team.

Not many months later the same trio accounted for nearby Lower Cathedral Spire. Then they began to wonder about the most spectacular of Yosemite's unclimbed pinnacles, the Lost Arrow. This smooth shaft splits off from the rock face to the right of Yosemite Falls. Its summit stands 1,300 feet above the base of the wall. In order to climb the Lost Arrow they had first to reach the notch between it and the wall. There were two possible approaches to the notch: a chimney that leads up from the base of the wall or a descent from the rim of the valley. In 1935 the Rock Climbing Section investigated both approaches and dismissed them as impractical. In 1936 Leonard wrote of the descent into the notch, "Roping down to the very edge of Yosemite Point, to the closest possible approach to the Arrow we obtained a view that

Summit of Higher Cathedral Spire. Bestor Robinson, Dick Leonard, and, on the right, Jules Eichorn. Courtesy Dick Leonard.

*Although trick piton placements and pendulums are commonplace today, they were then novel and daring.

134

Jules Eichorn on the first ascent of Lower Cathedral Spire, "the most difficult rock climb in America" (original caption). *Dick Leonard.*

was terrifying even to those who had climbed the Cathedral Spires. It was unanimously agreed that we would never attempt it."

When the Sierrans climbed the Higher Cathedral Spire, leader belays and piton placements were new and unfamiliar. Safety was always their prime concern, and even a short leader fall was considered risky. Thus, they made liberal use of pitons both as protection when climbing "free" and as a "direct aid" when they were unable to do so. As their confidence and technique improved in the following years, much that had required aid pitons, stirrups, and tension in the early days was climbed free. They still used pitons for safety, but "aid climbing" was soon looked upon as a last resort and not an end in itself.*

In the light of the growing expertise, the Lost Arrow, "the most fascinating unsolved problem in the state," took on a new allure. In 1937 Leonard and future conservation leader Dave Brower made a probe toward the Lost Arrow Chimney. They climbed some 350 feet to the foot of the chimney proper, yet the effort was purely exploratory. They were neither mentally nor technically prepared to launch an all-out push.

The other great problem of the day was the

*Today climbers hold that pitons and other devices may be used only for protection on a "free" climb. However, the distinction between free climbing and aid climbing has not always been so clearly drawn (certainly not in the 1930s). Europeans have generally accepted the use of a piton as a hand- or foothold on a free climb. For them aid climbing has meant the use of stirrups.

monolithic Half Dome, where Anderson's 1875 route remained the only way to the summit. The Sierrans made three attempts on the bald southwest face, but a close sight of the intended route discouraged them. Leonard later rationalized that the route "could not be climbed without excessive use of pitons as artificial aid. The undefined borderline between justifiable and unjustifiable use of direct aid would have to be crossed." The Lost Arrow Chimney and the southwest face of Half Dome were longer, more awesome, and more difficult than anything then climbed in Yosemite. They would have to wait for a new generation.

Unwilling or unable to force these routes, the Rock Climbing Section cast their eyes at other outstanding problems. The reputed twelve failures on Shiprock had not escaped them, and their attention was further captured by Robert Ormes's account in the *Saturday Evening Post.* Unlike Ormes, who only learned the strain a rope could hold when he fell on Shiprock, the Sierrans were accustomed to the intricacies of rope handling and aid climbing. They wholly accepted the use of pitons, not because their skills were inferior, but because their climbs in Yosemite demanded pitons.

In October 1939 a well-balanced team left Berkeley for their appointment with Shiprock. In those days a good belayer was almost as highly regarded as a good leader, and Raffi Bedayn was therefore a key member of the team. Apart from the food he provided from the family grocery, he was a reassuring second for an apprehensive leader. Dave Brower was the friction climbing expert. Slight John Dyer also had a special function: he would

Dave Brower on an early probe toward the Lost Arrow Chimney. *Dick Leonard.*

136

Dave Brower on the Berkeley practice rocks. Courtesy
Dave Brower.

come to the front of the rope when the pitons
barely held. The party was rounded out by Bestor
Robinson with his fund of stories and his keen eye
for gear.

Robinson had added something new to their
arsenal, expansion bolts. These were eye bolts
employed in the construction industry for fixings
in concrete. Robinson had used them around his
yard for a number of years, and the Sierrans tried
them out on the local rocks. However, stellite-
tipped drills and expansion bolts raised a problem
in mountaineering ethics; bolts unlike pitons could
be placed virtually anywhere. Was bolting a legitimate climbing technique? In "Shiprock," Robinson wrote, "We agreed with mountaineering mor-
alists that climbing by the use of expansion bolts
was taboo. We did believe, however, that safety
knew no restrictive rules."

The first night at Shiprock the Sierrans were
awakened by the screech of brakes and the sound
of voices. "This looks like them. Are you fellows
from the Sierra Club?" Mel Griffiths had driven
down to give them the benefit of his experience,
and they spent the next day scouting the route
with him.

On the first day of their attempt the Sierrans
passed the scene of Ormes's fall, remarking on its
obvious difficulties, and roped down a gully to a
large ledge below. This route possibility had also
occurred to the Coloradans, but they did not
follow it up, an oversight which Griffiths said "has
kind of stuck in my craw ever since." Brower then

The Sierrans steer their car over the desert toward Shiprock. *Dave Brower*.

led a delicate traverse to a short wall of rotten rock. Time ran out before Dyer gained many more feet, and they descended to their camp at the foot of the climb.

Unable to find an alternative, they were back at the rotten wall the following day. It was "a job of pure rock-engineering with two-man stands, pitons, foot slings and tension ropes." When the shadows lengthened and it was time to descend to camp, they had climbed only twelve feet of new ground. The conclusion was obvious. They would have to bivouac on the peak.

After a large breakfast they went up for their third day. Dyer finished off the wall, and Brower led a steep pitch. He was stopped cold by rotten rock within thirty feet of easy ground that led to the summit. That night they endured a four-man bivouac in a two-man tent. In the morning Robinson put a "ladder" of pitons up an expanding crack. The lower pitons dropped out as he drove higher ones. Then Dyer took over the lead and lassoed a horn of rock. At the top of the pitch he placed their fourth expansion bolt for a belay. Within minutes Shiprock was won.

It was an outstanding effort. The Sierrans were probably the only group on the continent capable of making the climb, and they did it with a bare minimum of expansion bolts. (Subsequent parties were to place many more bolts.) They were aware of the disreputable aura that surrounded the new techniques. Indeed, in their writings they pointedly called themselves "rock engineers," the abusive name that the conservatives had coined for technical climbers. On Shiprock they took a stand in open defiance of the conservatives, and the perspective of time has vindicated their attitudes and techniques.

During the 1930s the climbers on the East Coast

John Dyer on the rotten wall where a day's climbing resulted in a gain of twelve feet. *Dave Brower*.

Raffi Bedayn, John Dyer and Bestor Robinson settle into their bivouac on Shiprock. *Dave Brower*.

Dyer prepares to lasso the rock horn, the key to the summit of Shiprock. *Dave Brower*.

of the United States, the mountaineering establishment, generally looked upon the sport from a philosophical standpoint. Their climbing was still in the nineteenth-century tradition of the leisured gentleman mountaineer. The Californians were a home-grown group, owing no allegiance to hallowed traditions. They were the practical men of action brought up in the pioneer ethic. The intricacies of technical climbing were as attractive to them as they were abhorrent to the old school. Mountaineers like all men are the product of their environment.

After their success on Shiprock, the Sierrans pursued another of the hot climbing objectives of the day. This was Canada's Snowpatch Spire, the striking granite peak declared flatly impossible by Conrad Kain and a host of later luminaries. The most determined attempt was made by the German expatriate Fritz Wiessner in 1938. By midafternoon he and Dartmouth undergraduate Chappel Cranmer were almost at the level of the distinctive snowpatch at midheight on the southeast side. But with the advancing hour, Cranmer was reluctant to continue, and they retreated. Wiessner had dispelled the impossible hypothesis, but he thought the final wall would be predominantly aid climbing. He wrote that he did not want to make a climb which was "merely an affair of driving iron in the virgin rock."

With some nine unsuccessful attempts, the last by the well-known Wiessner, Snowpatch was talked of as the continent's number one climbing problem. In 1940 four Sierrans urged their car to the end of the logging road that gave access to the Bugaboos. They quickly concluded that Wiessner's route offered the best chance of success and set out on a reconnaissance. Bedayn and Canadian Jack Arnold passed Wiessner's high point and pressed ahead to examine the final wall. The prospect was not encouraging, and their companions decided against wasting any more time on Snowpatch. However, Arnold and Bedayn were not so easily put off. The only way to find out if a route would go was to come to grips with it.

They carried bivouac gear up to a high platform and huddled together through the night. The next morning they discovered a rodent had eaten a good part of their food. Leading up the key "Vein Pitch," Bedayn watched a small, well-fed rodent scampering over the rock. After several difficult pitches they scrambled onto the summit and swapped yodels with their friends on the glacier below.*

On Snowpatch and Shiprock the Sierrans convincingly demonstrated the excellence of their granite gymnasium, Yosemite Valley. Back in the valley, climbing was on the move. Successive attempts on the Lost Arrow Chimney, "the nightmare of all those who have inspected it closely,"

*Wiessner's estimation of the headwall was wrong. Above the snowpatch the climbing was piton-protected but entirely free.

inched the route upward. A new generation of climbers was making its mark. Typical of the newcomers were Fritz Lippmann, Robin Hansen, and their friends, the self-styled "goose gutters." The active encouragement of beginners was a strong tradition on R.C.S. outings. The goose gutters felt this cut too heavily into their climbing time. If the Sierrans scheduled a weekend meet, the goose gutters went elsewhere to avoid the crowds. However, this shift from group to individual climbing was not the real concern. What bothered the original R.C.S. members was the newcomers' extensive use of direct aid. It was an ironic twist. Aid climbing had brought censure on the original R.C.S. group. The older generation also considered the newcomers rash. They criticized their lax attitude to safety and reminded them of Leonard's dictum that should he ever fall, his first thought would be, "What will Underhill say about this in *Appalachia*?" The newcomers' Arrowhead Chimney climb (not to be confused with the still unclimbed Lost Arrow Chimney) was characterized by Shand as a route "which borders on the suicide climbs of the Wetterstein and the Kaisergebirge."

Were these criticisms the result of a lack of understanding between generations, or was something else involved? If Eichorn's group used pitons on the Higher Cathedral Spire, were not Lippmann and his pals entitled to find their own frontier? After his defeat on Shiprock, Coloradan Carl Blaurock had written, "Will someone find the key to the route by which the summit may be finally obtained, or if it is to be reached, will it be by methods not considered ethical?" Did the end justify the means? The debate was opened, but it was a debate that would have to wait. When Lippmann got down from the Arrowhead Chimney, Yosemite's age of innocence was over. It was December 7, 1941.

REFERENCES

Abraham, George D. *Modern Mountaineering.* London: Metheun, 1933.

Bedayn, Raffi. "Shiprock Finale." *T & T*, no. 254 (Feb. 1940):23.

————. "A Bugaboo No Longer." *AAJ* 4 (1941): 219.

Blaurock, Carl. "Shiprock Again." *T & T*, no. 237 (1938): 90.

Brower, David. "It Couldn't Be Climbed." *Saturday Evening Post*, Feb. 3, 1940.

————. "Yosemite Climbing Notes." *SCB* 27 (4) (Aug. 1942): 132.

Clyde, Norman. *Close-Ups of the High Sierra.* Glendale, Calif.: La Siesta Press, 1962.

————. *Norman Clyde of the Sierra Nevada.* San Francisco: Scrimshaw Press, 1971.

Dawson, Glen. "Mountain Climbing on the 1931 Outing." *SCB* 17 (1) (Feb. 1932): 113.

F. M. Fryxell Collection, Archives of Western History. Laramie: University of Wyoming.

Harris, Morgan. "Safety Last?" *SCB* 27 (4) (Aug. 1942): 65.

Leonard, Richard M. "Values to Be Derived from Local Rock Climbing." *SCB* 19 (3) (June 1934): 28.

———. "Piton Technique on the Cathedral Spires." *Appalachia* 20 (Dec. 1934): 177.

———. "The Cathedral Spires." *SCB* 20 (1) (Feb. 1935): 107.

———. "Half Dome." *SCB* 21 (1) (Feb. 1936): 96.

———. "Lost Arrow." *SCB* 21 (1) (Feb. 1936): 99.

———. "Lost Arrow." *SCB* 23 (2) (April 1938): 119.

———. "Lost Arrow." *SCB* 26 (1) (Feb. 1941): 138.

Leonard, Richard M., and David R. Brower. "A Climber's Guide to the High Sierra: Yosemite Valley." *SCB* 25 (1) (Feb. 1936): 41.

Leonard, Richard M., and Arnold Wexler. "Belaying the Leader." *SCB* 31 (7) (Dec. 1946): 68.

Maduschka, Leo. "Modern Rock Technique." *Mountaineering Journal* 1 (3) (March-May 1933): 156.

Michael, C. W. "First Ascent of the Minarets." *SCB* 12 (1) (1924): 28.

Robinson, Bestor. "The First Ascent of the Higher Cathedral Spire." *SCB* 19 (3) (June 1934): 34.

———. "Shiprock." *AAJ* 4 (1940): 54.

———. "The First Ascent of Shiprock." *SCB* 25 (1) (Feb. 1940): 1.

Shand, William. "Some Yosemite Rock Climbs." *AAJ* 5 (1944): 203.

Underhill, Robert L. M. "On the Use and Management of the Rope in Rock Work." *SCB* 16 (1) (Feb. 1931): 67.

———. "Mount Whitney by the East Face." *SCB* 17 (1) (Feb. 1932): 53.

Voge, Hervey. *A Climber's Guide to the High Sierra*. San Francisco: Sierra Club, 1956.

Wiessner, Fritz. "Snowpatch Spire." *AAJ* 3 (1939): 368.

Young, Geoffrey Winthrop. *Mountain Craft*. London: Methuen, 1920.

The Pacific Northwest and Alaska

The climbing centers of the continent were separated by hundreds, even thousands, of miles. During the prewar period transcontinental railroad travel was leisurely rather than rapid. The highway system was in its infancy, and most vacations were brief. When technical climbing arose in this period, it usually did so in isolation. Climbers in one area had to duplicate the learning efforts of those elsewhere and so evolved their own attitudes and techniques. This isolation was particularly true in the Pacific Northwest.

Before the rise of technical climbing the situation in the Northwest was similar to that in the Colorado Rockies. The more accessible peaks were climbed in the 1800s, and subsequent activity centered on repetition of the early ascent routes. In the Northwest the mountains of the interior remained unknown. The prominent and accessible volcanoes continued to hold the attention of mountaineers. Of these volcanic peaks one surpassed all others, 14,410-foot Mount Rainier. Plainly visible from Seattle, on a clear day it was a challenge to the people who lived nearby.

Such was the popularity of Rainier that first ascensionist Philemon Van Trump started a guiding business during the 1890s. He was emulated by Len Longmire, whose family developed a resort hotel on the south side of the mountain. Longmire's standard fee from Camp Muir to the summit was one dollar per person. The people who employed guides seldom had any previous knowledge of climbing. It was a once-in-a-lifetime experience for them, and, of course, they climbed by the simplest route. With the guides following the well-beaten path up the Gibraltar Route, no spark of genius came from that quarter.

There was one notable amateur climb during this plodding era on Mount Rainier: the first winter ascent by French alpinists Jacques Bergues, Jean Landry, and Jacques Landry in 1922. Winter climbing was unknown in Seattle, and the climb caused a stir in the local press. In later life Jean Landry reflected on the progress in mountaineering. The latter-day climbs were so much harder than those he remembered that he scarcely recognized himself as a climber. Yet the increase in standards came about largely as a result of improvements in equipment and technique. As he said to Molenaar, "The relation of challenge against capability has probably remained constant and so has, therefore, the moral reward of the climber's experience."

Although the guides on Mount Rainier occasionally included European professionals like the Swiss brothers Hans and Heinrich Fuhrer, they were essentially home grown. They evolved their own techniques for shepherding large parties up and down the mountain. Typically, a party of thirty to fifty people included one guide for every ten clients. The clients were fitted out with stout boots and an alpenstock. Ice axes were considered too dangerous a weapon to hand to novices, who were more likely to hurt themselves than cut steps in the ice. The lead guide tied into a heavy hemp rope, but not the rest of the party; they held it lightly in their hands. Its function was to keep them in line. The guides wore nailed boots in preference to crampons.

In 1929 a guide and his client slipped on an ice slope and died in a well-publicized accident. Crampons might have saved them, and regulations were drawn up requiring the guides to use crampons. In discussing the accident in 1929, Robert Underhill criticized the guides' lack of training. He pointed out that the heavy tourist traffic and the fee scale had brought about a "peculiar system of guiding," where it was profitable to have large parties of complete novices. Frank Willard, Rainier chief guide during part of the 1930s, recalled that the guides had to look after their clients from dawn to dusk and noted, according to Molenaar, "Guiding as you know isn't climbing."

If guided climbing was at a low ebb, amateur climbing was no better. The Seattle Mountaineers, the leading local club, were cautious to a fault. Their annual camp switched predictably from one volcanic peak to another, and a member's prowess was measured by the number of peaks climbed. They instituted "peak-bagging" awards: The more peaks climbed, the more impressive the award. The mechanical approach was highlighted by the Seattle Mountaineers' 1932 climbing code, written up by Playter. Rules were spelled out for leaders, climbers, and "rearguard": Obey the leader; start early enough to complete trip by daylight; do not relax vigilance at any time during the trip; and the catch-all, "Be prepared, and know how, to overcome unexpected difficulties." After twenty-five rules it was a surprise to read, "Remember . . . We climb for pleasure." The club's outings and aspirations defined what constituted mountaineering. It was not fertile ground for innovation, but, in spite of themselves, a new day was coming for the Seattle Mountaineers.

In the northern hemisphere the shadowed north sides of mountains carry the greatest accumulation of snow and ice. Due to glacial action during past ice ages the north faces are frequently the steepest and most forbidding. This is as true of Mount Rainier as it is of the Alps. Although the north face of Rainier is no match for the renowned alpine

The Seattle Mountaineers on Mount Saint Helens, 1917. Mass ascents were common in the Northwest from the turn of the century until the 1930s. Courtesy The Mountaineers.

north faces, the first probes onto it were analogous to contemporary efforts in Europe; the Mount Rainier aspirants were pushing back technical and psychological barriers. Starting from a lower base of skill, they were making a quantum advance.

The first of the north side features to attract attention was Ptarmigan Ridge, a mixture of problems on rock and ice. In 1933 a three-man team cut steps up 500 feet of steep ice. It was not a serious attempt, and the team turned back when it became apparent they could not reach the summit and return before dark. The following year team member Hans Grage joined up with Wolf Bauer, who had some slight experience of climbing in Europe. They retreated from their first attempt on Ptarmigan Ridge in the face of a driving storm, but undeterred, they were back two months later. They picked their way toward the ridge by flashlight, then chopped steps in hard ice by the cold light of a September dawn. Above the ice slope they paused to admire the shadowed depths of the north face proper, the Willis Wall, and were startled by the hiss and whir of falling rock and ice. Pressing against a rock cliff, they worked into an ice chute and climbed up under the cover of projecting rocks. Once past the chute, ninety

The north side of Mount Rainier. Ptarmigan Ridge rises from lower right to meet the ice falls of Liberty Cap Glacier. Liberty Ridge, center, is separated from Curtis Ridge by the shadowed Willis Wall. *Austin Post*.

minutes of rock climbing brought them to the upper glacier that leads to the summit plateau. The difficulties were below them, but they were not prepared to bivouac and had to descend.

Bauer returned in September 1935 with Boeing Company supervisor Jack Hossack, this time fully equipped with bivouac gear. If the climb took three days, they were ready. The low night-time temperatures kept the rockfall reasonably quiet, but Bauer and Hossack had to contend with hard late-season ice. After thirteen hours on the face, they reached the summit plateau, crawled into their sleeping bags, and cooked some hot pea soup.

The bold attempts on Ptarmigan Ridge had not gone unnoticed among the Seattle Mountaineers. Three weeks after the final success, a team organized by outdoor equipment buff Ome Daiber climbed another of the northern ridges, Liberty Ridge. After sixty-five years of negligible innovation, two outstanding climbs were made on Mount Rainier in the same month.

The Mountaineers gave prominent recognition to the new climbs. They realized that their home-grown techniques were inadequate and accepted Bauer's offer to conduct a climbing class. An avid skier, Bauer sent for the German literature on winter mountaineering and copied the European gear. By practicing before each class, he kept one jump ahead of his students. He made his first free-hanging rappel from a bridge in a city park.

The following week he had to demonstrate the technique at the Mountaineers' clubroom. While the keen-eyed students watched his every move, he launched out over the shaky handrail at the top of the main staircase and rappelled to the marble floor three stories below. Never again was he bothered by a rappel in the high mountains.

These instructional classes became a continuing event and performed a vital function in the Northwest. The Seattle Mountaineers were attracting a growing number of young people, but the old guard were not eager to pass their expertise on to the upstarts. It was difficult for newcomers to break into the select inner circle, but the climbing classes changed all this. Within a few years the old-time experts were left hopelessly behind.

Ice climbing on the first ascent of Ptarmigan Ridge. *Wolf Bauer*.

A common misconception among North American mountaineers of this era was that the big volcanic peaks were the Cascade Range. The rest of the range was supposed to consist of low, secondary peaks, heavily forested and of little interest. A few mountaineers were sufficiently curious to put this theory to the test. In 1932

Mountaineers' practice on "Big Rock," a glacial erratic on the outskirts of Seattle. One man rappels; another looks on while giving a casual belay. In the post-war years the area became a housing tract and Big Rock was buried in dirt. *Lloyd Anderson.*

Hermann Ulrichs was attracted to the North Cascades by enticing elevation marks on hitherto blank sections of the map. He soon experienced the dense forest part of the theory but equally, surely, refuted the secondary peak part. There were narrow crests flanked by rock walls and extensive glaciers. Few of the peaks topped 9,000 feet, but the height differential between valley bottom and summit was such that they were more exciting than the typical Sierra or Colorado peak.

Ulrichs was drawn on by the gradual revelation of the unknown as he penetrated the back country. Over a period of years he climbed some twenty new peaks, including Silver Star, and his example persuaded others to leave the over-familiar volcanic peaks and tackle the wilderness. As with the Interior and Coast ranges of Canada, the initial problem was the impenetrable jungle of deadfall and matted undergrowth over which and through which the climbers had to struggle. The arduous bushwacks, where climbers were frequently suspended above the ground by the undergrowth, provided a heightened sense of isolation and adventure. The peaks were often ascended by other routes than the simplest; the approach dictated the side that would be climbed.

In contrast to the Sierra and Colorado, many Cascade peaks were difficult on all sides. One such peak was Mount Goode. It repulsed a number of attempts by Ulrichs and others over the years and gained a considerable reputation. When they heard that a rival group from the Mazamas of Oregon planned an attempt, Seattle Mountaineers Bauer, Hossack, George MacGowan, and two others attacked Mount Goode in 1936. The climb was difficult, and Bauer placed a couple of pitons. Arriving on top first, he hastily built a rock cairn. Moments later he pointed to the cairn and de-

Hermann Ulrichs on the summit of Mount Edith, Canadian Rockies, 1925. His solo ascent of the northwest face of Mount Stephen two years later scandalized Canadian Alpine Club members. Courtesy Hermann Ulrichs.

jectedly announced to his comrades that the Mazamas had beat them.

During the prewar years almost all climbers were affiliated with the established mountaineering clubs. An unaffiliated climber was a rare bird, but there were exceptions. In 1937 a group of Rover Boy Scouts were informed by Scout headquarters that their climbing activities were more than the scouting movement could officially condone. The Rovers were more interested in the mountains than scouting. They formed the Ptarmigan Climbing Club and continued their far-ranging Cascade explorations. Jobs were hard to find in those years, and roaming the hills was cheaper than staying at home. In the summer of 1938 Ptarmigans Calder Bressler, Ray Clough, Bill Cox, and Tom Myers traversed the Cascade crest from Dome Peak to Cascade Pass, an area almost unvisited and unknown. This magnificent traverse, now known as the Ptarmigan Traverse, included several first ascents. It would have included Mount Goode on the eleventh day had their boot nails not completely worn out.

Another unaffiliated climber was Berlin emigrant Otto Trott. On a 1939 climb up the standard route on Mount Shuksan, Trott was surprised when his companion, Andy Hennig, laboriously cut steps up a moderate ice slope. Apparently, the ice climbing techniques developed in the Alps were unknown in the Northwest. Trott walked up and down the slope using the now usual crampon

Mountaineers group on summit of Mount Goode. Left to right: Jack Hossack, J. Halwax, Wolf Bauer and George MacGowan. Courtesy Wolf Bauer.

Typical Cascade weather on the first ascent of Forbidden Peak. *Lloyd Anderson*.

technique: ankles flexed, soles parallel to the surface of the ice, all points of the crampons biting the surface. The local climbers were keen to learn the new method, which Trott and Hennig applied on the first ascent of the west face of Mount Shuksan. On this climb they also employed ice pitons to protect the leader and bivouacked twice.

The most persistent climber of the prewar period was Lloyd Anderson, who later founded Seattle's Recreational Equipment Co-Op. He realized that in order to get up a Cascade peak, a climber had to chance the weather. He was prepared to carry on when the clouds clamped down and his teammates were thinking retreat. More than once while his companions descended through cloud and rain, he doggedly stayed on the mountain in the hope that one of them would come back. In 1940 he made the first ascent of Forbidden Peak with Jim Crooks, Dave Lind, sixteen-year-old Fred Beckey, and Beckey's thirteen-year-old brother Helmy.

These young recruits from the Seattle Mountaineers' climbing classes shared Anderson's dedication. Good weather or bad, they got away to the Cascades almost every weekend. Theirs was an informal, high-spirited approach that the older generation lacked. Walt Varney was a keen gymnast. He started a craze for doing front-flips while descending snow slopes. After a Mountaineers' outing, two dozen novices could be seen flipping down the mountain. It was a far cry from the twenty-five solemn rules for leader, climbers, and rearguard of a few years before.

The Northwesterners also went farther afield. "Unknowns" Hossack and MacGowan went to the Tetons in 1939 and pulled off a fine climb on the north side of the Grand Teton, the northeast couloir. In 1941 Anderson, Helmy Beckey, Rainier

Mountaineers' party that beat the Sierrans to the South Tower of Howser. From left: Tom Campbell, Lloyd Anderson, Lyman Boyer, Helmy Beckey. *Lloyd Anderson*.

guide Lyman Boyer, and Tom Campbell were in the Bugaboos in Canada. At camp they met a team from the Sierra Club, who told them of their plan to try for the prized South Tower of the Howser Spires. The Washington climbers remained non-commital. When the Sierrans approached the peak the following day, the Washingtonians were already well on their way to the top.

Alaska and the Yukon

While these climbers sought out the more challenging routes in the Pacific Northwest, another group accounted for the major peaks in Alaska and the Yukon. Far removed from the gentle Sierra Nevada, the compact Tetons, and the moderate-altitude Cascades, these are big mountains set in a hostile environment of glaciers and ice falls. They are the most magnificent and the most forbidding peaks on the continent. The major ranges are appalling in their sterility, few animals and plants survive there, and man himself has come only as a visitor, never to make a home. However, a few people responded to the unique call of the northern mountains and found a challenge unmatched by other ranges.

On the larger peaks the vertical relief from the surrounding glaciers to the summit is enormous. Indeed, the greatest vertical relief in North America is the two-mile-high Wickersham Wall on Mount McKinley. The weather is notoriously bad. Summer snowfalls of a foot or more within twenty-four hours are common. The frequent build-up of new snow makes glacier travel and climbing laborious. A waist-deep wallow quickly tires a person. Prior to the mid-1930s the mountains were deep inside a wilderness. The pioneers were forced to pack their equipment many miles, and there was little chance of a rescue unless it was to pick up a body.*

After the 1913 ascent of Mount McKinley there were no more climbing parties in the vicinity for twelve years. Even allowing for the disruption of

*By the mid-1930s bush pilots were prepared to land their ski-equipped planes on the glaciers. This simplified the overall climbing problem.

the First World War, the neglect of so many fine, untouched peaks seems odd. However, the best climbers of the day were involved in the Canadian Rockies, and technical climbing was nonexistent in the United States in the early 1900s.

The 1925 ascent of Mount Logan renewed interest in the far north and set the stage for a new era of exploration. The year after their Logan climb, Allen Carpé and Andy Taylor joined Columbia University medical professor William Ladd in a reconnaissance of Mount Fairweather, a beautiful peak sometimes visible from Glacier Bay. (It was ''fair weather'' if you could see the summit.) They ran out of time and supplies before they could establish themselves on the mountain.

The next try at Fairweather was led by Bradford Washburn, a young Harvard man with a toothy grin and a love of photography. Although he later became a master of planning and the best expeditionary leader in Alaska, his 1930 effort was less successful than Carpé's. Unprepared for the scale of Fairweather, he decided to spend the next climbing season in the Alps.*

Carpé returned to Fairweather in 1931 with Ladd, Taylor, and economist Terris Moore. At their highest camp they were twice poised for a summit push and twice stalled by storms. Supplies and morale were low, but Carpé was not prepared to give up without a fight. He looked around the tent at his companions and warned them that if they did not climb Fairweather, Washburn would be back the following year.

To conserve supplies, Ladd and Taylor descended, leaving their younger companions to battle it

*In 1929 Washburn and his guides made a noteworthy route up the Couturier Couloir of the Aiguille Verte. In the French mountaineering classic *Premier de Cordée*, a Bradford Warfield, Jr., is cast as an American with a passion for record times.

Mount Fairweather. The 1931 party climbed the left-hand skyline. *Austin Post.*

out with the elements. The wind was so violent that Carpé and Moore felt sure the tent would rip apart. Huddled inside, they took down the pole and clung to the flapping canvas through the night. When the storm passed, there were a couple of feet of new snow. In places they had to crawl on hands and knees to distribute their weight as they struggled toward the summit.

In 1932 Carpé organized a scientific expedition to Mount McKinley to study cosmic rays. It was nineteen years since climbers were on the mountain, yet by coincidence another party came that year. After making the second ascent of the highest summit, the Lindley-Liek Ski Expedition made their way toward the scientists' tents. The camp was deserted. The uneasy group continued down the glacier, and their fears were confirmed when they found the body of Carpé's companion, Theodore Koven. He had evidently fallen into a crevasse and died while trying to regain the tents. Of Carpé there was no sign.

At the time of his death, Carpé was one of the best expeditionary mountaineers on the continent. After early climbing in the Alps, he pioneered extensively in the Canadian mountains. Finally, he was irrevocably drawn to Alaska, which he wrote ''has haunted me for years.'' An independent-minded man, sometimes difficult to approach, he had been known to walk across glaciers without the precaution of roping to a companion. This carefree attitude has claimed many lives.

Bradford Washburn, left, and Bob Reeve before the flight to Lucania. Note the mass of camera gear. *Bradford Washburn*.

With a further season of alpine climbing behind him, Washburn returned to Alaska in 1932 to attempt Mount Crillon, a snow peak near Glacier Bay. Frustrated by bad weather, he returned the next year. Among his second group were a young racer on the U.S. ski team, H. Adams Carter, and two men whose names are linked with the struggle to climb K2, the world's second highest mountain, Charles Houston and Bob Bates. From a high camp some 6,000 feet below the top, the summit party climbed a 1,000-foot icefall and eventually reached a peak, but not the summit, which they could see half a mile away. It was a half mile they could not cross. The only alternatives were waist-deep snow and an avalanche slope. Carter and Washburn returned once again the following year and completed the climb under better conditions with a quick dash for the summit. On this occasion Houston was not with them. He was on the first ascent of 17,395-foot Mount Foraker southwest of Mount McKinley.

While the exploration of the Alaskan peaks was slowly pushed ahead, geographer and arctic specialist Walter Wood was active in the Canadian Yukon. In 1935 Wood, Swiss guide Hans Fuhrer, and two companions succeeded on Mount Steele, where their first attempt had been defeated by storm.

Two years after the ascent of Mount Steele, Bates and Washburn flew into the area for an attempt on the neighboring Mount Lucania. Bush pilot Bob Reeve made a perfect landing on the glacier only to discover a foot of slush covered by an ice crust. The plane was mired down. On the second day as an involuntary camper, Reeve tried to take off, but his skis broke through the crust. By the fourth day he was thoroughly tired of glaciers. He stripped everything out of the plane, changed the pitch of the propellor with a ball-peen hammer, and gave the engine full throttle. The plane bounced down a steep slope toward a glacial lake and into the air in the nick of time. Reeve later confided that that take-off had made a Christian out of him.

There were two other members of the Mount Lucania expedition, but Reeve made it clear there was no way he would fly them in or come and collect Bates and Washburn later on. To get back to civilization, they were left with two choices: either descend the Walsh Glacier or climb over the top of Mount Steele. Both alternatives finished with an extensive bushwack. Feeling that it would be unsafe for just two people to pick their way through the crevasses on the Walsh Glacier, they decided in favor of Mount Steele. If Wood and party had climbed up the ridge on the other side of the mountain, surely they could climb down it.

After two weeks of relaying loads, Bates and Washburn established a camp on the pass between Mount Steele and Mount Lucania. Their plan had been to make a speedy escape over Steele. However, they had more food than they could possibly

need or carry, so they decided to bag Lucania as well as Steele. Using one intermediate camp, they stormed up Lucania. Delighted as they were with this success, they were not out of trouble. Sixty miles of mountain, glacier, and swamp lay between them and safety. They threw away most of their food, a cooking pot, and nearly all their clothes. They even cut half of the floor out of their tent to save weight. After they had passed over the summit of Steele two days later, they removed the entire tent floor and sliced off the guy ropes. By the time they were hiking across the tundra, their food was almost gone, but fortunately they had not thrown away all their gear. They fed on red squirrels and a rabbit killed with their six-shooters.

Luck was with them. The weary pair met a pack-train and were soon eating huge quantities of sheep steak and lemon meringue pie at a trading post.

The era of the first climbs in Alaska and the Yukon was similar to that in other mountain ranges: The more prominent peaks were ascended by the simplest routes. The main problem was getting to the base of the mountain with enough supplies and determination to outlast the weather. It was unlikely that the climbers would be stopped by technical difficulties. Although the technical climbing was not as severe as contemporary efforts elsewhere, these mountains were by no means simple. In a Yosemite the difficulties centered on

On the first ascent of Mount Hayes, 1941. *Bradford Washburn*.

the ascent of a few hundred feet of rock. In Alaska problems of access, logistics, and weather demanded skills as much as did a Yosemite climb, and there was an overall seriousness that made Alaskan climbing a daunting business.

By the mid-1930s there were strong rock climbing technicians in the Sierra and the Tetons, and there were proven mountaineers in Canada, the Cascades, and Alaska. But what about a peak that combined the various kinds of difficulties? Would rock technicians pull it off? Or would mountaineers take the prize? The answer was not long in coming.

REFERENCES

Anderson, Lloyd. "The Climb of Forbidden Peak." *Mountaineer* 33 (Dec. 1940): 35.

———. "A First Ascent in the Bugaboos." *Mountaineer* 34 (Dec. 1941): 25.

Bauer, Wolf. "The North Face of Mount Rainier." *Mountaineer* 27 (Dec. 1934): 3.

———. "The Final Conquest." *Mountaineer* 28 (Dec. 1935): 3.

Beckey, Fred. *Challenge of the North Cascades*. Seattle: The Mountaineers, 1969.

Beckwith, Edward P. "The Mt. McKinley Cosmic Ray Expedition, 1932." *AAJ* 2 (1933): 45.

Borrow, Will H. "Via Liberty Ridge." *Mountaineer* 28 (Dec. 1935): 7.

Boyer, Lyman. "Another 'Unclimbable' Conquered." *Mountaineer* 31 (Dec. 1938): 30.

Carpé, Allen. "An Attempt on Mt. Fairweather." *Appalachia* 16 (Dec. 1926): 442.

———. "The Ascent of Mount Bona." *AAJ* 1 (1931): 245.

———. "The Conquest of Mt. Fairweather." *AJ* 43 (Nov. 1931): 221.

Child, William S. "Crillon, 1933." *AAJ* 2 (1934): 148.

Farquhar, Francis P. "Naming Alaska's Mountains." *AAJ* 11 (1959): 211.

Haines, Aubrey L. *Mountain Fever: Historic Conquests of Rainier* Portland: Oregon Historical Society, 1962.

Henderson, K. A. "Mount Rainier—and Guides: Comment." *Appalachia* 21 (June 1936): 34.

Hertz, Stuart B. "Everett Climb Pin." *Mountaineer* 25 (Dec. 1932): 30.

Houston, Charles S. "Denali's Wife." *AAJ* 2 (1935): 285.

Ladd, W. S. "Allen Carpé." *AAJ* 1 (1932): 507.

MacGowan, George. "Goode Conquest." *Mountaineer* 29 (Dec. 1936): 13.

Manning, Harvey. "Ptarmigans and Their Ptrips." *Mountaineer* 51(4) (1958): 48.

Molenaar, Dee. *The Challenge of Rainier*. Seattle: The Mountaineers, 1971.

Piontecki, Jack. "Climbing in the Bugaboos." *SCB* 27 (Aug. 1942): 122.

Playter, H. W., *et al.* "Code for Leaders and Climbers." *Mountaineer* 25 (Dec. 1932): 31.

Trosper, Wendell. "Mt. Rainier via Puyallup Cleaver: Sunset Amphitheater." *Mountaineer* 33 (Dec. 1937): 22.

Ulrichs, Hermann. "The Cascade Range of Northern Washington." *SCB* 22 (Feb. 1937): 69.

Underhill, Robert L. M. "The Accident on Mt. Rainier." *Appalachia* 17 (Dec. 1929): 388.

———. "Accidents." *Appalachia* 26 (Dec. 1932): 298.

Washburn, Bradford. "The Ascent of Mount Lucania." *AAJ* 2 (1938): 119.

———. "The Ascent of Mount Lucania." *AJ* 50 (May 1938): 95.

Wood, Walter A. *A History of Mountaineering in the St. Elias Mountains*. Banff, Alberta: Alpine Club of Canada, 1967.

———. "The Ascent of Mt. Steele." *AAJ* 2 (1936): 439.

Mount Waddington

On a climbing trip to Vancouver Island in 1925, Phyllis Munday was scanning the northern horizon with binoculars when her attention riveted on a distant peak. This chance sighting initiated a new age of exploration in the Coast Range of British Columbia, in which Phyllis and her husband Don were to play the major role. Apart from Mount Saint Elias in the far north, almost nothing was known of the peaks that stretch along the edge of the continent for 1,000 miles north from Vancouver. No climbers had penetrated into the heart of the region, and by the 1920s the Coast Range was pretty much dismissed as an alpine also-ran.

The first problem was to reach the alluring peak, and the sea seemed to offer the best approach. In the fall of 1925 the Mundays took a steamer up the British Columbia coast, landed at Ward Point, and started up a sketchy hunting trail. The brush had a malevolent air about it, and progress was slow. From a knoll overlooking the broad trench of the Homathko River, they got their first clear view of the spectacular peak they knew as "Mystery Mountain." On another trip the following spring they reached the glaciers surrounding Mystery Mountain or Mount Waddington as the 13,260-foot peak is officially named.

In 1927 the Mundays laboriously relayed equipment through the brush and up the glaciers. It was a full month before they were in a position to scout Mount Waddington's defenses. There was no easy way up the mountain. They tried a subsidiary southwest ridge, attempted to reach the east side, and finally set out for the west ridge. They were close to the lower of Mount Waddington's two summits by six o'clock, but they were not prepared to bivouac, and the weather was turning bad.

They were back for a fourth time in 1928, again attacking the west ridge. After fifteen hours of climbing from their high camp, they reached the northwest peak, but 1,000 feet away across a deep gash rose the true spire-like summit, "almost a nightmare in its grim inaccessibility, draped with plumes of huge, crumbling ice-feathers."

The Mundays then concentrated on the other fine peaks in the region, returning to it regularly over the next several years. Accompanied by Mount Logan expedition member Henry Hall and guide Hans Fuhrer, they made the first ascent of

The south face of Mount Waddington. The lower northwest peak is on the left. The final climb began in the right-hand couloir, crossed to the left side of the triangular snowpatch below the summit and so to the ridge. *Barry Hagen*.

Mount Combatant in 1933. But whatever they climbed, they saw the highest summit still untouched. With the added enthusiasm of Hall and Fuhrer, new plans were laid for Mount Waddington; however, by then they were not alone. Two other Canadian groups set out for the mountain in 1934.

Winnipeg climbers Campbell Secord and the brothers Roger and Ferris Neave approached Waddington from the Canadian interior. Since the southern approach had defeated the Mundays, they opted for the unknown northern side. The first morning at their 10,000-foot high camp they woke to a whiteout and did not get underway until late afternoon. They hoped to complete the climb by moonlight, but snow began to fall. Clouds and snow persisted through the next day, and their meager supplies dwindled.

They had to risk the weather or accept defeat. Through breaks in the clouds the three climbers caught glimpses of the final, 1,000-foot rock tower separated from them by a gaping bergschrund. The route lay on the right side of the tower, but they had to cross the schrund on the left. By two o'clock they had gained the rock and started to work right over icy ledges. Ropes and gloves froze, and night closed fast. At six o'clock they were still 800 feet below the summit. Rather than recross the terrible ledges, they rappelled straight down to the snow and spent a cheerless night in the bergschrund. A bold attack had been repulsed by impossible conditions.

While the Neave-Secord party was on the north, a British Columbia team tried to reach the summit rocks from the south. The gully they climbed would not go, and they had to descend. Telephone engineer Alec Dalgleish came down last. He was thirty feet above his companions when he slipped. His belayer held fast, but the rope parted over a sharp edge of rock, and Dalgleish fell 500 feet to his death. The accident contributed to the image of an impossible "killer mountain," as the press called it.

Last to try Mount Waddington in 1934 were the Mundays, Hall, and Fuhrer. They again climbed the northwest peak and descended some distance to look over the final tower. Although they were well equipped, they did not even attempt the "incredible nightmarish thing that must be seen to be believed." They had made their final bid. In writing about it in "Mt. Waddington, 1934," Don Munday implied that Waddington verged on the impossible, and Hall concurred. However, the assertion was far-fetched since they had never come to grips with the summit rocks. Three different groups of mountaineers had tried and failed. They had been handicapped by approach problems and weather, but their basic weakness was in rock climbing skill. Would a team of rock technicians fare any better?

The Sierra Club climbers had already knocked off a string of "impossible" routes in Yosemite. Mount Waddington was irresistible, and Richard Leonard and Bestor Robinson organized an expedition for 1935. They established a base camp on the lower glaciers and surveyed the south face. They lacked experience on snow and ice, so they passed over the couloirs, the obvious lines of weakness, in favor of the slower rock ribs. Their first probe was turned back by snowfall. Four days later sun-loosened ice chips showered down on them, and they turned back again. By then short of time and overawed by the problems of the south face, they decided to make a final try on the Mundays' west ridge route. They reached the lower peak, but a fresh storm prevented an attempt on the summit.

The Sierrans had never been on such a serious mountain. They were psychologically out of their depth, and their efforts were indecisive. However, they were getting the feel of the problems. If a party of expert rock technicians found the face free of ice, they surmised, then Waddington would be climbed. They were determined to return the next year.

They learned that a British Columbia group was also going after the peak. The two parties corresponded and agreed to coordinate transport arrangements but to work independently on the mountain. Unknown to both sets of Waddington hopefuls, still another effort was under urgent consideration on the East Coast. Fritz Wiessner had gone to Europe for the summer with the still unclimbed Walker Spur of the Grandes Jorasses in mind, but he was bombarded with telegrams from

Bill House and U.S. ski team member Betty Woolsey. They urged him to join them in a try for Mount Waddington before the Californians took the prize. Wiessner was intrigued. He wired his friends and took the next boat to New York. House corresponded with the Sierra Club climbers, and it was eventually agreed that because of their previous attempt they would have the first crack at the peak.

The three groups packed into the mountain side by side. Relations among them were entirely friendly, and they discussed the proposed routes together. The Sierrans were aware that the ice couloirs on the south face afforded the quickest access to the final tower. However, the overriding principle of their approach was safety at all times, and there was stonefall in the couloirs. They decided on a longer but, hopefully, safer route. The previous year they had set out from a camp 6,000 feet below the summit. They had agreed that *this* time they would place a high camp right under the south face as the Easterners were already doing, but pressed by the fast progress of the rival group and the possibility of a change in the weather, they decided to start for the summit right away. It was a major mistake.

Although they left camp early in the morning, the Canadians and the Californians only reached the foot of the south face by 8 A.M.; they had 2,400 feet of climbing ahead of them. The Canadians tackled the rock face directly under the summit

Bushwacking into Waddington. Bill House swats an insect as Wiessner brings up the rear. *Betty Woolsey.*

and gained 800 feet before they ran out of time. The Californians worked up the rocks to the right of the summit. By late afternoon they had climbed more than 1,000 feet, but unwilling to bivouac, they had to retreat off the face. Back on the glacier, they trudged wearily over to the Easterners' camp, where they were offered mugs of steaming chocolate. The drink was tainted with cooking fuel, but that mattered little. They gulped it down gratefully. The situation was self-evident; the Sierrans had made their bid, saying to the Easterners, "It's all yours; we're just not ready for it."

While they watched the progress of the rival groups that day, House and Wiessner planned their route. Shunning the longer and more involved rock ribs, they intended to climb the snow couloir leading to the notch between the northwest peak and the summit.

Early the next morning they climbed swiftly up the couloir. By midday they were above the level of the Sierrans' high point, but near the head of the couloir they were faced with 150-foot walls of steep, ice-glazed rock. No route lay there, and they had to descend.

That night the weather remained good. They set out again at 2:45 A.M. and switched their attack to the couloir between the summit and the "Fang" to its east. They had to climb the couloir before the day's bombardment began; rocks imbedded in the snow told them all they needed to know. When they reached the final tower, Wiessner appraised the situation,

Above us extended the last 1,000 feet of the south face in sheer forbidding-looking rocks, but the possibility of climbing it could be detected by anyone looking at it with a trained eye. I knew that the objective dangers* could be overcome, if this part of the climb was attacked intelligently and cautiously. Mentally and physically I was keyed up to the very high pitch which one reaches on certain occasions: at this time I knew that the summit would be ours. Determined, and feeling that no obstacle of a technical nature could stop us, I started on the rocks.

Almost immediately the climbing got harder. Wiessner took off his mountain boots and pulled

*Objective dangers are hazards over which a climber has little or no control, for example, loose rock, falling rock or ice, and snow and ice avalanches.

on a pair of the rope-soled, rock climbing shoes then popular in Europe. Searching for the simplest route and continually on guard against knocking rocks onto House, he led out the rope. After several hours of hard climbing they reached a 200-foot chimney-like depression. Wiessner led up fifty feet, then brought House up to a belay stance. The crux lay ahead: steep, ice-covered rock. Wiessner wormed onto House's shoulders, gripped the rock, and soon disappeared from view. House was anxious. He heard the screech of the wind on the summit ridge and now and then the welcome sound of hammer on piton. Then Wiessner shouted for him to come along, and struggling with the packs, he worked up over the bulge. At four o'clock two climbers belayed onto the tiny summit of the Coast Range.

They descended in 300-foot rappels. After one rappel the rope caught fast and Wiessner had to climb back up to free it. When they reached the gullies near the foot of the south face, it was dark. They had tied themselves in and begun the long wait till dawn when a rock avalanche shot down the couloir. It missed them by a few feet. They must press on at all costs! They carried on down through the night and reached their camp early in the morning. Behind them was the south face of Mount Waddington, the hardest climb in North America.

The struggle for Waddington was a reflection of mountaineering standards in North America. Al-though there were good rock technicians in Yo-semite and the Tetons, few had the combination of technical expertise and alpine experience demand-ed by a mountain such as Waddington. The Cana-dian mountaineers were hopelessly out of their element. The Sierrans felt that they needed ice-free rock, perfect weather, and a battery of pitons. But Wiessner had just the qualities needed. At the age of sixteen he had led climbs on the sandstone towers near his home in Dresden, Germany. This area had some of the hardest rock climbs then made, possibly the hardest in Europe. From there he went on to the rock walls of the Kaisergebirge and the Dolomites, where many Austrian and German climbers got their first experience of major climbs. He was also well acquainted with the technical and psychological problems of high mountains. He had made several good climbs in the Alps and participated in an expedition to Nanga Parbat. One of the leading German moun-taineers in the 1920s, he had a far wider base of experience than the home climbers.*

Wiessner knew all the techniques that were required on Mount Waddington, but more than technique it was his attitude that distinguished him from the other aspirants. Thoroughly con-versant with the new spirit that was sweeping through European climbing, he was prepared to

*Among the alpine climbs pioneered by Wiessner are the 1,000-foot southeast face of the Fleischbank and the north arête of the Furchetta in the Dolomites.

put more into the struggle, to accept certain risks, and, once the goal was set, to go all-out to the finish. The Sierrans recognized the difference between their safety-first approach and that of Wiessner. They were awed when he said it was worth risking your life for an important first ascent.

By 1942 many climbers were in the armed forces; however, the Beckey brothers were too young to serve. Fred was nineteen, and Helmy was about to turn seventeen when they set out for the unclimbed Tiedemann peaks in the Waddington region. They started with a third person, but he lost interest and dropped off the team. Three was already a slender party for what the brothers had in mind, but they had dreamed of the trip for a year and had taken the summer off. They had spent months gathering information, assembling their kit, and preparing the grub list. They had slept at the Vancouver docks while they packed the gear, and they were not about to turn back. In two weeks of effort they established their equipment on the icefields and then made a carry toward the Tiedemann peaks. The glaciers were so broken up that they felt overextended and gave up their original goal. They turned instead to the south face of Waddington as a consolation prize.

Mount Waddington had turned back about a

Bill House, left, and Fritz Wiessner on their return from Waddington. *Betty Woolsey.*

Fred Beckey at Mountaineers' climbing practice on Monitor Rock, in Seattle, 1939. This is almost certainly the first man-made climbing wall in the country. Three years later he and his younger brother made the second ascent of Waddington. *Lloyd Anderson.*

dozen attempts, and a man had died up there. It had demanded the utmost from Wiessner and House. What chance did the Beckey brothers have? It was true that they knew the south face had been climbed, but a second ascent can be as daunting as the first, especially if the first ascent party had a rough time. They did have one real advantage. They had carefully studied the earlier parties' accounts and knew their mistakes.

They made camp right under the south face. They watched the rockfall, and the day before the summit push they climbed over the bergschrund and into the couloir taken by Wiessner and House. It was not too steep for them; they could do it! With spirits buoyed, they started early the next morning. When they got to the difficult rocks of the summit tower, they changed into tennis shoes and slipped on homemade felt overshoes for a better grip on the wet rock. They reached the summit by evening and bivouacked just below it.

They deliberately timed their descent next day to reach the treacherous initial couloir at dark. Despite this precaution they heard the sickening crash of rocks. They flattened themselves against the slope and escaped the worst, but Helmy's knee was gashed. They moved out of the couloir, stopped the bleeding, and continued on down at daybreak.

The second ascent of Waddington was as remarkable as the first. It was no fluke. The Beckeys' knowledge about the route and careful planning were an obvious help, but the key was their attitude. They were keyed up to go; they did not know that they were given little chance. The old-line mountaineers were overawed by Waddington. The Beckeys were uninhibited by tradition. They were already widely experienced in the North Cascades. They had made more than fifty climbs, including many first ascents. They were used to three-day rain storms, to ice and rotten rock, to glaciers and unknown country. They were at home in the mountains.

REFERENCES

Beckey, Fred. "Climbing and Skiing in the Waddington Area." *AAJ* 5 (1943): 29.

Beckey, Helmy. "Mt. Waddington Climbed Again." *CAJ* 28 (1943): 172.

Carter, N. M. "The Fatal Accident on Mt. Waddington." *CAJ* 22 (1934): 46.

Hagen, Barry. "Mt. Waddington." *Ascent* 1(3) (May 1969): 20.

Hall, Henry S. "The 1934 Attempts on Mt. Waddington." *AAJ* 2 (1935): 298.

House, W. P. "The Ascent of Mt. Waddington." *AAJ* 3 (1937): 21.

"An Interview with Fritz Wiessner." *Ascent* 1(3) (1969): 15.

Munday, W.A.D. "Mt. Waddington." *CAJ* 17 (1929): 1.

———. "High Peaks of the Coast Range." *CAJ* 22 (1934): 1.

———. "Mt. Waddington, 1934." *CAJ* 22 (1934): 24.

———. *The Unknown Mountain*. London: Hodder & Stoughton, 1948.

Neave, F. "New Ways to Waddington." *CAJ* 22 (1934): 32.

Robinson, Bestor. "Mount Waddington." *SCB* 21(1) (Feb. 1936): 1.

Voge, Hervey. "Climbs in the Waddington Region—1936." *SCB* 22(1) (Feb. 1937): 29.

Wiessner, F. H. "The First Ascent of Mt. Waddington." *CAJ* 24 (1936): 9.

Woods, D. M., and R. M. Leonard. "Can Mt. Waddington Be Climbed?" *CAJ* 23 (1935): 28.

Worlds Apart

On his return from Mount Waddington Fritz Wiessner headed for Wyoming, where he made the second ascent of the north ridge of the Grand Teton. Then he convinced his companions to make a detour into northeastern Wyoming. He had heard of a spectacular rock tower and wanted to investigate. Devils Tower made an immediate impression. Its steep, columnar sides rose straight out of the dreary plain. He applied to the local Park Service officials for permission to climb it. They had never had a request of this nature and referred it to Washington. The request was refused. The Park Service was concerned about the consequences of an accident, but after an exchange of letters with the American Alpine Club, they agreed to let Wiessner make an attempt the following year.

In fact Devils Tower had been climbed years before in one of those colorful episodes that abound in the history of the West. It was all done in the spirit of patriotism and business enterprise. The setting was a Fourth of July picnic in 1893. The ascent was to be the chief attraction of a fair put on by ranchers Willard Ripley and Will Rogers.

They began their preparations a month before the celebration. They cut numerous thirty-inch wooden pegs and hammered them into one of the vertical joints on the side of the tower visible from the fairground. As they advanced up the crack, they joined the outside of the wood steps with a strip of two-by-fours and thus made a "ladder" roughly 350 feet long.

By July 4 all was ready. A crowd of 1,000 gathered. Some of them had come 125 miles from Rapid City, South Dakota, a week's roundtrip by horse and wagon. Like all good show business the events of the day built to a climax. After an invocation by a minister, Rogers started up the ladder. Within minutes he was on the summit, where he dramatically unfurled a large flag to the accompaniment of wild cheers from the onlookers.

Another chance to make a quick dollar happily occurred that day. Late in the afternoon the flag blew down and fluttered to rest on the dance floor. Ripley and Rogers cut it up and sold the pieces as souvenirs. Stars went for fifty cents apiece and portions of the stripes for twenty-five cents.

In 1937 Wiessner returned to Devils Tower with

Devils Tower. The Wiessner route works up cracks right of prow to reach the depression below the summit. *Ed Cooper*.

The ladder up Devils Tower as it appeared in the 1930s. Courtesy National Park Service.

Bill House and fellow Easterner Lawrence Coveney to attempt the first "real" ascent. Their reconnaissance was discouraging; a fierce gooseberry bush turned them back. The next day they attacked in earnest and overwhelmed the gooseberry bush with a three-man stand and leather gloves. A section of more conventional climbing brought them to the crux, an evil-looking eighty-foot crack.

Coveney and House were not optimistic and mentally went over the belay tactics that would be best in case of a fall. Wiessner was quiet and tense. Jamming one side of his body into the crack and holding himself in by heel and toe pressure, he methodically worked upward. Coveney and House watched every move, but Wiessner was a master crack climber. Before long he was over the worst stretch, and they relaxed. It was an extraordinary exhibition of climbing.

Once Wiessner was up, his companions had to struggle after him. Their pains were intensified by the comments of holidaymakers on the ground below, "Oh, the man's pulling him now." When the climbers got down, they were greeted by an enthusiastic, if ill-informed, crowd. They had to dispel the impression that they had used the rope to lasso spikes and then climbed up hand-over-hand. A spectator suggested that vigorous promotion would have drawn a larger crowd and been a boon to local business. As it was, latecomers missed the whole show.

Coveney climbs up to join Wiessner; behind them is the crux crack on Devils Tower. *Bill House*.

Devils Tower had been scaled by ladders and by "legitimate" means. It had been scaled for the flag and for profit, for sport and for the honor of a first ascent. In October 1941 there came the strangest ascent of all. George Hopkins parachuted onto the top. He ostensibly did it for a fifty dollar bet; in fact it was to publicize a planned attempt on a parachute jumping record. He intended to lower himself on a massive 1,000-foot rope. The jump went well, but not the descent. He was marooned on top.

Hopkins's fate attracted nationwide attention. Several climbers hurried to the scene to assist the rescue efforts, among them Paul Petzoldt, guides from Longs Peak, and Jack Durrance and friends from Dartmouth. When Durrance's group changed planes in Chicago, they were besieged by reporters. The reporters pleaded for photographs of the climbers draped with a ship's hawser and a laborer's pick axe, but were emphatically refused. While the climbers converged on Devils Tower, other plans were under consideration. The Goodyear Blimp left Akron, Ohio, for the expected four-day trip, and a pilot with a ski-equipped airplane declared himself ready to land on the tower.

Few persons were then capable of climbing Devils Tower, and the first rescue attempts got nowhere. When Durrance arrived, a thirty-foot ladder was in place, Hopkins had been on top for five days, and more than 1,000 sensation-seekers were in the area.

Durrance had made the second ascent of the Tower. As the best rock climber present, he would obviously take the lead, but none of the other climbers wanted to miss out on the glory. When he started up the rock, there were seven others roped up behind him! Petzoldt had apparently made a deal with the news media and insisted on climbing second in order to take action pictures. Their close pairing was unfortunate as the two had disagreed in the past*. When Durrance got to the crux, the rock was glazed with ice and his shoes slipped as he fought upward. He was furious when he glanced back and saw Petzoldt more interested in photographs than belays. During the rescue the camera was apparently sabotaged.

When the rescuers reached the top, they found Hopkins remarkably unconcerned. He was surrounded by supplies dropped from airplanes: blankets, hot-water bottles, a portable stove, coal, and enough food to stock a country store. But he was thirsty. His first request was for a swig of booze. Hopkins rapidly picked up the idea of rappelling and the whole group descended in the gathering dusk. Petzoldt guided Hopkins down while Durrance brought up the rear. The climbers had an understanding that they would not face the press until they were all off the Tower. The last rappels were illuminated by spotlights, and the eager crowd pressed close to the foot of the rock. While the rest of the party descended, Petzoldt and Hopkins met the press. (Petzoldt later maintained that he had waited for the others, but had missed them in the dark; Durrance believed that Petzoldt had deliberately rushed ahead to get in front of the cameras.) Hopkins was enthusiastic: ''This guy Durrance is sure some crackerjack on the cliffs.'' The newsmen were expecting a full complement of heroes, but the other rescuers faded into the crowd to avoid the publicity. Where were they? Durrance and his pals were tracked

*Durrance's and Petzoldt's relationship in the Tetons was not harmonious. One year the Dartmouth climbers applied for the guide concession held by Petzoldt.

George Hopkins, in flying suit, surrounded by his rescuers on top of Devils Tower. From left: Charles Gorrel, Jack Durrance, Paul Petzoldt, Henry Coulter, Ernest Field, Chappel Cranmer. Courtesy Henry Coulter.

down. They wanted none of the picture taking. They felt they were victims of a cheap publicity stunt, but the newsmen said it was all part of a day's work, and they relented. Pictures were taken, and the liquor flowed freely.

The bizarre series of events on Devils Tower tell us much about the status of climbing in North America. Ripley's and Rogers's bold effort was discounted by the climbers of the 1930s, who credited Wiessner with the first ''real'' ascent. Yet from the reactions of the crowd that watched Wiessner's climb, it is obvious that *they* would

Newspaper coverage of the Devils Tower rescue. Courtesy National Park Service.

have drawn no such distinction. To them it was all the same circus act. As far as they knew, everyone climbed peaks on a bet or a dare.

The news media naturally played up the drama of the rescue and expected the climbers to behave like heroes. Yet the climbers' reactions reflect an ambivalence toward publicity. Petzoldt was eager for the limelight, no doubt thinking of his guiding business. Durrance and his friends were aghast.

Devils Tower also provides us with a point of departure for a comparison between North American and European achievements. Were it located in the Eastern Alps, it undoubtedly would have been climbed around 1900 by "legitimate" means. (Any laddered ascent would have raised howls of protest among climbers.) Furthermore, if Europeans had witnessed Wiessner's ascent, they not only would have known how the rope was used but also would have appreciated the difference between the climbers' and the ranchers' ascents. After all, by the late 1930s the best-known German and Italian climbers were national celebrities.

The Alps Between the Wars

Although this work is concerned solely with North America, it is important to put home endeavors in perspective. We must be aware of what was happening in the Alps and try to understand why climbing had progressed so much further there.

The period between the wars was a time of remarkable advances in the Alps.*

Perhaps the single most important development was the democratization of the sport. This came about largely through the growth in rock climbing and the consequent emphasis on cliffs accessible to city dwellers. These were hard times in Europe. Instead of waiting for the dole, the young enthusiasts went to the hills. They had no money for guides and so built up their own skills. Typical of the areas where they climbed were the steep walls of the Austrian Kaisergebirge, rising up to 2,000 feet. Climbs there demanded the use of pitons for protection, and from that it was a short step to the use of pitons where natural holds were lacking.

Although the new rock experts made a series of difficult routes in the Kaisergebirge, it was not until they began to polish off famous walls in the Dolomites that their exploits created a stir in European climbing circles. On these walls they made full use of the techniques they had perfected on the practice rocks. However, their most important assets were dedication and a determination to break through psychological barriers. One of the most influential of the early Dolomite climbs was

---

*Americans played a minor role in the Alps. The most noteworthy contribution was made by Miriam and Robert Underhill, who pioneered several good routes with guides. Miriam also made a number of guideless, all-woman ascents of difficult routes.

the 1925 ascent of the 3,500-foot northwest face of the Civetta. Using just a handful of pitons, Germans Lettenbauer and Solleder dispelled the aura of impregnability surrounding this "Wall of Walls."

Coincident with the surge of rock climbing in the Dolomites was new interest in the Western Alps. There the pioneers had already climbed the obvious ridge routes. What remained were the rock and ice faces between the ridges. These faces were steeper, more difficult, and more dangerous than what had gone before. They made new psychological demands on the climbers who hoped to win them. Few climbs have created more of a sensation than the 1931 ascent of the North Face of the Matterhorn. It was a telling demonstration of what the rock experts were capable of doing. The traditional mountaineers could not ignore a route on the Matterhorn. The new men were in ascendance.

The pace continued to build, and they turned to faces their predecessors had not even conceived of as climbs. In 1935 three "last problems" were solved: the overhanging north face of the Cima Ovest in the Dolomites; and in the French Alps the much-sought-after north faces of the Grandes Jorasses and the Aiguille du Dru.

This period of European climbing was a new golden age, for there was an unprecedented explosion of talent. The climbers came predominantly from Austria, Germany, and Italy, with the Swiss and French playing a lesser role. The British, the "fully developed master men" of an earlier era, were left on the sidelines. On the cliffs of Britain, climbing standards advanced, but because of the structure of the rock this advance was achieved with a bare minimum of pitons; flakes and horns provided anchors for much of the needed protection. An occasional piton might safeguard a belay stance, but their use for direct aid was considered unsporting. An oft-quoted saying of the time was, "The sort of man who would drive a piton into English rock, is the sort of man who would shoot a fox." Apart from the moral question, the wholesale use of pitons would have "used up" the available rock and destroyed the sport by making it too easy.

The anti-piton attitude made good sense at home, but the British also applied it to the Alps. They had little feel for the new movements on the continent. They understood neither the need for pitons nor the new ethos in the Alps and seemed glad of it. Britain's prestigious *Alpine Journal* was a forum for diatribes against the new climbing. The editor, Colonel Strutt, could barely say anything positive about the ascent of the north face of the Grandes Jorasses, "It would be ungenerous in the extreme to withhold a certain admiration from this undaunted party's great exploit." A reviewer attacked a book by Italian Giusto Gervasutti for providing information on the "nailing of rock faces, since such methods have nothing in common with mountaineering," while British climber

Robert Irving explained in his book, "We can take no personal credit for this 'sportsman like attitude'; it is bred in us, just as a love of animals is bred in us."

As a result of this "sportsman like attitude" British alpinism went into almost total eclipse during the interwar years. This was unfortunate enough, but the British outlook also found its way across the Atlantic. Smith and Hickson in the *Canadian Alpine Journal* referred to the "cult of mechanized climbing" and distinguished "between a mountaineer and an acrobat or engineer 'armed with the instruments of road-breaking.' " Henderson, in *Appalachia*, the most balanced of the journals, was unable to stomach the North Face of the Eiger. He characterized the climbers as "mentally unbalanced."

The main, stated objections of the traditionalists were to the wholesale acceptance of pitons, to the seemingly fatalistic attitude toward danger, and to the nationalistic boasting that invariably attended the exploits. Yet the nature of the new climbs was such that pitons were not a substitute for skill. The best climbers of the day found them essential for safety and progress. Danger has been inherent in climbing since its inception; it is central to it. If the new climbers had a disproportionate share of accidents, it was because they were willing to accept greater risks in order to do their climbs. Finally, strident nationalism was sweeping through Europe. The German and Italian press used the climbers' exploits to focus national pride. Similarly, the British used the Mount Everest expeditions, and the Americans the achievements of aviator Charles Lindbergh.

The unstated objections of the old-line mountaineers are harder to fathom but had much to do with the disruption of the status quo. In Britain and North America climbing was a gentleman's sport. In Europe this was no longer the case. The new climbers frequently came from a working class background. Another hard blow was the fact that the newcomers had so obviously surpassed their elders. With their institutions under attack, the older generation rallied in defense of "the sport."

It is hard to say what effect these sentiments had on the emergence of technical climbing in North America. The majority of climbers certainly accepted the traditionalist viewpoint, but others broke loose. Jack Durrance in the Tetons and the Sierrans on Shiprock vividly demonstrated that they were uninhibited by tradition.

During the interwar years climbing in North America came nowhere near the standard in Europe. Conditions made this inevitable. By the 1930s climbing was an accepted sport in Europe. Here it was not. There were tens of thousands of climbers in Europe. In North America only a couple of hundred professional people made technical ascents. The development of local practice areas was well advanced in Europe. Here it was hardly begun. The Alps and the Dolomites were so accessible that the simple routes were already climbed, and climbers were seeking difficult routes. Here climbers were still making first ascents of virgin peaks. Finally, there was almost no exchange of ideas among North America's widely scattered climbing areas. Besides, there were few ideas to exchange.

The Mountains of Asia

The highest mountains on earth were a new frontier and posed significant new problems of scale, altitude, and extreme weather. The strong teams from Europe achieved major successes. Although Americans organized trips on a more modest, personal scale, they also made notable contributions. This was climbing more akin to the wilderness mountaineering of home. Highly evolved technical skills were less important than mountain know-how. Americans were thus on an equal footing with the Europeans.

In 1932 Terris Moore and civil engineer Richard Burdsall fought to the top of 24,892-foot Minya Konka, the highest peak in China prior to the annexation of Tibet. Four years later a strong Anglo-American party that included Adams Carter, Charles Houston, William Loomis, and Minya Konka veteran Arthur Emmons succeeded on 25,645-foot Nanda Devi. It was one of the best

prewar climbs and the highest mountain climbed until the 1950 ascent of Annapurna.

The next major Himalayan expedition had for its objective 28,250-foot K2. Under Houston's leadership, this 1938 group comprised Burdsall, Bob Bates, Bill House, and Paul Petzoldt, all men with proven abilities. The Duke of the Abruzzi's 1909 party had made the only previous attempt on K2. After a thorough, but time-consuming, reconnaissance the Americans chose the route attempted by the Duke, the Abruzzi Ridge.

The difficulties ranged against them were immense. The ridge reached two miles into the sky and was obviously steep; K2 has no easy side. Little was known about acclimatization to such high altitudes. Finally, there was the fear of a major step into the unknown.

Houston and his team climbed steadily and built up a ten-day supply of provisions at 23,300-foot Camp 6. Several of the lower camps were also stocked with food, but because of the climbing difficulties only one of the Sherpas was permitted to carry to the high camps. The climbers' supply line was precarious. The food margin at the top camp was slender, and they felt they needed two more camps to reach the summit. The weather had been unnaturally good, and they feared it would soon break. If it did, they would be forced to retreat.

Houston and Petzoldt reconnoitered the route to Camp 7, and the team spent a restless night at

Camp 6. Should they retreat while the weather held or press for the summit? In the end they compromised. They established Camp 7, but it was a two-man camp, and it was too low for a serious summit bid. The forceful Petzoldt reached 26,000 feet, and the team retreated.

With such a slender margin of resources, the decision against an all-out bid was prudent. However, when you strive for the ultimate, boldness and a willingness to risk all are sometimes necessary. Fritz Wiessner, who led a team to K2 the following year, had this boldness.

This group lacked the cohesiveness and all-round strength of Houston's party. Apart from Wiessner the only American to reach the upper camps was Dudley Wolfe, a strong performer but an inexperienced climber. Chappel Cranmer had heart trouble, George Sheldon was frostbitten, and Jack Durrance and veteran Tony Cromwell were unable to acclimatize.

Wiessner, Wolfe, and Sherpa Pasang Lama left for the upper camps. It had been agreed that the lower camps would be continually stocked, but unknown to the lead climbers no other American made it to the high camps. The vital line of supply broke down.

Wiessner and Pasang Lama climbed strongly on their summit bid. At 27,500 feet the summit was within their grasp when night approached. Wiessner wanted to climb through the night, but Pasang Lama insisted they descend. After a day of rest they made another attempt, which was frustrated by the loss of Pasang Lama's crampons. Then they descended to the next camp, where Wolfe waited in support. With insufficient supplies for a further attempt the trio descended to Camp 7. It was evacuated!

The three climbers shared one sleeping bag through a bitter night. In the morning Wolfe elected to stay behind. Wiessner and Pasang Lama carried on down to pick up supplies and get the Sherpas moving. As they descended, they found all the lower camps had been stripped. They spent a second night without sleeping bags and staggered into base camp. Wolfe was stranded at Camp 7!

A rescue attempt was mounted, but the ill-acclimatized Americans were unable to reach Wolfe. Six days after he had said goodbye to Wiessner, three Sherpas climbed up to his tent. Understandably demoralized, he was unprepared to descend and asked them to come back up the next day. After a day of storm the three Sherpas set out for Camp 7. Neither they nor Wolfe was ever seen again.

The evacuation of the upper camps was a tragic mistake. It was due to a Sherpa's belief that the summit team had perished. If Americans had been high on the mountain in support, it seems inconceivable that Wolfe would have been stranded.

In the aftermath of the expedition Wiessner was heavily criticized. This resulted in part from the statements of others on the expedition and in part from his unfortunate remark, quoted by the papers on his arrival in New York, "In mountain expeditions, as in war, one must expect casualties." While accurate, it gave the impression that Wiessner was indifferent to the rest of the party so long as he made the top. Although he had a hard manner in those days, his actions do not support this conclusion. When he and Pasang Lama were at 27,500 feet, he gave in to the Sherpa's plea to descend. He could have left his companion, as later Himalayan climbers have done, and carried on alone. He was going well enough to make the summit.

The War Years

North American climbing ground to a virtual standstill during the Second World War. Nonetheless, the war did have a few positive aspects as far as climbing was concerned. Climbers from all over the country enlisted in the mountain troops and got their first real chance to compare notes and explore problems of technique. As a result of the war effort new climbing gear was produced. At the end of the conflict it was cheap and plentiful for the first time.

In November 1941 the first mountain infantry batallion was activated and began training on Mount Rainier. Meanwhile, the Quartermaster Corps worked on specialized gear. Faced with the problem of supplying ropes to the troops, they tested every known rope fiber. The Plymouth Cordage Company was then manufacturing large-diameter nylon ropes for rope-driven sawmills. It made up a few nylon climbing ropes. These and other samples were subjected to a battery of tests including burial in the Panamanian jungle. The results were startling: Nylon was clearly superior. Not only did nylon have a higher breaking strength, but it had also an extraordinary ability to absorb dynamic shocks. The rope itself provided some of the desirable properties of the dynamic belay. When the combat troops in training at Seneca Rock, West Virginia, put nylon ropes to the test, they found them a genuine advance. Manila rope failed after some dozen test falls. Nylon rope held more than 150 falls.

Before the war, climbers usually got their pitons from Munich or had the local blacksmith make up a batch. Now a large domestic supply was needed. The only type available from Europe were blade pitons. For cracks wider than a pencil they were almost useless. The Corps designed a piton with a V cross-section that could span cracks up to three-quarters of an inch. It was the first angle piton.

European steel carabiners were tested and found to be painfully inadequate. A better model was produced. Toward the end of the war an aluminum carabiner was introduced. It was half the weight of the steel models yet equally strong. Aluminum carabiners never reached the troops in quantity because the bulk of the production was sidetracked to a warehouse in Utah.

Whatever the pressure of war, climbers remained true to their avocation. Mountain warfare specialist Adams Carter contacted the head of the French military mission in Washington, D.C., and arranged a climbing trip. The ostensible purpose was to test mountain equipment on Mount Washington. The real motive was a couple of days in the mountains.

The party consisted of General Béthouard, his two aides, and Americans Dick Leonard and Carter. They camped and climbed for a couple of days, and wherever they went, the French carried a leather briefcase. On the way back from the mountains they stopped for dinner at the Carter family home. As they lingered over a bottle of wine, they suddenly realized that their train was due. They piled their gear into a truck, sped to the station, and clambered on board the train.

The Frenchmen sat back, relieved. "We have a terribly important conference tomorrow," they confided. "If we missed it, it would cost us our jobs."

The general looked at his aide and said, "You have the briefcase, don't you?"

"Non, mon géneral," replied the colonel. He turned to his colleague and inquired, "You have it, don't you major?"

The briefcase had disappeared. All three officers turned a deathly white. At the next station Carter hopped out of the coach and ran to the baggage car. The briefcase was not among the pile of equipment. The train moved off. In desperation he opened a duffel bag, and there it was. A farm hand had evidently spotted the briefcase lying loose, the only time it was out of a Frenchman's hand, and crammed it into the duffel. When the train pulled into the next station, Carter reappeared with the brief-

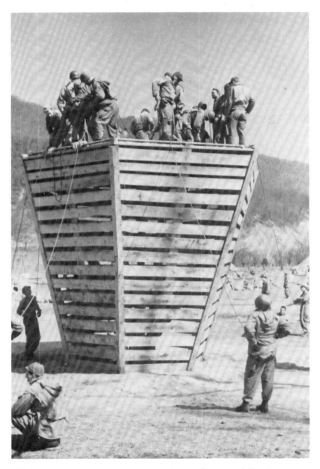

The belay tower built by the Army Corps of Engineers near Seneca Rock, West Virginia. Courtesy Jim Crooks.

case. The Frenchmen hugged him as though he just won the Tour de France.

They made the conference. Finally, Béthouard was to leave Washington, and Carter was invited to a magnificent farewell reception. As he started up the line toward the general, he recognized General Marshall and other notables in line behind him. Béthouard was delighted to see him and reminisced over the Mount Washington trip while the line grew longer and longer. Finally, he asked Carter if he knew what the briefcase had contained. Carter had no idea. "Why, it contained the French copy of the Normandy invasion plans."

Although the idea of specialized mountain troops was not universally popular in the military, the Tenth Mountain Infantry Division was formed in July 1943. During the fall of 1944 the allied advance into Italy was stalled at the foot of Italy's Apennine Mountains. It was essential to penetrate this barrier, but the enemy held the high ground. After two conventional attacks failed, the Tenth Mountain was ordered into battle. Under cover of darkness, their piton hammers muffled with cloth, they climbed up the precipitous side of Riva Ridge. The German defenders had not even considered the possibility of such an attack. They were taken by surprise, and the next day other enemy positions were overrun. Within a week the Apennines were breached. The road into the heart of Europe lay open.

REFERENCES

Cassin, Riccardo. "Italian Climbing Between the Wars." *AJ* 77 (1972): 149.

" 'Chutist Rescued from Peak." *Berkeley Daily Gazette,* Oct. 7, 1941, p. 1.

Coveney, Lawrence G. "Ascent of Devils Tower." *Appalachia* 21 (Dec. 1937): 477.

Daiber, Ome. "A Digest of World Climbs." *Mountaineer* 31 (Dec. 1938): 35.

———. "Climber's Digest. 1939 Review." *Mountaineer* 32 (Dec. 1939): 51.

Damesme, Maurice, and Tom de Lépiney. "The Early Years of the Groupe de Haute Montagne." *AJ* 75 (1970): 109.

"Devils Tower." *AAJ* 3 (1937): 107.

Durrance, Jack. "Emergency Ascent of Devils Tower, Wyoming." *Appalachia* 24 (June 1942): 123.

Dyhrenfurth, G. O. *To the Third Pole.* London: Werner Laurie, 1955.

"Eiger." *AAJ* 3 (1938): 224.

Field, Ernest K. "The Devils Tower Episode." *T & T,* no. 276 (Dec. 1941):167.

"Grandes Jorasses." *AAJ* 2 (1935): 420.

"Grosse Zinne." *AAJ* 2 (1934): 263.

Heckmair, Anderl. "Main German and Austrian Climbers Since 1930." *AJ* 74 (1969): 47.

"He'll Be down Before Nightfall." *Berkeley Daily Gazette,* Oct. 6, 1941, p. 1.

Henderson, K. A. "Alpina." *Appalachia* 21 (Dec. 1937): 528.

Hickson, J. W. A. "Reviews: Mountaineering." *CAJ* 23 (1936): 104.

House, William P. "Devils Tower." *AAJ* 3 (1938): 130.

———. "Mountain Equipment for the U.S. Army." *AAJ* 6 (1946): 225.

"Human Ladder Saves 'Chutist off High Peak." *San Francisco Examiner,* Oct. 7, 1941, p. 1.

Irving, R. L. G. *The Romance of Mountaineering.* New York: Dutton, 1935.

———. "Relativity in Mountaineering." *AJ* 49 (Nov. 1937): 153.

Jackman, Albert H. "The Tenth Mountain Division." *AAJ* 6 (1946): 187.

Joyner, Newell F. "Devils Tower." *Appalachia* 20 (Dec. 1934): 216.

Mason, Kenneth. *Abode of Snow.* London: Rupert Hart-Davis, 1955.

Moore, Terris. "The Minya Konka Climb." *AAJ* 2 (1933): 1.

Noyce, Wilfrid, and Ian McMorrin. *World Atlas of Mountaineering.* London: Thomas Nelson, 1969

"Reviews: Alpinismo." *AJ* 47 (Nov. 1935): 386.

Scott, Doug. *Big Wall Climbing.* New York: Oxford University Press, 1974.

Smith, F. H. "Reviews: Approach to the Hills." *CAJ* 27 (1939): 124.

Strutt, E. L. "Punta Margherita." *AJ* 47 (Nov. 1935): 356.

Ware, Wilson. "Italy: The Riva Ridge." *AAJ* 6 (1946): 208.

Wiessner, Fritz. "The K2 Expedition of 1939." *Appalachia* 31 (1956): 60.

Hard Rock, Hard Steel

In the years following the Second World War there was a gradual increase in climbing. With the rise in affluence and almost universal car ownership, a weekend in the mountains came within the reach of many. However, the key reason was undoubtedly the need for challenge. For a people concentrated in cities and suburbs, daily life had become predictable and routine. While the majority appeared to welcome this change, a few sensed a missing "something." Old-timers might reminisce over the rigors of ranch life, but at least that rugged existence satisfied the inner man. Office and factory work was disappointingly tame.

Paralleling the increase in absolute numbers was a rise in the level of skills. This advance was evident in all areas, but in none more than California. Perhaps this was no accident. California was beginning to assert itself as an industrial and intellectual giant, a land where new values were in the making. Here was the technology that promised a better future for mankind. Here also, though not yet fully recognized, was one of the finest climbing areas in the world, Yosemite Valley.

The San Francisco Bay Area Rock Climbing Section of the Sierra Club was at the forefront of prewar climbing and quickly regrouped after the war. There were familiar faces, and there were new ones. Many of the original generation, aged by the war and the passing of time, left the mountains to a new wave. Money and transportation were hard to come by in the immediate post-war years; therefore, local climbs in the vicinity of the Bay Area predominated. There was plenty of ex-army equipment. It was tough and serviceable, the best climbing gear yet seen on the continent. The dress code was informal but standardized. Vibram-soled army boots at five dollars were a great bargain for mountain wear while tennis sneakers were still considered tops for rock work. Baggy army pants festooned with pockets were made even more serviceable with the addition of a leather patch on the seat. The patch prevented rope burns from the speedy rappels that were in vogue. The top half of the outfit consisted of a work shirt, a shapeless sweater, and an army parka, all topped off by a green Tyrolean hat with a rakish feather.

Despite the restrictions imposed by time and money, the Sierrans were soon back in Yosemite. Two of the men from the glory days of the goose gutters, Robin Hansen and Fritz Lippmann, probed the three Yosemite problems that had repulsed the prewar climbers: the southwest face of Half Dome, the Lost Arrow Chimney, and the north face of Sentinel. These were not all-out attempts; the man prepared to make so bold an effort had yet to appear. However, the problems were defined. Who would solve them?

John Salathé, a slightly built Swiss wrought-iron worker then in his midforties, was having problems with his health and his marriage. Recalling his youth, he would get away to the mountains on weekends. Only there could he find the contentment that he had previously obtained from his work. He was under medical care, but in spite of the case full of pills and medicines, he felt steadily worse. Finally, he was convinced that his doctors were "a bunch of crooks and swindlers." The tranquility of the mountains and a book about natural living moved him to abandon conventional medicine in favor of a new regimen: climbing and a fruit diet.

He met a tall, energetic, flamboyant climber who lived near him, Ax Nelson. Nelson introduced Salathé to the R.C.S. The Swiss was different from the majority of the Sierrans. He was twenty years their senior, and he was a manual worker who lacked a college education. His peculiar and firmly held views on food and living marked him as an eccentric. Nonetheless, he was accepted, and he quickly became engrossed in learning the technicalities of climbing.

One of his early climbs was the Higher Cathedral Spire. As he led up the airy Bathtubs Pitch, his second had to pay an urgent call and asked Salathé to hold fast at the next belay stance. The rope eventually stopped running, and hearing Salathé shout "on belay!" the second set about his task. But the rope pulled tight, and with a stiff wind blowing he was unable to explain his situation. Salathé hauled in the rope and virtually pulled the hapless second up the pitch with his pack in his hands and his pants down around his knees. When he arrived breathless at Salathé's side, he was scolded in a heavy Swiss accent, "Dat's a helluva vay to climb. You got to button your pants!"

Older and less agile than his fellow club members, Salathé did not shine on tricky boulder problems. His interest lay in the intricacies of piton placement, where his craftman's affinity for tools gave him an advantage. One day he was stopped when the piton cracks ran out. Closely examining the wall, he noticed a blade of grass growing out of a minute crack. "By God," he thought, "if a piece of grass can come out, a piton can go in. So I takes a piton and drives and drives, but the piton chust bends."

Pitons were then made of relatively malleable iron. Employing his knowledge as an iron worker,

Salathé looked for an entirely new material: high-strength carbon steel. A discarded Ford Model A rear axle fitted the bill. He forged a piton from part of it and returned to the crack that had defeated him. As he later related it, "I took my piton and I pound and pound, and it goes into the rock." He had made a dramatic breakthrough. He began to forge pitons in a range of sizes emblazoned with the trademark of his Peninsula Iron Works, a P enclosed in a diamond.

Along with the other members of the R.C.S., Salathé was drawn to the unclimbed Lost Arrow. As the prewar climbers had recognized, there were two possible lines of attack: a direct ascent up the chimney from the base or a descent into the notch from the rim of the valley and then up the final spire, the Arrow Tip. In August 1946 Salathé arranged to meet two others for an attempt from the rim. His companions failed to show, but he was not so easily put off. He roped down to the notch and, unperturbed by the 1,200-foot drop all around him, began to solo climb using a self-protection system, something completely undreamed of by Sierra climbers at that time. With his special pitons he climbed about half of the 200-foot Arrow Tip, left a rock cairn, and retreated.

Salathé felt he had been let down deliberately by his friends, and he was probably right. Several big talkers made a show of wanting to climb the Lost Arrow, but when it came to the crunch, they were never available. When his fellow club members heard about the solo attempt, they had mixed emotions. Outwardly, they spoke of "crazy John," but inwardly they admired his audacity. Hoping to force him to abandon what appeared suicidal, they talked of expelling him from the group if the soloing persisted.

He was not about to give up. The week after his first effort, he approached John Thune saying, "John, I got a vunnerful climb." And to Thune's anxious query about the climb, "No, chust an easy one." That weekend the pair attacked the final spire of the Lost Arrow. As dark approached, Salathé was only forty feet from the top, but the rock was flawless granite and his rock drills were blunted. Thune insisted they retreat while they were still able to see.

Salathé would undoubtedly have returned to complete the climb, but before he could, a rival team swung into action. This four-man group had a new plan. Unable to match Salathé's skill at piton work, they intended to throw a weighted line over the Arrow Tip from the valley rim.

They spent their first day casting lines across the 150-foot gap until one finally lodged over the top of the spire. The next day two of the team roped down to the notch and worked up toward the line, which hung tantalizingly above them. They spent that night in the notch and resumed the attack the following day. When they reached the line, they used it to stretch a climbing rope across the gap between the spire and the valley rim. Using this rope secured

Yosemite Falls, flanked by ice, the shadowed Lost Arrow Chimney leading to the Arrow Tip and, near the right skyline, Yosemite Point Buttress. *Ed Cooper*.

at the rim, the two climbers mounted the spire by pushing up foot slings attached to the rope with prusik knots.* Man at last reached the top of the Lost Arrow. The ascent was quite daring, though not in the best traditions of the sport.

Not long after the "ascent" of the Lost Arrow, a team converged on the inviolate southwest face of Half Dome. Anderson's 1875 route now adorned with cables was still the only way up the dome. The southwest face begins steeply and then gradually tapers off in the final 1,000 feet. It was apparent that it would not "go" in a day, and of the climbing team only Nelson and Salathé were prepared to bivouac on the face. They got into the lead and stuck with it. Salathé's pitons enabled them to nail up hitherto hopeless cracks and thus avoid the need for bolts. The resulting two-day climb was a breakthrough for the postwar group and for Salathé and Nelson in particular. They succeeded on a climb that had turned back their predecessors. It was the first real advance since the ascent of the Higher Cathedral Spire.

The coincidence of living in the same city had brought Salathé and Nelson together, and they soon formed a powerful alliance. The older man was generally suspicious of others (he imagined that his wife was trying to poison him), but with carpenter Nelson he shared a common love of craftmanship. Both were staunch nondrinkers, an atti-

*A prusik is a sliding knot that tightens when loaded. When unloaded, it may be moved up the fixed rope. It has now been largely superseded by cam-action ascenders.

tude that set them apart from the light-hearted Sierrans. Both took climbing seriously: The object was to climb, not just talk about it. And while the other Sierrans encouraged Salathé to hold forth on his health theories, a subject always good for knowing smiles, Nelson was happy to share his partner's fare of prunes, figs, and cherries.

Salathé was totally committed to this diet, explaining that his aim was to cut down to "chust vun apple a day." On a winter ski trip the diet almost let him down. During the mountaineers' perpetual discussion of the merits of the equipment that weighed so heavily on their backs, Salathé kept kidding his companions about their cooking stoves: eat a fruit diet and such devices are unnecessary. One freezing night when they were all huddled in the tent cooking supper, Salathé meekly asked if he might borrow the stove. His companions sensed a triumph. Was his fruit diet unequal to the rigors of winter? No, Salathé explained, the diet was fine, but he needed to thaw out his dates.

Although the Lost Arrow was no longer inviolate, in Salathé's mind it remained to be climbed, preferably by the awe-inspiring chimney route that the prewar generation had aptly called "terrifyingly clear." Here he was not alone. Engineering instructor Chuck Wilts, a talented climber from Southern California, had already made a couple of strong probes into the chimney. Nelson and Salathé made careful preparations, mutually encouraging each other and united in their determination to show those Southern Californians a thing or two.

This rock climb, more continuously difficult than any previously attempted in Yosemite or even North America, would require innovations in technique, in equipment, and, most important of all, in commitment. From the progress to date, it appeared that the final climb would take about five days. The necessary gear, clothing, food, and water would have to be dragged up the chimney in the 100° F. heat of the Yosemite summer. The key question was not so much how to keep functioning, but whether it was possible to function at all under those conditions. Wilts and companion Spencer Austin were vitally concerned with having an adequate margin of supplies whereas their rivals' approach was to cut their weight to an absolute minimum.

As the summer of 1947 progressed, first one team and then the other went into action. After each effort they called up the others and swapped experiences, rubbing in their own superiority by such remarks as, "We passed your high point after four hours." As Labor Day neared, Nelson and Salathé were confident. They believed that the rival team was too concerned about replacing lost fluids and would never be able to haul their monstrous loads up the chimney.

During the early attempts Salathé and Nelson refined their methods. Yosemite climbers frequently used two ropes on tension climbs, alternately clipping the ropes into the carabiners (a technique which persists to this day in Europe), but for the Lost Arrow Salathé and Nelson reasoned that one climbing rope required less equipment and would suffice, a method that later became universal in North America. Then the usual technique for following aid pitches was to climb from piton to piton. On the Lost Arrow the second mounted a fixed rope with the aid of prusik knots, another method that would play an important role in later years.

Along with his pitons another unique weapon that Salathé fashioned was a hefty sky hook; the leader lodged the hook on small platforms and then stood up in a sling attached to it. He selected smaller bolts than those customarily used and, remembering the frustration of his earlier attempt on the spire, tempered the drill tips.

They stowed their food and bivouac gear, such as it was, in a burlap sack. When the leader finished a pitch, he heaved the reluctant beast up the chimney with a light line. They did without sleeping bags, sitting out the nights in a sweater and an extra pair of socks. Food was simply taken care of: fruit and nuts. Water posed a serious weight problem. Rather than take water to meet their usual needs, they cut down on their needs. By rigorously training to do without water, they got by on an allowance of little more than a pint per day. Today's Yosemite climber usually allows between three and four pints per day, and even this amount seems desperately short in the overpowering heat.

So much for the technical and logistical innovation. All of it was useless without the burning

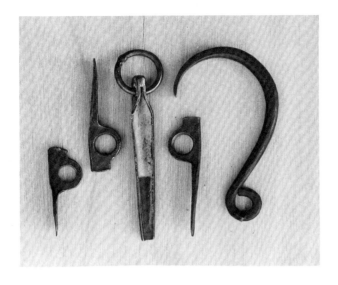

Equipment forged by Salathé: the sky hook used on the Lost Arrow, three hard-steel "Lost Arrow" pitons, and a rare ring angle. (Dick Irvin collection.) *Chris Jones*.

ambition, the force of will, that tips the scale on any great endeavor. They were well equipped. Salathé seemed oblivious to danger, and Nelson summed up his attitude this way, "One cannot climb at all unless he has sufficient urge to do so. Danger must be met—indeed it must be *used*—to an extent beyond that incurred in normal life. That is one reason men climb; for only in response to challenge does a man become his best."

Over the Labor Day holiday Salathé and Nelson set out on their third attempt on the Lost Arrow. The familiar lower pitches went quickly. By the middle of the the second day they passed their rivals' high point, which Wilts and Austin had taken two and a half days to reach. Salathé worked up a wall of decomposed granite. He showed his canny nature by knocking holes in the rock, through which he threaded rope slings, and by stringing together a number of poor pitons to make a passable hold. (By his resourceful use of aid Salathé presaged the aid climbing specialists of the early 1960s.) He stuck with this lead through the

afternoon and finished it the next morning. He had been at it for eight hours.

With their carefully limited supply of eighteen pitons and a dozen carabiners, the leader frequently ran out of equipment and had to descend and clean out the lower pitons. Progress was painstakingly slow. On the third day they made only 200 feet, but as they huddled together in the bivouac, Salathé confided to Nelson his happiness at being there with "our great friend," the Lost Arrow. On the morning of the fifth day the weary pair climbed the last few feet to the summit.

The thirst and suffering had been terrible at times, and Salathé exclaimed, "Ve ver pooped out till ve thought ve ver dead." Yet the climb was a great spiritual adventure for him. It was a vindication of his lifestyle, a time when he felt the "good angels" were with him.

By reason of the difficulties, the length of the climb, and the commitment required, the ascent of the Lost Arrow Chimney was a landmark in North American climbing.

One year after the Lost Arrow climb Salathé and Nelson went up to look over the 1,500-foot north face of Sentinel Rock. However, the first climbers to really come to grips with the face were a new group. Students Al Steck and Bill Long were the prime movers, ably backed up by physicists Phil Bettler and Jim Wilson. As with the Lost Arrow there was no all-out attempt right away but rather a series of probes. In a two-day effort in May 1950, Long and

On the Arrow Tip, John Salathé watches Ax Nelson rappel back into the notch. Courtesy Dick Houston.

Bettler reached midheight, the top of the Flying Buttress, before they retreated. The Great Chimney loomed menacingly above their high point, and they expressed doubt about the climbing possibilities on the smooth Headwall that barred the way into the chimney. With the competition intensifying, Steck and Wilson got into condition by cross-country running before they launched the first all-out try that June. But Wilson was disabled by muscle cramps, and they were forced to come down.

Steck had an advantage over the rest of the field. He had climbed in the Dolomites, where he made the first ascent by an American of the famous Comici route on the north face of the Cima Grande. Thus, he had already climbed an awesome wall, and he knew that a higher standard had been reached in Europe.

Over the 1950 Fourth of July weekend the Sierra Club group planned a trip into the High Sierra. Steck had greater things in mind, but with Long committed to assist on the club trip, he was without a partner who he felt was up to the demands of Sentinel. Although not a close friend, he knew Salathé's stubborn tenacity. Sensing a chance to steal a march on the rest of the field, he telephoned him. The climb was on.

In two days they were on top of the Flying Buttress and climbing into the unknown and into the appalling summer heat.* Salathé spent ten

*Today it is widely appreciated that the summer months are too hot for extended climbs in Yosemite, but during this era you climbed when you had a few days' vacation. Thus, July Fourth and Labor Day were opportunities not to be missed, even if it meant almost passing out in the heat.

hours on the lead over the Headwall and into the Great Chimney. As they hung on the wall, they looked down on tiny figures languishing in the Merced River. With only a few mouthfuls of water each day, they were unable to eat, and Salathé abandoned his can of dates in the Great Chimney. (This hallowed can remained in the chimney for many years until a thoughtless souvenir hunter removed it.)

As they feared, they could not force their way directly up through the Narrows section of the chimney. Salathé made a bold lead on the outside wall; the top was in reach. On the fifth day they

An exuberant Salathé and Nelson after their ascent of the Lost Arrow Chimney. Courtesy Dick Houston.

Bill Long takes tension from the rope on an early attempt on the north face of Sentinel Rock.
Allen Steck.

pulled onto the summit. The climb demanded everything they had, but Steck explained, "There is nothing more satisfying than being a pioneer." The last of the great Yosemite problems of the day had been solved.*

Salathé was in his fifty-first year at the time of the Sentinel climb. In the following years his climbing tapered off. In the mid-1950s he returned to Switzerland, where he lived alone in a mountain chalet and subsisted on the native plants. In the 1960s he was in North America once more, living out of the back of an old truck. He spent the winters near the Mexican border and followed the sun during the summer, but he seldom visited Yosemite Valley, the scene of his three great climbs. He felt that the new regulations and camping fees were the creation of swindlers, an imposition which this great-hearted and simple man could not put up with.

In looking back on Salathé, we see a characteristic that typified the innovators whose achievements are admired today. They conceived the climbs that they wished to do, and from this conception they evolved the necessary methods to do the job, whether the methods were daring leads, the acceptance of high mountain bivouacs, or the creation of a superior piton. The men and their spirit preceded the methods.

*Salathé had said that he would not attempt Sentinel because it was too hard for him. It is likely that he never would have gone up on the wall but for Steck's invitation. Once there, he climbed superbly.

John Salathé gathering herbs in Switzerland, 1957.
John Thune.

The 1950 Sierra Club group that established two routes on Mount Waddington. Note ex-Army baggies and basketball shoes. Back row, left to right: Ray de Saussure, Jim Wilson, Bill Dunmire, Al Steck, Phil Bettler. Front row: Bill Long, Oscar Cook, Dick Houston. *Phil Bettler*.

Gear used on the first ascent of Castle Rock Spire, High Sierra. Note the drill, hangers and Star Dryvin bolts; in this system a metal sleeve was expanded by the bolt. Nylon tape slings are used in preference to metal-runged stirrups, and the gear is rounded out by the ubiquitous hat. *Phil Bettler.*

After the ascent of the north face of Sentinel, the Bay Area group turned to other problems. Their guiding light was Steck, whose alpine experiences greatly impressed his contemporaries, none of whom had ever set foot in Europe, let alone climbed in the fabled Alps. However, they seldom got to Yosemite more than a few weekends a year. Partly as a consequence of their infrequent visits, their skills remained at a level where they were unable to assess the possibility of another advance. Free-climbing standards were static, and aid climbing was still a slow, clumsy affair. Although they pioneered several new climbs, notably the east buttress of El Capitan and Yosemite Point Buttress, they never reached the level of inspiration of the Lost Arrow Chimney and Sentinel. Indeed, none among them tried to repeat these climbs. The field waited for a new generation.

REFERENCES

Hansen, Robin, and Fritz Lippmann. "Some Yosemite Problems." *SCB* 31(7) (Dec. 1946): 118.
Nelson, Anton. "Half Dome, Southwest Face." *SCB* 31(7) (Dec. 1946): 120.
———. "Climbing the Lost Arrow." *SCB* 32(5) (May 1947): 1.
———. "Five Days and Nights on the Lost Arrow." *SCB* 33(3) (March 1948): 103.
———. "Sentinel Rock, Northeast 'Bowl.'" *SCB* 34(6) (June 1949): 147.
Steck, Allen. "Ordeal by Piton." *SCB* 36(5) (May 1951): 1.
Swift, Robert. "Class VI Climbing in Yosemite Valley." *Appalachia* 31 (Dec. 1957): 441.

The Southern Californians

Three Los Angeles teenagers came to Yosemite in 1953 intent on making the second ascent of the north face of Sentinel. They met Al Steck in Camp 4 and aggressively pressed him for information about the climb. He was put off by their arrogance and, unable to remember the precise details, gave a diffident reply. The three then talked to Bob Swift, Steck's companion on the Yosemite Point Buttress climb. They posed a trap question about Sentinel, to which they already knew the answer. Swift had no idea of the answer and took a guess. It was the wrong guess. "That proves what we are thinking," one of them replied; "Steck is giving out misinformation. He doesn't want the climb repeated."

Their attitude hardly endeared the Southern Californians to the Bay Area group. Indeed, on their first visit to Yosemite Royal Robbins, the best climber and cockiest of the three had arrogantly asked the locals, "What have you guys got around here worth climbing?" In the eyes of the Bay Area group his actions marked him as an intense, humorless competitor.

The Bay Area climbers did not know that the eighteen-year-old Robbins had a reason to be cocky. He was the best rock climber in California and, although perhaps unaware of it at the time, the best in North America. On his home ground, Southern California's Tahquitz Rock, he had made climbs that far surpassed those in Yosemite for sheer technical difficulty.

When he and his pals, Jerry Gallwas and Don Wilson, came to grips with Sentinel, they brought a new level of skill to Yosemite and drastically cut the climbing time from five days to two. For Steck and Salathé Sentinel had been a tension climb with free sections. For the Southern Californians it was a free climb with sections of aid. They were nonetheless impressed by the climb and particularly by Salathé's lead on the outside wall at the Narrows, a pitch which they and later parties climbed directly. With this introduction to Yosemite we might suppose that they would soon make their own climbs in the valley, but because of the demands of jobs and school, the travel involved, and their own prefer-

ence for Tahquitz, the Southern Californians visited Yosemite infrequently.

Tahquitz Rock

In order to put their superior skills into perspective, we shall trace events on their home ground. Situated near the mountain town of Idylwild, Tahquitz Rock is a warm-looking crag of superb granite. Its southern location spared it the ice- and water-polish that characterizes Yosemite. The rock is rougher, knobbier, and so less slippery. The earliest climbs were made in the 1930s, and the emphasis was immediately different from that in Yosemite. There was just a single outcrop; ambitious pioneers had to force new routes between established lines.

Under Tahquitz conditions skills rose appreciably. In fact, the hardest prewar rock climb in the country was made there. This was Glen Dawson's Mechanics Route, climbed without the bolt and angle piton commonly used on later ascents. In the postwar period the Los Angeles Sierra Club group again concentrated on the area, then only a three-hour drive from their homes. The combination of a close-knit group, excellent rock, and a friendly environment, as opposed to the forbidding walls of Yosemite, helped to raise the standards. There were so many difficult routes by the early 1950s that the locals had to devise a new system for rating them.

The Sierrans used a six-point scale to assess the difficulty of a route. In this scheme classes 1 through 3 denoted hiking through exposed scrambling, class 4 signified roped climbing where belays were required, class 5 denoted piton-protected climbing, and class 6 was reserved for tension climbing. Although there is a progression in difficulty from class 1 to 5, this was not necessarily the case between class 5 and 6. The top two ratings referred to different *methods* of climbing. (However, the class 6 pioneers *did* regard tension climbing as more difficult than class 5. It was on steeper rock, demanded a new technique, was thoroughly exhausting, and appeared to be dangerous.) The Tahquitz climbers subdivided their class 5 routes into easy, moderate, and difficult. This soon became inadequate, and they devised the so-called Decimal System. They selected a group of well-known routes, and several people arranged them on a scale of difficulty from 0 through 9, that is, 5.0 through 5.9. Where there was the widest agreement, routes were selected as the "standards." As

Tahquitz Rock, training ground of a new generation of California climbers. *Burt Turney*.

new routes were climbed, they were compared with the standards and the rating decided by concensus. The Tahquitz climbers also split class 6 climbs into similar decimal categories, but by the early 1960s this nomenclature was superseded by the European designations A1 through A5.

A rating system is a valuable tool. It enables climbers to gauge whether they are up to a route and, also important, to gauge their performance against that of others. In the following years the Decimal System was applied to other areas and other situations. Thus, 5.7 at Tahquitz is theoretically similar to 5.7 in Colorado or Canada. Although climbers love to argue over the validity of the ratings in various areas, it is this author's observation that the system is fairly uniform.* The rating of key climbs will be given in the text from this point on. The rating is that at the time of the first ascent, or shortly thereafter, and may not reflect current practice. A route that originally required aid may now be climbed free.**

When Robbins arrived at Tahquitz in the early 1950s, the best climbers were consistent 5.8 per-

formers, whereas in the rest of the country 5.7 was about the maximum level. Yet the better climbers had not really pushed themselves. The time was ripe for an aggressive climber to break through. Robbins had already scrambled about on rocks with school friends, using a massive rope stolen from a trucking company, and he soon created a stir among the Sierrans. On small practice rocks he attempted the hardest routes without the upper belay commonly used, and he had the audacity to apply the gymnastic moves from bouldering to Tahquitz. His rapid progress was barely interrupted by a leader fall in which he broke an arm. He was soon the best climber in the area, but it was not all plain sailing. He was so far ahead of his contemporaries that some felt he was reckless, a criticism universally applied to innovators. Several of the old guard came down heavily on him, ostensibly over the safety issue and also perhaps because they found him hard to get along with. However, longtime pioneers John Mendenhall and Chuck Wilts sided with him, pointing out that what might be dangerous for an unexceptional climber was safe for Robbins.

His 1952 ascent of the Open Book was a major step. This 200-foot right-angle corner had been climbed on pitons and wood wedges, but Robbins led the route completely free and in so doing introduced the 5.9 standard to North America. Once he made the break, several others joined him in climbing at this level, including Mendenhall and

*When Canadian Jim Baldwin returned from Yosemite in the early 1960s, he brought with him wild tales of expertise. The Vancouver climbers at Squamish Chief unknowingly set the rating system 0.2 below the actual level, thus adding to their inferiority complex. They could never seem to work up to 5.9!

*Representative prewar climbs may be rated as follows: at Tahquitz, Mechanics Route (5.8); in Yosemite, Higher Cathedral Spire (5.7 A2); in the Tetons several Durrance routes at 5.7; in the East the Bradley-Gilman (5.7) on Cannon Mountain; in Canada, Snowpatch Spire (5.6 A2).

Wilts. Mendenhall's staying power was remarkable. In 1930 he was perhaps the first person to consciously belay in the Sierra when he climbed the Northeast Gully on Laurel Mountain. Wilts not only was a strong contender for the Lost Arrow Chimney (Salathé greatly admired him) but also had made the first free ascent of the Higher Cathedral Spire (5.8).

An engineer by profession, Wilts took the concept of alloy steel pitons a step farther than Salathé. He milled "knife-blade" pitons out of chromium-molybdenum alloy steel for use in incipient cracks. The new pitons were literally the thickness of a knife blade, yet under ideal conditions they held up to 2,000 pounds. Another frontier in aid climbing lay open.

The Yosemite climbers of the era were occupied with overcoming the valley walls. At Tahquitz there were no such awesome challenges; the locals became obsessed with the numbers of the rating system and with the method and style of an ascent. To get up a route was not enough; it had to be done with a minimum of strain and fuss. A step in this direction was the elimination of tension from aid climbing. Using nylon webbing stirrups or aid slings that held the foot snugly, they discovered that they could easily hold themselves into the rock by locking one leg behind the other. This relieved the leader much fatiguing strain from the rope and as a bonus put less strain on the pitons.

With these advances in technique, it is little wonder that the Southern Californians made such a fine effort on the north face of Sentinel Rock. But, curiously, the person who applied these advances to pioneering new routes in Yosemite was not a Tahquitz specialist. Over the 1954 Easter vacation Jerry Gallwas introduced a newcomer to the pains of climbing. Mark Powell was over-

weight and hopelessly out of condition. He trailed far behind as Gallwas set a wicked pace up the talus to the Lower Cathedral Spire. Gallwas climbed the route free while the exhausted Powell clung to aid slings and took tension from the rope as he clawed his was up the rock. On the descent to the valley floor Powell had visions of cold beer. Gallwas considered this weakness lamentable. He

Chuck Wilts with a primitive piton-testing rig.
Frank Hoover.

said that beer was no food for climbers and gave his opinion that Powell would never make a climber. Perhaps this denial of Powell's ability was the spur that did the trick. He went on a starvation diet and was soon down to fighting weight. He was athletic and determined, and spent four months in Yosemite later that year. In 1955 he climbed extensively at Tahquitz and formed an alliance with Gallwas and Wilson that led to a new era of climbing in the Southwest.

From Spider Rock to Totem Pole

After the ascent of the volcanic plugs Shiprock and Agathlan (1949), there was almost no pioneering in the Southwestern desert. The most spectacular spires were sandstone and were thought to be hopelessly friable. However, magazine pictures of these surrealistic spires attracted Gallwas and Wilson, and in 1955 they made a scouting trip to Canyon de Chelly National Monument. Looking across the canyon from the rim, they were fascinated by the stark beauty of 800-foot Spider Rock, reputedly the highest free-standing spire in North America. It had already repulsed several attempts by Coloradans, and the Southern Californians determined to have it. When Powell saw their pictures, he needed no further convincing.

During Easter week the following year the three conspirators left Los Angeles for the desert. As they approached the canyon rim overlooking Spider Rock, Gallwas and Wilson theatrically held back so that Powell would absorb the chilling effect of the moonlit spire alone.

Spider Rock, Canyon de Chelly National Monument, Arizona. The route lies up a crack on the opposite side. *Ed Cooper.*

For climbing blank sections they had three-eights-inch diameter bolts. Although these required a larger hole than the quarter-inch bolts favored for granite, they could be placed in the soft rock in a few minutes. Unhappily the climbers removed several bolts with their fingers! The first day's work went slowly. They were unprepared for the sudden cold of a spring day in the desert and spent the next day warming themselves in the sun. It was not until the fifth day that Powell made the last moves onto the summit. In the light of current climbing prohibitions in the desert areas under the jurisdiction of the Navajo people, it should be noted that the Indians were intrigued by this first ascent and often came to watch. One of them hoped to repeat the ascent and asked the climbers if they would leave their ropes.

Encouraged by this success, the three tracked down the location of a spire they had seen featured in an advertisement, Cleopatra's Needle, New Mexico. Over the following Labor Day weekend Wilson placed a ladder of pitons up a crack in the 250-foot spire. The rock was as bad as they feared. Forty feet from the top he ran out of equipment. As he backed down, a piton shifted. Unclipping his slings, he backed down again. The next piton rotated in the crack. He quickly stepped down again, and this time he was held, his heart pounding with fear. When they returned to the final pitch the next morning, each pin had to be re-driven.

The last spire on their list of "must" desert climbs was the Totem Pole in Monument Valley, a precarious shaft of red sandstone so thin relative to its 300-foot height that the idea of its existing at all was faintly absurd. Nonetheless, two attempts had already been made on the pencil-shaped Totem Pole by Coloradans by the time the Californians turned their attention to it. They spent four days on the harrowing ascent of this most difficult of the three spires.

After this climb the companions went their separate ways. Wilson dropped out of climbing and disappeared to the East Coast. After one more major climb Gallwas also went on to other things. Powell alone remained dedicated to the sport. His contemporaries, although keen weekend climbers, never lost sight of the importance of completing college and getting a good job. Powell was different. He threw himself into climbing completely and abandoned college. He spent the entire summers of 1956 and 1957 climbing and supported himself between times by laboring and meter reading. This was a major break with the past. It marked the change from the career man who climbed on weekends to the climber who supported his habit as best he could. Several of Powell's contemporaries resented his wholesale dedication to climbing. They considered it a waste of his college potential and characterized him as a "climbing bum."

Two of the first ascent party silhouetted against the Totem Pole, Monument Valley. *Bill Feuerer.*

During the mid-1950s the general level of Yosemite climbing was inexpert. In 1956 two unsuccessful attempts were made to repeat the southwest face of Half Dome, while such hoary favorites as the Higher and Lower Cathedral Spires counted some four ascents each. In contrast to this mediocre performance Robbins and Southern Californian Mike Sherrick made the third ascent of Sentinel's north face, and Powell established a stunning free climb, Arrowhead Arête (5.8). Powell's pace was quickening. The next summer he and Wally Reed put up several good climbs, most notably the Powell-Reed Route on the northeast face of Middle Cathedral, the first breach in that somber wall. With these ascents Powell effectively brought Tahquitz standards to Yosemite. He free-climbed to the limit, and where he had to use aid, he forced himself to move up on marginal A4 pitons. He made his climbs in a bold, forthright manner, leading them straight off without repeated reconnaissance.

Powell referred to Arrowhead Arête as "possibly the most continuous difficult fifth-class climbing in this country," and he was probably correct. He knew that in terms of absolute difficulty it fell short of several Tahquitz climbs. The key to his statement is "continuous." The decimal ratings have an inherent shortcoming. A one-pitch Tahquitz route and a two-day Yosemite route may have the same rating. The system makes no allowance for the length of a climb, the continuity of the difficulties, the commitment, the remoteness, and other quali-

Mark Powell on an early ascent of the Lost Arrow.
Bill Feuerer.

ties. Yet it is these ingredients that make up the total climb. Powell therefore added a grade to the rating system in an attempt to give an overall assessment of a route. In this system a Grade I is a climb that takes a few hours, a Grade III takes most of a day, and a Grade V may take from one to one and a half days. The most demanding climbs of the day were the Lost Arrow Chimney and the North Face of Sentinel, both Grade V. A colloquialism that came into use later is "big wall," meaning a multiday rock climb. The Lost Arrow Chimney was the first big wall in Yosemite although today's climbers would not regard it as such because it is commonly climbed in a long day.

Powell combined an athletic asceticism with a robust liking for women and booze, and he found the Southern Californians a bunch of prudes. More to his liking were a group that surrounded civil engineer Warren Harding, who, already an avid sports car driver, in the early 1950s became a climber after he read a book about a ferocious alpine climb, the West Face of the Dru. Harding sensibly decided that he would never go to the extremes of the West Face of the Dru and therefore would never get into real trouble. Little did he know how the future would turn out.

One May morning in 1954 Harding was roused from his bed on top of a boulder by stranger Frank Tarver and talked into trying the imposing, unclimbed north face of Middle Cathedral Rock. Tarver knew others were already ahead of them on the rock, but climbing rapidly, they eventually caught up. It was perhaps fortunate the two ropes combined. Harding and Tarver were short on gear, whereas the others were heavy on gear but light on experience. The coincidence of two parties setting out for the same route on the same day underlines the fact that although the mid-1950s was a period of little activity in Yosemite, there was a definite rivalry among the better climbers for the outstanding problems of the time, a rivalry that has intensified over the years.

In 1954 Harding teamed up with Bob Swift and Tarver to make the second ascent of Lost Arrow Chimney. Concerned that his beloved Jaguar would not get enough exercise while he was on the climb, Harding arranged for a woman friend to give it a daily spin. Each day during the climb he paused and smiled when he heard the car winding up through the gears. One day, instead of the throaty roar of shifting into a higher gear, there was a grinding crash. Harding's smile vanished. "Oh no," he cried, burying his face in his hands. After the epic four-day climb he learned that his car was intact; the crash had been a garbage truck dumping a load of trash.

Slight and wiry, Harding was able to worm inside cracks where bulkier climbers had to flail away on the outside. On the Lost Arrow Chimney he worked out a new pitch, the Harding Slot, while his lead of the Worst Error, a dark 300-foot crack on the imposing Elephant Rock, helped establish him as the most daring crack climber of the day.

Harding also gathered a reputation as a wine lover. Once, after a bout of drinking in Camp 4, he and his comrades gently faded into oblivion. When they woke in the morning, Swift had an empty wine jug for a pillow and Tarver was lying face down in the dirt. Both had killing hangovers. Harding shot out of his sleeping bag and with a glint in his eye proudly announced to his miserable companions, "Passed the sustained drinking test. Not a trace of a hangover!"

By the mid-1950s technique and confidence advanced to the stage where another step forward in climbing the big walls of Yosemite was possible. The next challenge was obvious, the 2,000-foot northwest face of Half Dome. Perhaps because of its height and its commanding position at the far end of Yosemite Valley, Half Dome has a uniquely aloof and mysterious air about it. Although the nothwest face appeared hopelessly bald in the center, there was a definite weakness on the left side.

Several parties sniffed around the base of the route, climbed a few pitches, and declared that it

The great days in Yosemite. Warren Harding, center, in his Jaguar with Mark Powell and Bea Vogel, 1957. *Frank Hoover.*

The northwest face of Half Dome. The 1957 climb began on the far left side, traversed in at mid-height to follow the line between sun and shade and moved left once more at the summit overhang. *Tom Gerughty.*

would "go." After a similar preliminary scouting of the Lost Arrow Chimney and Sentinel Rock, the tactic had been to make successive probes up to around midheight. By the time Half Dome was actively under consideration, a team came forward ready to go all-out from the start: Southern Californians Robbins, Gallwas, and Wilson, and another climber with a big reputation, Harding.

Harding and Robbins had first climbed together at Tahquitz. Harding was the hard man from Yosemite and Robbins the local expert of Tahquitz. After making a lead, Harding belayed Robbins up a succession of aid pins. While Robbins was cleaning the last pin, two of the three belay anchors suddenly popped out. Harding frantically hammered on the remaining pin, which looked like it it was moving, and Robbins hastily redrove the pin he had just removed. It was a close call. At almost the precise moment that they were re-anchoring to the rock, a friend on the ground shouted up that it was getting late. When would they be down? Without a trace of emotion in his voice Robbins replied that everything was just fine; they were almost up. Harding was impressed by Robbins's absolute control in a tight situation; he had to be made of hard stuff. Robbins was equally impressed by Harding's apparently casual attitude toward belaying and safety. He thought to himself that Harding must be made of hard stuff. Both men were right.

On the joint Half Dome attempt the early pitches went slowly, and after three days the climbers came down. Significantly, Harding and Robbins had wanted to press on. Following this rebuff, plans were made to return the following year, but they never materialized.

Powell was also interested in Half Dome. He hoped his desert companions, who had already been up on the climb, would invite him along, but they remained noncommittal and seemed to exclude him from their plans. The answer was to form a separate team. He joined Harding and aircraft engineer Bill Feuerer for the attempt. They assembled their gear in late June 1957, but in vain. When they reached Yosemite, Robbins, Gallwas, and Sherrick were already established on the route.

The Southern Californians had made thorough preparations. Gallwas forged some ten hard-steel pitons patterned after Salathé's as well as angle pitons that would span cracks up to three inches. They crammed their extra gear into a mail bag and carried a total of 1,200 feet of rope in case of a forced retreat.

Late on the second day Robbins was hard at work completing the rightward traverse onto the main part of the face. He placed a piton, called for slack, and descended fifty feet on the rope. Then he pendulumed back and forth across the sheer wall until on his fourth attempt he was able to grasp a good handhold. He left a fixed rope and rejoined his companions. The key section of the climb was made. When they crossed the "Robbins Traverse" the next morning, they left the fixed rope to insure the possibility of a retreat. (There is a strong tradition of "irreversible" traverses in climbing, most notably the Hinterstoisser Traverse on the Eiger. Although the idea is no longer a strong one, it once was a potent fear.)

The constant mental strain, the uncertainty of the outcome, and the fear that they would have to

Jerry Gallwas on Half Dome. *Mike Sherrick*.

Mike Sherrick in Yosemite, 1956. He was recovering from a broken leg sustained in a ski accident. *Frank Hoover*.

go directly over the summit overhangs tolled heavily on the three climbers. They were psyched by the scale of the climb. Robbins, who had borne the brunt of the leading, was mentally exhausted on the fourth day and took a complete rest while Gallwas eked out 300 feet of progress. Sherrick was shattered and did no leading during the final two days.

After their fourth night on the wall they crammed all their excess gear into the hauling bag and cast it into space. They watched fascinated as the bag cartwheeled and plunged down. Without once touching the wall, it smashed into the ground they had left five days earlier.

Not far above their bivouac rose the dread summit overhangs. Fortune was with them; a fifty-foot "Thank God" ledge led off to the left. Leaving a relatively secure stance, the leader worked out over one of the most appalling voids in climbing. It was like stepping out of a skyscraper onto a one-foot ledge. Eventually, the impending wall pressed him off balance, and he had to continue by hanging from his arms, his hands gripping the crack behind the ledge.

After five tense days the three climbers reached the summit, their hands scarred and grimy, their faces drawn and lined with dirt, their mouths and throats tormented by the ever-present thirst. It was a hard-won victory, the most demanding big wall climb in North America and the first Grade VI on the continent. Waiting to greet them on top with beer and sandwiches was Harding, whose own team, bitterly disappointed, had arrived just too late to take the prize.

REFERENCES

Burton, Hal. "They Risk Their Lives for Fun," *Saturday Evening Post*, Feb. 25, 1956, p. 58.

Harding, Warren. "Worst Error." *SCB* 44(7) (Oct. 1959): 76.

Powell, Mark. "Arrowhead Arête." *SCB* 42(6) (June 1957): 58.

———. "Middle Cathedral Rock Northeast Face." *SCB* 43(9) (Nov. 1958): 78.

Roper, Steve. "Four Corners." *Ascent* 1(4) (1970): 26.

"Royal Robbins: Interview." *Mountain*, no. 18 (Nov. 1971), p. 27.

Sherrick, Michael. "The Northwest Face of Half Dome." *SCB* 43(9) (Nov. 1958): 19.

Smith, James. "Tahquitz Rock." *SCB* 23(2) (April 1938): 111.

Wilson, Don. "The First Ascent of Spider Rock." *SCB* 42(6) (June 1957): 45.

———. "Cleopatra's Needle." *SCB* 42(6) (June 1957): 63.

———. "The Totem Pole." *SCB* 43(9) (Nov. 1958): 72.

Wilts, Chuck. *A Climber's Guide to Tahquitz and Suicide Rocks*. New York: American Alpine Club, 1970.

Ungentlemanly Behavior

The climbing developments in California during the postwar decade were the most far-reaching on the continent. Yet because of the isolation of the climbing centers and the parochial attitude of the climbers during the period, the new ideas were not spread around. During these years, parallel but separate advances took place in what were then the other two important rock climbing centers: New York's Shawangunks and Colorado.

Apart from his climbs on Mount Waddington and Devils Tower, Fritz Wiessner is best remembered in American climbing for his discovery of the Shawangunks. New York members of the Appalachian Mountain Club occasionally spent the weekend on the 200-foot granite cliffs of Breakneck Ridge facing the Hudson River. After a violent thunderstorm one day in the spring of 1935 the sky cleared, and from Breakneck Ridge Wiessner saw a long line of cliffs away to the north. The following weekend he and his friends set out over country roads to find the elusive cliffs. Before the weekend was over, they made the first climb at the Shawangunks. Because of its proximity to New York City, the excellence of the rock, and the extent of the cliffs, this area among the many on the East Coast would become the predominant climbing ground. When in the 1950s East Coast climbing finally ceased to be merely a pastime for eccentric gentlemen, it was at the Shawangunks that the sport took off.

The Shawangunk cliffs differ from Yosemite Valley in several ways. A seven-mile-long escarpment, they rise out of rolling, pastoral New York countryside. There is no feeling that one is at the periphery of a mountain range. The cliffs average 200 feet in height, and good access is provided by roads and trails. Finally, the quartz-conglomerate rock is wholly unlike Yosemite granite. There are few cracks, chimneys, or friction problems. Instead, there are near-vertical faces, horizontal ledges, and ceilings produced by the horizontal bedding that characterizes the area.

The small scale of the Shawangunk cliffs and the friendly surroundings freed the climbers from certain of the psychological stresses common in Yosemite and led to a situation akin to Tahquitz: a total concentration on the mastery of technical problems. The locals became experts on their home ground, but when they eventually went to other areas, they discovered that their specialized tech-

Hans Kraus in the mid 1950s. Note "Turswiry Hat."
Courtesy Hans Kraus.

niques were not always applicable. However, the Shawangunk climbers had their revenge. Outsiders with reputations were sometimes stopped cold by a fierce-looking roof of only moderate difficulty.

After the 1935 discovery of the Shawangunks, development went ahead slowly. World War II disrupted the normal flow of events at the cliff although Fritz Wiessner continued his regular visits. During this time he made the acquaintance of an orthopedic surgeon from Austria, Hans Kraus. Already an accomplished climber, Kraus was rock-starved and eager to climb with Wiessner. Several excellent routes resulted from their partnership. High Exposure (5.7), a daring and exposed climb conceived by Kraus, is perhaps the classic of the area. In 1946 Wiessner established what was then the most difficult route in the area, Minnie Belle (5.8). The first pitch, a steep inside corner, demanded the utmost in crack climbing technique.

Yet Wiessner never felt that Minnie Belle or his other Shawangunk climbs equaled those he had made on the sandstone towers near Dresden, Germany, during the 1920s. By the time he was actively exploring the Shawangunks, he was in his midthirties. No longer the energetic youth of his European days, he now owned a business and had family responsibilities. The competition, that vital spur to extending oneself to the limit, was almost nonexistent. Everywhere that he and Kraus looked, there were new climbs, many of them simple. Why risk their necks?

By the mid-1940s the more obvious routes had been pioneered. The climbers turned their sights on the overhangs, and Kraus drew on his experiences in the Dolomites. European climbers used pitons freely for progress as well as protection, and in 1946 he introduced aid climbing to the Shawangunks. It was a significant contribution. Apart from innovations produced at home, it gave the Easterners experience of a technique they later used in the Western mountains. Wiessner, however, was philosophically against aid climbing and would not permit his partners to use aid; he was also opposed to publicizing the sport in magazines.

During these immediate postwar years the number of dedicated Shawangunk climbers remained small, perhaps twenty, almost wholly within the Appalachian Mountain Club. Although they welcomed newcomers, their social net was limited. One of their prime concerns when the climbing season got under way in the spring was who, if any, of last year's recruits would stick with them for another year. One who did was Bonnie Prudden, a climber of considerable skill who became Kraus's regular partner and was later known for her writing on physical education. Prudden was one of the few women of the day who performed, and survived, in what was then an almost exclusively male preserve. As such, she engaged the interest of her fellow club members; a favorite story concerns the naming of the climb Boston.

After they had completed a new route, Prudden and partner Dick Hirschland sat at the top of the cliff relaxing and taking in the view. She was explaining the whereabouts of a friend's summer place. With her thighs as an improvised map she pointed out the geography of the region and remarked that the place was situated between Providence and Taunton, Massachusetts. Hirschland broke in, "I wish I was in Boston."

In 1950 the Shawangunk scene remained essentially identical to that ten years earlier. Kraus and Wiessner were still the kingpins. The milieu was sociable and pleasant but stagnant. Yet change is inevitable. In 1951 a wiry Princeton undergraduate, Jim McCarthy, appeared in the area and worked his way through the established routes. As Wiessner had moved out of the New York region,

McCarthy soon had only one superior, Kraus. Already a legend in the area, Kraus recognized McCarthy's ability and drive and gave him every encouragement. Thus nurtured by Kraus, McCarthy progressed quickly and before long supplanted his mentor as the best technician. A small group of climbers headed by Kraus and McCarthy now kept somewhat apart from the main A.M.C. contingent, whom they found depressingly conservative. This separateness helped McCarthy attain the enviable position as the new top man at the cliffs. His followers waged a subtle psychological battle against the A.M.C., and their stories of desperation convinced the A.M.C. climbers that McCarthy climbed at a level far above their own. The tactic was so successful that McCarthy's routes attained an aura of impregnability out of all proportion to their difficulty.

Not long after McCarthy had taken over Kraus's mantle another newcomer arrived, not from the Ivy League background of Princeton but from Cooper Union in New York City, not from the well-heeled families that produced the majority of Eastern climbers but from an ethnic city block on Long Island. Although without McCarthy's athletic build, Art Gran was a born competitor and easily mastered the best of the older climbs, though not McCarthy's new "horror" climbs. Gran introduced some of his New York companions to climbing, notably a group from the City College Outdoor Club. Although they were nominally affiliated with the A.M.C., they also kept apart from the

"Appies" as they mockingly termed them. The feeling was probably mutual. On one side there were the brash newcomers, some with undesirable accents, on the other side the gentlemanly Appies.

There was no coincidence in the fact that McCarthy now climbed in higher gear. He could feel the barbarian hordes hard on his heels, and in 1957 he established Yellow Belly (5.8), then the hardest route on the cliff. He began to push especially as Gran and his pals were repeating his routes and finding them only a shade harder than the previous ones.

A major thrust in free climbing is the elimination of the aid used by earlier climbers; it is a fine feeling bettering your predecessors. (In absolute terms today's climbers easily surpass their predecessors; the real test of a climber lies in judging their capabilities against the prevailing standards of the day.) McCarthy worked hard to cut out the aid then commonly used. He established a new norm with his free ascent of Broken Sling (5.8). In common with everyone else at the cliff, Gran looked upon Broken Sling as an ultimate horror. Only when one of McCarthy's crowd told him he had led equally difficult routes was Gran able to overcome the aura of the route and set about climbing it. Broken Sling was such a noted super climb that when it became clear others might begin to repeat the route, Dave Craft reputedly chopped off a key hold to keep away the riffraff.

As the 1958 season got underway, McCarthy and Gran could eye each other as equals—and rivals. McCarthy launched out on a series of classics, the "Land" climbs, with his Birdland and Roseland (5.9). Gran contributed the fierce Retribution (5.9). It was a hard-fought battle between lawyer and fitness buff McCarthy and the voluble and demonstrative Gran. The latter worked hard to project the image of a top climber. Gesturing arms, subtle footwork, and contorted body positions accompanied his accounts of the desperate moves on his latest climbs. These performances earned him the nickname, Art "The Move" Gran.

Confrontation

The Shawangunks lie on private land, the Mohonk Trust. In 1958, to control access to the cliffs and the litter problems, the owners began to require a climbing permit. The permit idea was developed in liaison with the A.M.C., and the Appies went on to institute a sign-out system. Only leaders qualified by the A.M.C. were supposed to lead a rope on the cliffs. The system was intended to make climbing safer and reflected the peculiar American philosophy of protecting the citizen from himself.

In the Shawangunks the growing number of nonaffiliated climbers had little use for regulations. The City College of New York group was now a potent force. Gran and mathematician Claude Suhl interested several others: local resident Dave Craft and a Californian already marked as a romantic wanderer, Gary Hemming. To emphasize their philosophy, the group styled themselves the Vulgarians; and vulgar they were. The emergence of this new and ungentlemanly group of inner-city people was viewed as an unpleasant threat by the bucolic Appies.

In the spring of 1959 a Yale student was killed in a climbing fall. He was not a qualified leader. In the aftermath of the accident it was learned that the Mohonk Trust's liability insurance would be raised. The A.M.C. felt responsible for the insurance problem and feared a crackdown on climbing. They proposed that only qualified persons be allowed on the cliffs. The A.M.C. alone would approve a person's abilities; on reaching a certain proficiency, a climber would be eligible for a yearly permit priced at a stiff ten dollars.

There is no doubt that the Appies were motivated by good intentions, but much mischief has been committed under the guise of good intentions. The new regulations not only arose out of concern for human life, but they were also another stage in the ongoing confrontation with the Vulgarians. Patrols walked under the cliffs to check up on climbers. A party stood a good chance of being ordered off if the second was not a "qualified second."

The Vulgarians were not about to comply with all this nonsense. Climbing represented a freedom to them not an extension of society's restrictive ways, and they escalated the confrontation. Their weekend hangout was the nearby Wickie Wackie campground. Here they raised all sorts of hell: frenzied jumping on a wooden footbridge, which made a terrific racket; riotous parties; swearing at friend and foe alike; and at the cliffs themselves, much to the disgust of the Appies, uncouth beer drinking. The Vulgarians were on an orgy of vulgarity, and their attitude toward the Appies could be summed up by "up yours." After an evening of drinking at Charly's, the favorite bar near the cliffs, they urinated on the departing Appies from the roof. One night an intense hate session led to more drastic action: A car supposed to belong to the most officious of the Appies was turned over. It was the wrong car, but the point had been made. The Vulgarians were ascendant. The Appies retreated as arrogant youth had its day.

The emergence of the Vulgarians as a potent force was a breakthrough in East Coast climbing. No longer were climbers drawn exclusively from the professional classes. The significance of the new climbers was not that persons from humbler backgrounds were more willing to scuff their hands on the rock or live rough but that the newcomers were not tied to the past. The typical A.M.C. member of the day went through a long period of learning and eventually led at a mediocre level. That was the way it had always been. The Vulgarians wanted to climb at the top level right away, and before long several did.*

In spite of the drama of confrontation, technical progress at the Shawangunks continued apace; qualified or unqualified, the Vulgarians and their fellow travelers were the best performers. By now the harder climbs were so demanding that they were worked on in stages. Rather than complete a new route in one shot, it was common for several climbers to go up and down until confidence was built up and fear controlled. The person who connected the route up, generally the one who had the idea of the climb, took most of the glory.

On one occasion Gran was invited, or perhaps conned, to help McCarthy and his henchmen on a new route. McCarthy's partner Craft made the first few moves. He was lowered exhausted to the ground, and the lead was handed over to Gran. The unwritten game plan called for Gran to work

*Persons drawn from the working class also arrived on the California and Colorado climbing scenes during the 1950s. Their arrival considerably widened the pool from which potential climbers could be drawn and provided a vital new impulse.

on the placement of a bolt. When exhausted, he too was to retire and leave the field to McCarthy, who was anxiously waiting in the bullpen below. Much to McCarthy's chagrin, Gran managed to stay with it and press on to the top of the fierce Never Never Land (5.9)

Yet, always friendly rivals, the two combined in 1960 to put in a finale to the Land climbs, Land's End. Despite the setback on Never Never Land, 1960 was McCarthy's year. He produced an undoubted masterpiece in M.F. (5.9), a personal breakthrough and a route where his seconds struggled hard to follow.

Throughout the 1950s the Shawangunks remained isolated from the other climbing areas in the country. Sure, the locals knew that there were diehards who specialized in crashing up and down boring snow peaks in the Northwest and Canada, but were there any *real* climbers? Slowly the word filtered through, and an occasional outsider showed up; rumor had it that there were a handful of super-climbers in California.

Set on investigating the rumors, the first Vulgarian expedition took to the field in 1959: four city kids in a hulking Oldsmobile. They were bound for the fabled Canadian Bugaboos and the "Golden West." After driving for days through the American heartland, they crossed the emptiness of North Dakota, a land of space and distance foreign to them. Long after dark they pulled off the road and rolled out their sleeping bags on the prairie.

Late that night a highway patrol officer stopped to check out their car. Awakened by the officer's probing flashlight, Gran's earnest question in his solid Bronx accent was, "Say, mister, is it all right if we sleep on your lawn?" It was all right; the city kids were in the clear, and the Vulgarians were on their way to devastate new fields.

John Turner
and the Club de Montagne Canadien

For the majority of climbers the Shawangunks *were* East Coast climbing. Although climbers at other areas failed to match the progress at the Shawangunks, a Montreal-based group made definite contributions. As frequently happened, this group arose independently of outside contacts. It also arose somewhat through the Boy Scouts, another common thread in the story. Ben Poisson was inspired to climb by a merit badge recently introduced by his scout troop. The badge was awarded for a daring adventure, such as climbing a mountain, and was called the Annapurna badge. (The Quebec scouts looked to mother France for inspiration, and the French had recently made the ascent of Annapurna, the first of the world's 8,000-meter peaks to be climbed.) A fellow scout recalled seeing some cliffs near Val David, fifty-five miles from Montreal. The pair studied a French climbing book and took to the field. They first climbed L'Arabesque on the Mont Césaire cliffs and later attacked the isolated pinnacle of L'Aiguille at Mont Condor. On the latter they found pitons left by unknown predecessors. They improvised carabiners by looping sash cord around the climbing rope and through the eyes of the pitons.

In 1955 Poisson and his friends met a tall newcomer solo-climbing down a difficult route. Like themselves, Claude Lavallée had begun to climb on his own, improvising as he went along. Poisson and Lavallée went on to revitalize the local Club de Montagne Canadien when an outsider arrived who was to affect their thinking profoundly.

John Turner had left Britain to escape the military draft. A chemist by training, his thick glasses and unruly mop of black hair gave him a studious university air. Powerfully built, Turner was a fanatic for weight training; he once dropped his weight-lifting bar through the floor of his apartment. He was already an accomplished climber, and when he met the Club de Montagne, their revival was in full swing.

While the Quebec climbers looked to France for guidance, newcomer Turner was steeped in the British tradition. In order to safeguard his leads, he ingeniously threaded rope slings inside cracks or placed them on rock horns—any trick to avoid a piton. Lavallée, the most gifted of the locals, was impressed by Turner's purity of approach: daring leads with minimal protection. Although a taboo

Claude Lavalleé on Shockley's Ceiling, Shawangunks. Quebec climbers used the chest tie-in common in France. *Imre Michalik.*

against the indiscriminate use of pitons spread through the Club de Montagne Canadien, Turner's ideas failed to influence East Coast climbing. He was a prophet before his time.

When Turner and Lavallée visited the Shawangunks, they concluded that the locals were only too ready to use pitons when the going got rough. The locals felt that Turner knew next to nothing about protection and safety. Both views had validity; each group was a product of its own traditions. While some might feel that too many pitons were employed at the Shawangunks, others could point to a couple of bad leader falls for which Turner became renowned.

Although quiet by nature, Turner lived dangerously. He drove his old VW at a constant flat-out speed with a heart-stopping, four-wheel drift around corners. (Driving as if in a Grand Prix was also part of the British climber's tradition.) On a weekend climbing trip Turner was once cut off at the highway toll booth. Furious, he pulled the luckless driver from his car and punched him. Justice was served; Turner was summarily arrested.

The Club de Montagne made several trips to the Shawangunks each year, but their best efforts took place on cliffs nearer home. Turner was a strong crack climber, and on the steep 450-foot granite of New Hampshire's Cathedral Cliffs he established what was perhaps the hardest and most serious route on the East Coast. In 1958, sharing the lead with Gran, he put up Repentance (5.9). The route

went unrepeated for ten years, though not for lack of attempts.

Colorado Rock

In common with their counterparts in California and the East Coast, postwar Colorado climbers were isolated from events in the rest of the country. Skills had lagged behind during the prewar years, and the area continued as something of a backwater during the 1940s and mid-1950s. A contributing factor was the self-image of the local climbers. They thought of themselves as mountaineers rather than rock specialists. They played

John Turner. *Julie Podmore.*

down technical competence on small cliffs and emphasized instead the values of peak climbing. But mavericks arise! In 1949 Tom Hornbein showed the determination so evident in the dramatic traverse of Mount Everest some fifteen years later when he put up an overhanging aid climb, the Northwest Passage, on Boulder's jagged Flatirons. Four years later, partnered by Cary Huston, Hornbein led a vicious, unprotected lieback on Longs Peak. Years after, the Hornbein Crack (5.8) was only mentioned in hushed voices.

In the postwar era the potential of the Boulder region as a rock climbing area was scarcely realized. Several of the most obvious local problems remained unsolved while the superb climbs in nearby Eldorado Springs Canyon were untouched. For example, the 150-foot overhanging west face of the Maiden (5.7 A3), a showpiece spire on the Flatirons, was not climbed until 1953, when Dale Johnson, Huston, and Dave Robertson pulled over the last bulge and onto the summit.

The neglect of the Boulder cliffs was due in part to the greater appeal of nearby Rocky Mountain National Park. The park offered more of the "real thing": high peaks, snowfields, airy pinnacles, and rock faces up to 1,000 feet high. Of the mountains in the park Longs Peak remained the predominant objective. Here the Stettner's amazing 1927 climb, now often combined with a continuation up the 1950 Window, was the touchstone. Nonetheless, several of the better Colorado climbers were more intrigued by the glamour and tradition of the Alps than by the problems at home, and all they knew of Yosemite was that it was a national park.

In this unpromising atmosphere Ray Northcutt, fiercely determined and a fitness buff, began to probe the third buttress on the 800-foot north face of Hallett Peak. Success eluded him until 1956, but the resultant climb was the most demanding in the state (III, 5.7).* The mental pressures of the third buttress made a strong impression on Northcutt. The smooth walls that fell away to the ground brought to mind well-memorized pictures of the alpine horror climbs of the day, the Eigerwand and the Cima Grande. It was an overdrawn comparison. The climb did represent an advance over previous Colorado routes, though it was by no means the equal of Yosemite's Lost Arrow Chimney, made almost ten years earlier.

Ignorant of events in Yosemite, Northcutt's partner, Harvey T. Carter, began to boost the third buttress as one of the hardest routes in the country. The climb enjoyed a considerable reputation, but it fell from its pedestal three years later in 1959. Intent on making the second ascent of this "hardest climb in Colorado," Teton veterans Yvon Chouinard and Ken Weeks hiked up to a bivouac

---

*In 1947 Joe Stettner, Jack Fralick and John Speck established what was then the best route in the state: the 1,200-foot east face of Monitor Peak in the San Juan Mountains. Northcutt's third buttress was the first climb to surpass Stettner's.

Ray Northcutt poses for a hero shot.
Courtesy Ray Northcutt.

at the foot of the route. Intrigued to see how the climbing would go the next morning, they started up the first pitch at four in the afternoon. They found little difficulty and decided to carry right along. As night fell, they arrived on top of the vaunted third buttress.

An inquisitive and far-ranging climber, Carter went to Yosemite. He was one of the first outsiders with an established reputation to do so. The smooth, merciless Yosemite cracks were foreign to him, and he failed to make an impression on the harder climbs. The locals were pleased to have confirmation of their feeling of superiority, but they were not so pleased when they learned that Carter had removed the register from a well-known peak in order to study it. Yet worse was to come. *Summit* magazine* published a letter from Carter that belittled Yosemite and its climbers. He so enraged the locals that for years afterward Yosemite climbers were automatically hostile toward visiting Coloradans. The common feeling was, "Let's roast 'em."

About the time of Carter's unfortunate foray to Yosemite, another Coloradan, Layton Kor, happened to see a movie that showed climbing. A few days later the tall, lanky bricklayer sauntered over

*Founded by two fundamentalist Southern Californian women in 1955, *Summit* was for many years the only magazine in America that dealt with climbing. A parochial mélange of hearty backpacking sagas, robust climbs, homey poetry, and other odds and ends, *Summit* is an American original, put down, yet loved by climbers.

to a local rock intent on giving the sport a try. Equipped only with street shoes, he slipped off the rock. He got nowhere and concluded that, as in the snow climbing he had seen on the film, climbers progressed by cutting steps. Armed with a geological hammer, he returned to the rock and painstakingly hacked his way up a few feet. This method was even worse; there had to be a better way. He signed up for an introductory course offered by the Colorado Mountain Club, and in hardly any time he had outdistanced his instructors. He took to the sport like no one else they had ever seen. He had a voracious appetite for rock, any rock in any weather. He climbed almost every day and quickly ran out of partners who could stand the pace. The solution was simple; he would climb alone. His contemporaries laid bets as to how long he would live. But he fooled them; he simply got better. In 1958 he ran into Northcutt, who fancied he saw in Kor the same demonic qualities possessed by Hermann Buhl, the legendary Austrian super-climber of that era. Events were to prove how correct was Northcutt's intuition.

Longs Peak has always been a focal point for Colorado climbers. The peak occupies the same position in the eyes of local climbers as Mount Rainier does in the Northwest. In the same way that Mount Rainier has been the scene of notable advances in climbing expertise, so has Longs Peak and in particular its east face. The evolution of climbing on the east face has followed the classic pattern seen throughout mountaineering. The secure-feeling chimneys on the periphery were the first to be attempted (Alexander's and North in the 1920s); then leaving the chimneys, climbers worked the interconnected series of weaknesses bordering the faces (Stettners Ledges and the Window); finally the main faces came under attack. On Longs Peak the real problems of the east face are two 900-foot sweeps of granite separated by the large ledge, Broadway. By the late 1950s neither the upper nor the lower wall had even had a serious attempt registered against it, though by now they were furtively talked about as the next wave.

With his success on Hallett Peak behind him, Northcutt looked at the lower of these two walls and in 1958 twice launched probes onto it. He then teamed up with Kor. The two trained rigorously that winter and the following spring. They were out on the local rocks almost every day, keying themselves up for an advance into the unknown; they meant business. In the summer of 1959 they made their first try on the east face. After they had pushed the route past the prominent band of overhangs on the lower wall, they were caught in an afternoon storm. They retreated off the face, securing the distance gained by leaving fixed ropes. Some weeks later they climbed higher yet, where they were stopped by a water-worn blank section. Rather than bolt his way over blank rock, North-

cutt made a daring traverse to the right. Here barely 300 feet from the top their supply of wide-angle pitons was too depleted to force the issue. Once again they retreated, and once again the route was secured with fixed ropes. Northcutt was not to be denied; in mid-July he and Kor finally completed the Diagonal (V, 5.9 A3). Northcutt, the driving force behind these attempts, had established what was clearly the most difficult climb in Colorado. It was the culmination of his climbing career.*

Above and to the right of the Diagonal lies an even more seductive wall, the appallingly steep and smooth Diamond. Dale Johnson dearly wanted to attempt the Diamond, but he made a tactical error; he applied to the local Park Service officials for permission. No one had ever applied for permission in this way before, and the Diamond was obviously a difficult proposition. The Park Service reasoned that the request was evidence of the extraordinary nature of the undertaking. They labeled the proposed climb a stunt, denied permission, and declared the Diamond off limits to all comers.

For the group of up-and-coming climbers led by Kor, the closure of the Diamond was perhaps no

---

*Although the Diagonal was not equivalent to the 1957 northwest face of Half Dome, it was a major advance in Colorado. Northcutt and Kor knew almost nothing of developments in Yosemite, and in terms of commitment and achievement their route was not far short of the Half Dome climb.

The east face of Longs Peak. Broadway runs across the center of the face, dividing the lower wall from the Diamond. The marked routes are, left to right, Stettners Ledges, the Diagonal and the Diamond. *Ed Cooper*.

great matter. They felt cocky about their skills. As far as they knew, they had no rivals for the climb; when they were ready, it would be waiting for them. By this time they had heard of Yosemite, but they had the impression that Yosemite climbers were only interested in bolt routes up blank walls. (The bolting theory was widely believed for years because of the inordinate publicity generated by certain "bolt-heavy" Yosemite climbs.) This apparent emphasis on bolts appeared ridiculous to the Coloradans, and they looked upon Yosemite climbers as an aberration.

The Coloradans were caught up in the legends and methods of the Alps, and were convinced that speed of movement was everything in mountaineering. Consequently, Kor and his companions went at climbing as if it was a footrace and devoured virgin rock near Boulder at a frantic pace. The two principal areas of interest were Boulder Canyon, with its 100- to 300-foot granite climbs, and Eldorado Springs Canyon, where brilliantly colored, depressingly steep sandstone provided faces up to 500 feet high. Indeed, so determined and successful was Kor's campaign in Eldorado Canyon that in a couple of years it became *the* place for the aspiring Colorado hard man. In 1959 Kor turned to Redgarden Wall, the biggest face in the canyon, and forced a route to the top of Tower 2. By virtue of the continuity of the difficulties, the ascent of T2 (5.9 A1) was a breakthrough in Colorado climbing. Within a few months Kor established two classics on Redgarden Wall, Yellow Spur and the Grand Giraffe; he was off and running and never looked back.

In order to experience the aura of the Alps firsthand, Kor and Northcutt planned a big summer in the Italian Dolomites for 1960. However, Northcutt had begun to acquire other interests, and Kor had to make the pilgrimage alone. The first venture to the Alps was a thin one. He lived on a diet of cream buns and beer, apparently the only foods he knew how to order. He cut his dismal trip short and returned home. To vent his frustrations, he headed to Canada, where he put up good routes on Bugaboo and Pigeon Spires in the Bugaboos. Then he rounded out the summer with a visit to the still mysterious Yosemite.

By 1960 the Yosemite climbers were convinced that they were the best in America, and with good reason. They were. The few outsiders who had come to the valley had been humbled, even though they were preceded by stories of how good they were back home. (The outsiders undoubtedly were good back home, but there is a marked difference between top dog in the bush league and top dog in the competitive big league of a Yosemite). When Kor arrived in the valley, strong memories remained of a previous Coloradan, Harvey T. Carter. The majority of the Yosemite climbers were college-educated; a few of them may have looked patronizingly at bricklayer Kor, gleefully anticipating his being rapidly "burnt off" by a diet of fearsome Yosemite cracks. But not Kor. He asked the location of the hardest climbs, and to the consternation of the Yosemite pundits he did them. Yosemite's aura of supremacy took a nasty jolt.

Back home in Colorado that same year sparks also flew. It was forcibly brought home to the locals that there were other good climbers in the

Layton Kor in Eldorado Canyon, Colorado.
Larry Dalke.

country. A California team stole the first ascent of the Diamond from under their noses. It was a bad year for false pride.

The fact that the Diamond had been off limits for so long had, of course, added to its notoriety and prestige. In 1959, the year before the successful ascent, a California team had camped under the face waiting for a break in the weather. They had simply not bothered about permission. Had they managed to climb the face, they probably would have been arrested. Over the following winter two of this team, Bob Kamps and Dave Rearick, assembled an impressive list of reasons why they should be allowed to attempt the Diamond. The Park Service, swayed by Northcutt and Kor's success on the Diagonal, relented.

Kamps and Rearick were well prepared. They came fresh from a month of Yosemite climbing and acclimated to the 14,000-foot altitude of the Diamond by repeating Northcutt's Diagonal. With the assistance of a support party (which the Park Service demanded for safety reasons), they carried their loads up the North Chimney and left them on the ledge, Broadway. From there the foreboding steepness of the Diamond, wreathed in clouds and weeping rivulets of water, offered no encouragement; they retreated to the comfort of the Chasm Lake hut for the night.

By 9:30 A.M. the next day they had regained Broadway and were on their way up the ever-steepening face. As they climbed the lower part of the wall, belay stances became less and less substantial. On the fifth lead a build-up of afternoon clouds suggested the possibility of a storm to the wary Californians, and they rappelled down to their bivouac on Broadway.

But no storm came. After a luxurious night's sleep, they prusiked up fixed ropes to their high point in the orange light of dawn. The second day brought difficult piton placement in a steep slot filled with irregular blocks. They noticed with awe that the haul bag hung out from the wall and came up without touching the rock. That night was spent huddled on a two-foot ledge. On the third day they were slowed by blocks of ice in the summit chimney, but they pressed anxiously for the top and arrived shortly after midday (V, 5.7 A4). On hand to greet them were several hardy newspaper reporters who had hiked up the back way in search of a scoop. The climb of the "forbidden" face on the widely known Longs Peak caught the popular imagination, and the victors were treated to a succession of parades, banquets, and television appearances.

The bold grab of the Diamond by "unknown" outsiders chastened the Colorado climbers. Resentment over the affair lingered on for several years. However, as Johnson and Northcutt had by now faded from view, only Kor was capable of initiating a climb of this magnitude, and he had spent the summer away from the home front. The moral was obvious. The Californians, far from being bolting fanatics, were a force to be reckoned with. They might swoop down at any time to pick off climbs that "belonged" to Coloradans. It was a lesson that Kor did not forget.

The end of the 1950s marked the termination of the postwar era in American rock climbing. The era saw important patterns of development echoed in California, Colorado, and the East Coast. Climb-ers were still few in numbers and increasing only gradually. However, the breakdown of social barriers allowed the entry of a new element. The brash newcomers were impatient with yesterday's methods, yesterday's gods. Under this new impetus, standards, techniques, and the psychological frontier were pushed ahead. By the end of the era the chronic isolation and parochial attitudes of the climbers also began to change; climbers were now curious about what was happening elsewhere. The summer of 1960 was an important one for the spread of ideas. Kor and the Vulgarians made the pilgrimage to Yosemite; Californians took the Diamond from the Coloradans and showed up in the Shawangunks. And 1960 was also

Summit of Longs Peak after the Diamond. From left: Ted Dutton of the *Denver Post*, Dave Rearick and Bob Kamps. Courtesy Bob Kamps.

important from another standpoint. The rock climbers were now curious about alpine climbing. Yosemite regulars visited the Tetons, where their technical ability amazed the locals. Kor, the Vulgarians, and climbers from the Pacific Northwest converged for a big season in Canada's Bugaboos. With the rock climbers of 1960 we will now turn to the strange world of alpinism.

REFERENCES

Accidents in North American Mountaineering. New York: American Alpine Club, 1960.

Ament, Pat, and Cleveland McCarty. *High over Boulder.* Boulder: Pruett, 1970.

Carter, Harvey. "Letter to the Editor." *Summit* 3(7) (July 1957): 29.

Dornan, David. *Rock Climbing Guide to the Boulder, Colorado, Area.* Boulder: Outdoors United, 1961.

Dumais, Dick. "Shawangunks." *Mountain*, no. 21 (May 1972), p. 23.

Fricke, Walter W., Jr. *A Climber's Guide to Rocky Mountain National Park.* Boulder: Paddock, 1971.

Gran, Arthur. *A Climber's Guide to the Shawangunks.* New York: American Alpine Club, 1964.

Hébert, André. *Alpinisme au Québec.* Montreal: Editions du Jour, 1972.

Johnson, Dale L. "Two New Routes on the Maiden." *T & T*, no. 440 (Aug. 1955), p. 139.

Loughman, Mike. "Letter to the Editor." *Summit* 3(11) (Nov. 1957): 21.

Northcutt, Ray. "Hallett's Peak." *Summit* 3(1) (Jan. 1957): 17.

———. "A First Ascent on the North Face of Hallett Peak." *AAJ* 11 (1959): 233.

———. "The Diagonal, East Face of Longs Peak." *AAJ* 12 (1960): 129.

Poisson, Bernard. *Escalades, Guide des Parois Région de Montreal.* Montreal: La Cordée, 1971.

Rearick, David. "The First Ascent of the Diamond, East Face of Longs Peak." *AAJ* 12 (1961): 297.

Rubin, Al, and Paul Ross. "Vox for Vulgaria." *Mountain*, no. 21 (May 1972), p. 18.

Sessions, George. "Letter to the Editor." *Summit* 4(4) (April 1958): 23.

Walton, Harold F. "Through the Window." *T & T*, no. 386 (Feb. 1951), p. 15.

Wiessner, F. H. "Early Rock Climbing in the Shawangunks." *Appalachia.* 33 (June 1960): 18.

Williams, Richard C. *Shawangunk Rock Climbs.* New York: American Alpine Club, 1972.

The North Face

High on a wall in the North Cascades are two tiny figures. The upper one crampons up an ice gully and hammers in a belay piton. He sets his pack on a ledge and hurriedly pulls up the rope. His shout "On belay!" is almost lost in the amphitheater of the wall. As the second climbs up, the leader checks his watch and the build-up of afternoon clouds. Will the weather hold? Will they make it down tonight?

This is an alpine team at work on a mountain wall. Is what they are doing really different from rock climbing, or is it the same thing with a handicap of pack and mountain boots?

The essential difference is one of environment.

The rock climber operates on outcrops and foothills. The environment is a friendly one. Approaches to the crags are rapid, and descents are often no more than a hike down a well-trod path. Weather is seldom the unpredictable force of the mountains. If the party is caught in a rain squall, a few rappels will bring them down to the ground. Rock climbing is gregarious. There is seldom any "solitude of the hills" but rather an experience shared with other parties in the area.

The alpine climber contends with a harsh environment. The approach commonly takes the better part of a day or more, and the descent may be a difficult undertaking in its own right. The consequences of a storm may be serious, and there is the probability of rock and ice falls. In the event of an accident there is seldom anyone in the area to call out a rescue group. Often there is none to call; the alpine party must be self-sufficient.

The rock climber has reduced the overall difficulties in order to concentrate on the technical problems of the rock. It is apparent that major advances in skill will take place on rock climbs. The alpinist faces such an array of difficulties that the chief concern is getting up. The need to move fast precludes working on a difficult technical problem for several hours. The differences in overall experience and outlook are such that rock climbers and alpinists frequently keep to their own specialties. The rock climber is the purist. Technique is paramount; approach hikes, heavy packs, bivouac gear all impede the action. The alpinist accepts these impediments because they are part

231

of the total experience, but a twenty-foot boulder problem may leave him cold. He needs all-round skill, not a flawless climbing technique.

Having made these distinctions, it must be admitted that the dividing line between "rock climb" and "alpine" is often arbitrary. The Diamond on Longs Peak, which we have dealt with under Colorado rock climbs, is as alpine as most Teton climbs. Several Teton routes are not alpine at all. In borderline cases it is helpful to consider the climbers' self-image. Kamps and Rearick made a "rock climb" on the Diamond because they were rock climbing specialists. Teton climbing may be treated as alpine because the climbers viewed themselves as mountaineers.

The first postwar alpine climb to concern us epitomizes everything alpine. There is no ambiguity over Devils Thumb. The 9,077-foot peak is one of the most dramatic in the Alaska Coast Range. A shaft of light-colored granite thrust out of the Stikine Icecap, it is readily seen from the Inside Passage. In 1937, the year after his Waddington climb, Fritz Wiessner penetrated into the icecap. He was accompanied by Donald Brown and Bestor Robinson, leader of the Sierra Club party on Mount Waddington, but this strong party achieved nothing. Continued bad weather frustrated their climbing plans.

After the teenage Beckey brothers so daringly made the second ascent of Mount Waddington, Wiessner and Fred Beckey corresponded and swapped experiences. The subject of the alluring Devils Thumb came up, and they agreed to attempt the peak when the war was over. Early in July 1946, Beckey, Brown, and Wiessner relayed loads toward the Stikine Icecap. Thrashing through the underbrush of devils club and slide alder, Wiessner slipped and twisted his knee. He continued to the icecap, but climbing was out of the question for him. The disconsolate team headed back to the coastal port of Wrangell.

Beckey had planned a trip for later in the summer with Mount Rainier guide Bob Craig. He wired Craig and ex-mountain-troop-instructor Cliff Schmidtke to drop everything and get up to Alaska. A week later the optimistic trio disembarked from a little boat, making the weekly run up the Stikine River to Telegraph Creek, B.C., and made their way to the equipment cache. To their amazement it was pilfered. Mountain goats had devoured much of the food, including the powdered milk, container and all. Luckily for the goats they were far away, but three ptarmigan were not so fortunate. Schmidtke felled them with stones.

Before tackling Devils Thumb, the trio climbed Kates Needle in a marathon twenty-two hour roundtrip. Then bad weather set in. With an intervening dash down to the Stikine River to fetch supplies, it was more than a week before they could reconnoiter the east ridge of Devils Thumb. When they left camp at 3 A.M., clouds were moving in once more. Reckoning they had time for

Devils Thumb, Alaska-British Columbia border, with Cat's Ear Spire at left. The east ridge forms the right skyline; the 1946 party climbed snow and rock on the near side of the east ridge. *Dick Culbert*.

a quick look, they pushed up the initial snow slopes and cached an assortment of gear. Soaked by icy rain, they sat out the next day in camp and expected still another day of bad weather. They were surprised the following morning by clearing skies. Away from camp at midmorning, they worked up the southeast face and gained a notch in the east ridge. They changed into tennis shoes and battled wet rock along the narrow and exposed ridge. Rock and ice pitons came into play on the hardest sections. At dark they were well positioned for the top, but the morning sky revealed another change in the weather. They stamped their feet to restore circulation, gathered up their equipment, and headed toward the top. Within minutes snow was falling. The consequences of becoming pinned down by a storm were all too obvious. Reluctantly, they retreated off the mountain.

It was a vicious storm that blew in and confined them to camp for the next three days. When it was over, avalanching snow cut short their third attempt on Devils Thumb. Time was running out. In three days they had to catch the Stikine River boat on its weekly run to civilization. Doggedly, they set out once again at 3 A.M. Quickly, because of their familiarity with the route, they reached the narrow summit just past midday. They had made the first highly technical climb in Alaska.

Beckey was next attracted to Brussels Peak, an isolated 1,000-foot limestone tower in the Canadian Rockies that had defeated the best prewar climbers. Boldly standing out on the skyline of the Banff-Jasper highway, Brussels provides an example of the difference in technical standards that exists between the mountains and the local rocks. Had Brussels been situated in Yosemite, it would have been climbed in the late 1930s because the rock climbing was well within the capabilities of the prewar climbers. Yet Brussels is in the mountains. After a long, arduous approach, the dark and gloomy cliffs of rotten rock wreathed in cloud are quite a different proposition from Yosemite's sun-warmed granite. By 1948 the list of those who had turned back on Brussels read like a *Who's Who* of American climbing.

Among the defeated was Frank Smythe, a mountaineer in the traditional British mold who had been a power on the prewar Mount Everest attempts. He was based in the Rockies as an instructor with the Canadian mountains troops. After the war he returned to attempt the second ascent of Mount Alberta but retreated in foul weather. He was much impressed by the difficulties of the climb and the lack of belays on the steep limestone. On Brussels Peak he was twice turned back and gave his opinion that it was harder than any peak in Europe.

Posing the age-old question whether Brussels was climbable, Smythe wrote in 1948, "Not by normal mountaineering methods—not, that is, without taking the life in the hands and that is *not* mountaineering. Only, I think, by 'direct aid' methods—that is, by the employment of pitons (iron spikes) and the other paraphernalia of the mountaineering steeplejack."

Steeplejacks or not, an indecent number of good teams tried and failed on Brussels Peak. In 1948 parties led by John Oberlin and Fred Beckey were turned back. When Teton guide Jiggs Lewis and photographer Ray Garner went into the peak, they learned that John and Ruth Mendenhall were ahead of them with a week's supply of food. Near the base of the peak Garner and Lewis met the Mendenhalls coming out. They had retreated at the "first step." The mountain was waiting, and Garner was hellbent on climbing it. He had obtained an advance on a movie to be titled *First Ascent.*

On their initial reconnaissance Garner and Lewis passed the first step, the previous high point. After a rest day they returned to the fray with Ed George. Weighed down by bulky camera equipment, they made slow progress and were caught by a thunderstorm above the first step. Lightning was striking all around them, and Lewis wedged himself into a crack. Although not then appreciated, a crack is the last place to shelter from lightning; electrical discharges follow lines of weakness. Happily, the lightning died down, and the climbers eased out of their hiding places. Within sight of their goal, they faced a difficult decision. Prudence suggested retreat, but if they

had been prudent they would not have been on Brussels in the first place. While George waited, Garner and Lewis pushed on to the top.

The retreat was a disorderly affair harassed by wind and snow. When they reached George, he was suffering from exposure. In their numbed and exhausted state, they abandoned two ropes as they fled the mountain. Garner summarized the epic on Brussels Peak, "We had taken the old black devil, and we had taken him under very difficult conditions."

But not according to Frank Smythe. In his book *Climbs in the Canadian Rockies,* he took issue with the four expansion bolts and pitons used, saying that those who used them "have not the courage or capacity to climb without." Smythe's principal complaint was that pitons eliminated all risk. He conjectured, wrongly, that on no part of the upper climb "could either of them have been killed." (This was a reversal on his previous stand on risk taking.) He argued, "Supposing it was the regular thing for all mountaineers to use pitons on their climbs, would it not be a sign of the degeneracy of man?"

Pitons were by then accepted throughout the climbing community excepting the British and Canadian Alpine clubs. We might dismiss Smythe's views as dyed-in-the-wool conservatism, but he went on to raise a crucial point, "It is knowing where to draw the line that counts in life. Does the sportsman take an automatic weapon to kill his tiger? He does not. He shoots with the same weapon as his ancestors." The problem is one that has perpetually troubled mountaineers. Where *does* a sportsman draw the line in using the new equipment that is constantly becoming available? An engine is disallowed in a yachting race, yet a compass is essential. So mountaineers consider helicopter-assisted climbs unacceptable and a rope fundamental. In between there are many shades of gray.

Pitons and Aid Climbing in the 1950s

It is important to distinguish between pitons used as protection and pitons used as direct aid. Smythe did not do so; he disliked them in any form. However, in 1928 he was on the first ascent of the west buttress of North Wales's Clogwyn d'ur Arddu. The leader placed a piton, and Smythe noted, "I must own to a vast feeling of satisfaction on finding myself attached to it."

As climbers attempted more difficult routes, it became essential to arrange adequate protection. The British rock climbers of the interwar period relied on primitive methods while their European counterparts used pitons. In Britain skills improved slowly while in Europe they advanced dramatically. American climbers of the 1950s used numerous protection pitons on routes where today's climbers will need less protection. Of course, due to increasing skills, a scary lead by 1950s standards is less troublesome today.

The 1950s climbers were also quick to use aid where they could not free climb. Today most of the routes done with aid during that era are climbed free, and it is considered bad form to force a route with aid where a more competent climber, or even tomorrow's climber, may be able to do without it. The current attitude may suggest that the 1950s climbers used aid too freely. To appraise the situation, we should look at the problem through their eyes.

Aid climbing was then known as "sixth class." The very name "sixth class" hinted that here was something beyond the ordinary. From the dramatic books on the great climbs of Europe the leading American climbers learned that *sesto grado* was the ultimate in difficulty, a world where sleepless bivouacs, storms, and tragedy combined in an almost unimaginable Wagnerian world of suffering and heroism. If you wanted to climb the north walls of the Alps (and who in fantasy at least did not?), then aid had to be mastered.*

*A distinction must be made between a European *sesto grado* or VI and an American Grade VI. The European gradings are equivalent to our *class* rating system; their V corresponds to 5.7, and their VI to 5.9. A European VI gives no indication of the length or seriousness of the climb. This information must be gleaned from the route description or, of course, a *look* at the climb. The French, however, *do* add an overall assessment to the rating. In their system *Extrêmement Difficile* is comparable with our Grade VI.

In the 1950s difficult climbing was relatively new in North America, and aid climbs were only attempted by the best climbers. Everyone was a novice on aid, and almost every aid climb was an all-out experience. Standing in slings attached to a piton driven up under a roof was very exciting. What if the piton pulled out? Suppose you fell from the lip of a roof and hung in space suspended from your waist. Could you get back onto the rock, or would you suffocate? The fears were real. Although the earlier climbers dealt with the identical piece of rock as today's climbers, they confronted an entirely different set of problems. They were entering a new world and inventing the sport as they went. Because of them and the immense fears they overcame, today's climbers are able to extend the frontiers still farther.

In 1949 Fred Beckey turned to the peaks of the Juneau Icefield north of Devils Thumb. Other climbers had been into this spectacular area. When the leader of a rival group heard of Beckey's plans, he wrote ordering Beckey to keep away from "his" peaks. It was the incentive Beckey needed.

Once in the area of the dramatic Michaels Sword and Devils Paw, the party was prevented from making any climbs of note because of two weeks of bad weather. Beckey and Graham Matthews then flew north for a prearranged meeting with another group. However, this group was stalled by floe ice in Disenchantment Bay; they had made even less progress than the Juneau party. After urgent discussions it was agreed to cut their losses and head down to the Juneau Icefield. A few of the group flew south while others bartered their service as fishermen for passage on a fishing boat.

Among the climbers that finally assembled on the icefield were Henry Pinkham and the irreverent humorist Bill Putnam. On this second Juneau trip there was again plenty of bad weather. While Putnam and others passed the time playing bridge, Beckey kept up a barrage of jokes and comment. Patience wore thin, and he was banished from the communal tent. When the weather finally cleared, Beckey and partner picked off Michaels Sword, and Putnam, Pinkham, and two others went after the Devils Paw.

The gaping bergschrund that defended the Devils Paw took a couple of hours to negotiate, and the nervous Pinkham had to be urged across by the time-honored vigorous pull on the rope. With Pinkham balking at the exposure, it was late in the afternoon before the party reached the col that gave access to the summit. After checking out the route, they returned to camp.

The following morning the team set out again. By tacit agreement Pinkham remained in camp. The climbing was difficult all the way to the summit, and the trio did not arrive back in camp until past midnight. Generous-hearted Pinkham was the first to greet the victors.

Despite his failure on the Devils Paw, Pinkham

had an impressive roster of climbs behind him. When the august council of the American Alpine Club received his membership application, it included one of the finest climbing records they had reviewed for some time. They were only too delighted to recruit members of such caliber and passed on the applicant with enthusiasm.

Pinkham's sponsors listed his address as Petersham, Massachusetts, where they had arranged with the postmaster to forward any mail. This proved to be their undoing. After the council meeting, club secretary Bradley Gilman was writing up the minutes at his home in nearby Barre, Massachusetts. In going over the applications again, it struck him as odd that he had never met or even heard of Pinkham. If so experienced a mountaineer were in the neighborhood, he would surely know him. Puzzled, Gilman went over the application in detail. The only climber he could associate with Petersham was practical joker Putnam. Suddenly it dawned on him that the unsuspecting hierarchy of the club had elected Putnam's malamute dog to membership. The matter was held over to the next council meeting, at which time the council reversed themselves on Pinkham's application, yet not without a touch of regret. His climbs were all genuine, and his politics would be no threat to the status quo.

The North Cascades

During the postwar decade the Cascades were the least understood of the major alpine areas in North America. With a wealth of unknown ground to discover, the local climbers tended to stay put, and the area was little visited by outsiders. An exception to the lack of outside understanding of the

The Seattle climbers' weekend, circa 1950. From left: Don Wilde, Fred Beckey, Pete Schoening. Courtesy Fred Beckey.

area was Mount Rainier, a popular pilgrimage for mountaineers from all over the country. To most outsiders the graceful bulk of Mount Rainier rising beyond Seattle *was* the Cascades; their interest went no further. But Rainier is only a fraction of the story. The most interesting alpine regions lie in the North Cascades up to and across the British Columbia border, where the peaks carry names such as Challenger, Fury, Slesse, and Shuksan. This region is the most alpine of all climbing areas in the lower forty-eight states.

Fred Beckey was chief among those looking for the hidden climbing gems in the North Cascades, a labor in which he was joined by a succession of partners, most of whom could not, or would not, stay the pace. Among those who stuck to it were Pete Schoening and Ralph Widrig. All three shared a fondness for the unclimbed rock spires that were then all the rage. Predominantly Seattle residents, Beckey and his pals were working their way through school or held regular jobs. Consequently, they were doing something unusual in North America, weekend alpine climbing. After work on Friday the marathon began with a hectic drive over highway, dirt road, and finally logging road. Saturday they fought the brush on long-forgotten mining trails or through trackless valleys to reach a high camp. At the first light on Sunday came the climb, then the descent back to the car and the long drive through the night. Numb with fatigue, the drivers rolled their cars more than

once. The climbers sometimes arrived back in Seattle about the time responsible citizens were going to work. Beckey was twice awakened during Monday morning sales meetings.

An essential goal in climbing is to maintain a degree of uncertainty, especially where people are trying to advance the limits of the sport. A critical climber might have protested when he read an article called "An Alternative to Planned Bivouacs" in 1951 about a new system of fixing ropes on routes. An umbilical cord of rope was strung from the gradually advancing high point all the way to the safety of the ground. With the climbers able to retreat and return to their high point at will, bivouacs on the face were a thing of the past. On the traditional alpine climb with bivouacs, the advocates of the new system pointed out, there

were the ever-present dangers of bad weather isolating the climbers, of "physical and mental deterioration . . . improper rest and food," and of the constant nervous strain. With fixed ropes, climbers could start each day from a comfortable base camp, and they were no longer at the mercy of storm. In short, the climb was "more enjoyable." However, enjoyment is not the hallmark of great climbs.

It can be argued that fixed ropes enable people to attempt climbs which are beyond them, using the classic alpine approach, climbs which they should leave to others. It can also be argued that in this case fixed ropes were a sensible approach. These routes were worked on mostly on weekends.

Typical of the climbs put in with fixed ropes was

the 1,800-foot east face of the North Peak of Mount Index. At 5,900 feet, Mount Index is one of the lower Cascade peaks on which trees, brush, heather, and lichens may be as difficult as and certainly more exasperating than the rock itself. Beckey had prospected the brushy lower section of the climb in 1941. He returned in 1951 with Schoening and others, and the route was established to around midheight over two separate days. With ropes in place, just one day was needed for the final push to the summit (IV, 5.7).

The majority of the Cascades climbs were still done in the classic manner. The two routes initiated by Dave Harrah on the 4,000-foot north face of Mount Johannesburg stand out as good classical mountaineering. Beckey's and Schoening's 1950 traverse of the three peaks of Mount Index (V), where the Middle Peak was climbed for the first time, was a bold undertaking.

In spite of these efforts, adventurous mountaineering was far from established in the Cascades by the mid-1950s. Outsiders regarded the area as backward and conservative. Although much of this reputation was due to hearsay and lack of understanding, there were some grounds for it. The Northwest was the home of what might be termed the "American Climbing Theory." Badges were awarded and special symbols placed beside one's name in the club journal for climbing a few simple peaks. Caution was the word in climbing practice. Parties of fewer than three or four persons were considered unacceptably risky by the Seattle Mountaineers (as a result of this taboo several climbers appear as makeweights on the pages of the club journal), and the traditional ten-point crampon was preferred over the newer and more efficient twelve-point variety. Tools such as pitons and crampons were used primarily for added safety, not to extend the limits of the possible. This was hardly the atmosphere to nurture young tigers.

To the east of the traditional Cascade climbing centers and divorced from them were ranchers Gene Prater and Dave Mahre and their friends in the Sherpa Climbing Club of the Ellensburg-Yakima area. They opened up a series of routes on their home mountain and the premier peak of the central Cascades, granitic Mount Stuart. Notable among these routes were the Ice Cliff Glacier (1957) and the Grade IV northeast face. Keenly interested in ice climbing, they turned their sights on the north side of Mount Rainier.

The general lack of climbing achievement in the Northwest can best be gauged from the fact that on Mount Rainier the best climbs of the 1930s, the Ptarmigan and Liberty ridges, had not been attempted during the following twenty years. It fell to Prater and his friends to make the second ascents and in 1957 to climb the ridge that bounds the Willis Wall, the much sought-after Curtis Ridge.

The Sherpas were dissatisfied with the performance of the existing ice climbing gear. They welded their hinged, twelve-point crampons into a solid unit, which was more effective when kicked into hard ice. They then had the confidence to climb wholly on the front points. Front-pointing was first used by Austrian and German alpinists in the 1920s. This technique demands steady nerves and strong calf muscles as the whole body weight is concentrated on the front of the boot. Under the influence of Bavarian immigrant Marcel Schuster, the Sherpas developed the idea of two-man rope teams rapidly leap frogging up steep ice from one stance to the next. The theory was that the momentum kept muscle fatigue to a lower level than the traditional methodical advance with step-cutting.

With their fondness for mixed rock and ice climbing, the Sherpas had to deal with rockfall. Up to this time the usual protection was a newspaper or extra mitts stuffed under a wool hat. Mahre and Prater used construction hard hats on climbs. They were possibly the first Americans to do so.

Other climbers who fell outside the conservative mold were John Dudra and European Fips Broda. In the winter of 1955 they climbed remote Mount Slesse (V). Beckey was also entirely his own man. In 1957 he climbed the much discussed Coleman Glacier Headwall on Mount Baker, the landmark volcanic peak of northern Washington. Hoping as always for the first ascent, Beckey was astonished to see footsteps when he exited from the face. Ed Cooper's party had beat him to the climb. Beckey was ever on the lookout for promising partners, and he soon had Cooper in tow. Over the next few years they put up a series of good climbs together, including the northwest face of Forbidden Peak and the north face of Mount Baring.

In 1951 Schoening and Richard Berge had established the route partway up the third of Baring's four final steps. In spite of repeated attempts, on one of which Berge fell to his death, no one had been able to push the route higher. In 1960 Beckey and Cooper were joined in another attempt by Don Claunch (Gordon), a man who went through cycles of interest in religion and mysticism. He once made a mysterious solo attempt on Alaska's Mount Saint Elias, approaching the mountain from the sea by row boat. In preparation for Baring, they spent several days cutting a trail through the brushy cliffs of the lower wall, fixing ropes over the worst sections. On the second day of their summit bid they reached the previous high point, sixty feet up the third step, where they spent six

Sherpa Climbing Club, early 1950s. From left: Gene Prater, Dave Mahre, Bill Pater. *Gene Prater.*

Dave Mahre climbing hard snow-ice on front points.
Gene Prater.

hours trying to place a bolt in the "flint-hard" rock. After a heated argument with Claunch, Beckey left for his job in the city on the morning of the third day. Cooper and Claunch spent several more fruitless hours drilling bolt holes until they managed to place a knife-blade piton. It took them two days to complete the lead, and it was not until the fifth day that they were on top.

The Tetons

With their familiar skyline of picture-postcard mountains and their stirring history of great men and great deeds, the Tetons have some of the atmosphere of the Alps. Ever since the achievements of Underhill and Durrance the range had been the preeminent area of high standard mountaineering on the continent. In general, the prewar climbers did not return after the war, but their achievements were strongly felt. Several of their routes remained unrepeated until the mid-1950s, and Durrance's climbs were looked upon as bordering the limits of the possible. The question was not whether the postwar mountaineers could surpass Durrance, but whether they could equal him.

The Grand Teton is the peak that first captures the eye. If you are a mountaineer, the somber north face will rivet your attention. North faces occupy a special place in mountaineering history. The advances in the Alps during the 1930s took place to a large extent on the northern precipices of peaks such as the Matterhorn and Grandes Jorasses. There is a definite mystique about these cold and lifeless walls that the sun seldom touches.

Since Durrance and the Petzoldt brothers had climbed it in the 1930s, the North Face of the Grand Teton had moved from climb to legend. It is important to understand the aura that surrounds certain climbs and mountains at various stages in the evolution of climbing. Imagined fears and difficulties may be even more of a barrier than real ones. The reputation of a route may be sufficient to keep people off it for years. When the courage is finally summoned and the goal committed, the climber may lie awake at night, stomach tense and heart racing. Deep inside, he may be defeated before he comes to grip with the route. The retreat later in the day is a foregone conclusion. No less than any other individual, the climber must believe in success before it will happen.

Two guides who cast longing glances at the North Face of the Grand Teton were Art Gilkey and Dick Pownall. Durrance and the Petzoldt brothers had traversed off to the north ridge below the final headwall. For a new generation the challenge was the headwall. Spurred on by news of a rival party, Gilkey and Pownall joined forces with Ray Garner in 1949.

Late one August evening they placed a high camp on the Teton Glacier in the shadow of the North Face. At the first light they were working up through chimneys and cracks, snow and ice. Loose rock lay on the ledges, and water ran over the face. The only sounds to break the silence of the vast northern amphitheater were their own communications and the occasional whirr of falling rock. They were alone on the notorious North Face. Here and there they came across relics of earlier parties: rusted pitons left by Petzoldt and

North Face of the Grand Teton. The 1936 party traversed to the north ridge via the second ledge. In 1949 the climbers stayed on the face until the fourth ledge and in 1953 they provided a direct finish. *Gene White.*

Durrance, an abandoned carabiner, a piece of rope sling. By midafternoon they were below the unknown upper portion of the wall. Pownall led up to a narrow ledge and tried to traverse along it into a chimney. But the ledge tapered to nothing, and he could not make the move around the corner. Unwilling to give in, he placed a piton and with tension from the rope wormed around the corner and into the chimney. At 10 P.M. the three climbers struck a match to sign their names in the summit register.

The strongest climbers of the day had spent seventeen hours on the face. There were stories of desperate pitches and slipping tennis shoes. There was falling rock and ice. The reputation of the climb, referred to in awed terms as "The North Face," was firmly established. It was a never-to-be-repeated horror that was joked about rather than seriously considered. But by 1953 a new group of Teton climbers were ready to test the "climb of climbs": Park ranger Richard Emerson, who learned his climbing in the Tenth Mountain Division, and guides Willi Unsoeld and Leigh Ortenburger. Emerson was in the lead at the traverse. Edging along the ledge, he peered around the corner and glimpsed one of Pownall's pitons. He snapped into it at full reach, then hung from his arms and moved arond the corner. He had led the notorious "pendulum pitch" free without realizing it. Just below the summit they straightened the route even further by climbing the "V

gully." The final touches were added to the classic North Face.

In this same summer of 1953 Ortenburger and fellow guide Mike Brewer made the second ascent of Durrance's west face of the Grand Teton (IV) while Emerson, Ortenburger, and Don Decker put up a superb climb on Mount Moran, the long and elegant south buttress (IV, 5.7 A3). Durrance's climbs were at last equaled, and Emerson, Ortenburger, and Unsoeld established themselves as the new powers in the Tetons. Theirs was a thorough mountaineering skill. Emerson and Unsoeld went on to major feats in the Himalayas, and Ortenburger became America's foremost Andean climber.

The North Face of the Grand Teton continued to dominate the range and to hold the budding hard man in its sway. Because it is a straightforward route today, we should know why it was then so important. The North Face *looked* terrible, and it inherited the alpine north wall mystique. From accounts of the quasilegendary ascents it was known that falling ice and rock were to be expected, and American climbers had yet to come to terms with this hazard. Although the climb is straightforward under good conditions, in bad weather it can be a harrowing experience. It was the harrowing experience that climbers heard about, expected, and indeed *wanted* to believe in.

It made sense for ambitious climbers with short vacations, or a few weeks between school and

Willi Unsoeld on the North Face of the Grand Teton, 1953. *Leigh Ortenburger*.

summer jobs, to head for the accessible Tetons. If any area in North America could be thought of as a mountaineering center, it was here. An important sense of continuity was provided by the professional guides. They were dedicated climbers, thankful for the money and the chance to live in the mountains. For years the leading climbers were either guides or Park Service rangers. Much prestige attached to both jobs. It was quite something to be a climbing ranger or Teton guide.

Every summer a keen group was on hand for hard climbs and good times. A Dartmouth contingent that centered around Barry Corbet and Jake Breitenbach carried on the Teton climbing tradition begun by Durrance. Loosely associated with them were Bill Buckingham and John Dietschey. Their home was an abandoned Civilian Conservation Corps camp, a special place at the foot of a fabled mountain range. Bivouacked inside a disused incinerator for the 1957 season and getting by on fifty cents a day were Southern Californians Yvon Chouinard and Ken Weeks. They were drawn into climbing by nest-raiding experiences as falconers.

The longer and more obvious climbs in the Tetons had largely been pioneered by the mid-1950s. The emerging Teton climbers had a strong background in rock climbing. They turned to the subsidiary peaks and canyon walls and initiated an era of specialization on rock. The deliberate search for difficult rock was something new in the Tetons, long regarded as the center of United States alpinism. For a brief period these new routes were deemphasized in written reports because of the feeling that they belonged "more to the art of rock climbing than to mountaineering." Typical of the areas under attack were the steep northern walls of Garnet Canyon, the southern ramparts of Disappointment Peak. These climbs were not intended as routes to the summit of Disappointment Peak but were hard climbs for their own sake. Once on the plateau at the head of the canyon, most parties headed down. Ranging up to 1,000 feet, the better climbs included Irene's Arête (5.8) in 1957, where Dietschey was partnered by one of America's best women climbers, Irene Ortenburger, and in 1958 Chouinard's and Bob Kamps's Satisfaction Buttress (5.9 A2).

Coincident with the new climbers, the general level of competence in the Tetons was rising. A record was set in 1958 when the North Face of the Grand Teton and the south ridge of Mount Moran both had five ascents. However, there was by no means a flood of climbers, for there were seldom more than twenty residents in camp at any one time. If newcomers arrived disgorging ropes and boots from their car, they were soon surrounded by the residents. The climbing community was so small that they would either know them personally or at least have some acquaintance in common. Before long a pot of tea was on the boil, and everyone got in on the latest news and rumor: A party was overdue on the north ridge; Mount Robson was yet to be climbed that year and conditions were reckoned to be awful; the Harvard team was supposed to be knocking off first ascents in the Wind Rivers; and the guy in campsite twelve was just back from the Alps and selling off European gear.

Fred Beckey occasionally made brief appearances in the Tetons between sorties in Canada, the Northwest, and elsewhere. His true mountaineering genius, his ability to move rapidly over difficult ground, is illustrated by a bet that he made in 1959. The bet was whether he and Chouinard could climb a new route on Mount Owen from the campground and get back before dark. All the way up the climb, the Crescent Arête, Chouinard had to hustle to stay with Beckey. On top Beckey decided the obvious descent was by the Northeast Snowfields, at that time more ice than snow. They sailed past another party, who were setting up rappels from ice pitons. Hours after

Just off the North Face, Richard Emerson, Willi Unsoeld and Leigh Ortenburger pause on the summit of the Grand Teton. Courtesy Willi Unsoeld.

they collected their winnings, a small band crawled into camp and related how two madmen had come streaming out of nowhere on the dread Northeast Snowfields.

In 1960 Yosemite climbers Royal Robbins and Joe Fitschen arrived to check out the Tetons. Cocky and confident, they raced up several of the hard Teton rock climbs. The locals were impressed, but the visit had more positive results than merely burning up routes. It led to an important crosscurrent of ideas and helped end the chronic insularity of both areas. Teton regulars were very active that year. Ever on the lookout for major lines on the big peaks, Ortenburger picked off the Grand Teton's Northwest Chimney (IV, 5.8), where he was partnered by his wife Irene and local resident Dave Dornan. A few days later Chouinard, Fitschen, and Robbins repeated this climb and finished up via the hardest pitches of Durrance's west face. The winds of change were blowing in the home of American mountaineering.

The Mountains of Canada

During the postwar years mountaineering in Canada's inland ranges continued much as before. Ever willing to beat a new track, the hardcore Canadian explorers continued to search out peaks and ranges that others were unwilling or incapable of going after. Tough and grizzled ex-major Rex Gibson and Sterling Hendricks were typical of the breed. However, as the 1950s began, technical

Mount Robson. The ice-encrusted Emperor Ridge is at left; the normal route picks its way through the icefall on the right. The two branches of the Wishbone Arête are directly below the summit. *Ed Cooper.*

skills remained at a low level. The Canadians had yet to put an all-Canadian party onto the summit of their nemesis, Mount Waddington. In the Rockies Mount Robson resisted all attempts. After a gap of thirteen years climbers again reached its coveted summit in 1953. The lack of success on Robson was excused by the explanation that the peak was out of condition. It may be conjectured that the mountaineers were more out of condition. Mount Robson could not have resisted determined attacks for so long.

Ever since Walter Schauffelberger narrowly failed on Robson's Wishbone Arête in 1913, numerous attempts had been launched against it. In 1951 Fred Ayres and John Oberlin were stopped short of Schauffelberger's high point by granular snow lying over ice. Had Ayres succeeded, it would have been a fitting climax to a career that ranged from Robson to the Southwest, the Alps, and the Andes. A modest man, by the mid-1950s he had one of the most impressive mountain records in America, a record largely unknown and wholly unsung.

In 1955 Ayres had a good climbing season in the Rockies partnered by Don Claunch and Californian Dick Irvin. Irvin was one of the first climbing bums. He was also one of the most adventurous. He evolved a two-year cycle of climbing: a summer in North America, a winter in the New Zealand Alps, the next spring in the Himalayas, followed by climbs in the Alps on the journey home. It was a grueling schedule.

With good weather in the Rockies during the first part of August 1955, Ayres and his companions began to think of Mount Robson. Claunch was hot to climb the Wishbone Arête, but Ayres could not be talked into yet another try. He and Irvin climbed the Kain Route. Claunch found willing partners in Tahquitz specialist Mike Sherrick and UCLA medical student Harvey Firestone. They set up a camp on Robson's west flank and then waited on the worsening weather. On the second morning they moved across to the base of the mile-long ridge. With Sherrick making the hardest leads, the first day's climbing took them to a notch just below the two branches of the Wishbone. On the second day Claunch led up ice slopes to the ice-crusted gargoyles for which Robson's Wishbone and Emperor ridges are famous. Sheer ice slopes fell away to either side of the narrow arête; almost every gargoyle had to be taken directly. Time slipped away. Finally, stopped by a bulging ice wall 300 feet from the summit, they bivouacked where they stood.

They spent a cheerless night wondering how they were going to force the last few rope lengths. Force them they must. Retreat from such a position was unthinkable. At dawn the three shivering climbers, swathed in every last piece of clothing, got to grips with an ice chute. Claunch cut steps and placed pitons until he came to the crux, a vertical pitch of loose snow and rotten ice. After twenty-five feet of precarious stemming, he felt a wind blowing ice crystals in his face. It could only

Don Claunch on the Wishbone Arête. Deeply religious, he carried a bible throughout the climb. *Harvey Firestone.*

mean one thing. The windswept summit was just ahead. Forty-two years after Schauffelberger's gallant bid, the Wishbone (V) was at last climbed. Yet this fine climb did not open the eyes of others to the potential for technical climbing in the Canadian Rockies. The Rockies had a well-deserved reputation for rotten rock and a high proportion of "dog routes."

With the surge in rock climbing, the new climbers turned instead to the Bugaboos. Several of these peaks had been declared impossible. When that was disproved, it was said they had only one route. The reputation for difficulty, the compactness of the group, the reasonable access, and the superb granite attracted a growing number of "heavies" from all over the continent. Hans Kraus and Jim McCarthy came from the East, Bill Buckingham from the Tetons, and John Turner from

Montreal. The Bugaboos were the place to be.

Urging their Oldsmobile over the logging road that leads to the Bugaboos, the Vulgarian team arrived in 1959. Art Gran had an important rendezvous with impoverished Seattle climber Ed Cooper, who had the enviable knack of subsisting on soda crackers and chicken noodle soup. In preparation for their meeting, Cooper had written Gran listing every piece of equipment he owned including details of a secret weapon, a seventy-foot aid sling for solo climbing.

Prominently visible from Boulder Camp, the habitual climber's camp in the Bugaboos, are two showpiece peaks of the group, Bugaboo and Snowpatch spires. Both present menacingly steep eastern faces toward camp, faces on which to write part of the story of American climbing. Cooper and Gran's objective was the 1,300-foot east face of Bugaboo Spire. They spent several days climbing and fixing ropes to within 500 feet of the summit but then lost heart in the face of the continual difficulty and danger.

Even finer than Bugaboo is the east face of Snowpatch, which Cooper would have tried, but his former partner Fred Beckey had beat him to it. They had had a falling out and were now in active competition. Cooper continually tried to outfox Beckey. When they met, they fenced around the question of where each had just been. One would nonchalantly let slip the notion that he was just "hanging around" for a few days with nothing particular in mind. At the first opportunity the other would sneak off to get the jump on his rival.

Beckey and Munich alpinist Hank Mather spent four days hammering their crude assortment of homemade pitons and wood wedges* into the first four leads on the sheer lower part of Snowpatch's east face. They fixed ropes over this ground and then reached the summit in two and a half days of continuous effort (V, 5.7 A2). It was the most impressive rock wall yet climbed in the alpine mountains of North America.

An originator of the fixed-rope school in the Northwest, Beckey was isolated from the new skills and techniques of Yosemite. He chose to approach this alpine climb in a fixed-rope frame of reference. It was perhaps unfortunate that the subsequently published action pictures showed the climbers prusiking up their ropes rather than climbing. As skills advanced in later years, it became fashionable to joke about Beckey's fixed ropes. Had the best Yosemite climbers of the day climbed Snowpatch instead of Beckey, it is debatable whether they would have resorted to fixed ropes, but they remained in Yosemite. Beckey had

the vision and determination to climb such faces in the mountains.

No less illustrious than the previous year's climbers were those who showed up in the Bugaboos in 1960. Taking up residence in a narrow slit under a boulder was a lean and determined Cooper. Although later known as a connoisseur of bizarre literature, he lasted out a spell of bad weather this year on a heavy diet of Whitehead, Santayana, and Russell. Then he went back onto the face of Bugaboo Spire alone. On his third day on the face a drill bit jammed inside the holder. He had to use the same bit over and over until it was reduced to a useless fragment. With his supplies almost exhausted and his piton hammer coming apart, he went down for more equipment.

At camp he was surprised and not a little relieved to see his old partner Art Gran. They completed the route in slightly more than a day of climbing. Had Cooper stuck it out alone, it would have been a remarkable achievement.

Avid, impatient Layton Kor was also in the Bugaboos during the 1960 season. Back from his dismal venture in the Alps, he knocked off the east face of Pigeon Spire and the north face of Bugaboo in quick succession. A new day was coming to Canadian climbing.

---

*Sized from one to four inches, the wood wedge is a cheap and easily made alternative to today's angle piton. Wedges never found much favor in North America but are still used in Europe at the present time.

Snowpatch Spire. The 1940 route lies up the extreme left margin. The Beckey-Mather route on the east face reaches the left-hand summit directly from the glacier. *Ed Cooper*.

REFERENCES

"An Alternative to Planned Bivouacs." *Mountaineer* 43 (1951): 35.

Ayres, Fred D. "An Attempt on Mt. Robson." *AAJ* 8 (1952): 368.

Beckey, Fred. "New Climbs in the Alaska Coast Range." *AJ* 56 (1947): 139.

———. "In Spirit Land." *AAJ* 7 (1950): 441.

———. "Bugaboo Adventures." *AAJ* 12 (1960): 17.

Beckey, Fred, and Edward Cooper. "The North Face of Mount Baring." *AAJ* 12 (1961): 302.

Claunch, Don. "First 1953 Ascent of Mt. Robson." *CAJ* 37 (1954): 72.

———. "Ascent of the Wishbone Arête, Mt. Robson." *AAJ* 10 (1956): 1.

———. "The Wishbone at Last." *CAJ* 39 (1956): 92.

Cooper, Edward. "Bugaboo Spire, East Face." *AAJ* 12 (1961):383.

Craig, Robert. "Stikine Odyssey." *Mountaineer* 93 (Dec. 1946): 38.

———. "West of the Stikine." *CAJ* 30 (1947): 29.

Emerson, Richard M. "Class 6 in the Tetons." *SCB* 39(6) (June 1954): 27.

Garner, Raymond C. "The First Ascent of Brussels Peak." *AAJ* 7 (Jan. 1949): 115.

———. "The North Wall of the Grand." *AAJ* 8 (1951): 61.

Harrah, David. "A Fine Conditioning Climb." *AAJ* 8 (1952): 347.

Irving, R. L. G. "Trends in Mountaineering." *CAJ* 40 (1957): 53.

Kraus, Hans. " 'Artificial' Climbing in the Bugaboos and Cascades." *Harvard Mountaineering*, no. 13 (May 1957), p. 31.

Mendenhall, John D. "Climbing in Jasper Park, 1948." *SCB* 34 (June 1949): 144.

Molenaar, Dee. *The Challenge of Ranier*. Seattle: The Mountaineers, 1971.

Ortenburger, Leigh. "North Face of the Grand Teton." *AAJ* 9 (1954): 173.

———. "South Ridge of Mt. Moran." *AAJ* 9 (1954): 181.

———. "Disappointment Peak, South Ridges," *AAJ* 11 (1959): 307.

———. "Grand Teton, Northwest Chimney." *AAJ* 12 (1961): 375.

———. *A Climber's Guide to the Teton Range*. San Francisco: Sierra Club, 1965.

Putnam, William Lowell. "Across the Icefield to Juneau." *Appalachia* 27 (1949): 415.

Schoening, P. K. " 'Fixed' Routes on Faces." *AAJ* 8 (1952): 343.

Sherrick, Michael. "A New Route on Mount Robson." *SCB* 41(10) (Dec. 1956): 19.

Smythe, Frank S. *Climbs in the Canadian Rockies*. New York: Norton, (n.d.).

———. *Rocky Mountains*. London: Adam and Charles Black, 1948.

Thorington, J. Monroe. *A Climber's Guide to the Rocky Mountains of Canada*. New York: American Alpine Club, 1966.

Mount McKinley

We turn again to the inhospitable mountains stretching from the Alaska panhandle to Mount McKinley and the Alaska Range. These northern mountains are a distinct group from the climbing standpoint. They are the biggest, least accessible peaks on the continent, as far removed from the Shawangunks as the 10,000 meters is removed from the 100-meter dash.

Mountaineers may approach Alaskan climbing in two different ways. They may regard it as alpinism under worse conditions; the coefficient of suffering is higher. Or they may regard it as expeditionary climbing, a cousin of Himalayan mountaineering, where a party will spend several weeks establishing a line of camps up the mountain. The summit is then taken in a quick dash from the highest camp. In the prewar years both approaches were used in Alaska although the more prominent climbs were usually undertaken in expedition style. On the long and generally straightforward routes then climbed, supplies could be ferried from camp to camp during indifferent weather. When the postwar mountaineers turned to these peaks, they had the precedent of expedition climbing before them.

Apart from Mount McKinley's obvious distinction as the "big one," the superb aerial photographs by Brad Washburn focused interest on this peak. The first six ascents of McKinley's highest summit had all been made by essentially the same route, that discovered by the Sourdoughs. From his 1942 ascent and his overflights, Washburn was able to ferret out several attractive new possibilities. In 1951 he led the team that pioneered the West Buttress. This straightforward climb was nonetheless important.* With the use of air-dropped supplies, it soon became the "normal route," if any route on such a serious mountain may be thought of as normal. It opened the mountain to a new generation of enthusiasts.

To persons more familiar with peaks like Mount Rainier and Mount Whitney, the 120-square-mile massif of Mount McKinley is hard to comprehend. Moreover, the two separate summits and the complicated array of ridges and faces offer a myriad of distinct routes. Climbers from the University of Alaska set two ambitious goals for 1954. One team would approach from the south and attempt the first-ever traverse of the peak. Another team would try for the west buttress of the North Peak, the route probed by Dr. Cook in 1903. Both routes

---

*No difficulty ratings will be given for Alaskan climbs. No one has yet rated these climbs, and the author is reluctant to set standards by intuition. Further, perhaps half the climbs mentioned await a second ascent. A concensus of opinion is yet to be reached.

The south face of Mount McKinley. The Thayer Route traverses the foreground ridge, descends into Thayer Basin and climbs out to the right skyline. The west rib is at the left and the Cassin Ridge in the center of the face. The direct south face takes an ill-defined rib to the right of the Cassin Ridge. *Bradford Washburn.*

promised technical climbing more difficult than any previous Mount McKinley climb.

McKinley Park ranger Elton Thayer led the traverse party, which included climbing instructor George Argus, Dartmouth graduate Les Viereck, and McKinley veteran Morton Wood. By air-dropping their supplies, they were able to travel light on the forty-mile approach up the west fork of the Ruth Glacier. Ahead stretched the five-mile-long south buttress undulating between 13,000 and 15,000 feet as it led up toward the South Peak. A steep ice slope barred the way, and a week of intense effort was required to get the party onto the ridge. Then the climb went smoothly. In another week they traversed the ridge, descended into Thayer Basin, and climbed up to join Karstens Ridge 3,000 feet below the summit.

On the more typical Mount McKinley climb of that era camps and supply dumps were established along the route. The camps provided a haven during storms and were used on the descent. But Thayer's party relayed all of their gear as they advanced; they left no secure line of retreat behind them. The day after they reached Karstens Ridge, they made a quick dash to the summit and then began the descent.

Conditions were bad on the traditional Karstens Ridge route. The snow was too soft for effective anchors from an ice axe, and the underlying ice was too broken up for ice pitons. Thayer came down last, safeguarding the party from the rear, but skirting a ridge crest, he slipped. His rope-

mates were on belay, but his momentum swept them along. Pitching through the loose snow, they fell 900 feet down the slope. Only Wood was unscathed. Viereck had chest pains, and Argus a possible leg fracture. Thayer, whose dream the climb had been, lay dead.

The sun set behind the North Peak, and the temperature plummeted. They had to make camp at once. Wood and Viereck chopped a platform on the slope and maneuvered Argus inside a tent, which they then erected around him. There they remained for six days hoping that Argus would improve and that search planes would see the messages stamped out in the snow.

After the fall they had pitched the tent where they could, but the obvious avalanche danger of the spot eventually compelled them to move. They wrapped Argus inside air mattresses, sleeping bags, and tents and lowered him down the nerve-wracking slope.

The next day an airplane flew overhead but failed to see them; the search was concentrated on the other side of the peak. If Argus was to be saved, Viereck and Wood would have to go for help. They left him the bulk of the food and set out. After three days of almost nonstop hiking, they met park rangers. Argus had been waiting alone on the mountain for a week when a rescue party finally reached him.

The first traverse of Mount McKinley was a bold undertaking. But was the accident avoidable? The climbers had been on the mountain for three

Mount Deborah from the south. The 1954 party approached from the west and gained the corniced south ridge at the saddle which appears to be just below the summit. They took six hours from here to the top. The east ridge, right, has so far turned back all attempts. *Austin Post.*

weeks and had just come down from the 20,000-foot region. Fatigued and offguard after the summit was behind them, it was humanly impossible for them to take every precaution. A momentary lapse was all that was needed.

Thayer might have been stopped by a solid belay, but at that time no effective loose-snow belays existed. Today a shovel-shaped aluminum plate, a "deadman," is often used in poor snow. However, the deadman does not necessarily make snow climbing safer today. As safety devices are improved, climbers extend their frontiers. A climber of Thayer's imagination will always be pressing the frontier.

The other University of Alaska party was also on Mount McKinley at the time of the accident but did not learn of it until after their climb. The team on the west buttress of the North Peak included Donald McLean and Charles Wilson from the university, seasoned Alaskan climber Bill Hackett, German climber Henry Meybohm, and Fred Beckey. They placed six camps on the climb from the glacier at 8,000 feet to the North Peak. Although their route was technically more demanding than any previous McKinley climb, they reached the top in two weeks. They hoped to climb the South Peak, but a storm kept them pinned at their highest camp.

On their return to Fairbanks, Beckey and Meybohm learned that Austrian mountaineer Heinrich Harrer was in Alaska. Harrer had achieved lasting recognition in the climbing world for his partici-

pation in the 1938 ascent of the Eigerwand. He would be a strong partner for the peaks they had in mind: 12,540-foot Mount Deborah, 100 miles east of Mount McKinley, and 14,573-foot Mount Hunter, directly south of Mount McKinley.

With 7,000 feet of relief these peaks do not match McKinley's 10,000 to 12,000 feet, nor do they pose equivalent problems of acclimatization. Nevertheless, they are subject to similar weather and are more continuously difficult than any climb then made on McKinley. They may be compared with McKinley because they posed an equivalent psychological barrier.

Beckey and his companions waited until evening to crampon up an avalanche-prone couloir on Deborah's west flank. By early morning they placed their first camp. They slept the following day, then moved their camp to the foot of the western summit slopes that evening. The next morning they climbed up toward the crest of the south ridge. The ridge was a wild prospect. It was severely corniced and dropped away sharply on both sides. It is sometimes possible to avoid cornices by passing to one side or the other, but on Deborah the faces were too steep. The climbers had to work directly up and down the cornices for six tense hours on the half-mile-long ridge. They reached the summit twelve hours after they left camp.

All three were impressed by the difficulties on the ridge, declaring that it was the most sensational ice climb they had ever done. After this, the

Heinrich Harrer on the south ridge of Mount Deborah. *Fred Beckey*.

five-day ascent of Mount Hunter was icing on the cake.

During the mid-1950s local Alaskan climbers made informal trips into the more accessible regions on a weekend basis, and Mount McKinley was climbed once or twice a year. Mount Logan and Mount Saint Elias came under attack, and several of the most difficult unclimbed peaks, notably the Moose's Tooth and Mount Huntington, were probed.

It was not until 1959, however, that climbs were made that again advanced the standards in Alaska. The first of these, like many a climbing trip, was conceived in a bar. In the flush of a hard-won victory, four happy, inebriated Teton guides talked themselves into an attempt on the south face of Mount McKinley.

In June 1959 Barry Corbet, Bill Buckingham, Jake Breitenbach, and Pete Sinclair urged their beat-up cars, Millicent and Bulldog, over the dusty and debilitating Alcan Highway.

The decision to try the west rib of the south face was provoked by an article by Bradford Washburn which described the south face of McKinley as having "the best of all possible future routes." The Teton guides had carefully studied Washburn's pictures. Nonetheless, as their bush pilot faded into the distance and left them alone with reality, the view of their 10,000-foot route was demoralizing. A rock buttress rose sharply out of the glacier and led into a heavily corniced snow ridge. The ridge finally gave onto the upper 5,000 feet of snow gullies and rock ridges.

After a week of effort they gained the top of the rock buttress by a difficult ice gully and pitched their third camp on a platform hacked out of the ice. Concentration Camp was a cramped and squalid place tacked onto the edge of nothing.

The climbers watched the daily build-up of clouds apprehensively and worried over their escape route through the ever-changing icefall down below. There was 8,000 feet still to go, and nearly all of their seventeen hundred feet of rope was in place in the ice gully. They hoped the climbing would ease, but a reconnaissance made it plain there was hard ice climbing ahead. They

Outside Don Sheldon's hangar in Talkeetna, Alaska; Jake Breitenbach, left, Pete Sinclair, Bill Buckingham and Barry Corbet. Note the ex-Army "Korean" vapor-barrier boot. These boots virtually eliminated frostbite on Alaskan peaks. However, they are too clumsy for highly technical climbing. Fritz Goro, *Time-Life*.

were already unpleasantly extended, but in order to press on they would have to remove the fixed ropes safeguarding the gully.

Why risk it? Thoughts drifted to a quiet evening at a Dartmouth alehouse, to the Tetons in summer. When up against irrevocable decisions, climbers are forced to examine their motives. If they are ambivalent, they will probably call it a day and go down. At Concentration Camp they weighed the difficulties of retreat against the climb. Finally, with renewed determination they cleared half of the fixed ropes from the ice gully and headed up into the unknown.

Relaying loads and leapfrogging the ropes to safeguard the hardest sections, they climbed 2,000 feet of steep ice in one long day. Above them a broad snow ridge blended into the upper face. For the first time in several days they were confident. In two more days they reached the point where they hoped to cut across to the West Buttress on the descent. They left a cache of equipment and headed for the summit with minimal gear. The following morning, because of their rapid pace up the mountain, they were not properly acclimated to the 20,000-foot height. They gasped for every breath when they staggered onto the summit.

The clouds that had been building for days finally closed in, and snow fell as they retreated to their highest camp. When they looked out of the tent the next morning, there were eighteen inches of new snow, and it was still coming down. The obvious ridge they had so easily followed on the way up was indistinguishable from several others.

Their cache would soon be buried and lost. They hurriedly packed up and descended into the murk. They had not gone far before they realized they were on the wrong ridge! They climbed back up to the last remembered landmark. After a number of false starts, they located the right ridge and the ice axe barely visible above the smooth mound of snow that covered the vital equipment cache. Taking directions from the cache, they plunged down the side of the ridge and groped through a whiteout to the West Buttress. Four rising young

La Pérouse. The 1959 route started at the base of the central rock rib and passed the summit ice seracs on the left. *Leo Scheiblehner.*

climbers had completed the most demanding route yet on Mount McKinley.

The 1960 *American Alpine Journal* honored the climb by carrying the description as the lead article. Tucked away at the back of the journal was a scant note on another Alaskan climb. This was on La Pérouse, a 10,750-foot peak in the Mount Fairweather region. Although on a low peak, the route went 7,000 feet directly up a rock-and-ice face menaced by avalanches. The leader was Leo Scheiblehner, an Austrian alpinist of the first rank.

In Europe he made numerous solo climbs, including a three and a half hour ascent of the Comici route on the north face of the Cima Grande. In North America he and Fred Beckey made a notable climb of Mount Hood's Yocum Ridge under winter conditions.

During the 1959 summer Scheiblehner and Richard Griesmann worked as guides for a geological party in the Fairweather region, and Scheiblehner set his hopes on the southeast face of La Pérouse. Because of the avalanche danger, he

reckoned to climb through the midsummer Alaskan night. The two climbers started at 3 P.M., after the sun left the face, and rapidly climbed the straightforward rock ridge that forms the lower quarter of the route. The steep snow and ice above was in perfect condition for cramponing, and they made fast time to an ice-covered rock slab at midheight. It proved to be the crux of the climb, hard and difficult to protect. Past it, they gained the upper 3,000 feet of ice and, in a race with the morning sun, broke out of the face at 5 A.M.

Scheiblehner looked upon La Pérouse as a scaled-up alpine climb. He compared it with the north face of Les Courtes, a demanding ice climb in the French Alps. To him a fast, all-out push was the obvious and safe thing to do. But in the Alaskan context the climb was extraordinary. It took a steep face, and it was done without reconnaissance, fixed ropes, or camps. It was a climb ahead of its time.

Even more provocative than Washburn's remarks on Mount McKinley's west rib were his comments in *Mountain World* on the "great central bulge in the fabulous 10,000 foot South Face of the mountain." The climb was so steep and difficult and so exposed to storms that Washburn advised that "none but the most uniformly experienced and powerful team should even think of attempting it." In his opinion it was the greatest remaining pioneer ascent in North America.

Who could fail to appreciate the significance of the south face? Who would make an attempt after such a build-up? Perhaps intimidated by the reputation of the south face, no home teams came forward.

Away From Home

In order to bring North American climbing during the 1950s into more of an international framework, we shall consider briefly American achievements abroad. Topflight American climbers seldom visited the Alps during the era, and when they did, they were eager to repeat the classic climbs. The Andes and the Himalayas were more in line with the wilderness mountaineering of home, and there the achievements were more outstanding. In the Andes, Dave Harrah's and James Maxwell's 1950 ascent of Yerupaja was a fine effort on a peak that had defeated previous parties. The 1952 ascent of Salcantay by Fred Ayres, George Bell, Graham Matthews, David Michael, and French alpinists Claude Kogan and Bernard Pierre was one of many fine Andean climbs that the four Americans made along with Andy Kauffman and Leigh Ortenburger.

In the Himalayas the decade of the 8,000-meter peaks began with the epic 1950 ascent of Annapurna by the French and is best known for the 1953 ascent of Mount Everest by a British team. In 1953 the Americans were also in the field. The Third American Karakoram Expedition set out for K2.

Ever since the two attempts on K2 in the late 1930s, Bob Bates and Charles Houston planned to return. Their dream appeared a reality when eight climbers reached 25,500-foot Camp 8 and prepared to place an assault camp and go for the summit. Then tragedy struck. During the enforced immobilization of a four-day storm, a blood clot developed in Art Gilkey's leg. There was imminent danger of the clot lodging in his lungs or heart. His only chance for survival was immediate evacuation. His companions lashed a tent around his sleeping bag and began to lower him down the mountain. After a harrowing descent Bob Craig left his teammates and climbed across to the meager site of Camp 7 to prepare a tent platform. Moments later George Bell slipped. He pulled Tony Streather from his steps, and as they fell, they dragged Bates, Houston, and Dee Molenaar with them. In a flash they realized that nothing could stop them. It was all over.

Just before the fall Molenaar had anchored to one of the ropes that secured Gilkey, and belaying Gilkey was the implacable Pete Schoening. Somehow both ropes of falling climbers snagged on Molenaar's rope, and somehow Schoening withstood the impact of five falling climbers.

The shattered and numbed team anchored Gilkey to the slope and crossed over to the site of Camp 7. When they had pitched the tents, they went back for him. On the other side of the rock rib that separated him from the camp, they were greeted by a haunting sight. Instead of Art Gil-

key's cheerful face there was nothing but snow and wind. An avalanche had swept him away.

Once more K2 defeated an American team. Another attempt was planned, but an Italian expedition climbed the peak in 1954. It was not until 1958 that an American party succeeded on an 8,000-meter peak, the only such first ascent that fell to Americans. Lawyer Nick Clinch organized and led the group to 8,068-meter Hidden Peak (or Gasherbrum I), where the summit pair was Schoening and Andy Kauffman. Two years later the irrepressible Clinch led an expedition to 7,828-meter Masherbrum, where Bell and Willi Unsoeld reached the summit.

In absolute terms North American achievements in foreign ranges were modest. But the key point to bear in mind is that American climbers had so much to do on their own continent. It was *unnecessary* to climb abroad. The Europeans fielded several strong teams in the Himalayas and Andes each year. They had to travel halfway around the world to find new ground, but the Americans had more than they could manage at home.

REFERENCES

Accidents in North American Mountaineering. New York: American Alpine Club, 1955.

Bates, Robert H. "The Fight for K2." *AAJ* 9 (1954): 5.

Beckey, F. "Mt. Deborah and Mt. Hunter: First Ascents." *AAJ* 9 (1955): 39.

Buckingham, William J. "The Western Rib of Mount McKinley's South Face." *AAJ* 12 (1960): 1.

Houston, Charles, and Robert Bates. *K2, The Savage Mountain*. London: Collins, 1955.

McLean, Donald H. O. "McKinley, Northwest Buttress." *AAJ* 9 (1955): 70.

Scheiblehner, Leopold. "East Face of La Pérouse, Fairweather Range." *AAJ* 12 (1960): 113.

Sinclair, Pete. "The West Rib of the South Face of Denali." *Dartmouth Mountaineering* (May 1960): 7.

Thayer, Elton. "King Peak." *AAJ* 8 (1953): 410.

Viereck, Les. "Mount McKinley from the South." *Dartmouth Mountaineering*. (April 1956):28.

Washburn, Bradford. "Mount McKinley: The West Buttress, 1951." *AAJ* 8 (1952): 213.

———. "Mount McKinley Alaska." In *The Mountain World, 1956/57*. London: Allen & Unwin, 1957.

Wood, Morton S. "The First Traverse of Mt. McKinley." *AAJ* 9 (1955): 51.

Wood, Walter A. *A History of Mountaineering in the St. Elias Mountains*. Banff, Alberta: Alpine Club of Canada, 1967.

Yeasting, Bob, and Bill Niendorff. "King Peak: Yukon Expedition 1952." *Mountaineer* 47 (Dec. 1952), p. 41.

El Capitan

Yosemite Valley. It is the Fourth of July weekend in 1957. The heat is oppressive, and the campgrounds are overflowing. The roads are crowded with cars that make their way from viewpoint to store and back to viewpoint. Tourists idly drink Coke and tap in time to the radio as they cruise up and down. They are in Yosemite for a good time. The scenery may be a bonus, but many of them would just as soon be at Las Vegas. They look upon Yosemite as an outdoor amusement park. There is a sense of bored pleasure seeking in the air.

This sense of ennui contrasts with the urgency of three grimy young men. They, too, seem oblivious to the scenery, but they are not bored. Harding, Feuerer, and Powell have just been aced out of Half Dome and are earnestly discussing their next move. A climbing revolution is about to take place in Yosemite, a revolution that in less than ten years will put American climbers at the forefront of the sport and influence mountaineering all over the world.

After grumbling around the valley in a "fit of egotistical pique," Harding decided to cap the Half Dome climb by a harder one. He looked across at the 3,000-foot south buttress of El Capitan and emphatically stated, "I'm gonna climb that goddamn line."

His concept was audacious. Yosemite climbers had never seriously considered El Capitan, for it was outside their frame of reference. With its uniform smoothness, its lack of resting places, and above all its overpowering size, it represented a new dimension in American climbing. It would obviously require a new approach. In anticipation of progress on the order of 100 feet a day, the trio agreed to work upward by a series of well-stocked camps linked together and to the ground by fixed ropes, somewhat analagous to Himalayan climbing. Once in place, the ropes could be climbed by slings and prusik knots, and the camps restocked with food and gear from below.

Harding and his friends scrounged what gear they could and set to work. The initial leads were hard. The blind or "bottoming" cracks buckled their pitons. They were forced to place several bolts in order to reach the first real ledge on the climb, Camp 1, 300 feet up the wall. Hard steel

El Capitan. The routes indicated are, from left: Dihedral Wall, Salathé Wall, Muir Wall (which begins to the left of the Salathé), and Nose. *Ed Cooper.*

Climbers in the Stoveleg Crack, Nose, on the second ascent. *Tom Frost.*

pitons would have been a godsend. Powell tried to trade for some Salathé pitons, but they were already collector's items, and he managed only to obtain a couple.

From Camp 1 they worked right and pendulumed into the awesome 400-foot Stoveleg Crack. Only four of their pitons were large enough to span its two-inch width. These were made from the sawed-off legs of a gas stove unearthed in the Berkeley city dump. When the leader had placed all of them, he lowered himself from the top piton and cleared out those below. This "leapfrogging" was a touchy business; the leader was poorly protected once he extracted the lower pitons. Stoveleg Crack was a scary place.

After seven days they descended. Although their gear was badly mauled, they were on their way. Their ropes stretched 1,000 feet up the wall. On the ground they ran into an unexpected problem. Rubber-necking tourists had brought traffic to a standstill. The crusty chief ranger banned any further activity on El Cap during the peak tourist season from Memorial Day to Labor Day. Little was achieved apart from the replacement of borrowed ropes. In the fall, disaster struck. Powell smashed his ankle on a simple climb.

Through the winter Feuerer worked hard developing specialized gear. Although an ingenious craftsman, he had an unfortunate capacity for error. He was nicknamed the Dolt. He made several types of piton including an adjustable model consisting of two parts locked together by

His haul rope hanging free, Chuck Pratt nears the end of the lead under the Great Roof, Nose. *Tom Frost.*

bolts. To ease the horrendous task of supplying the lead climbers with food and water, he built a cart out of aircraft parts and bicycle wheels. It would be loaded with gear and winched up the face by a capstan arrangement.

When they got back on the climb in the spring, they put the "Dolt Cart" through its paces. It had a tendency to go belly-up and was less than a sensation. The ground party in charge of loading the cart continually tried to please the climbers with new goodies. One blistering day they sent an ice-cold six-pack of beer up to Camp 2 (Dolt Tower). Harding and Powell took one look and knew better. Feuerer downed a couple of cans. After a moment's pause he sprang to his feet and announced that he was going to learn to fly. In spite of flying and the Dolt Cart they advanced the

route to midheight before the summer recess insisted on by the chief ranger.

During the summer, rifts appeared in the team. With Powell partially disabled, Harding felt they were too weak to carry off the climb and invited others. Feuerer became disenchanted with climbing, quoted the Bible in letters to Harding, and left the team. In order to set Powell's broken ankle, the doctor fused the bone. Hampered by his disability, Powell was unable to play a major role in the climbing; on the first attempts he had done the bulk of the leading. Disturbed by the influx of newcomers and feeling less and less part of the climb, he withdrew.

With his original partners out of the picture Harding drafted whomever he could. Most climbers did not want to be involved in such a long, drawn-out affair, and several of those who went up on the wall were overwhelmed by the scale and the exposure. El Capitan was a psychological frontier. About this time Royal Robbins almost became involved. Or did he? Robbins recollects that he got a postcard from Harding inviting him on board, an invitation he declined. Harding recalls a telephone conversation with Robbins. During the conversation Robbins reportedly said that, as Harding was not making much progress, he was thinking of getting up a team. He would use Harding's equipment as far as it went and then go for the top. And what was Harding's reaction to that, he wanted to know. "Fine by me," replied Harding and then after a distinct pause, "but exactly *what* would you say you had done?"

In any event Robbins never appeared on the rock, and in September 1958, Harding was back

The scale and exposure on El Capitan was sufficient to demoralize most contenders. This is the view looking down the Nose from the belay position at the end of the Great Roof. *Tom Frost.*

with a large party. In appalling heat they pushed the route upward only a couple of hundred feet in nine days: from the vicinity of El Cap Tower (Camp 3) to Camp 4 1,900 feet above the ground. Among other trials there was a logistical problem; the lead men consumed food and water faster than the haulers could bring it up. After this protracted struggle and two short skirmishes, the chief ranger gave Harding an ultimatum: either get up by Thanksgiving or abandon the climb. This unenforceable deadline did not bother Harding and Wayne Merry, who now emerged as his strongest partner. It was exactly their attitude as well; they were pretty sick of the whole affair.

Early in November with Rich Calderwood and George Whitmore in support, Harding and Merry set out on a determined bid. From Camp 4 they worked out under the Great Roof, a feared pitch that turned out to be reasonable, and up into the dihedrals that lead to the summit. Days passed. They established Camp 5 and then 6. On the evening of the ninth day a storm provided a welcome relief from the ceaseless hammering, the exposure, and the constant nervous tension. Holed up in Camp 6, Harding and Merry took stock of the situation. Below them they reckoned Whitmore was near Camp 4 ready to ferry up loads, and they knew that Calderwood had already had his fill of El Capitan and had gone down. Ahead they reckoned one long day might see them over the top.

On the morning of their eleventh day they heard a yodel from the top. Harding shouted a strangled reply through a mouthful of food. When they heard his squawk, his waiting friends became anxious. They decided the climbers were in a desperate fix and lowered them a rope. It was the last thing that Harding and Merry wanted. They had not come this far to be hauled off. They intended to finish under their own steam. In vain they yelled up to their friends to get the "goddamn rope" the hell out of the way. The weather looked to be worsening, and Harding determined to go all out for the top and work through the night if necessary. By the light of his headlamp he drilled bolt holes in the overhanging headwall. Ironically, as he did, the rope hung within easy reach. He stuck to the lead without relief and placed twenty-six bolts. Just after sunrise he pulled himself over the top. El Capitan had been won, an enduring testament to man's spirit and a landmark in American climbing.

In between bouts on the south buttress, or the Nose, of El Capitan Harding turned to another impressive Yosemite wall, the 1,200-foot east face of Washington Column. He used the east face as a test ground for new gear, and like the Nose it required several attempts and several partners before the successful ascent.

During the late 1950s a small community of climbers centered in Berkeley. They spent varying amounts of time in and out of the university. In

1959 a Berkeley group attempted the 1,000-foot west face of Mount Conness, a high mountain wall outside Yosemite Valley. On the second pitch, leader Don Goodrich pulled away a large block. As he fell, the block fell with him, and he was seriously injured. His companions did what they could for him. Some stayed with him; others raced down for a rescue party. A stretcher team arrived early the next day, but Goodrich died before he reached the waiting ambulance. It was a dark moment for the close-knit group. When they returned to their house in Berkeley, "the Pad," the silence was oppressive. Before long they accepted the situation, and one of them voiced an unspoken thought, "We might as well divide up his gear."

Death in the mountains seldom acts as a deterrent. In fact the reverse is often the case. Disaster stamps a climb with a certain cachet and may make it even more appealing. Climbers who would not normally have dreamed of leaving the confines of Yosemite Valley soon had their sights on Mount Conness. However, it was Harding who made the climb later that year. A strenuous chimney pitch was memorable. Harding was way out above his last protection when he called down to his ropemates that he was running out of strength. Methodically, he began drilling a bolt hole, but he felt himself drifting to sleep! Finally, he rested against the bolt and began laughing feverishly.

By 1960 the east face of Mount Whitney's satellite peak, Keeler Needle, was a hot topic among Yosemite Valley climbers. Again Harding pulled off the 1,500-foot climb (V), which he made with a motley crew that included "Desert Frank," whom he had just met in the Yosemite bar.

These noteworthy High Sierra climbs made almost no impression on the Yosemite climbers. Yosemite was the center of their universe, and they were not to be distracted. There were new faces on the scene, and the pace was quickening. Among the newcomers were Berkeley residents Chuck Pratt and Steve Roper. Pratt had tremendous talent as a free climber and quickly climbed at the top standards. He partnered Harding on the final push on Washington Column. The gangly Roper had climbed the local Berkeley rocks since he was fifteen. At high school he tried to interest his classmates in climbing and once coaxed a companion up into a tree. Climbing was safe, said Roper, if you knew the correct procedures. He tied the hesitant neophyte into a rope for a demonstration. He was to jump off while Roper held him on a tight belay. He jumped, and Roper grasped the wrong rope. The lad hit the dirt with a thud.

Mortified, Roper clambered to the ground. There was no sign of life. He must bury the body and leave home! But as he stood transfixed, he heard a faint moan. The ex-climber eventually recovered from a dislocated back.

In 1959 Pratt and Roper joined Bob Kamps in an attempt on the massive 2,000-foot north face of Middle Cathedral Rock. Fast on aid and skilled at free climbing, the newcomers completed the route in a rapid two and a half days (VI, 5.9 A4). It stands in marked contrast to Harding's protracted efforts on the Nose and Washington Column.

A new group of Southern Californians also arrived at the end of the 1950s. Teton climber Yvon Chouinard came in an old truck that doubled as a mobile workshop. On a small forge in the back of the truck he turned out hard-steel pitons patterned after Salathé's. With the money from the sale of pitons and income earned as a private eye, he could climb for half of the year. His companion Tom Frost was an engineering student at Stanford and

Chuck Pratt, left, and Warren Harding just down from the east face of Washington Column, 1959. *Steve Roper.*

more in the mold of the typical 1950s climber.

In 1959 Chouinard and Frost attempted a new route on isolated Kat Pinnacle. After he had gained fifty feet on the overhanging rock, Chouinard came to hairline cracks where his smallest knife-blade pitons buckled. He yelled down to Frost that they needed a short, solid piton that would chop its way into the rock. Back on the ground, they worked on the design of a new piton. Frost came up with a basic hatchet-like shape, and Chouinard refined the details. It was about the size of a postage stamp. The business end was the thickness of a knife blade and penetrated only a quarter-inch into the rock. With several of these Realized Ultimate Reality Pitons, or rurps, Chouinard and Frost made the crux pitch on Kat Pinnacle (A4). It was the most difficult aid climb in North America. The tiny rurp played a key role in ushering in a new standard of aid climbing in Yosemite. It enabled the use of previously hopeless cracks, where before bolts had to be placed.

Yosemite climbers were forced to sharpen their aid climbing skills by the nature of the rock. Instead of the deep, parallel-sided fissures common in other granitic areas, Yosemite has many shallow, bottoming, U-shaped cracks. For these problem placements the climbers evolved a bag of tricks: two or more pitons nested together to pack into a shallow hold; blunt, sawed-off, soft-iron European pitons; pitons driven sideways or eye first; protruding pitons tied off near the tip to reduce leverage.

While the newcomers moved strongly onto the Yosemite scene, the leader of the previous group of Southern Californians served in the U.S. Army. Royal Robbins was demobbed in 1960, left his conventional past in Los Angeles, and moved into the Pad in Berkeley. Instead of his former leisurely

Yvon Chouinard and Tom Frost set out to repeat the first four pitches of the Nose, 1960. Their innovative Realized Ultimate Reality Pitons, rurps, enabled them to eliminate several bolt placements. *Bill Feuerer.*

pace he climbed with a new ferocity. His whole personality and motivation seemed to change. Before he entered military service, he held a steady job as a bank teller. Good clothes and partygoing were among his interests; an early marriage emphasized his orientation to typical city values. Nonetheless, during this time he was torn between the accepted symbols of success and an undefinable something else. When he left the army, others had surpassed his achievements in Yosemite. It was getting late. The slow paced 1950s had been swept aside. Excellent climbers seemed to be behind every boulder. Robbins reentered the climbing scene with a sense of mission.

The year of Robbins's reappearance in Yosemite was an important one. Chouinard and Frost established a classic big wall route when they climbed the elegant west face of Sentinel Rock (VI) in two and a half days. Robbins and Joe Fitschen made an aid climbing horror with Arches Direct (5.9 A5), where one pitch took Robbins ten hours and two falls to complete. Yet the most ambitious project of all was a "continuous" ascent of the Nose of El Capitan without the use of fixed ropes. Harding's party had fixed ropes (subsequently removed) all the way up the climb. With the route known and the 125 or so bolts in place, Robbins, Fitschen, Frost, and Pratt intended to repeat the climb without the security of fixed ropes.

The Nose route includes several pendulum maneuvers, and a pendulum is not always reversible. Once they were well up on the wall, there would be only one way to go: upward. A retreat would require the placement of bolt anchors for many rappels down blank sections of the wall. It was an unthinkable prospect.

They reckoned on ten days for the climb, and a doctor hardly encouraged them when he said he doubted they could survive on their meager ration of water. In every sense the climb was an adventure. A rescue was not to be considered. There was neither the expertise to carry off a rescue nor sufficient rope on hand to reach down to them from above. In order to cut down the risks they made a pact that they would only rappel with a prusik-knot belay for safety, a precaution they would not normally have taken.

Working in pairs, the two teams alternated days of leading and hauling. Late on the third day Pratt rappelled toward Harding's Camp 3, El Cap Tower. Without warning his rappel arrangement flipped off the rope. The prusik knot cinched and

Royal Robbins, left, and Joe Fitschen sort out the hardware for the second ascent of the Nose, 1960. Note the load-hauling pulleys and the four rurps, with slings attached, near Robbins's cup. *Tom Frost.*

saved his life. Through the next days the struggle continued into the Gray Bands, up past the Great Roof, and onto the upper section of the face. On the afternoon of the seventh day the four climbers pulled onto the summit. Virtually every climber in Yosemite was there to welcome them. Champagne flowed, and a euphoric summit party got under way. It was good to be in Yosemite and a climber, especially after the "most magnificent and complete adventure of our lives."

Not long after the second ascent of the Nose, Harding was at a party with the victorious team. Pratt came over and warmly shook his hand. Robbins and Fitschen maintained their distance. Harding was aware of an antagonism from the new elite. With both real and imagined pressures on him, he was determined to "show them."

On New Year's Eve 1960, he led off up one of the most unlikely valley walls, the 1,000-foot west face of the Leaning Tower. A continuous overhang from top to bottom, the face is almost devoid of cracks in the lower one-third. On the first pitch Harding loosened a flake, which toppled over and lacerated his head. His companions rushed him to the hospital, where the doctor bandaged his head and told him to take it easy. He went straight to a party.

In 1961 Harding and his companions returned to the Leaning Tower on four separate occasions. They placed fixed ropes as they advanced and drove 110 bolts in order to complete the climb. With its oppressive overhang and blank rock, the

Leaning Tower was a new departure in Yosemite. Yet the bulk of Yosemite climbers looked upon the route as a regressive step. They had dismissed the face from consideration because of the obvious need for bolts. Their goals lay in the other direction: to minimize bolts and fixed ropes. Harding, however, was not a resident valley climber. He kept out of the mainstream of Yosemite thought. He climbed whatever took his fancy without worrying over the ethics of the case. The pity of the affair was that Harding and his critics had more grounds for agreement than disagreement. The misunderstandings prevented them from appreciating each other's true merits.

This era in Yosemite is best remembered for the first routes on the big walls. Because of their spectacular nature, these climbs overshadowed all else. However, the climbers did not spring full-fledged onto the walls. They mastered technical skills on shorter but demanding routes.* Powell introduced this style of climbing to the valley, but after his accident he never quite regained his previous position in Yosemite. He concentrated instead on Tahquitz Rock, where he pioneered at a high standard through the 1960s. Yet his influence on the rising generation of Yosemite climbers was profound.

*Big wall climbing evolved faster in Yosemite than in the Dolomites, the most comparable European area. Unlike Yosemite, the Dolomites have no tradition of short climbs where standards are pushed to the limit. When a Yosemite climber confronted A4 nailing 2,000 feet up a wall, he had already done a similar pitch nearby.

They emulated his climbing, his sparing use of aid, and perhaps most important his lifestyle. Powell's greatest legacy was not in his individual climbs, good though they were, but his devotion to the sport. He was the first Yosemite climber to center his life around the sport; to adopt it as a way of life.

Pratt was the natural successor to Powell. The route that haunted him was the Worst Error. From a swimming hole in the Merced River, he gazed up at this imposing crack on the side of Elephant Rock. Harding had used aid from a bolt, but he *had* to do it without. After his all-free ascent (5.9), he became obsessed by two 400-foot cracks in an alcove just to the right. Unlike the big walls, where several climbers shared the physical and mental strain, everything here depended on just one person, the leader. He twice climbed up to the base of the shallow, overhanging jamcrack that is the final pitch of the left-hand crack, but both times his seconds were unable to follow. On his third attempt in the fall of 1961 he led Mort Hempel up the fearsome pitch. Crack of Doom was the first 5.10 in Yosemite.

In a few short years the standards and techniques of Yosemite climbing had taken a dramatic leap forward. Yet for the principals involved, climbing was by no means the whole story, nor even the most important party. Perhaps the key element was that through climbing and living in Yosemite they found a sense of community and purpose they did not feel in the outside world.

During the early years of the sport, climbers

subscribed to society's norms. They were a group of hardy outdoorsmen much like sailors or skiers. The 1950s marked the appearance of a new breed: the working class climber, and the four-months-a-year climbing bum. Instead of looking toward a college degree and a career, this new breed lived from year to year. They had a clear sense that they were "different." The Yosemite climbers created a gulf between themselves and the despised "tourists." It was easy to look down upon them and the suburban impedimenta that they brought into the valley, to compare their seemingly vacuous life to the climbers' spartan, dedicated existence.

At high school and in society at large the key factor was "fitting in." At school organized sports were the thing, together with the car syndrome, and all that it stood for: drive-in movies, soda fountains, and "cruisin' Main." Almost without exception the Yosemite climbers rejected this version of life, and just as surely it rejected them. At a time when it was virtually unthinkable, many of them dropped out of school. Pratt's case was typical. A physics major at Berkeley, he detested the mandatory ROTC with its uniforms and parades. When he changed out of his uniform one afternoon, all the frustrations of school life came to a head. To hell with it, he thought, I'm off to Tahquitz. He never looked back.

Once they dropped out, they felt all manner of pressures. Their parents were humiliated and hated the rejection of their own values, the grubby Yosemite existence, and the casual laboring jobs.

Nor were the climbers appreciated in the valley. They were a pest to the Curry Company, the park concessionaire. They were dirty, and they lounged around the coffee shop. They gave the park an unsavory air. The outside pressures on the climbers created a feeling of *us* against *them* and helped to build the cohesiveness of the group.

Situated directly across from the north face of Sentinel Rock is Camp 4, a dusty area of boulders, trees, and campground tables. By mid-April of each year a dozen or so of the faithful had set up camp for part or all of the six-month climbing season. Camp 4 was their spiritual home, their bastion against the outside world. There they met others who had been through their own crises, others who understood. There was a ritual importance to life in this camp, this valley. A phrase that summed up their feeling was "living at one with the dirt." And from the Christian idea of deliverance through toil, they spoke of purification through suffering on the granite walls.

By day Camp 4 was almost deserted, but in the evening small groups gathered around the kerosene-lighted tables to compare notes, discuss climbs, and put the world to rights. If circumstances demanded, an impromptu party materialized.

One evening Mike Borghoff led a group in a brazen chorus. Around midnight an irate tourist visibly shaking with rage demanded they stop. Harding staggered to his feet and danced around the fire wine bottle in hand in a gesture of defiance. The tourist threatened to call the rangers and fled the scene. The party resumed with gusto. Within minutes a green truck with a flashing red light pulled into Camp 4. A ranger hopped out and strode purposefully toward the group. Close behind came the gleeful tourist.

In reply to the ranger's stern complaint, Harding suggested that he could explain everything, but he stumbled and crawled toward the ranger. Then events took an unexpected turn. The ranger's face suddenly broke into a smile, and he exclaimed, "Why, you're Warren Harding, I've never met you." He warmly shook the hand of the rapidly sobering Harding, who gravely replied, "Yes we were meaning to call you. We were having a quiet evening when a man in khaki pants started bothering us." The tourist vanished, and the party continued into the small hours.

Although climbing is inherently dangerous, there were no fatal accidents in Yosemite Valley until the 1960s. This is in marked contrast to the Alps, where death is a matter of routine. The difference is explained by the far smaller number of persons at risk, the lack of objective dangers, and the protection afforded by hard-steel pitons. American climbers were also more cautious; those on the hardest routes were qualified to be there. Although death was kept in the background, it was part of the climbers' metier. Not a few climbers knew the Marquis de Portago's dictum, "There are only three real sports: bull-fighting, motor-racing, and mountain climbing." Death in the mountains has a fascination, and a heroic image attaches to those involved in such a dangerous activity.

In 1960 one of the first fatal accidents occurred in the valley. A teenage climber fell into the Arrow Chimney while rappelling into the notch at the base of the Lost Arrow Spire. Harding volunteered to retrieve the body, but the Park Service considered the risk unjustified. In deference to the relatives they closed the route for one year. The closing was inconvenient for Chouinard and Roper who had looked forward to trying for the first one-day ascent of the chimney. It was a consolation to brag that whoever went up first would get the victim's climbing gear.

After the prescribed one-year moratorium, the pair started up the Lost Arrow Chimney. They were uneasy over what lay ahead. Roper was particularly concerned about Chouinard's reaction because of his Catholic background. After a few pitches Chouinard yelled down "remains" and tossed off a spherical object. All appeared to be well. It was Roper's turn to lead on the pitch they knew would take them past the body. Apprehensive and tight-lipped, he swung onto a ledge covered in human remains. He was terrified by the sight and hurried on without stopping. Just then Chouinard yelled up, "What's it like?" It was a tense moment. Roper blurted out, "His goddamn parka doesn't fit me."

In his account of the second ascent of the Nose, Robbins wrote that a younger generation would pioneer a route on the unclimbed southwestern face of El Cap. Yet it did not have to wait for a younger generation. Just one year later Frost, Pratt, and Robbins had the project firmly in mind.

All three had independently seen the possibility of the route. Its beauty was that it linked the relative weaknesses on the 3,000-foot face. The climb would not require anything on the order of the 125 bolts placed on the Nose. If few bolts had to be placed, the total climbing time would be cut, and this suggested an attempt more in the nature of a continuous ascent than a fixed-rope climb. Even though it was admitted that Harding and his companions had adoped the only possible tactic when they pioneered the Nose, climbers now wanted to cut down the reliance on fixed ropes and bolts.

From their experience on the northwest face of Half Dome and on the Nose, Frost, Pratt, and Robbins planned a bold strategy for their new route, the Salathé Wall. They would climb to about one-third height and descend leaving fixed ropes. They would then prusik up the ropes, cast them off, and go for the summit. As Robbins stated the position, they wanted ''to keep the element of adventure high with at least a moderate amount of uncertainty. It was perfectly clear to us that given sufficient time, fixed ropes, bolts and determination, any section of any rock wall could be climbed.'' It was not so much *what* one climbed, but *how* one climbed it that was important.

Over four days Frost and Robbins established the first part of the route to Heart Ledge. Pratt went to the city and filched more hardware. When he returned, the push began. After they dropped off their ropes, they had 2,000 feet of rock ahead of them as difficult as any yet climbed in the history of the sport. From Heart Ledge they worked left into a crack system that split the face and up to an

Tom Frost starts out under the roof on the pitch that leads to the headwall, Salathé Wall. Courtesy Tom Frost.

overhanging headwall 300 feet below the top. Their tactic was for the second to remove the pitons as he prusiked up the leader's rope. The third man in turn prusiked up a free-hanging rope. On the sixth day Robbins had to follow up the final lead on the overhanging headwall. He knew that he would swing out into space if he cast off from the belay. Gingerly he let himself out from the wall until he reckoned he had nullified the effect of the overhang. When he let go, he caroomed out over 2,500 feet of air. He was barely able to hold back a yell of terror.

Later in the day the three climbers came to a steep crack that was obviously the final pitch. As a gesture, Frost gave Pratt the honor of the last lead. Little did they suspect that after six days and thirty-five pitches it would be one of the toughest leads on the climb. When Pratt made it in style, the achievement was sealed (VI, 5.9 A4). They had used just thirteen bolts and free-climbed about a quarter of the route.

Robbins and his circle were a clear cut above the other valley climbers on the big walls. It was hard for an outsider to break in because almost no one else was mentally prepared for an El Capitan. Chouinard felt deliberately excluded by Robbins, yet believed he belonged to the inner circle. The first *continuous* ascent of the Salathé Wall would prove his worth. In 1962 he persuaded Roper to join him in a try for this prestigous first. But the element of fear was so great, the sense of commit-

Chuck Pratt, above, belays, while Tom Frost de-pitons the headwall, Salathé Wall. Robbins must follow by prusiking up the free-hanging rope. *Royal Robbins.*

ment so overwhelming, that at Heart Ledge Roper refused to go on. To settle the matter, he jettisoned one of the haul bags. In the fall TM Herbert joined Robbins and Frost on the Salathé, but storm and illness turned them back above Heart Ledge. In October Robbins and Frost pulled off the climb.

In 1957 Yosemite climbing began to break away from the lack-luster midfifties. Powell was establishing difficult (5.8) free climbs, and Half Dome and El Capitan ushered in Grade VI. By the early 1960s the first steps had been taken to 5.10, and Grade VI was on everyone's mind.

REFERENCES

Chouinard, Yvon. "West Face of Sentinel Rock." *AAJ* 12 (1961): 363.

Harding, Warren J. "El Capitan." *AAJ* 11 (1959): 184.

———. "East Face of Washington Column, Yosemite." *AAJ* 12 (1960): 124.

MacDonald, Allan. "Realm of the Overhang." *SCB* 47(9) (Dec. 1962): 5.

Robbins, Royal. "Climbing El Capitan." *SCB* 45(9) (Dec. 1960): 47.

———. "The Royal Arches Direct." *SCB* 46(8) (Oct. 1961): 56.

———. "The Salathé Wall." *SCB* 47(9) (Dec. 1962): 106.

———. "The Salathé Wall, El Capitan." *AAJ* 13 (1963): 332.

Roper, Steve. "Middle Cathedral Rock, North Face." *SCB* 45(9) (Dec. 1960): 92.

———. *A Climber's Guide to Yosemite Valley.* San Francisco: Sierra Club, 1964.

———. *A Climber's Guide to Yosemite Valley.* San Francisco: Sierra Club, 1971.

"Royal Robbins: Interview." *Mountain*, no. 18 (Nov. 1971), p. 27.

"Warren Harding: Interview." *Mountain*, no. 9 (May 1970), p. 15.

Layton, the Great 'Un

With the coming of the 1960s the insularity of the various climbing areas on the continent slowly disappeared. A key reason was the fascination that the half-mythical outside regions and legendary climbers held. How hard were the climbs? How good were the climbers? Facts were hard to come by. There were no first-rate magazines devoted to the sport (*Summit* was never entirely on the ball), and club publications emphasized mountaineering, not the nitty-gritty world of the local rock climber. News and gossip therefore traveled a transcontinental grapevine. A few climbers made a point to visit the scattered climbing centers. They were sure of a warm welcome, hard climbs, and evenings filled with talk of people and mountains that ranged from California to the East Coast and across to the Alps.

One of the first of the legendary outsiders to arrive on the East Coast was Layton Kor. Local climber Dave Craft came up to the Shawangunks to greet him. Craft arrived late Friday afternoon and walked into the favorite hangout. The barman directed him toward six-foot-four of enthusiasm wolfing down quantities of beer and ice cream. He had found his man. Kor was partly smashed and overjoyed to meet a "Gunks" climber. He insisted they do a climb right away. Oblivious to the fading light, he impelled Craft out of the bar and onto the rock. The legend was real.

No less distinguished a visitor was Yvon Chouinard, who climbed in as many areas as he could. The more he visited, the more equipment he sold. He was "initiated" by resident hard man Jim McCarthy, who had the habit (shared by others in their own domain) of sticking outsiders on desperate climbs in order to impress them with the superiority of the area and its climbers. He led Chouinard to Never Never Land. McCarthy climbed in polished style and arrived triumphantly at the sloping belay ledge eighty feet above the ground. Second man Pete Geiser saw that all was well and took him off belay. Suddenly the dirt on the belay ledge broke away under McCarthy's feet, and he plummeted earthward. Geiser snatched up the rope and brought him to an abrupt halt within feet of the deck. Seemingly unperturbed by his narrow escape and his undignified midair position, he looked around the group of anxious spectators. He fixed his eyes on the startled Chouinard and majestically intoned, "Welcome to the Shawangunks."

McCarthy was renowned for the falls he took and other disasters. In the late 1960s he fell out of Stoveleg Crack on El Capitan. Anxious not to appear an outsider by overdriving his pitons, he had placed them with the approved "couple of light blows." The lower ones ripped out, and he plunged down, fracturing his right arm before he was stopped by the rope. A group of climbers quickly organized a rescue, and Chouinard was on the lead rope. When he reached McCarthy, his first words were, "Welcome to Yosemite."

From contacts with Chouinard and others in the early 1960s the Shawangunk locals heard about the rising standards in California. In particular they heard that free climbing had advanced to the 5.10 level, and they were eager to prove that they, too, could hack the new standard. McCarthy realized that a 5.9 climb with a couple of aid moves, when done all free, was an obvious candidate for the new rating. His first notable successes were Retribution and Nosedive in 1961. The 5.10 standard definitely arrived the next year when he free-climbed Matinée, a route put up by Chouinard. Art Gran was also pushing the standards, if not quite at McCarthy's level. He was the first to repeat the notorious M.F., which defeated both Chouinard and John Turner. When Gran was not busy climbing, his fund of desperate stories projected the image of a dedicated hard man.

McCarthy's speciality were the overhangs which were then the frontier of Shawangunk climbing. One needed a strong grip and stronger nerves to launch out from under a roof and onto a steep headwall. On the other hand, Turner, who was defeated by the ceiling on M.F., was a crack climbing specialist. With his friends from Montreal he opened up Pokomoonshine, a 400-foot cliff in upper New York State. Typical of Turner's routes was Bloody Mary, an intimidating lieback crack with jagged rocks at its base. On his first attempt he climbed poorly protected for 100 feet to a niche. Second Dick Willmott was suffering from a surfeit of blueberries, vomited, and fell out of the lieback. When Turner roped down, a falling stone cut the head of a female companion, so naming the climb. On the second attempt Turner again reached the niche; this time Willmott was washed out of the lieback by a sudden thunderstorm. The pair finally mastered Bloody Mary with fellow Britisher Dick Strachan. (Strachan made a solo ascent of Turner's nearby F.M., a feat which contributed to the feeling that Turner's circle was unsafe.) McCarthy wanted to repeat Bloody Mary, but he was psyched by its aura of unprotectability. Not until 1971 did he made the second ascent.

Turner was also first to put in high standard routes at Bon Echo, a 300-foot crag rising out of Ontario's Lake Mazinaw. Although most of his routes were completed at the first attempt, he took four tries to climb the unrelenting line of the Joke (5.9). On the first attempt he took a huge fall and

John Turner on Garter, Pokomoonshine, 1960. *Jerry Pryor.*

ended us suspended 100 feet above the lake with a broken leg. The second attempt was frustrated when the only available boat sank; on the third he got past the crux but was so drained by the effort that he rappelled off; on the fourth all went well. On the last two attempts he placed a single knife blade piton to protect the crux. It popped out when second Strachan pulled on it. Not only did Turner put up rock climbs as demanding as any in the country, but he did them with minimal protection, and he did them singlehandedly. He did not operate in the competitive atmosphere of a Tahquitz or an Eldorado Canyon, where several good climbers advanced the standards together. He operated out of the mainstream and received almost no recognition beyond his immediate circle.

During the early 1960s the Vulgarians dominated the social and climbing scenes at the Shawangunks. You either loved them or detested them. Several weekends a year the cliffs resounded to a snarling collection of VW buses, Chevies, Triumphs, and what-have-you as the Vulgarian-sponsored Shawangunk Grand Prix took to the dirt roads. The Grand Prix had a staggered start. If a driver caught up to another car on the tortuous Wickie Wackie road, he blinked his lights and in theory was let by. Other groups were also active in the Gunks. A more flexible band of Appies had appeared, as well as numerous college outing clubs, among which the MIT group was predominant.

The various groups had their own hangouts,

social structure, and dress code. Affiliations were obvious at a glance. The Appies opted for a "tweedy," country gentleman look: knickers, a Pendleton shirt, and a beret. The MIT climbers, on the whole a colorless lot, often affected the curious hairstyle favored by sporty engineer and scientist types, a full beard and a crew-cut. They dressed in unsightly army fatigues adorned with a maze of pockets. Their canvas army belts were ringed with blanket pins from which hung out-of-date soft-iron pitons. The soft-iron pitons marked the MIT crew as "unhip." The Vulgarians had quickly adopted the chrome-moly pitons of Yosemite fame.

The Vulgarians had their own code. In the Brando-Kerouac image they wore Levi's and T-shirts. A few of them were the proud owners of imported French down jackets. Except among climbers these quilted jackets were then unknown in North America. They suggested that their owners were members of the elite, who climbed the great north faces making innumerable bivouacs on the way, or at least had plans to do so.

The symbolism of the down jacket was echoed in other ways. Lacking their own strong traditions, the young American climbers of the early 1960s were well up on the trends in the Alps. Few European climbers were more revered than those who attempted the Eigerwand in the 1930s. Several Eastern climbers had well-thumbed copies of Heinrich Harrer's Eigerwand history, *The White Spider*. In the photographs the granite-faced men invariably endured a terrible storm. Just as invariably they wore a close-fitting cap. The hard men of the Gunks adopted this thin cotton cap as their own.

Originally a motorcycle cap, it was worn to prevent injury from a "minor stonefall." Hans Kraus picked it up in the Dolomites and intro-

Vulgarian crew at Pokomoonshine: Front, left to right: Claude Suhl, John Weichsel, Al DeMaria, Roman Sadowy. Top: Dick Williams, Brian Carey. Courtesy Dick Williams.

duced it to the Shawangunks, where it was known as a "Turswiry Hat." The origin of the name is part of the curious body of Vulgariana. The City College climbers were also active cavers. Roman Sadowy had memorized a passage from a melodramatic account of the exploration of Schoolhouse Cave, West Virginia, which described the arch-hero as a "terse, wiry leader." Sadowy referred to the better Shawangunk climbers as terse, wiry leaders, and they all owned cotton caps. A 1958 article in *Sports Illustrated* featured "high-angle specialist McCarthy" complete with Turs-wiry Hat. From then on its value was even more pronounced.

Gran was unofficial spokesman for Eastern climbing. On one of his first visits to Yosemite he was deeply engaged in a discussion with Robbins on the topic of just *who* were the hard men in their respective areas. "Well," said Gran in all serious-ness, "in the Gunks you can tell the best climbers by the hats they wear." It sounded absurd, but it was true. The ever-earnest Robbins was taken aback and impressively replied, "In Yosemite you can tell the best climbers by the routes they do."

During the mid-1960s the number of Shawan-gunks climbers increased, but it was sufficiently small that the dedicated climbers knew each other at least by sight. One day Gran overheard a stranger say he had just done the fierce Land's End. "You did Land's End?" Gran demanded incredulously. The newcomer replied that was the case. Gran retorted, "You couldn't have. I don't even know you." Yet the number of persons capable of leading at the standard of Land's End continually edged upward, a progress stimulated by the appearance of Gran's Shawangunk guide-book in 1964. The guide helped to demystify the existing routes and brought about a period of con-solidation. The majority of the classic lines had been climbed, and attention turned to repeating the best routes and to eliminating aid.

The Vulgarians developed close bonds. In the late 1950s several of them had moved into New York's Lower East Side, then in the formative stages of the coming bohemian period. By the mid-1960s city life began to pall. Although climb-

A typical Vulgarian gross-out; Dick Williams makes the first nude ascent of Shockley's Ceiling, Shawangunks. *Art Gran*, courtesy Ed Cooper.

ing was now less important to the original Vulgarian group, they retained an identity with the Shawangunks, the scene of their intense, ribald youth, and they moved up to the country near the cliffs. They had college educations, and the move meant they had to take whatever jobs they could. The trade of a city job for a life in the area of the Shawangunks was gladly made. There they lived free from the expectations of the hustling world for which they had so little sympathy.

Colorado Rock

When Layton Kor returned to Colorado from his 1960 cross-country trip, his enthusiasm knew no bounds. His revelations of hard climbs and hard climbers opened the eyes of the Coloradans and particularly fellow fanatic Bob Culp. They had met when Northcutt and Kor came down from the Diagonal. Kor, tall and gangly, spoke excitedly of the difficulties while the compact, trim Northcutt said little. Kor was oufitted in ridiculous knickers that stopped above his knees and socks that stopped below them. A red beret perched on his head. Northcutt's clothes gave him just the right air of authenticity, and his red beret was set at a jaunty angle. Not long after the meeting Culp bought a red beret.

It was apparent to Kor and Culp that there were fantastic climbers in Yosemite, let alone Europe.

They had best sharpen up their act. They were enmeshed in the history of the sport and determined to bring that history to life in Colorado. In his autobiography *Lonely Challenge* Austrian mountaineer Hermann Buhl emphasized that climbers had to solo in order to realize their full potential. This was gospel to Culp and Kor, who began to solo ever more unlikely routes. In an effort to experience the continued difficulty of a major alpine climb, they knocked off Hallett Peak's second and third buttresses in a six-hour dash. (Kor later soloed the third buttress in about ninety minutes.)

Just when the climbing future looked bright and plans were laid for a summer in the Alps, Kor was bedridden with severe chest pains and shortness of breath. Doctors diagnosed the problem as the lung fungus San Joaquin Valley fever but had few suggestions in the way of treatment. The prognosis was that Kor might die, might recover, or might spend the rest of his life in bed. In casting about for a better idea, Kor heard of a spirit healer in Texas who believed in a starvation diet. He determined to go. His friends thought it was madness; he was signing his death warrant. They chipped in to send him to the Mayo clinic, but his mind was made up, and off he went to Texas. After more than a month he returned. He had wasted away to a gaunt 110 pounds, but he breathed freely.

His recovery may have been prolonged by his

lettuce and carrot diet. At lunch stops on climbs he would devour a couple of heads of lettuce and exclaim to no one's conviction, "You should try it. Lotsa energy in lettuce." Convalescent or not, his pace picked up. In 1961 he and Culp attempted the smooth 1,500-foot northwest face of Chiefshead, an outstanding problem in Rocky Mountain National Park. Climbing as though inspired, he led a difficult 160-foot pitch with one shaky piton for protection. Like so many of his climbs, this 5.9 pitch gained an enduring reputation for desperation.

Kor was on form as never before and ranged over the cliffs and mountains of Colorado and the Southwest, climbing everything in sight. He was fascinated by the sandstone towers of the desert and made early ascents of the three classic spires pioneered by the Southern Californians: Spider Rock, Cleopatra's Needle, and the Totem Pole. He went on to make his own contributions encouraged by astrophysicist Huntley Ingalls, who enthused over the spires as "significant summits unique on the face of the planet."

Before Kor's onslaught got underway, Californians Kamps and Pratt made the second ascent of Spider Rock. According to Navajo legend its summit is littered with the bones of children the Spider Woman devours. After an uneventful climb Kamps and Pratt entered the town of Chinle, curious to see if they had caused a stir. At the ranger headquarters they learned that the Navajos were furious over the desecration. He should have known better, but on the way out of town Pratt stopped at the local trading post. It was full of Navajos. The conversation died away, and all eyes fixed on him. The only sound was his quickening heartbeat. As he moved toward the door, a massive Indian loomed up out of the shadows and demanded:

"Did you climb Spider Rock?"

"Why yes," returned Pratt reaching for the door, "now that you mention it, I did." But worse was to come.

"What did you find on top?"

Every ear strained for the reply. His mind raced.

"We found a pile of bleached bones on the top."

The silence was absolute. He began to ease open the door. The huge Indian took a step toward him, "What do you take me for—a fool?"

The room burst into uncontrolled laughter, and the humbled Pratt slid out the door.

The Californians attached a ritual importance to their cross-country trips. Beat writer and sometime mountain climber Jack Kerouac was one of their heroes, his *On the Road* one of their favorite sagas.

Late one fall Chouinard took off from the East in a drive-away car. It was in bad shape, and he had spent all his money on gas and repairs when he reached Boulder. There he met Pratt, and with the help of a borrowed credit card they coaxed the car into Albuquerque, New Mexico. Unknown to Chouinard the car had been stolen and later recovered in New York. By the time he delivered it, he was a month late. The owner was furious and refused to repay his expenses.

Flat broke, Pratt and Chouinard started to hitchhike home. In Grants, New Mexico, they were picked up by high school kids joy-riding in their parents' car. The local police hauled the car over and were suspicious of the down-at-heel climbers. They were held in jail for seventy-two hours while the police checked their fingerprints.

After their release they took a bus to a nearby town and tried to catch a ride. No one stopped, so they stole into the railroad yard. They spotted a car transporter headed west and made themselves comfortable in a pick-up truck playing the radio and laying low while the miles slipped by. In Winslow, Arizona, a security guard noticed the pick-up's steamed windows, and the luckless pair were again hauled off to jail. The judge offered them ten to thirty days if they pleaded guilty. If they pleaded not guilty, they would be charged with trespass and get six months. They served fifteen days. When Pratt arrived home, the sky had fallen. His army induction notice awaited him.

In 1961 Kor and Ingalls planned to attempt the Priest, a sandstone spire twenty miles east of Moab, Utah. They were joined in the attempt by longtime desert devotees Fred Beckey and Harvey Carter.

Holed up in Colorado Springs, Carter kept apart from the main thrust of Colorado climbing. Once a year he staged a "Soft Rock Climbing Championship" on his local boulders. Since he knew the set pieces by heart—indeed he set the course—he consistently emerged the champion. The Boulder climbers thought the championship was a joke and left it severely alone, but one year a Boulderite could not resist the temptation. He sauntered over to the competition site and struck up a conversation with a coed. The young woman reverently pointed to a muscled figure at grips with the rock and said, "That's Harvey Carter. He's the world's greatest climber."

Before Carter and Beckey arrived in the Moab area, Kor and Ingalls picked off nearby 400-foot Castelton Tower. Then all four climbed the Priest in two hard days. In 1962 Colorado University student George Hurley joined Kor and Ingalls on the 650-foot Titan. The lower part of the route led up a single 300-foot crack system, where they learned to deal with the soft, mud-caked rock. They hammered and chipped it away in order to place pitons in the underlying rock. They spent two days fixing ropes up to the Finger of Fate and completed the route with one bivouac (V, 5.8 A3).

The Titan, Utah. The 1962 route takes the shadowed wall beneath the Finger of Fate, then lies near the right skyline. Harvey T. Carter and party climbed the sunlit face in 1971. *Ed Cooper.*

Kor and Ingalls next enlisted the long-time mentor of Boulder climbers, Steve Komito, for 300-foot Standing Rock. Although short, the climb was a nightmare of rotten rock and A4 pitons. From Standing Rock and other climbs Kor gained a reputation as a master on bad rock. The worse conditions got the more eager he became. He was probably the best all-round rock climber in the country in his ability to get up any given piece of rock.

Climbing continued apace on the rock walls around Boulder. As elsewhere in the state Kor outdistanced all others. The only person near his level was Culp, who carried the longtime appelation, "Colorado's number two climber." The pair established a milestone in Boulder climbing with Naked Edge in 1962 (5.9 A3). This superb 900-foot climb combined maximum difficulty with a bold line. For years it was the showpiece route of the area.

Kor worked as little as possible and as a consequence had more time for climbing than anyone else. He climbed with anyone, just so long as his second would hold on to the other end of the rope.

His favorite hangout was the Sink in Boulder, a popular bar with Colorado University students. All he needed to see was someone wearing a parka. A favorite story has him in the Sink one evening when he had just made the acquaintance of a newcomer. Impatient to get going, he enthused over a "fantastic climb" he had spotted. He insisted they do the route by flashlight. Before long he shouted encouragement as their two tiny shafts of light made their way upward.

Kor climbed so fast and confidently that his

Kor leads off from the Finger of Fate, Titan.
Huntley Ingalls.

partners were glad to leave him the bulk of the leading. This arrangement suited him perfectly. He wanted to be in the lead all the time. The more overawed his sometimes green seconds were, the more he relished the situation. He occasionally added a touch to the second's anguish. At a belay ledge on the overhanging face of Steamboat Rock he found a few bird feathers. As Mike Covington gingerly prusiked up, Kor leaned over the edge with the feathers stuck in his hair and let out a shriek. Covington went white.

Kor's special domain was Rocky Mountain National Park, where he put up the second route on the Diamond, Yellow Wall (V, 5.8 A4) in 1962. His partner Charles Roskosz was not "authorized" to be on the Diamond and was fined ten dollars by the Park Service. The next year Kor and Robbins climbed the Jack of Diamonds in a sixteen-hour dash. More a legend than a piece of rock, the climb went unrepeated for years. The Diamond itself had a reputation for seriousness that did not begin to fade until the 1967 ascent of D-7 (V, 5.6 A2) After Larry Dalke, George Hurley, and Wayne Goss pioneered this route there was a Diamond climb without a horror pitch. By the 1970s the once formidable Diamond became a regular event.

Late in 1962 Kor again laid plans for a blitz of the Alps. He had to make amends for the dismal venture two years before. As it happened a season in Yosemite got in the way of the European trip. By now a few Colorado climbers paid an annual visit to the fabled valley. The outsiders looked on Yosemite with a mixture of awe and envy. It was widely believed that the Californians were blessed in some supernatural way. (Mike Borghoff imagined a race of blond giants; instead he met Harding and Powell curled around a jug of wine.) The feeling was reinforced when the outsiders arrived in Yosemite. The locals were fit and suntanned and ruthlessly efficient on the Camp 4 boulder problems. They dressed alike in shorts and white T-shirts, adopted the same patterns of speech, and

Charles Roskosz, left, and Layton Kor after the first ascent of Yellow Wall, the Diamond. *Cleve McCarty.*

were prone to philosophical discussion. They were impressively serious and intellectual.

The subtleties of the Yosemite scene were not lost on the Coloradans. One returned with the regulation shorts and T-shirt and a touch his friends thought was a bit much: a volume of Nietzsche stuck prominently out of his back pocket.

The Californians were also coming to Colorado in force. Dave Rearick, who had arrived as an outsider to climb the Diamond, now came to live in the Boulder area. With his Tahquitz background of pushing the limits of free climbing, he led Kor's T2 in 1962 (5.9). Robbins passed through the same year. The locals were awed. He had just climbed the Salathé Wall and was off to conquer the Alps. Because of his technical supremacy and his distant manner, he was the butt of many stories. There was the time when he reputedly rose to his feet in Camp 4 and announced, "Tomorrow we have decided to climb the Salathé Wall." The statement was followed by a round of applause.

Another Robbins story was apparently coined during this visit to Boulder. He and his wife Liz were at a party. He spoke on a variety of topics, and by the time he left there was a look of wonder on people's faces. The oracle had spoken. The bemused expressions were shattered when a Boulderite mimicked Liz Robbins, "Look, Royal, there's a mouse."

To which the grave, deep-throated reply was, "That's not a mouse; that's an elephant."

And an enraptured Liz, "Oh Royal, you know *everything*!"

Unkind, but a reflection of the way he was seen by his peers and would-be-peers.

Royal Robbins, left, and Pat Ament in Yosemite, 1968. *Steve Roper.*

He was back in Boulder in 1964. With his teenage protégé Pat Ament he made free ascents of Eldorado's Yellow Spur (5.9) and Athlete's Feat (5.10) at Castle Rock. The latter was a major effort. At the crux Robbins said he just had strength for one more try. Although he took a fall, he made the lead.

Ament first appeared on the Boulder scene around 1961 with his high school pal Larry Dalke. They got stuck on Yellow Spur in the dark and were rescued by Kor. He recognized their determination and soon had them in tow on new routes. Ament announced that in two years he would be a better climber than Kor and set out to make good his prediction. After he climbed with Robbins, he emphasized the elimination of aid. However, his egotism and drive to succeed estranged him from many, and he drafted a succession of youngsters onto his rope. These unsuspecting seconds belayed while he worked out moves. In this manner he built up his knowledge of a route and ultimately strung together the moves to make a free ascent.

Dalke was also highly motivated and patterned his climbing after Kor. By the late 1960s he was the fastest and most skilled aid climber in Colorado. His free climbing was also remarkable as evidenced by his 1964 ascent of the Green Spur (5.9).

In 1965 Ament began to work on what was an obvious test piece, the vicious, overhanging Supremacy Crack. He eventually climbed it with a top rope, and when Robbins was in Boulder the next year Ament made the lead (5.11). Robbins made a strong try to follow but was held on the rope. The fact that he could not follow Ament's lead does not mean that he had been surpassed. There is a marked difference between "wiring" a route and doing it on sight. Although it was the first 5.11 lead in the country, the new standard had not yet arrived. The top-roped workouts removed the ascent from the traditional field. Not until the 1970s did climbers lead 5.11 without reconnaissance.

As climbers strove to eliminate aid, it became important to define the exact meaning of the term. In the early 1950s Tahquitz climbers counted *any* assistance from the rope, pitons, or other protection points as aid. This ethic eventually spread

Larry Dalke on the first ascent of The Invisible Wall, Longs Peak. *Layton Kor.*

across the continent although the date of its acceptance varied. In the Shawangunks, for example, climbers had originally followed the Dolomite tradition where aid meant stirrups; using a piton for a handhold was not considered aid. When Ament pioneered his all-free ascents, he sometimes failed to abide by the finer nuances of style. A hasty grab for a piton was easily overlooked in the flush of victory. But whatever blemishes certain of his ascents may have in modern eyes, he was one of those most responsible for the push into 5.10.

The flat grassland to the west of the Rockies is an unlikely setting for a major climbing area, but if you know where to look, you will see a low cliff band. When you are almost upon the cliffs, you realize that what you see is the far side of a 2,000-foot chasm, the Black Canyon of the Gunnison River. While newcomers ventured onto his hardest Eldorado Canyon routes, Kor was busy in this far more serious setting. After an exploratory climb in 1961 he rushed over with a fistful of pictures to see Culp. That evening they piled into Kor's rickety Ford and raced to the canyon.

When they reached its floor, they picked an 1,800-foot buttress for their first climb. They anticipated the steep granite would need a lot of aid and had brought huge quantities of gear and water. By early afternoon they were on top.

Kor relished the canyon's somber half-light and its oppressive feeling. Here was an area that rivaled Yosemite Valley in the magnificence of the

Larry Dalke, left, and Pat Ament on the first ascent of Temporary Like Achilles (5.8 A4), Eldorado Canyon. *Cliff Jennings.*

The Black Canyon of the Gunnison, Colorado. *Gene White.*

climbing situation. The partners he introduced to the canyon seldom lasted more than one climb before they became spooked. However, Larry Dalke was different. This was where Kor climbed, and this was where he would climb. They made several outstanding climbs which rivaled anything in Yosemite save El Capitan. Kor said little about the canyon; he did not want to attract a bunch of Californians. Before his campaign was over, he pioneered some dozen routes including the 1965 Green Slab (VI, 5.8 A4) with Brian Marts and South Wall of Chasm View (VI, 5.9 A4) with Dalke.

Throughout his career Kor was haunted by the great climbs of the Alps. Late in 1965 he left for Europe and a try at the most talked about Alpine problem of the day, the Eiger Direct. The climb was a triumph and a tragedy. John Harlin fell to his death. Although Kor was not among the five persons who reached the top, he made a major contribution to this historic ascent. When he returned to America, his goals were changing. He had climbed extreme routes for nearly ten years; how long could he last? He was also delving into religion and drug experiences. There was one major climbing effort to come. Perhaps as compensation for not being on the final push on the Eiger, he teamed with Wayne Goss in what may be regarded as a symbolic finish to his exploration in Colorado, the first winter ascent of the Diamond. This two-day climb in March 1967 was a prodigious undertaking, made almost unbearable by the intense cold. The Enos Mills Wall was the first big wall in North America climbed in winter. With this ascent Kor broke clear of the spell of extreme climbing. There were hard climbs now and then, but he was committed to religion.

Wherever today's climbers go in Colorado, they are likely to find that Kor has been there before.

Kor's contribution to the sport was unprecedented. The enduring personality of the era will always be the lanky figure striding along at full speed exclaiming over some climb he has just spotted, "It's simply *got* to be climbed."

REFERENCES

Ament, Pat, and Cleveland McCarty. *High over Boulder.* Boulder: Pruett, 1970.

Cote, Joseph, and Karen Cote. *A Climber's Guide to Cathedral and White Horse Ledges.* Joseph Cote, 1969.

Covington, Mike. "Diamond Commentary." *Mountain,* no. 40 (Nov. 1974), p. 17.

Culp, Bob. "Boulder Rock Climbers: Faces of the Sixties." *T & T,* no. 623 (Nov. 1970), p. 238.

Dumais, Dick. "Shawangunks." *Mountain,* no. 21 (May 1972), p. 23.

Fricke, Walter W., Jr. *A Climber's Guide to Rocky Mountain National Park.* Boulder: Paddock, 1971.

Gran, Arthur. *A Climber's Guide to the Shawangunks.* New York: American Alpine Club, 1964.

Ingalls, Huntley. "We Climbed Utah's Skyscraper Rock." *National Geographic* 122 (Nov. 1962): 705.

Kor, Layton. "Black Canyon of the Gunnison, Green Pillar." *AAJ* 15 (1966): 146.

———. "On the Granite Wall." *T & T,* no. 583 (June 1967), p. 4.

———. "Climbing in the Black Canyon of the Gunnison." *Climbing* 1(1) (May 1970): 10.

"One Man's Way to Reach the Summit." *Sports Illustrated* 9(16) (Oct. 20, 1958): 18.

Pratt, Chuck. "The View from Deadhorse Point." *Ascent* (May 1970): 37.

Roper, Steve. "Four Corners." *Ascent* (May 1970): 26.

Rubin, Al, and Paul Ross. "Vox for Vulgaria." *Mountain,* no. 21 (May 1972), p. 18.

Sopka, John. "Five New Routes in the Black Canyon of the Gunnison." *AAJ* 13 (1963): 493.

Williams, Richard C. *Shawangunk Rock Climbs.* New York: American Alpine Club, 1972.

The Eiger
of North America?

In climbing as in life the grass is greener on the other side of the fence, particularly if there is a "Keep Out" sign on the fence. The forbidden has a strong fascination to the human mind. When authorities decree that certain peaks are not to be climbed, those peaks take on a new luster.

In 1936 in the aftermath of tragedies on the North Face of the Eiger, the Swiss cantonal government of Berne banned attempts on the face. The ban was wholly ineffective. It drew the sensation-hungry, deterred no one, and was dropped within a few months. The European nations never again tried a similar tactic. In the United States outright bans and restrictive regulations are not uncommon: the prohibition against climbing El Capitan during the tourist season, the closure of the Lost Arrow Chimney, the taboo on the Diamond. Why the difference in attitude?

Europeans look upon an individual's life as his own concern. The state does not attempt to protect a person from their own actions even if those actions are potentially lethal. In North America the state often does intervene between the individual and his destiny. It takes the role of the all-seeing protector. The motorcyclist must wear a helmet;

the scuba diver who lacks a certificate may not have air cylinders recharged; the motorist who does not care for seat belts is assailed by buzzers and lights, and the car will not start. In areas under the jurisdiction of the National Park Service, there have been both outright bans and restrictive regulations. The regulations have covered what a person may attempt, with whom, at what time of the year, and with what equipment. The intent has been to reduce accidents and keep away the inexperienced. Yet their success is questionable and their effect pernicious.

Challenge and judgment are the essence of climbing, and regulations attempt to remove both. They prevent less experienced climbers from making the very decisions that will afford them the experience they seek. In addition, regulations imply that climbers do not know when to wear protective helmets or use the rope. The important mountaineering decisions are not those made by a ranger at park headquarters but those necessitated while a climb progresses: evaluations of the route, the strength of the party, changing weather conditions, and so on. Those who draw up the regulations are not usually active climbers, and thus it is no surprise that they hope regulations will save lives. They fail to realize that danger is inseparable from mountaineering. There will always be accidents.

By virtue of its location near Seattle and its accessibility, Mount Rainier has been the scene of tragedies and near tragedies to inexperienced people. From the ranger station at Paradise the summit seems within easy grasp. More than one tyro has set out for the top with street shoes and a cheery wave. In the case of these nonclimbers some regulation is probably desirable, just as it is desirable to have a guard rail around Niagara Falls. However, during the 1950s the Rainier authorities imposed stringent regulations on bona-fide climbers. One of these was the notorious equipment check. A caustic bunch of rangers checked off a person's gear against a master list that contained every conceivable and some almost inconceivable items. The grand finale was the ice axe test. A ranger siezed the axe, supported it between two rocks, and jumped on it. If the shaft broke, too bad. Other axes, presumably tested, were available from the nearby guide concession. Of course, climbers occasionally got the best of it. One quietly produced a newly developed all-metal axe. Legend relates that the overzealous ranger spent the rest of the week hobbling around on a sprained ankle.

One summer Steve Roper and three friends came up from California to climb the usual route on Mount Rainier—pretty small beer for this strong party. They persuaded the authorities that they were "qualified" to make the climb only after considerable discussion. Roper's ice axe had "rental" written upon it, and with a hint of glee a ranger cracked it in half. Not a little chagrined, Roper duly rented another axe which, significantly, was not subjected to the same test. After the ranger advised them of the various regulations, including the mandatory use of the rope above the 10,000-foot level, the Californians set off. The simple climb was quickly made, and on the descent they ran and glissaded down the snow beside the well-marked tracks of countless parties. Unknown to the climbers, the rangers practiced long-distance law enforcement through a pair of binoculars. One of the party was unroped. When they entered the ranger station to check in from the climb, a grim-faced Smokey-the-Bear figure read them the section and act. Before they were allowed to leave the park, the law breaker was hauled before a "kangaroo court" and fined twenty-five dollars.

The regulations were restrictive and annoying enough on the regular route, but on the sinister northern flank of Mount Rainier they were repressive. Besides the equipment check, a team had to have a minimum of four members and a standby party in support. However, the regulations were almost self-defeating. To come up with a competent party of four in those days was no

simple matter, and dubious climbers were sometimes tagged onto a rope. The procedure under-
mined the total strength of the party but satisfied
the rules.*

The Willis Wall

Rising between Mount Rainier's Liberty and Curtis
ridges and capped by a 300-foot ice cliff, which
spews off avalanches, is the grim Willis Wall. To
the budding hard men of the Cascades the north
face of Mount Rainier looked scary, steep and
rotten. It looked like the great faces of the Alps. It
would have to be climbed.

In the early 1960s a group of Seattle climbers
hung out at the Pizza Haven in the university
district managed by machiavellian Eric Bjornstad.
An inveterate collector, he had acquired a wooden
camel, a few thousand keys, and 6,000 old bottles
(most of which were subsequently destroyed in
the Seattle earthquake). Bjornstad was generous
with both pizzas and the latest climbing gossip.
One of the climbers who occasionally dropped by
was the mysterious, scraggly-looking Charlie Bell.
It was never clear to the Seattle bunch just where
Bell came from or where he got his money, but at

that time he received regular unemployment
checks in the mail. Since he listed his occupation
as "Mandarin Chinese translator," his easy life
seemed destined for a long run.

One day at the Pizza Haven Bjornstad confided
to Bell that Ellensburg climbers Dave Mahre, Gene
Prater, and others were about to launch a "secret"
attempt on the Willis Wall. They were afraid the
Park Service would deny permission for it, so they
signed out for nearby Liberty Ridge. Bjornstad
invited Bell to come along as part of the required
support party.

The morning of the attempt dawned cloudy, and
before long the climbing party came down and
announced they were giving up the project. Bell
rested during the bad weather and munched the
Baby Ruth bars that were his staple diet. The next
day was as beautiful as the previous one was bad,
and he decided to reconnoiter the route for the
others. The closer he got to the wall, the more
reasonable it looked. Early in the afternoon he
began climbing up moderately angled snow on the
right side of the face. He was on a rib that stood
out from the face and thus felt safe from the rock
and icefall that occasionally rattled down to either
side. The higher he got, the easier the climbing
looked ahead. Almost imperceptibly the reconnaissance turned into a real attempt. That night he
bivouacked, and by the middle of the next day he
was up the feared Willis Wall. It had been an
uncommonly pleasant, straightforward climb. Of

*The Park Service was not wholly responsible for the sad state
of affairs. The rules were drawn up in consultation with the
region's mountaineering and mountain rescue organizations.

Charlie Bell on the Robson Glacier. *Ed Cooper.*

course, he had to get down. He knew that to traverse the mountain and descend by the normal route would be dangerous because of hidden crevasses. To avoid the crevasse probem, he descended Liberty Ridge and bagged another "first."

A day or two later Bell turned up at the Pizza Haven. Bjornstad jokingly inquired, "Hey, what did you do? The Willis Wall?" The answer left him dumbfounded. When he heard the details, he began calling around town with the news: Charlie Bell *soloed* the Willis Wall!

The Seattle and Ellensburg climbers were amazed. Few of them knew Bell, and those that did considered him an average performer. How could he have knocked off a climb they regarded as the next frontier? Bell was delighted at the sensation he had caused and readily agreed to Bjornstad's suggestion that he lead a second ascent. A half dozen well-known climbers accompanied Bell back to Mount Rainier eager to repeat the climb and see the evidence firsthand. Unfortunately, the day was hot, and the obvious avalanche danger caused them to abandon the attempt. It was an understandable action, but it did not help Bell's story.

Several of the climbers thought Bell was vague about the route he had taken. They could make out footsteps on Liberty Ridge but not on Willis Wall. Beckey wondered why Bell had no high altitude sunburn and dismissed the ascent as nonsense. The seeds of doubt were sown.

Bell left Seattle. The following summer, word of the widespread doubt reached him, and he decided that the simplest thing to do was to repeat the climb with a camera.

In 1962 Ed Cooper and Mike Swayne attacked the extreme left side of the crumbling Willis Wall. Unroped, they climbed rapidly to the top. They noticed a lone figure moving to the foot of the wall far below them. One day after they made their triumphant entry in the summit register, Bell entered the details of his second solo climb. Because the bergschrund at the base of his previous route was impassable, he had taken a different and more dangerous line. He climbed diagonally left from near the base of Liberty Ridge, crossed a prominent avalanche chute, and joined the west rib, his earlier route, about two-thirds of the way up. In his camera he had, or so he thought, irrefutable proof of his climb.

When Cooper got down, he wrote an article about his "illegal" climb for a Seattle newspaper. He included his caustic views on the regulations. The Park Service was badly needled. Rangers were dispatched to the summit to obtain the incriminating evidence. Imagine their surprise when they discovered a second crime: Bell's solo climb! Warrants were issued for all three lawbreakers. Swayne was picked up and held in jail until he paid the $150 fine, but Bell and Cooper managed to lay low until the flap subsided. However, there was no escape. Cooper was seized and handcuffed by federal marshals in Yosemite a few years later. Bell eventually forfeited fifty dollars to clear his name in the matter of *U.S. vs. Charles H. Bell.*

After his second ascent of the Willis Wall, Bell had his pictures developed, and a few people even took the trouble to look at them. The diehard sceptics easily explained away the pictures; he had hired a plane or had traversed directly across from Liberty Ridge. Undeterred, he prepared careful accounts of his climb. *Summit* refused the material,

The climbing days behind him, Ed Cooper turns to photography. *Jim Stuart.*

saying that solo climbs were not the sort of thing for their readers. The *American Alpine Journal* did not reply.

In 1970 the climb was unknowingly repeated by Seattle climbers Alex Bertulis and Jim Wickwire, who made the first winter ascent of the wall. Their photographs matched Bell's, and his second climb was established beyond doubt.* The enigmatic Bell became something of a cause célèbre. The role of the persecuted innocent seemed to fit him well.

Dave Mahre returned to the Willis Wall in 1963. He and his companions had been watching and studying the wall for five years. They had charted the safest route, and conditions were right. With Wickwire, Don Anderson, and Fred Dunham, Mahre completed the second route on the Willis Wall proper (IV or V). It is regrettable that the 1964 *American Alpine Journal* referred to the East Rib as "the first *legal* ascent."

*The author accepts Bell's unproven 1961 first ascent of the west rib proper.

In the rest of the Cascades good climbing continued apace. Beckey and Cooper, former friends, now turned competitors and tried to beat each other to various unclimbed plums. Beckey took the north face of Mount Fury, Cooper the north face of Mount Terror. On Mount Adams Cooper and Swayne climbed the east face. They were followed the next year by Beckey and protégé Dan Davis on what Beckey claimed as the east face "direct." Davis and physics major Pat Callis climbed the North Peak of Mount Index in winter in a four-day round trip. However, the highlight of the early 1960s took place across the Canadian border on remote Mount Slesse.

The instigator of the 1963 climb of the northeast buttress of Slesse, one of the finest routes in the Cascades, was old warrior Beckey. He was partnered by fashion photographer Steve Marts, who had fallen under the beneficial influence of the new attitudes in Yosemite Valley. Marts wanted to make a clean break with the fixed-roping that was still prevalent in the Northwest. He made it clear to Beckey that they should tackle Mount Slesse in alpine style. Their initial attempt was cut short after their first bivouac, when daylight revealed nothing but dense clouds. They retreated rather than risk the possibility of a storm on the peak. A few weeks later they returned to the buttress with Bjornstad and reached the summit on the morning of their third day.

About this time Bjornstad opened his own coffee

bar, The Eigerwand, in the university district. The place was elegantly furnished. Because of Bjornstad's reputation as a "gentleman burglar," his friends pressed him for the history of its magnificent marble coffee tables; surely he had not bought them. No, Bjornstad explained, he had not bought them. He had liberated the marble slabs from the men's room of the abandoned city jail.

By 1965 a new group of climbers began to make their mark in the Cascades. Like Marts, they determined to dispense with fixed ropes. Beckey

Dan Davis on the North Peak of Mount Index, January, 1963. *Pat Callis.*

was reputed to have ropes hanging on a half-dozen climbs. The ropes served to establish the routes as "his." A standard joke among the younger climbers, when asked what they had in mind, was that they were "off to hang a couple of ropes." The forceful newcomers also worked to cut down on the aid used by their predecessors. They exploded up the traditional routes on the granite crags of the Wenatchee River's Tumwater Canyon, their major practice area. Chief among them were Tom Hargis and powerfully built, impetuous Jim Madsen.

The young turks were attuned to the latest in climbing, and in the mid-1960s the latest was Yosemite. They went to the valley and brought home new attitudes and new desires. They found a wall in the Cascades comparable with the big walls of Yosemite: the 1,200-foot east face of Liberty Bell. The first attempts on the face were made by Marts and architect Alex Bertulis, who had made a ten-day traverse of the Picket Range in 1963. Marts returned in 1965 with University of Washington climbers Don McPherson and Fred Stanley, perhaps the strongest free climber of the period, to establish the Liberty Crack (V). The pace of exploration was quickening. Bertulis and Mc-Pherson climbed the Independence Route (VI, 5.8 A4) over four hard days in 1966. Two weeks later Bertulis, Madsen, and two others made a new finish to Liberty Crack. Bertulis took a couple of falls on the third lead when sky hooks slipped off. He gave up exhausted, and Madsen stormed into the A4 lead, breaking his hammer in the process. After their hammock bivouac, another hammer had disappeared. With only two hammers left and unknown ground ahead, Bertulis's companions wanted to retreat. He persuaded them to stick with the climb, and they reached the summit on the

The north face of Mount Slesse. The 1963 route ascends the buttress which starts at the lower right. *Steve Marts.*

Leif-Norman Patterson, left, Fred Beckey, Hank Mather and Alex Bertulis on top of the Squamish Chief after the first ascent of the Northwest Passage, 1965. With outstanding climbs in Europe and the Americas, Norwegian-born Patterson is among the most accomplished mountaineers in North America. From *Vancouver Sun,* courtesy Alex Bertulis.

morning of the third day. After a series of successes in Yosemite, Madsen and Kim Schmitz returned to Liberty Bell in 1967. The desirable central line on the east face remained unclimbed. Fred Beckey's rotting fixed ropes were cut away (by "irresponsible bastards"), and the pair completed the third route on the face, the so-called Direct (VI, 5.9 A4).

The hard climbs in Tumwater Canyon and on Liberty Bell signaled a new level of technical expertise in the Northwest. The newcomers might have initiated an advance in alpine climbing. No such advance occurred. Yosemite, with its easy approaches and greater prestige, siphoned off the best young climbers. The North Cascades presented formidable barriers of access, weather, and remoteness to its suitors. Ambitious plans were laid but seldom came to pass. In order for alpinism to progress significantly in the 1960s, the new skills learned at the rock climbing centers would have to be conscientiously applied in the high mountains. An influx of new faces and new ideas was needed in the slow-moving alpine world.

The Tetons

During the early 1960s the Tetons were the goal of American mountaineers. There were seldom repeated alpine classics, hard rock climbs, and exciting new routes. The most discussed unclimbed route on the high peaks was the Grand Teton's Black Ice Couloir. The problem was not so much that technical difficulties had defeated earlier climbers, but that the climbers had not got to grips with the couloir. The steep couloir was different. It offered ice climbing in a range where such climbing is rare. It posed significant dangers from the rockfall that funnels into it from either side. At this stage in the evolution of North American moun-

Ray Jacquot in the Black Ice Couloir, Grand Teton.
Herb Swedlund.

taineering, climbers had yet to come to terms with objective dangers. Deliberately climbing under these conditions might appear to verge on madness. However, bearing in mind such factors as temperature and time of day, an experienced climber can judge the dangers. Objective dangers add another dimension to the total mountaineering problem. To accept objective danger calmly, to weigh the risks, and to judge when conditions are right were major challenges for alpinists of the 1960s.

The Black Ice Couloir was high on the lists of several ambitious climbers, especially because the strong Chouinard-Weeks team turned back in the face of rockfall. Fear of the unknown and the dangers kept the climb a talking point until 1961, when engineering student Ray Jacquot teamed with Yosemite climber Herb Swedlund, who was in his first season as a Teton guide. Both had read Harrer's *The White Spider*, the gripping history of the Eigerwand, and were keen to find out what north walls and ice climbs were all about.

They knew that Europeans begin ice climbs at night. Freezing is at a maximum, snow is firm, and the early start allows the climbers to be well on their way before the sun loosens ice-imbedded rocks. Jacquot and Swedlund approached the couloir by moonlight and were on the ice by 1 A.M. Swedlund had worn crampons only once before, but his confidence increased as they advanced up the dread slope. He was irritated when Jacquot seemed to dither about on a lead, but when it was his turn, he slipped on the verglas-coated rock. No rocks fell, and after eleven tense hours they were up (IV).

Jacquot and Swedlund were the heroes of the hour. They explained that the climb had not been an ordeal, but others did not bother to listen. Like the North Face in earlier years it was talked about rather than repeated.

Although the Black Ice Couloir was climbed only once in the next four years, other alpine routes were highly prized. For the ambitious alpinist the North Face of the Grand Teton was an almost obligatory ascent. The Teton regulars prided themselves on their superiority to the Northwest "snowsloggers," and they concluded that the Tetons were the tough alpine scene in North America. A similar feeling of superiority prevailed among the best climbers in other areas. The Northwesterners thought they were the best mountaineers. The Shawangunk climbers and the Californians each thought they were the best on rock. There was so little interchange that it was easy for you and your mates to be convinced that you were at the forefront. Although Teton climbers lagged behind the Californians in rock skills and although their alpine routes were no better than those in the Cascades and Canada, their conclusion was largely correct. In the Tetons difficult alpine ascents were commonplace. Elsewhere they were uncommon.

When Yosemite climbers came to the Tetons in the early sixties, they brought with them the attitudes of California climbing. They caused a mild sensation by wearing shorts on mountain routes, and they knocked off several hard rock climbs with ease. The locals were eager to improve their skills. In 1961 Barry Corbet, Dave Dornan, and Dick Emerson completed the northwest face of Teewinot (IV, 5.8 A3) while Dornan and Swedlund climbed the South Buttress Right on Mount Moran (IV, 5.8 A1). Activity intensified on Moran, and six new routes were established in 1962. Dornan, Chouinard, and Jim McCarthy made No Escape Buttress (IV, 5.9). Pete Sinclair, Bill Buckingham, Guide Pete Lev, and Leigh Ortenburger climbed the north face (IV, 5.8). Perhaps the highlight of the season was Chouinard and Tom Frost's route on the northeast face of Disappointment Peak (IV, 5.9 A3).

The search for large-scale rock climbs led several people to the nearby Wind River Range. These granite peaks were one or two full days' hike from the road and were far less frequently visited than the Tetons. Climbers tended to go there for a holiday rather than to blaze new paths. Climbing standards there lagged behind the Tetons. Although a route might be an advance in terms of Wind River climbing, equivalent routes had already been made elsewhere. The Wind Rivers have a history of their own, but like Squamish Chief, the High Sierra, and much of the Rocky Mountains, they have contributed little to the development of North American climbing.

Of course, there are exceptions to such statements. In the Wind Rivers Chouinard and Art

Jim McCarthy on No Escape Buttress. Mount Moran. *Dave Dornan.*

Gran's 1961 route on the northwest face of East Temple appears equivalent to contemporary Teton climbs. Almost as soon as they set up their first bivouac, they were hit by a rainstorm. Rivulets of water ran down the face and over their bivouac sack. After a miserable night they were greeted by a dismal, watery dawn. They pressed on through steady rain and reached the top by late afternoon.

The most impressive Wind River wall is the 1,800-foot north face of Mount Hooker. The 1964 climb (VI) gave three and a half days of hard going to a strong trio of Californians: Royal Robbins, carpenter Dick McCracken, and Charlie Raymond. It was more severe than any rock climb yet made in the Tetons.

In the mid-1960s there seemed to be a pause in high standard Teton climbing. The alpine routes had lost much of their mystique, and the rock climbs were obviously not the match of those in Yosemite. Part of the reason for the pause was a lack of new ground—there were already some twenty routes on the Grand Teton. But there was an important new fact in American climbing, for the center of gravity had moved away from the Tetons. Yosemite was the new standard.

The Tetons were far from finished. They were still the mountains where many Americans pursued their alpine careers, they had difficulty and challenge enough to satisfy anyone, and they continued to serve as a training ground for expeditionary climbers. They were also the scene of new developments. In the winter of 1965 a Salt Lake City group climbed Mount Owen, and the following year they accounted for Mount Moran. They chose to climb these peaks in winter because they were familiar with the range. They were certain they could climb them in summer. By climbing in winter they lengthened the odds.

The Tetons were the only real mountaineering center in North America. Cascade climbers came predominantly from the nearby cities. In Canada you might not see another party for days. In the Tetons the regular visitors, the rangers, and the guides gave continuity and atmosphere to climbing in the area. At the Climbers' Camp aspirant mountaineers were sure to meet others and profit from good advice. They might talk with some of the big names in American climbing.

There was more to the Tetons than just climbing. These were intensely lived years in young lives. The latest climbing gossip was bandied about, spontaneous parties erupted, and the climbers' perennial quest for "tourist chicks" was vigorously pursued. There was a sense of camaraderie and of exploring new frontiers. Life in the Tetons was simply better and more brightly focused. It was a sad day when you headed out of the Tetons at the end of the climbing season.

Several college-educated climbers determined to live there year round. They had looked at the conventional "good life"; to them it was an abyss. Breitenbach, Corbet, and others worked as ski patrolmen and guides, ran motels, did any job to enable them to live where they belonged. They searched for a more idealistic life, and in the Tetons fleetingly they found it.

Dave Dornan on South Buttress Right, Mount Moran. *Pete Lev.*

Since the late 1950s a select group had gathered on summer nights to play music. These "Teton Tea Parties," presided over by talented musician Bill Briggs, came to have a special significance to the initiated. The music, the mountains, the communion were a potent brew. As their fame spread, more people were drawn to the parties, and the inevitable decline set in. Briggs tried to recapture the magic of the early days by insisting that everyone be silent, but it was in vain. The Vulgarians saw the tea parties as an opportunity for sport. They disrupted the church-like atmosphere with swearing, firecrackers, and finally the "Vulgariphone." They placed the far end of this fifteen-foot pipe over burning oil and then blew down it. The Vulgariphone shot out a flame accompanied by a sound that can only be described as an elephant fart.

The Vulgarians imported the Shawangunk Grand Prix to the Climbers' Camp and tore around the perimeter. There were riotous parties and monster campfires. Such antics went against the grain. The Park Service was upset by the "unconventional behavior" in the camp. Climbers overstayed the fourteen-day limit and were a nuisance. There was evidence of drugs. In 1966 the Climbers' Camp was closed.

The Mountains of Canada

As the 1960s progressed, it became apparent that future advances in North American alpine climbing would increasingly take place in Alaska and Canada. The Tetons and the Cascades had served until then, but they suffered from several flaws. They lacked major faces similar to those on which the stirring alpine climbs had taken place, and snow and ice conditions in the Tetons, at least, were seldom truly alpine. They lacked the scale of the Alps and the seriousness. The leading American climbers knew that the Tetons and the Cascades were not the ultimate experience. Was this experience waiting in Canada?

Chouinard and Ken Weeks went to Canada to answer this question in 1960. Their equipment was wretched, their clothes were torn, and they were broke. To get gas money, they hiked along the highway picking up discarded bottles worth a few cents apiece. To get food, they made an arduous ten-mile round trip into an Alpine Club of Canada camp, where they scavenged sacks of flour, carrots, and potatoes. Then they toiled into the Bugaboos with their heavy loads. The resident climbers were glad to exchange expensive dehydrated food for a couple of honest-to-goodness spuds. Chouinard and Weeks were ready to go.

Easily visible from the main street of Jasper, Alberta, there rises a dark and brooding wall, the 4,000-foot north face of Mount Edith Cavell. Together with Dan Doody, a climber at his best when things got rough, Chouinard and Weeks hung around the base of the immense wall. It was their ideal: "a technical climb," Chouinard wrote, "under alpine conditions with objective dangers." They accepted—indeed sought—objective dangers

The four-thousand-foot north face of Mount Edith Cavell. The 1961 route goes up the Angel Glacier, right, then climbs the rib directly below the summit. The 1967 route ascends ribs to the subsidiary left-hand summit. *Ed Cooper.*

as part of the total challenge. The weather was stormy. Merely looking up at the face was enough to churn the stomach. The climb went undone, but it did not go away.

During the following winter they made plans for another attempt. Weeks went into the army (he later went AWOL and hid out in the Tetons), and his place was taken by Beckey. This year there was money to spare. Doody had negotiated a film contract with the Canadian National Railways (C.N.R.), and the three lived in style at the C.N.R.'s opulent Jasper Park Lodge.

On the wall they were greeted with rockfall that would plague them for the rest of the climb. Wherever possible they belayed under projecting rocks. At one place Chouinard hesitated before he committed himself to the shooting gallery. Doody provided the needed spur, "I'll do it, if you won't." It was getting dark when the trio finally reached a ledge big enough to sit on.

In the morning the sky was completely overcast, and a steady rain fell as the climbers got under way. Flashes of lightning threw the face into garish relief. Beckey had climbed brilliantly the first day, taking the majority of the leads, but now he was badly rattled. Again Doody was the calm voice of reason that pulled the team together.

Leading on rotten ice, Chouinard peered down through a break in the clouds. His companions were huddled against the slope. Below them was the void. It came to him in a flash: This was truly like the pictures of the Eigerwand. Just below the summit was a steep band of wet, rotten shale. Pitons were useless. After a tense eighty-foot lead with no protection, Chouinard grasped the summit snow ridge. His feet slipped when he tried to move up. Beckey and Doody watched his every movement. If he came off, their feeble belay would be ripped away. Chouinard tensed up. "Oh God," he thought, "what a place to get it!" In desperation he looked to the side. A patch of snow gave hope of overcoming the final lip. He worked his way across and quickly stood on the summit (V).

The north face of Mount Edith Cavell was a major event in American climbing. Not only was a difficult climb made under poor conditions, but the climbers had to overcome the fear that surrounds a major push into the unknown. The team was drawn from the Northwest, California, and the East Coast. They brought with them the mix of qualities needed to advance the sport: experience gained throughout the continent, skills honed in local areas, and a willingness to accept objective danger. Perhaps it was just coincidence that the objectively dangerous Willis Wall and Black Ice Couloir were climbed this same year, 1961. Perhaps it signaled the beginning of a new attitude.

Beckey and Chouinard completed their Canadian season with a visit to the Bugaboos, which had become the alpine rock climbers' mecca. They were drawn by the mysterious western faces of the Howser Spires, the largest and most remote walls in the area. With Chouinard's Yosemite experience a decisive factor, they climbed the west buttress of the South Tower in one and a half days. The route was the equal of the east faces of Snowpatch and Bugaboo spires that were climbed a couple of years earlier with siege tactics. Yosemite philosophies and techniques were having far-reaching consequences.

Mount Robson

The spectacular peaks of a mountain range invariably attract attention. The straightforward routes are soon climbed, and latecomers are forced onto more difficult lines. Advances in mountaineering often occur on the most sought-after peaks. It happened on Mount Rainier, Mount McKinley, the Grand Teton, and Mount Robson. The Wishbone Arête was almost climbed in 1913, and the Emperor Ridge was seriously attempted in 1931 by Robert Underhill, both before their time. Repeated attempts on the two routes were made over the following years. In 1959 two parties were stopped by the tusk-like ice formations on the final stretch of the Emperor Ridge.

In 1961 two climbers bivouacked at the foot of the major difficulties on the Emperor Ridge. Tom Spencer had climbed Robson by the regular route two years before. His partner was snow ranger Ron Perla from Alta, Utah. Their alpine records were unimpressive; according to the conventional wisdom they had little chance. But they did not know that they were supposed to fail. Their determination and their naïvety were apparent when they left their bivouac. The mountain was capped in cloud, and windblown snow plastered the rock. They advanced. By early afternoon they gained the notorious ice-encrusted, knife-edge ridge. Huge faces fell away to either side, and they could get no adequate anchors. They doggedly continued, and late that evening they reached the summit. Two "unknowns" had pulled off a route that had kept away big-name climbers. Perhaps their biggest advantage was that they *were* naïve. They were not overawed by the oft-repeated Robson stories.

With the ascent of the Emperor Ridge (V) all the more obvious sides of Mount Robson had been climbed save the north, although several attempts had been made on the 2,000-foot snow and ice face. On one try Beckey and Cooper climbed to midheight before anxiety over the stability of the snow caused them to retreat. The next day their route was obliterated by an awesome slide.

Beckey went to the Bugaboos in 1963 with fellow Washington climbers Pat Callis and Dan Davis. There was a loose understanding that they would go to Robson together later, and Beckey went over to the Howsers. When he returned to Boulder Camp, he was surprised to find the others gone. On the way into Robson he heard they had climbed the face. Like the Emperor Ridge climb its significance lay in the climbers' willingness to undertake such a route on so feared a peak. The pair had made technically equivalent ice climbs in the Cascades but never on a Robson.

Beckey was keenly disappointed to miss out on Robson's north face. Yet he made some twenty-five first ascents all over the continent in 1963, about average performance for this most prolific of American climbers. In March 1965 he made the first winter ascent of Mount Robson. His compulsive pursuit of unclimbed peaks and faces made him second only to long-haul truck drivers in annual mileage. Much of this driving was occasioned by his concern over the weather. One Beckey story has him leaving Seattle and driving 150 miles south toward Mount Adams. The weather began to sour, so he turned around and drove back through Seattle toward British Columbia and Mount Slesse. Near the Canadian border he again became anxious about the weather. He urged his companions to turn back and head for Liberty Bell. Even as they hiked into Slesse, Beckey continued to talk about alternate plans.

Beckey's preoccupation with the weather began well before a projected climb. He would call the long distance information operator in, for example, Jasper, Alberta, to discuss the conditions on Mount Robson. Once on the climb, distant clouds were regarded as a threat. More than one partner was busily climbing when interrupted by Beckey's insistent, "Whadya think on the weather . . . think we should go down . . . whadya think?"

Wherever climbers went in the fifties and sixties, it was entirely possible they would come across one of Beckey's hard-working cars parked at the roadhead—perhaps the pink T-bird. In the back seat would be a few old copies of *Playboy*, odds and ends of climbing gear, and a box full of maps and photographs, the secret new climbs that he unearthed from obscure sources and zealously guarded from prying eyes. On the dashboard would be his address book: a half-dozen garish postcards from a Las Vegas casino covered with the phone numbers of the women he seemed to know in every state.

One time when climbers met Beckey along the trail with a recruit in tow, the conversation went roughly like this,

"Hi Fred, where've you been?"

"Oh you know," came the evasive reply, "back of the Divide."

"Yeah, I know, but what were you on?"

It was a ritual game. The questioner knew that Beckey would not tell where he had just been, and Beckey *knew* that he knew. Beckey gave one of his conspiratorial grins. After he grilled the others for any information they had, the parties went their separate ways. As if driven by some inner demon that allowed him no peace, Beckey strode off into the distance, his mind on his women and his mountains. A climber since the 1930s, a man with an ageless wanderlust, he is a legend in his own time.

Shawangunk climbers were active in both the Bugaboos and the Rockies during the 1960s. Gran was the inspiration for much of this activity. He was defeated by a storm on the west flank of Mount Alberta, but in 1964 he and John Hudson climbed the west face of Mount Brussels in one and a half days. In 1965 Gran, Hudson, and Pete Geiser attempted the imposing 4,000-foot east face of Mount Chephren. A rock avalanche swept down the evening before the climb, and the sheer size of the face almost demoralized them. They were away by 4 A.M. with Gran in the lead. He remained in front throughout the two-day climb (V). It was his finest achievement in the mountains.

The Canadians

The postwar Canadian climbs we have so far considered were established by Americans. Where were the home climbers? The situation in Vancouver will help to illustrate. The 1961 ascent of the Grand Wall on nearby Squamish Chief produced no appreciable local following. Here was a major cliff with hardly a soul on it an hour's drive from a large city. Several good Europeans were drawn to the area. They came from a spirited climbing scene and expected to find a like-minded group in Vancouver. At Alpine Club of Canada meetings they were regaled with slide shows of "700 bloody dandelions" and asked if they would like another

cup of tea. Enthusiasm turned to disillusion. Instead of the good-natured banter that had been so much a part of climbing at home, they met indifference. After a few climbs several strong performers drifted out of the sport. Those who persisted often wondered where all the fun had gone.

Across the Rockies in Calgary the situation was not so deadly. Although the Canadians looked upon cliff climbing as gymnastics and pitons as unsporting, an Austrian group were active in the area during the 1950s. Their chief contribution to local climbing was the discovery of Yamnuska, a limestone crag of Dolomitic steepness. Located east of the main chain of the Rockies, this mile-long cliff enjoys reasonable weather and may be climbed on year round. In 1957 Austrians Heinz Kahl, Hans Gmoser, and Leo Grillmair put up the 1,000-foot Diretissima (5.7), a climb that gathered a big reputation.

By the early 1960s the Austrians had given way to a new group. The leading light of this high-spirited Calgary band was expatriate Englishman Brian Greenwood. He and Canadians Don Vockeroth and Lloyd MacKay were largely responsible for the next series of climbs at Yamnuska. Vockeroth came from Drumheller, Alberta, a region noted for dinosaur remains. He hated to back down off a climb. One day when Vockeroth had been in the lead for a couple of hours, second Greenwood grew more and more uncertain of the prospects and tried to talk him down. Vockeroth stuck with it.

Finally, Greenwood yelled up, "You're a god-damn brontosaurus."

"A what?" came the reply.

"A brontosaurus. Big body and a small brain."

The Canadian mountains were yielding excellent climbs that combined technical problems on rock and ice with objective dangers and overall seriousness, but somehow they never seemed to match up to the sheer desperation of the Eiger-wand legends.

Rising aloof and sheer near Lake Louise, the 4,500-foot north face of Mount Temple was regard-

Brian Greenwood on the south face of Mount Watkins, Yosemite Valley. *Chris Jones.*

ed as the Eiger of North America. Various attempts had been launched on it over the years. In 1962 Greenwood probed the lower pitches. A few days later Chouinard and Shawangunk climber Doug Tompkins headed up toward the Dolphin, a prominent snowfield on the lower face. Chouinard woke up during the bivouac and looked out at the night sky. A weather front was moving in. The situation was serious; any falling rock or ice would be funneled on top of them. They descended in the dark, getting off the lower slopes just as the sun hit the top of the face. Moments later a rockfall obliterated their tracks.

In 1966 Greenwood was back on Mount Temple again with Heinz Kahl and Charlie Locke, though Kahl was forced to drop out because of illness.* The key to a direct route to the summit was the wall directly above the Dolphin. When Greenwood and Locke reached this upper wall, they found it to be different from the impression they had formed of it from below. Their ledges turned out to be snow slopes, and the hoped-for chimneys were water-worn grooves. They were both disappointed and relieved that they could not tackle the wall directly. They veered to the right and reached the summit after a wet bivouac. Once again the climb was perhaps not an Eiger, but the achievement was significant. The pair had committed themselves to a forbidding mountain wall.

The ascent of Mount Temple's north face acted as a catalyst. The next season in the Canadian Rockies was a full one. Chouinard's party made a second route on the north side of Mount Edith Cavell and climbed the north face of Mount Assiniboine. Robbins partnered Hudson on a major

*Although he suffered from leukemia, Kahl kept on climbing. His name will always be associated with his final project, Mount Temple's north face.

The north face of Mount Temple. The 1966 route lies in the shadowed bowl under the right side of the summit ice cliffs. Greenwood and Locke climbed immediately right of the large snowfield in the lower half of the face (the Dolphin). *Ed Cooper.*

Rampart wall, the north face of Mount Geike, and then audaciously soloed the 1961 route on Edith Cavell. Calgary climbers MacKay, Vockeroth, and Ken Baker pulled off the east face of Howse Peak. The story of technical mountaineering in North America had begun in the Canadian mountains. As the seventies neared, these once-fashionable peaks came back into favor.

The alpine climbers of the 1960s advanced the limits considerably beyond those of the previous decade. In particular, they probed the steep mountain walls that earlier climbers had shunned. The intermixing of climbers, ideas, and ambitions from across the continent, the acceptance of objective hazards as part of the challenge, and the application of skills worked out at rock climbing centers all contributed to the progress. Rock climbing was well advanced in areas such as the Bugaboos and the Tetons, and standards were not far short of the Alps. If mixed climbs on rock and ice lagged behind the sensational alpine achievements, the reasons were not hard to find: the few participants, the remoteness of the peaks, the lower base level of skill, and the preoccupation with rock climbing.

Expert climbers had burst on the alpine scene. The decade also witnessed another major push. First-rate alpinists expanded their activities to Alaska and the Yukon. It is to this story that we shall now turn.

REFERENCES

Anderson, Don N. "Mount Rainier, Willis Wall." *AAJ* 14 (1964): 169.

Beckey, Fred. "West Face of South Tower of Howser Spire." *AAJ* 13 (1962): 57.

———. "Mount Adams, East Face Direct via Victory Ridge." *AAJ* 13 (1963): 469.

———. "Mount Redoubt, East Face, Ramparts." *AAJ* 15 (1966): 159.

———. *Challenge of the North Cascades.* Seattle: The Mountaineers, 1969.

Beckey, Fred, *et al. Climber's Guide to the Cascade and Olympic Mountains of Washington.* New York: American Alpine Club, 1961.

Bertulis, Alex. "The East Face of Liberty Bell." *AAJ* 15 (1967): 291.

Bjornstad, Eric. "North Face of Mount Slesse." *CAJ* 48 (1965): 152.

Chouinard, Yvon. "The North Wall of Mount Edith Cavell." *AAJ* 13 (1962): 53.

Cooper, Edward. "Mount Adams, East Face." *AAJ* 13 (1962): 205.

Davis, Dan. "The North Face of Mount Robson." *AAJ* 14 (1964): 64.

Dornan, David B. "Mount Moran, East South Buttress." *AAJ* 13 (1962): 219.

Gran, Art. "East Temple." *AAJ* 13 (1962): 220.

———. "West Face of Mount Brussels." *AAJ* 14 (1965): 324.

———. "The East Face of Mount Chephren." *AAJ* 15 (1966): 41.

Greenwood, Brian. "Mount Temple's North Face." *AAJ* 15 (1967): 287.

———. "Calgary Climber." *AJ* 75 (1970): 101.

Hudson, John R. "The North Face of Mount Geikie." *AAJ* 16 (1968): 60.

Jones, Christopher. "Canadian Rockies North Faces." *AAJ* 16 (1968): 56.

Locke, Charles. "Mount Temple: North Face." *CAJ* 50 (1967): 73.

McCracken, Richard K. "Mount Hooker's North Face." *AAJ* 14 (1965): 347.

Madsen, James. "Liberty Bell, Direct East Face." *AAJ* 16 (1968): 134.

Molenaar, Dee. *The Challenge of Rainier.* Seattle: The Mountaineers, 1971.

"Mount Moran, First Winter Ascent." *AAJ* 16 (1968): 148.

"Mount Owen, First Winter Ascent." *AAJ* 15 (1966): 142.

"Mount Robson." *AAJ* 12 (1960): 139.

Ortenburger, Leigh. "Grand Teton, Black Ice Couloir." *AAJ* 13 (1962): 216.

———. "Mount Moran, 1922–1962." *AAJ* 13 (1963): 410.

———. "Disappointment Peak, Northeast Face." *AAJ* 13 (1963): 488.

———. *A Climber's Guide to the Teton Range.* San Francisco: Sierra Club, 1965.

Robbins, Royal. "Cutting Canadian Capers." *Summit* 14(8) (Oct. 1968): 14.

Sinclair, Pete. "Behold Now Behemoth." *Ascent* 1(2) (1968): 5.

Smutek, Ray. "The Great Willis Wall Controversy." *Off Belay* (April 1972): 48.

Spencer, T. M. "Emperor Ridge, Mount Robson." *AAJ* 13 (1962): 235.

———. "Robson by Emperor Ridge." *CAJ* 45 (1962): 106.

Stanley, Fred. "Liberty Bell Mountain, East Face." *AAJ* 15 (1966): 132.

Vockeroth, Don. "Howse Peak: East Face." *CAJ* 53 (1970): 36.

North to the Future

Alaskan climbing moved ahead in the 1960s without the benefit of a local nucleus. Unlike in the Tetons and Cascades there was no group of Alaskan climbers who set up camp year after year. Instead, a team would fly in, attempt their preset objective, and fly out. Climbers came from every part of the continent, but they continued to come in small numbers. There were probably more climbs in a week in the Cascades than in a year in Alaska.

Why then do we devote another whole chapter to Alaskan climbing? Not because we are mesmerized by the "importance" of big mountains but because several Alaskan climbs have been of great quality. In a typical Alaskan venture the idea is sparked among a group of friends. Months of planning and hard work build dedication to the goal. When the team arrive at the base of the peak, they are focused on their objective far more than mountaineers on a typical climbing vacation. As a result of this combination of intensity of purpose and ambitious choice of objectives, several persons have made their finest climbs in Alaska.

Europeans were also keen to explore these wild Alaskan peaks. They had read Brad Washburn's comments on the central bulge of McKinley's south face. In 1961 a group from the Italian Alpine Club led by Ricardo Cassin took up the challenge. Perhaps the most brilliant alpinist of the decade prior to World War II, with his historic "firsts" on the Grandes Jorasses, the Cima Ovest, and Piz Badile, Cassin was now in his early fifties, but his skill and determination were still very much with him.

The Italians traveled to Talkeetna, a collection of rundown buildings and two airstrips where they met bush pilot Don Sheldon. One of the best known of that hardy, individualistic breed, Sheldon was a brash yet endearing character. He and his Talkeetna rival Cliff Hudson were as much a part of the Alaskan climbing scene as the peaks themselves.*

As they flew into the mountain, Cassin carefully pinpointed the landing zone. Sheldon carefully told him it was the wrong place. Cassin insisted.

*Hudson and Sheldon had a falling out over poaching customers from each other. One time Sheldon radioed to a group waiting to be flown out by Hudson that he was away in Anchorage. He did not know when Hudson would return but would be happy to fly them out, which he did. Hudson claimed that he had been near Talkeetna all the time.

Climbers and gear were dropped off, and Sheldon flew away. A couple of days later he returned to check on their progress. Much to Sheldon's secret delight, Cassin meekly asked if he would ferry them to the proper landing place.

The Italians tackled the climb in a different manner from home teams. They set up fewer camps and returned to base after a stint on the face, as opposed to staying on the face and moving up from camp to camp. This difference in approach illustrates the role that precedents play in climbing. Home teams emulated earlier Alaskan climbers while the Italians looked on the south face as a scaled-up alpine problem.

A week of complicated route finding and difficult climbing preceded the establishment of their first camp on the face. Above, things moved rapidly. In three more days the lead climbers reached the 17,000-foot site of the third and highest camp. Three days later all six climbers were at this camp. The weather was clear, but a cold wind whipped snow into their clothing as they set out for the summit. At 11 P.M. numbed fingers fumbled with frozen pack straps. In the surreal Alaskan twilight the Italian and United States flags were raised on the summit.

The descent began immediately. Twenty-three hours after they left Camp 3, the exhausted climbers crawled back into their tents. Jack Canali's feet were in bad shape. His friends prepared hot drinks and tried to cheer him, but he was too experienced to be fooled. He knew the consequences of severe frostbite.

While they slept fitfully, a question weighed heavily on every mind. How would Canali manage the difficult descent? At two o'clock the wind died, and Cassin decided they must go down. Canali could not get his boots on, but Luigi Alippi passed him his reindeer boots and made do with extra socks in his overboots. By the time they were ready, the weather had deteriorated, and the descent was postponed.

With Canali's disability and Alippi unable to use crampons, the storm-bound descent the following morning demanded absolute concentration. Cassin was unwilling to stop at Camp 2; a matter of hours could save Canali's feet. He and Annibale Zucchi shepherded Canali through mist and snow to Camp 1. They rested a night before the final battle through powder snow to base camp. It had been snowing for three days without an appreciable break. Two days later Canali and two companions were under treatment for frostbite in an Anchorage hospital. Remarkably, no fingers or toes were lost.

The Italians had made the boldest and most continuously difficult climb in Alaska. Yet they seriously misjudged Alaskan conditions. They came equipped with knickers, knee socks, and ordinary alpine boots. The frostbite was a mild penalty.

The next year two English climbers came to

attempt the superb Moose's Tooth. The "normal" group for such an objective would have been at least four persons. One might point to their plan as an example of audacity; the more likely explanation is that the two did not know any better.

Barrie Biven first met Tony Smythe over a dinner of fish and chips in an English cafe. They parted an hour later with an agreement to climb in Alaska. Frank Smythe's son had been a Royal Air Force pilot and used to commute to the Welsh crags on weekends in his jet fighter plane. He wanted to earn money for the Alaska trip by working in Canada. To do so, he had to obtain emigrant status, and he told the authorities he was a pilot. They listed him as a clerk. In Ottawa he took odd jobs and bought an automobile "about twenty feet long."

When Biven arrived in April they heaved their gear into the trunk and set off. The punishing journey along the Alaska Highway was more than they bargained for. The car that cost $160 shed a door, half the generator, a rear spring, and most of the engine oil. They were flat broke when they limped into Whitehorse, Yukon Territory, but luck was with them. They found work in a silver mine and finally reached Anchorage in July. There they lost no time. In one day they bought their food in a supermarket, traveled to Talkeetna, flew into the mountain with Sheldon, and started climbing. The Moose's Tooth was a "mere 10,355 feet," and they saw what appeared to be a simple route.

After seven hours of climbing, they bivouacked. On the second day they continued over easy ground until they were caught in a rainstorm and endured a miserable bivouac with nothing but a plastic tarp for shelter. The next morning the weather was better, and they struggled through rain-soaked snow to the lower summit. Slowly they worked across the mile that separated them from the main peak, but unfortunately there was a sharp gap in the ridge. The gap confirmed the inevitable. The naïve Englishmen had underestimated Alaskan weather, Alaskan snow conditions, and Alaskan peaks.

During the following week Biven and Smythe climbed Mount Dan Beard and prepared to leave. They had told Sheldon they could not afford the cost of a flight. Instead they would walk out the seventy-odd miles. After six days on the Ruth Glacier they were confronted with a raging river. They cut some small trees and lashed them together to make a raft. It took twelve hours to construct and lasted three minutes in the water. Then they set out through the brush to reach a railroad twenty-five miles distant. They made about two miles in an afternoon of effort. The brush was hopeless, so they gambled on another raft. When this raft struck driftwood, they struggled to a sandbar, where they watched helplessly while the raft broke up in the current.

They had lost their gear and were marooned in the middle of an awesome river. They had been without food for three days, and tasks like collecting driftwood for the fire quickly tired them. Their second morning on the sandbar they decided to wait one more day in the hope that a plane would spot their fire. The next day they would try to ford the river, a desperate move in their weakened condition.

Luck was still with them. That evening a pilot saw the smoke from their fire, flew by to check out the situation, and radioed Sheldon to pick them up in a float plane.

After Sheldon plucked them out of the river, they ate from early evening to just past midnight in a Talkeetna cafe. The proprietor seemed to look upon feeding them as a challenge. He finally defeated them with an apple pie about a foot and a half across. The Englishmen knew about the high prices in Alaska, and they expected the bill would be around thirty dollars. When they were told it was two dollars apiece, they protested; the owner was robbing himself. But he was adamant, "I guess some folks eat more, and some folks eat less."

New Hampshire's 6,288-foot Mount Washington may seem a long way from Alaskan mountains in both geography and climate, but in the winter Mount Washington has weather as bad as any in Alaska. Winds over 200 miles per hour have been recorded. Snow and ice climbing on Mount Washington can be a survival exercise, and it was an exercise familiar to the Harvard Mountaineering Club. Club members were reared on a tough diet of weekend rock climbs and Mount Washington. Combined with the club's strong esprit de corps, this training meant that good, well-rounded climbers came along rapidly.

The club had a long tradition of Alaskan ventures, and honorary member Bradford Washburn was keen to promote new projects in the north. In 1963 seven students planned a climb up the center of McKinley's largest flank, the 14,000-foot Wickersham Wall.

The Harvard climbers of the time traveled around the country in a secondhand Cadillac hearse. On one trip they were stopped by a suspicious policeman. He insisted there were too many people in the front seat; some would have to get in the back. Then he walked to the back of the hearse and opened it up. There were fourteen Vassar women inside.

For the trip to Alaska the Cadillac hearse was passed over in favor of a VW bus, which the Harvard climbers coaxed up to McKinley Park. The park rangers were less than enthusiastic about their proposed climb, but the Harvard team had not come 4,000 miles to compromise; they hiked into their base camp and set to work.

In order to take advantage of the more favorable condition of the snow, they climbed at night. Each night the lead climbers were rotated. The others relayed the loads. When the lead rope returned, they brought tales of horror pitches ahead. The

pair who took over were determined to prove *they* could do it, and the next night they pressed ahead until they, too, became exhausted and psyched by new obstacles. The friendly rivalry kept up the momentum of the climb, and they reached the summit two weeks after leaving base camp. The route was not the equal of the Italian's south face, but it was an excellent effort by a young group, most of whom went on to even more demanding routes.*

In a commendable effort to further technical mountaineering, the American Alpine Club asked Jim McCarthy to pick a strong team and a demanding objective; the club would foot the bill. According to McCarthy, the plan was for the "best

*The Harvard climbers did not make the first climb on the Wickersham Wall. A month earlier Hans Gmoser led a Canadian party up the right side of the wall in a week of rapid climbing.

American climbers to attempt the biggest wall they could find in a remote area." The team of McCarthy, Layton Kor, Royal Robbins, and another Yosemite expert, Dick McCracken, were certainly among the best climbers. The Logan mountains in Canada's Northwest Territories are remote, but because of their milder climate they are more like the Wind Rivers than the Alaska Range. Furthermore, their objective could not be described as "the biggest wall"; at 1,800 feet the southeast face of Proboscis was no bigger than several Wind River or Bugaboo climbs. But it was steep and difficult, and the select group required three days to climb it.

Although the southeast face of Proboscis was a hard climb, it failed to match the hopes of its sponsors. By 1963 an 1,800-foot granite wall held few terrors for a Robbins, who later said in *Moun-*

tain, "If you've been doing it for years, climbing a steep granite wall for three days just isn't adventure anymore—you know you can do it."

Proboscis is also interesting because it is the only time during this period that we meet the best rock technicians of the day and this, as we noted, on an atypical northern climb. The hard men of the East, Colorado, and California were conspicuous only by their absence. Surely, we might conclude, if *they* had gone north, home teams would have picked off the prizes! This is unlikely. Mountains attract those best suited to them. The qualities that make an outstanding cragsman are not necessarily the qualities that get you up Mount McKinley.

If the Proboscis climb did not reach new heights, other events of the early 1960s brought American climbers to the attention of their European counterparts. The single most dramatic event was the 1963 traverse of Mount Everest by Tom Hornbein and Willi Unsoeld, one of the finest Himalayan climbs of the decade. In addition, Americans made several impressive routes in the French Alps due in large part to skills imported from Yosemite. Stories about El Capitan also filtered across the Atlantic. This burst of activity from a continent regarded as an also-ran in world mountaineering made the Europeans take notice. *La Montagne,* journal of the French Alpine Club, enthused, "By their accomplishments in the Alps, their first ascents in the Mont Blanc region, and their traverse of Everest, American climbers have reached the top rank in international climbing. In our view this is the most noteworthy event of 1963."

The European Attack

The Europeans were also becoming interested in the mountains of North America. In 1964 a French expedition set out for Alaska. The strong party of eight was led by the outstanding French mountaineer of the era, Lionel Terray. Their principal objective was unclimbed Mount Huntington, a striking peak first tried by Beckey in 1957. After knocking off Huntington, they planned to climb the Moose's Tooth and forge a new route on the south face of Mount McKinley. Like the Italians and the English before them, the French underestimated the Alaskan peaks.

When they flew into Huntington, they came face to face with the realities of Alaskan climbing. The temperature hovered around −10° F., and a keen wind whipped across the snow. In two days they established an ice cave at the base of the northwest ridge but then progress slowed. Terray had never seen such tough ice. On the ninth day he was out in front, balanced across a crevasse, when the snow broke from under him. He lost his balance and shot down a slope of bare ice.

At the instant of the fall, climbing partner Soubis was adjusting his crampons. The belay rope lay idle in the snow. There was no chance Soubis could anchor it. It reeled out and then stopped. Terray had dragged a line behind him to be used as a fixed rope. Moments earlier climbers below had attached this line to a snow picket, and the chance anchoring was all that saved Terray from the "big ride."

The fall wrenched his arm and put the leader out of action. The climb was more difficult than expected, and the team descended to base for fresh supplies and equipment. They returned to the ridge without Terray. However, he was determined to get back in the fray. Nine days after his accident he stood on the summit with his companions.

After this climb carried out in atrocious weather, the French were in no mood to complete the rest of their program. When Sheldon flew in, he brought two attractive women with him. Urged on by Sheldon, they staged an impromptu dance on the glacier. The humor of the situation was lost on the weary French. They stared glumly ahead.

Four Munich climbers also had their eyes on Huntington in 1964. This party led by Walter Welsch included toolmaker Klaus Bierl, apprentice guide Arnold Hasenkopf, and heavy equipment operator Alfons Reichegger. Because the French were already at work on Huntington, the Germans turned to the nearby Moose's Tooth. They made an attempt from the south but were stopped by steep, decomposed rock at the same point reached by an earlier American party. Then they turned to

the west ridge, previously tried by Biven and Smythe.

While they rested in camp, an American team arrived. The two groups amicably agreed to join forces and placed an advance camp where the ridge steepened. However, the Americans could not match the Germans' pace and soon dropped behind. The Germans reached the top in twenty-two hours of continual climbing.

Within a few years Europeans had made major climbs on La Pérouse and McKinley, and had picked off as well the outstanding Moose's Tooth and Mount Huntington. Home teams either had not tried these climbs or had failed on them. What accounted for the disparity? The Europeans were first-rate alpine and expedition climbers; several of them were among the best in Europe. The Italians and French were virtually subsidized national teams. The members were honored to be chosen, and the people back home expected success. Finally, the Europeans were not overawed by Alaska. Indeed, they were overconfident.

The French forestalled not only the Munich team on Huntington but also two of the Harvard Wickersham Wall climbers. Don Jensen and Dave Roberts turned instead to the Hayes Range and Mount Deborah. Mount Deborah was much finer than their photographs had indicated, and they devoted all their energy to the 3,000-foot east ridge. Short on food and dogged by the weather, they nonetheless fixed ropes over a third of the

Mount Huntington. The ridge climbed by the French rises from left to right; the Harvard route ascends the indefinite left-tending rib under the summit. The peak in the middle distance is The Rooster Comb and beyond it the Moose's Tooth. *Bradford Washburn.*

route before the magnitude of the undertaking became all too obvious and they retreated.

Home climbers again failed while the Europeans made difficult climbs. However, the European ascents of Huntington and the Moose's Tooth were in the traditional vein; the climbers took the simplest routes. The following year home climbers succeeded on lines that were among the most difficult on their respective peaks.

Wiser from their experience on Mount Deborah, Jensen and Roberts enlisted fellow students Matt Hale and Ed Bernd for an audacious route on the west face of Mount Huntington. The cream of French alpinists had given everything to fight their way up the northwest ridge. What chance did four undergraduates have on a more difficult route? After ten days on the face they were less than a third of the way up, and half of their allotted time was gone. In their third week they saw the upper part of the route for the first time. The summit was within grasp. Three days later Hale and Roberts were climbing up to the highest camp when Hale slipped. The anchor piton ripped out, and both climbers rolled down the slope. Suddenly they stopped. The rope had snagged over a rock nubbin. Though badly shaken, they carried on and late that night joined their companions on the final push to the summit.

The next day they began the arduous descent. The only reasonable option was the route they had come up, which involved rapelling down fifty-odd pitches. A rappel is a deceptive procedure. There

is no margin for error. Without warning Bernd's rappel failed, and he fell to his death.

We did not hear about these Harvard climbers in the Shawangunks or on alpine routes. Just how accomplished were they as technical climbers? Certainly they were not in the front rank, but by the mid-1960s there was a wide base of proficient climbers. They were solid on 5.8 and got up the odd 5.9 pitch, and on ice they had probably done as much as anyone on Mount Washington. Although not top performers on the local crags, they were technically well qualified.

The same sense of "unknowns" applies to most of the team that made the other outstanding climb of the year. The driving force behind this project was medical doctor Dick Long. His experience harked back to the Yosemite of the 1950s as did that of his companions, Al Steck and Jim Wilson. During the fifties Long had been to Mount Logan. A memory that haunted him was the central southern ridge, a six-mile-long nightmare that rises over two vertical miles. With the steady advance of climbing standards over the years, the formerly unthinkable ridge gripped Long's imagination. Could it be done?

Before the Logan trip Long and Steck were joined by John Evans, who paid part of his college tuition by wrestling alligators at South Dakota's Reptile Gardens. Together they climbed the north-

Matt Hale at an equipment cache on the west face of Huntington. Note free-hanging fixed rope. *Don Jensen.*

Mount Logan. The Hummingbird Ridge rises directly in front. *Walter Wood.*

west face of Half Dome and·pioneered big wall routes in Yosemite and the High Sierra; the year after the Logan trip Long and Steck made the third ascent of the Salathé Wall with Steve Roper. Although they would not meet these types of problems on Logan, their achievements demonstrate that they were up on the Yosemite big wall skills. More important, they demonstrate that they were not easily put off by scale or difficulty.

Long surreptitiously got hold of a set of aerial photos of the ridge of Logan from Boyd Everett, who hoped to lead a rival Eastern group. When Long's friends saw the photographs, they thought he was joking. But he was not; his answer was that they were as good as any climbers in the world. The team was rounded out by ski racer Paul Bacon and electrical engineer Frank Coale.

No expense was spared to obtain the best equipment, and the party got together for a shakedown on California's Mount Shasta. They drove all night to the peak and discovered they had left behind the majority of their food. After the first day's climbing, Steck and Wilson slept in an experimental home-made tent. During the night a storm front moved in. Snow piled on the tent until it was about to collapse. Steck crawled outside and began to shovel snow as if his life depended on it. His frenzied shouts to Wilson to get the hell out and give a hand were answered by grunts. Wilson was acting as a guinea pig for one of Dr. Long's drugs. The trial program continued the next day. Wilson

worked up a bulge on ice pitons. The pitons ripped out, and he fell, gashing his head. Perhaps the Mount Shasta fiasco should have served as a warning, but they persisted.

The method of attack on Mount Logan was ingenious. A lead pair fixed ropes while the following climbers moved up the gear. A camp was established, used as a base of operations, and then moved higher. The fixed ropes were removed from below and used to safeguard the way to the next camp. The climbers, their 4,000 feet of rope, fifteen gallons of fuel, and thirty days' food advanced up the monster ridge. The enormity of the undertaking weighed heavily on them. More than once there was sentiment for going down, but a few always insisted they continue. After two weeks they established their second camp. They were behind schedule, and prospects for the summit looked bad. They took a vote and agreed to carry on until the food was down to a nine-day ration. At the end of the third week they were at the point of decision. They must either go on over the top or commence the unthinkable retreat down the ridge. They carried on. One month after the climb began, they reached the summit of Mount Logan. The fifteen or so pounds each man lost was one indication of the intense effort they had made. When Wilson returned his son asked, "Dad, was it as rough as Shasta?"

With landmark ascents on Mount Huntington and Mount Logan the year was a notable one in

American climbing. Two parties had pushed the limits of the possible.

In the 1960s not only were there unclimbed peaks of the stature of Mount Huntington and the Moose's Tooth, but several mountain ranges were unknown. In June 1962 *Summit* published a picture of spectacular mountain walls, the Riesenstein of British Columbia. The picture created a stir among American mountaineers. The major ranges of British Columbia were reasonably well defined. Where were the Riesenstein? Climbers dug through libraries and pored over photo collections. Finally, Vulgarian Al DeMaria found the key. *Summit* had been hoaxed. The peaks were seventy miles southwest of Mount McKinley, were known as the Cathedral Spires, and had never been visited.

Although these peaks are only in the 8,500-foot range, they rise up to 5,000 feet above the surrounding glaciers. When DeMaria and his friends flew into the area in 1965, they were stunned. The peaks were sheer on all sides. There were *no* simple routes! The strong party made only a small dent in the potential of the area.

The following year a Harvard group were in the Cathedral Spires. It included Roberts, Rick Millikan, a Wickersham Wall veteran and a grandson of Everester George Mallory, Alaskan climbing bum Art Davidson, Dave Johnston, and Peter Meisler. Davidson lived out of the back of a truck and lived mostly on cottage cheese, peanut butter, and raisins. During the Alaskan winter he kept warm by reading books and nursing endless cups of coffee

Jim Wilson ascends a fixed line on the Hummingbird Ridge. The route traversed the gendarme and background ridge. Courtesy Al Steck.

in restaurants. This group, too, were intimidated by the Cathedral Spires. Their primary goal was the highest peak in the range, 8,985-foot Kichatna Spire. The modest height was no measure of difficulty, and progress on the route was slow. Then a twelve-day storm set in. Enclosed by the forbidding walls and damp from living on the glacier, the climbers' morale sank. Davidson and Millikan could not reestablish themselves at a high bivouac on Kichatna Spire until the end of their third week. They dropped part of their stove and were thus without water in the morning, but on the summit day the loss was a minor irritant. After ten hours they stood on the top.

Winter on Mount McKinley

In 1965 a predominantly Japanese party repeated the final section of the Thayer Route on Mount McKinley. During the climb Shiro Nishimae and Art Davidson became intrigued with the idea of climbing McKinley in winter. The problems were tremendous: the cold, the weather, and the short days of the Alaskan winter. But the problems *were* the appeal. No such climb had ever been attempted in Alaska. The two persuaded Colorado equipment manufacturer Gregg Blomberg to lead the venture. After a period when it seemed on the point of collapse, the party was rounded out by six-foot-seven forester and climbing bum Dave Johnston, orthopedic surgeon George Wichman, and biologist John Edwards. Before departure French mill worker Jacques Batkin, who climbed Mount Huntington in 1964, and his Swiss companion Ray Genet joined on.

The climbers landed on the Kahiltna Glacier in January 1967 and packed their loads toward the West Buttress. The glacier was covered with new snow and seemed safe. More by omission than by conscious decision, they traveled over it without the precaution of roping together. A few days later Batkin perished in a hidden crevasse.

They were badly shaken by Batkin's death, and there was sentiment to call of the trip. After a period of indecision they returned to the climb, but all was not well. They had varying degrees of commitment and lacked a sense of unity. Leader Blomberg was perhaps most affected by the accident. His heart was no longer in the project.

Hope alternated with despair. The men struggled with the mountain and their inner selves. After almost four weeks they positioned a summit team, but this team included weaker members of the party. When a second group climbed up to the high camp after the hoped-for summit day, they found that the others had not even left the tent. Again morale sagged, and only Nishimae's firm sense of control kept the party together. Later five climbers set out for the top, but Blomberg felt below par and returned to camp with Nishimae. Early in the evening Davidson, Johnson, and

Genet stood on the darkened summit. It was still dark when they arrived back at 18,200-foot Denali Pass, where they had cached bivouac gear. A 1,000-foot descent and a mile of level going separated them from their companions at the ice cave below. They were tired, and the descent in the dark would be treacherous. They decided to bivouac at the pass. The decision seemed reasonable, but it turned into a nightmare.

They were awakened by a wind that threatened to rip away the parachute that covered them. The temperature was in the vicinity of $-40°$ F., and they estimated the wind at 100 miles per hour. The combined effect gave a wind chill temperature of around $-150°$ F. Their position was desperate. In the hope of escaping the wind, Johnston left their miserable bivouac and clawed his way to the far side of a rockpile. Davidson and Genet remained where they were, but their determination was sapped by the cold, the altitude, and fatigue. In a moment of weakness they lost their grip on the parachute, and it was snatched away by the wind. The cold penetrated farther into their sleeping bags, and the wind threatened to blow them down the mountain. They wedged themselves between rocks, but it was hopeless. During their battle with the wind they had exposed their hands and lost the use of their fingers. Their survival depended on Johnston. They struggled over to him. Grimly determined, he hollowed out a small cave and helped his companions inside.

Unknown to the three at Denali Pass, Blomberg and Nishimae tried to reach them that day. The wind drove Nishimae back when he was less than 100 feet from them. He saw a sleeping bag flapping in the wind and was sure that all three were dead. He kept his thoughts from Blomberg.

When the three at Denali Pass awoke the next morning, the wind was as intense as ever. Only a meager meal relieved the endless hours. The following day the situation was worse. The food was virtually gone, and they were out of fuel to melt snow for drinking water.

By the afternoon of the third day at Denali Pass their only hope lay in finding a gallon of gas that Johnston had cached three years earlier and spotted again a few days before. Who would go for it? Johnston had dug the cave, cooked, and fed the others. He had done his share. Davidson and Genet's hands were in poor shape, and unlike Johnston they did not know the exact location of the gas can. Each man was lost in his private hell, guilt-ridden if he did not go for the gas, yet afraid to face the wind and cold. Eventually, Genet pulled on his boots and went out into the swirling snow. He used two ice axes to hold himself into the slope and crawled over to the cache. Not long after the trio had their first liquid in thirty-six hours.

On the morning of the fourth day the wind had lost much of its force. They would have tried to break for the lower camps, but in their condition it was impossible. They remained in the cave, and passed the day in a listless, half-wakened state. Although there was now plenty of gas to melt snow, they drank a minimum amount of water. They had only one tin can, in which they cooked and in which they passed their urine out of their cave.

The following day the wind died down completely. They pulled on frozen equipment and crawled out of their icy hole. Instead of a view down the mountain there was nothing but cloud. Descent in a whiteout was hopeless. They returned to the cave.

The sixth day the clouds lifted, and the weary trio set out for the lower camps. They found the highest camp abandoned, and when they reached the next lower one, it too was deserted. Unknown to them, their friends had descended and signaled a passing plane. As the weakened climbers continued their descent the next morning, a helicopter landed nearby. The ordeal was over.

No review of Alaskan climbing in the sixties would be complete without reference to Vin Hoeman and Boyd Everett. Hoeman was the first person to climb all the fifty states' high points, but his real love was the Alaskan mountains. He was out summer and winter, making more Alaskan ascents than any contemporary climber. One of his notable climbs was a traverse of the Alaska Range by way of the summits of McKinley and Hunter. He amazed visiting climbers when he gave them capsule histories of their ascents. He kept records on virtually every climber who visited Alaska. Much of this data was gathered for a projected guidebook. He not only knew the exact order in which the first 180 persons had stepped onto the summit of Mount McKinley, but he had also calculated their average age to be 29.3 years. For the purpose of his guidebook he decided that a "significant" summit had to rise at least 1,000 feet above a col. This eliminated innumerable peaks that were little more than bumps on ridges. The distinction was needed, but Hoeman took it too much to heart. He was forever foregoing worthwhile climbs in order to storm off after a distant but significant rubble heap.

New York investment analyst Boyd Everett was renowned for flying out to Alaska in his Brooks Brothers suit. He changed into his climbing gear in Sheldon's hangar. His genius was planning. He rightly observed that although Alaskan climbers usually attributed their defeats to bad weather, the real causes were poor organization and low morale. After a series of fine climbs which included new routes on Mounts McKinley and Saint Elias, he conceived an ambitious triple attack on McKinley's south face in 1967. His group would repeat the finish of the Thayer Route on the right flank and the Italian route up the central bulge, and they would establish a new route between them, a so-called direct south face.

The new-route team was a powerful one. The

Boyd Everett in Alaska. *Gray Thompson.*

year before Denny Eberl and Gray Thompson made the second ascent of the north face of Edith Cavell. A year later they were to become the first American rope to climb the North Face of the Matterhorn. Roman Laba had been on several rugged Vulgarian trips, and Dave Seidman was a fast-rising Dartmouth climber.

The major problem with the proposed new route was the avalanche danger. Two other groups had looked at it and given up. Shortly after they arrived at the base of the wall, Eberl and Thompson had to run for their lives when an avalanche swept the face. When the snow dust cleared, the place where they had been standing was covered with ice blocks.

Nonetheless, they persisted. At about the halfway point Eberl and Thompson saw the telltale storm signs of lenticular clouds. They had two choices: camp where they were, slightly protected by a rib, or descend twenty pitches to a lower camp, about a third of the way an obvious avalanche chute. Eberl insisted they descend.

Thompson insisted they stay, "Goddamnit, Denny, the storm probably won't be big anyway, and this rib is pretty safe from small slides. Besides, look at that wall above the couloir. All that stuff is loose as hell."

"You're crazy," replied Eberl, "this place is going to get *creamed*. Look at that face above us."

The argument raged for forty-five minutes. While they argued, they managed to snarl 300 feet of nylon rope. They hurled it down the mountain and shook their fists as it disappeared. Finally Thompson agreed to descend. As they started down, an avalanche let loose, and rocks pulverized their descent route. Their fixed ropes were largely destroyed, and the air was thick with the acrid smell of rock dust, but the decision was made, and they carried on down. That night the rib where they might have stayed was overrun by avalanches.

The storm lasted fourteen days and pinned the climbers at widely separated campsites. When it was over, Eberl and Thompson climbed up to their companions at a higher camp. It was so cramped

Dennis Eberl on the direct south face of McKinley.
Gray Thompson.

that the garbage dump, the toilet, and the ice used for meltwater were all in the same place. Laba and Seidman had a pot of soup ready, and while they sat discussing their next move, Eberl complained about toilet paper in his soup. Seidman looked into the bowl with concern. Brightening, he fished out the offending object and went back to his own bowl. Eberl was speechless. Then he shrugged and went on eating.

The weather turned better, and the climb was pushed ahead. The climbers reasoned that to go on was no worse than to go down. Three rock buttresses high on the face were bypassed to the side. After a month of grim confrontation they made their way onto the top.*

While the triple attack was in progress on Mount McKinley, Jensen returned to Mount Deborah with a strong party including Art Gran and Wickersham Wall veteran Pete Carman. There was almost continual storm, and they spent twenty-four days under the face. They had no real chance to test the difficulties of the climb and were unable to improve on the previous high point. There were no lead articles in the climbing journals, no congratulations on a great success. Deborah was a failure. But it is often from the failures that we gauge much of the story of climbing. A determined effort on a fearsome climb is more revealing than a

*This was Everett's last Alaskan expedition. In 1968 Everett, Hoeman, Seidman, two other Americans, and two Sherpas were overwhelmed by an avalanche on the Himalayan giant, Dhaulagiri.

Direct south face team, from left: Roman Laba, Gray Thompson, Dennis Eberl, Dave Seidman. Courtesy Gray Thompson.

predictable success. Unhappily for the student of mountaineering, failures are often kept quiet, not because of shame, but because the climbers hope to return and do not want to draw attention to the route.

Some of the boldest efforts in climbing are never recorded. They exist for a time as oral tradition and then are lost forever. Who knows what they could reveal of man's struggle against the mountains and against himself?

Defeat. A climber looks up at the east ridge of Mount Deborah. Art Gran.

REFERENCES

Abrons, Henry L. "A New Route on the Wickersham Wall." *AAJ* 14 (1964): 47.

Bleser, Warren. "McKinley's East Buttress." *Summit* 11(6) (Sept. 1965): 12.

Blomberg, Gregg. "Winter Ascent of Mt. McKinley." *Summit* 14(1) (Jan.-Feb. 1968): 2.

Cassin, Riccardo. "Up the Impossible Wall." *Life*, Aug. 25, 1961, p. 51.

———. "The South Face of Mount McKinley." *AAJ* 13 (1962): 27.

"La Chronique Alpine." *La Montagne*, 46 (Feb. 1964), p. 192.

Davidson, Art. *Minus 148°*. New York: Norton, 1969.

DeMaria, Alvin, and Peter Geiser. "Ascents in the Cathedral Spires, Alaska." *AAJ* 15 (1966): 25.

Evans, John, and Allen Steck. "Mount Logan's Hummingbird Ridge." *AAJ* 15 (1966): 8.

Everett, Boyd N. "The Organization of an Alaskan Expedition." Privately printed for Harvard Mountaineering Club, 1966.

Gordon, Don. "Attempt on Wickersham Wall, Mount McKinley." *AAJ* 13 (1962): 196.

Gran, Arthur. "Mount Deborah, Attempt on East Buttress." *AAJ* 16 (1968): 121.

Hasenkopf, Arnold. "Deutsche Alaska: Kundfahrt." *Alpinismus* (Oct. 1964): 49.

Hoeman, Vin. "Grand Traverse of the Alaska Range." *Summit* (April 1968) 14(3): 14.

———. Unpublished ms. for Alaska Guide; Alaska Data File.

Irvin, Richard. "Mountaineering Notes, Western Alps." *SCB* 48 (Dec. 1963): 99.

McCarthy, James P. "The Southeast Face of Proboscis." *AAJ* 14 (1964): 60.

Maraini, Fosco. "The South Face of Mount McKinley." *AJ* 68 (1963): 108.

Millikan, Richard G. C. "The Wickersham Wall: 1963." *Harvard Mountaineering* no. 17 (May 1965): 27.

Read, William A. "The East Buttress of Mount McKinley." *AAJ* 14 (1964): 37.

"Riccardo Cassin: Interview." *Mountain* no. 22 (July 1972), p. 32.

Roberts, Dave. "An Attempt on Mt. Deborah." *Harvard Mountaineering* no. 17 (May 1965): 15.

———. "Mount Huntington: West Face." *AAJ* 15 (1966): 1.

———. "Five Days on Mt. Huntington." *Harvard Mountaineering* no. 19 (May 1967): 21.

———. "Challenges in the Cathedral Spires." *Summit* 14 (5) (June 1968): 20

———. *The Mountain of My Fear*. New York: Vanguard Press, 1968.

Roberts, Dave, and Richard Millikan. "Kichatna Spire." *AAJ* 15 (1967): 272.

"Royal Robbins: Interview." Mountain no. 18 (Nov. 1971), p. 27.

Seidman, Dave. "Mt. McKinley . . . The Direct South Face." *Ascent* 1(2) (1968): 18.

Smythe, A. G. "The Moose's Tooth." *AJ* 68 (Nov. 1963): 262.

———. "A Limey's Adventure in Alaska." *Summit* 15(9) (Nov. 1969): 2.

Soubis, Jacques. "La Conquête du Mont Huntington." *La Montagne*, no. 49 (Oct. 1964), p. 261.

Steck, Allen. "Ascent of Hummingbird Ridge." *Ascent* 1(1) (May 1967): 3.

Terray, Lionel. "Mount Huntington." *AAJ* 14 (1965): 289.

Thompson, Gray. "McKinley's 'Centennial Wall.' " *Summit* 14(2) (March 1968): 3.

Welsch, Walter. "Auf Eisriesen in Alaska." *Der Bergsteiger* (Nov. 1964): 120.

———. "The Moose's Tooth." *AAJ* 14 (1965): 299.

The Granite Crucible

During the early 1960s Yosemite Valley was an unknown quantity. The locals quietly, almost furtively, advanced the standards of American climbing, but the climbing world remained blissfully ignorant. Outsiders read about Harding's ascent of El Capitan in the 1959 *American Alpine Journal,* but over the next three years the *Journal* was curiously silent about Yosemite. The lack of information and the long, drawn-out ascent of the Nose made it a hard place to fathom. However, a few outsiders came to see for themselves. And not only see. They started to climb the walls.

None of the earliest visitors was ready for the mental and technical demands of El Capitan, but in the spring of 1962 Ed Cooper and Canadian Jim Baldwin came for the express purpose of making a new route on El Cap. The year before, they had established the Grand Wall (V) on Squamish Chief, a gaunt, 2,000-foot cliff near Vancouver, British Columbia. On the Grand Wall, in the Cascades, and in the Bugaboos, Cooper demonstrated he had the mind for big walls.

To the climbers in Robbins's circle the bizarre events surrounding the Grand Wall meant that the outsiders already had two strikes against them when they arrived in Yosemite. First, Cooper and Baldwin took about a month to fix ropes on the Grand Wall. In some places, they bolted up alongside perfectly usable cracks. Suitable pitons were unavailable locally, and Cooper maintained that it was simpler to bolt than to manufacture pitons. Second, because of Squamish Chief's location above a highway, the lengthy ascent attracted wide interest. One weekend a reputed 12,000 cars crowded into the area. The climbers were celebrities in nearby Squamish, which enjoyed a tourist boom. They were furnished with free food and lodging, which delayed the climb even more. They went up on the wall, placed a few pitons, fiddled around with the ropes, and then hurried down to dinner and the bar. They had never had it so good!

The publicity appalled the Yosemite regulars, for whom the sport was a personal affair above sensationalizing. It appeared to them that Cooper was another Harding in his striving for publicity. Indeed, much of the antagonism toward Harding was over the publicity issue. (When Harding and Robbins hiked toward Half Dome in 1955, they

Warren Harding makes the big time: billboard outside Bishop, California, 1963. *Meredith Ellis Little.*

met a group of tourists. While Robbins hid behind a boulder, Harding enthusiastically described their plans.)

Robbins's attitude toward Cooper was hostile from the start. He sent underlings to convey messages and made a point of not speaking to him. What galled Robbins was the way the outsiders immediately started to fix ropes on El Cap. He felt they should climb lesser routes to establish their right to preempt such a prize. The locals were upset that outsiders were climbing what they themselves were reluctant to do until they could carry it off in the correct style. At least, these were the reasons espoused by Robbins. The more likely cause of the annoyance was the idea that outsiders might launch out on a new route on Yosemite's finest wall without flinching at the magnitude of the task.

Cooper and Baldwin chose a daunting route. Their Dihedral Wall would follow an unrelentingly steep and direct line up a series of leaning corners. After the first lead there were no more stances for 1,000 feet. They whittled away at the climb through the spring. Up and down they went, sometimes not even reaching the previous high point. The climbing was difficult and the exposure sensational. Baldwin confessed, "Going up there day after day eats your mind. I'll get a little smashed the night before and convince myself that it'll be raining in the morning."

They climbed 900 feet before Baldwin had a heart-stopping accident. His prusik knots slipped, and he slid 100 feet before he stopped where the rope was anchored to the wall. His hands were burned from clutching the rope, and his prusik knots were nearly worn through.

Because of the summer climbing ban on El Cap, they could not get back on the route until the fall, and during the summer it was rumored that Robbins might go up on it when he returned from the Alps. Pushed into action, Cooper and Baldwin were back on the wall in September. Their party was materially strengthened by the addition of Californian Glen Denny. They advanced their fixed ropes to the 2,000-foot level and then returned late in November to complete the route in a six and a half day push.

The locals were a proud bunch. They had definite ideas about what was good style and what was not. Several people took exception to the Dihedral Wall. They liked neither the fixed ropes nor the long siege. However, the exemplary Salathé Wall had itself been fixed over the lower third. It was not so much that Cooper fixed ropes that was open to criticism, but that he established them so far up the route and took so long to do it. The locals' concern over climbing ethics can be looked upon as an attempt to keep climbing adventurous, to prevent the rocks from being overwhelmed with rope. It can also be looked upon as a competition where the elite cry foul on the less experienced.

The Yosemite experts were rattled by the Dihedral Wall; it was an unpleasant crack in the Yosemite façade. The façade had already been weakened by Layton Kor, who had stormed up several difficult routes. In 1963 he planned a trip to the Alps, but the lure of Yosemite proved too great.

The early season weather was dreadful. While most of the climbers hung around the coffee shop, Kor headed up toward the Steck-Salathé on Sentinel. It was caked with snow and ice. No one had attempted a big wall Yosemite climb in winter, but Kor was nothing if not an innovator. He half-seriously commented, "I want to see if I'm afraid to die." Apparently he was. After a couple of desperate leads he and his partner came down.

Kor teamed with several fast-rising newcomers. One was Berkeley math student Eric Beck. As soon as Beck got his scholarship grant, he went to Yosemite, where he fell under the influence of climbing guru Steve Roper. Roper was in with the big shots and had a fund of outrageous stories. The wide-eyed newcomers received a steady stream of comment and ribald advice.

Big-wall impedimenta; Glen Denny at the top of the Dihedral Wall. *Ed Cooper.*

Like most of the Yosemite regulars who climbed for six months a year, Beck was perpetually poor. One way to solve the money dilemma was to "scarf" discarded food in the cafeteria. One day at breakfast Beck reached for an abandoned cereal bowl. At the same moment the owner returned. "Hey, that's ours," he complained. When he got a better look at Beck he had second thoughts and added, "Here, you can have it anyway." Not long after this episode the head busboy saw some climbers eyeing the leftover sausage. He grabbed the sausage and brought it over. The climbers warmed to their new ally, and he found them a congenial lot and told his underlings to give them any leftover grub. Life was pretty soft until the busboy became a climbing bum.

The bad weather continued into the spring of 1963, but Kor was impatient. He had to have his own route on El Capitan. He and Beck established ropes over the lower third of their intended route, the West Buttress. Beck was new to big wall climbing and was awed by the exposure and the scale. One time when he arrived at a belay stance and it was his turn to lead, Kor said, "The next pitch looks really scary"; and in a keen, expectant voice, "bet I can lead it pretty fast if you want to take the next one."

With the bad weather and the continual nervous strain, Beck was not overanxious to go up on the wall. Suffering from a "mind inversion," he backed off the climb, and Roper joined Kor to finish it. They fixed ropes to midheight and then completed the route in a three-day effort.

Kor and Roper made a well-matched pair. Both were lively personalities with a love of black humor, and both were fast aid climbers. They and Denny next prepared to attempt the third ascent of the Nose. Robbins and his friends had made the second ascent in seven days. Kor and company

Several people gave a hand on the Dihedral Wall; here Steve Roper is at a hanging belay. Note the formidable mass of gear. *Ed Cooper.*

were out to cut the time to shreds. (Robbins scoffed when he heard their ambitions.) They reached the foot of the wall in the dark. At the first hint of daylight Roper pounded in a piton. Three and a half days later they were on top.

Roper was an avid speed climber. In an ostensibly uncompetitive sport the time taken to complete a route was a simple method of comparison. The Steck-Salathé on Sentinel Rock was at this time a standard test piece among the better climbers. Robbins had done the route five times and eliminated all but forty feet of the aid. On his last trip he cut the time to ten hours. On their first trip up the Steck-Salathé Roper and Frank Sacherer shaved two hours off Robbins's time.

When the jubilant pair arrived back in camp, a subdued Robbins offered his congratulations and magnanimously opened a bottle of champagne. The chronically shy Sacherer had never tasted champagne before and remarked that it tasted like Coke.

Two days later Robbins and Frost ate an early breakfast in the Yosemite cafeteria and let it be known that they hoped to be back in time for lunch. They made it back just too late for lunch. After breakfast they had hiked up to Sentinel Rock, climbed the Steck-Salathé in "three hours and fourteen minutes," and returned. Robbins had made his point.

Ed Cooper was back in Yosemite in 1963. He had interested the *Saturday Evening Post* in a story on a projected new climb on Half Dome. Although they

were unaware of the pending contract, the Yosemite regulars knew Cooper's penchant for publicity. That very spring he had informed the media of another projected Yosemite climb, and they had not forgotten the Grand Wall ballyhoo. Cooper and Berkeley hot rod enthusiast Galen Rowell spent a few days fixing ropes on the lower pitches and then descended in poor weather. They expected to return and finish the job when Rowell's exams were over.

No one had been more put out by Cooper's Dihedral Wall climb than Robbins. When he saw what was happening on Half Dome, he recognized an opportunity to even the score. As Cooper and Rowell descended to the valley, Robbins and Dick McCracken went up to the base of Half Dome. They set out in doubtful weather, and after four

days of difficult climbing they were on top of the Direct Northwest Face (VI, 5.9 A5).

Certainly Robbins had done the climb in a finer style than was Cooper's intent, but opinion was sharply divided as to whether his action was admirable. It was the last straw for Cooper. Without bothering to collect his equipment from the base of the climb, he left for New York and a new life as a stockbroker.

1963 was a productive year for Robbins. One week after the Half Dome climb, he and McCracken were on another Grade VI, the East Side of Upper Yosemite Fall. Perhaps his finest effort was during four stormy days in May, when he made the second ascent of Harding's Leaning Tower route (VI) alone. It was the first solo ascent of a major Yosemite wall.

The Valley Scene

In the early sixties there were typically ten to twenty climbers in residence in Yosemite. Of this number only two or three were from outside California. By the midsixties the number of climbers doubled, and outsiders were beginning to outnumber the locals. Two events helped to bring about these changes: the demystifying of the routes that followed the 1964 publication of Roper's *Climber's Guide* and the belated recognition of Yosemite climbing in mountaineering publications. The *American Alpine Journal* barely mentioned Yosemite during the early sixties. The magnificent Salathé Wall was covered in a four-sentence note tucked away at the back. Rock climbing was vaguely considered not quite "on."

In 1963 the *Journal* made amends. The first four articles were devoted to Yosemite. Most influential was Chouinard's "Modern Yosemite Climbing," which began, "Yosemite climbing is the least known and understood and yet one of the most important schools of rock climbing in the world today." The article opened the eyes of climbers throughout the country to the revolution that was sweeping through the valley. Written with conviction and passion, it was full of advice for the out-of-state climber, who learned that he would not be accepted "until he proves he is equal to the better climbs and climbers. He is constantly on trial to prove himself."

Chouinard ended with a stirring call to arms, "Yosemite Valley will, in the near future, be the training ground for a new generation of super-alpinists who will venture forth to the high mountains of the world to do the most esthetic and difficult walls on the face of the earth." This prophecy had the right ring to it. Whether it was accurate will be for a later generation to judge.

Back in the nitty-gritty of Yosemite Chouinard noted "an aura of unfriendliness and competition between climbers, leaving a bitter taste in the mouth." Of course, competition and sport are closely linked. The climbers acted out Western man's precepts in the framework of Yosemite: get ahead; make something of yourself. Robbins was firmly on top of the pecking order. A remote, hard-to-fathom figure who took himself seriously and liked to appear well read, he constantly put himself on trial to maintain his position.

One afternoon at the Climber's Camp in the Tetons, Robbins was hanging around with the Vulgarians when someone suggested a push-up contest. Within moments people were straining and sweating on the ground, but not Robbins. He disdained to join in. Not long afterward, so the story goes, one of the Vulgarians was walking outside the campground when he saw a naked torso rhythmically heaving up and down. He gingerly crept forward, eagerly expecting to see a couple making love. To his surprise the torso belonged to Robbins—practicing push-ups.

Eric Beck, archetype Yosemite climbing bum, who stated: "at either end of the social spectrum there lies a leisure class." *Tom Gerughty.*

Sometime later Robbins was again enjoying a bull session with the Vulgarians. During a lull in the conversation he seized his chance, "Hey, you guys, do you want to have a push-up contest?"

Competition was part of a greater whole. The beauty and meaning of the Yosemite experience were more important. By late fall of 1963 only Baldwin, Beck, and Berkeley climber Chris Fredericks remained in Camp 4, trying to hold onto a year of precious memories and shared experiences. They spent their last money on coffee in the cafeteria, a scheme which allowed them to stay dry and consume unlimited amounts of sugar and cream. Finally, they went to the rangers and inquired if departing tourists had left any food. They had: a motley assortment of half-used catsup, cookies, mustard, and other leftovers. The climbers eagerly took their spoils back to Camp 4 to the men's room, the only place with a heater. There they assigned points to each item according to its survival potential; cookies rated higher than mayonnaise. Beck summed the points and divided by three. The bargining commenced, and each man eventually left with an armful of odds and ends. They held out one more week.

The young Berkeley group were back the next year. The rapidly emerging technical force among them was graduate physics student Frank Sacherer, an intense, tight individual whose concentration on climbing and physics was fanatical. He climbed like a man possessed and deliberately forced himself to use minimal protection. On one occasion he was way above Beck's belay stance without a single intermediate piton. Beck anxiously called up to him to put in a piton. Sacherer spat back, "Shut up, you chicken shit."

Sacherer directed his energies toward eliminating aid and was scrupulous in his demands that his partners not "cheat." After leading the first free ascent of the ominous Crack of Despair (5.10), Sacherer belayed his second from deep inside the crack. Tom Gerughty was in his first month as a climber. As he struggled up the crack, he took a quick rest on a bolt. Sacherer heard his panting slow down, sensed what had happened, and mercilessly yelled, "Get your foot off the bolt, Gerughty!"

In short succession he led Gerughty up the fingertip crack on the Dihardral and up the overhanging jamcrack on the right side of the Hourglass. Sacherer cursed when their rappel rope hung up on the descent from the latter climb. In a burst of fury, he climbed back up the rope hand over hand.

All-out; Frank Sacherer on the first ascent of Ahab (5.10), a flared, overhanging chimney at the base of El Capitan. *Tony Qamar.*

Frank Sacherer in a typical Yosemite crack. *Tony Qamar.*

Pratt and Robbins had been the star free-climbers of the early 1960s, but Sacherer surpassed them. They had a deliberate, controlled style; his was to get mad at the rock, and he often appeared on the verge of falling. If Pratt initiated 5.10 in Yosemite, it was Sacherer who brought it to fruition. When Pratt and Fredericks repeated his Hidden Chimney on Bridalveil Fall—East Side, they had to struggle hard to get up. Perhaps the best free-climbing achievement of 1964 was Pratt and Sacherer's one day ascent of the 1,200-foot Lost Arrow Chimney (V, 5.10). Sacherer later said, "The day you do the Arrow Chimney is the day you do more work than any other day of your life."

The next year Sacherer had to spend more time at his physics books. To stay in shape, he and Beck undertook a vigorous course of training. When they got back to Yosemite, it was with telling effect. They eliminated eighty aid pitons on Middle Cathedral Rock's Direct North Buttress (V, 5.10) and created a stir when they did the west face of Sentinel in a day, the first one-day ascent of a Yosemite Grade VI.

By 1966 Sacherer was through. He realized that if he kept up this pace, he would probably be killed. His nerves were frayed, and there was an offer of a good job in Europe. His companions carried on the free climbing boom: Pratt and Fredericks on the poorly protected Twilight Zone, and Fredericks on English Breakfast Crack. In a different vein Beck soloed the northwest face of Half Dome. The next years saw a consolidation of Sacherer's achievements, but it was to be some time before free-climbing standards were raised once more.

Tahquitz Rock

While the Berkeley group pushed the standards of free climbing in Yosemite, Bob Kamps and Tom Higgins made a similar advance at Tahquitz Rock. First, however, they had to equal Robbins's landmark achievements. One of their first breaks was free-climbing the Blankety-Blank (5.10). Robbins heard about the feat and came back to duplicate it. Much to the delight of the locals, he slipped a couple of times, and his peaked white cap, almost a Robbins "trademark," came floating to the ground. Yet when Higgins and Kamps repeated several of Robbins's climbs, their respect only grew. Higgins took a long fall from the top of a nasty pitch on Robbins's El Camino Real.

In 1964 Higgins established Jonah (5.10), a climb that takes a blank, unpromising line, but rather than setting the stage for another advance, this climb seemed to Higgins to be the culmination of his Tahquitz explorations. The best natural lines had been climbed, and Jonah and his later Sham shared stances with already established routes. Though technically dazzling, the newer routes lacked the character of the classic climbs and had a contrived air about them.

Bob Kamps at the practice rocks. *Frank Hoover.*

Tom Higgins on the first ascent of Jonah,
Tahquitz Rock. *Bud Couch.*

Tahquitz remained the number one climbing area in Southern California, yet it curiously lacked the characters and legends that have enlivened other important rock climbing centers. In keeping with the Southern California mania for driving, Tahquitz was a commuters' rock. Unlike its New York counterpart, the Shawangunks, it never developed a strong social scene.

Back on the Walls

The year 1964 was not only notable for free-climbing advances; it was a heavy year on the big walls in Yosemite. Early in the season Pratt and Robbins made the second ascent of the West Buttress of El Capitan. In June Robbins was joined by Frost in the five-day second ascent of the Dihedral Wall. On the Dihedral Wall Robbins adapted the Jumar, a cam-action device developed for crevasse rescue, to big wall climbing. As in prusiking, the second followed a pitch by "Jumaring" up the anchored climbing rope; however, Jumars are far quicker to use than prusik knots. Jumars were also used to move loads up the wall. The haul rope passed through a pulley, and a Jumar was used to brake the load. A sling was attached to the haul rope with a second Jumar, and the climber stood down heavily on the sling to move the load. Before this innovation two methods were in general use. One was to haul the bags, typically weighing thirty to

forty pounds, hand over hand; in the other, a climber prusiked up a fixed rope with a haul bag suspended from his waist. These and other refinements in technique, such as the reinforced nylon "belay seat" and the nylon bivouac hammock, which provided some semblance of comfort in the middle of a featureless wall, helped the climbers in several ways. They speeded up the climbing, made it less arduous, and gave the climbers the confidence to attack ever-more demanding routes.

In the summer of 1964 Warren Harding returned to Yosemite, intent on climbing one of the few remaining virgin walls, the south face of Mount Watkins. He interested Pratt in the project, and they set out to recruit a third. However, the experienced were not interested, and the interested lacked the necessary experience. They had resigned themselves to a two-man effort when Chouinard, fresh out of the army, arrived in camp. He immediately signed on.

It was mid-July, and the temperature in the shade was in the midnineties. On the south face of Mount Watkins there was no shade, and the white granite bowl of the face acted like a giant reflector. They entered an inferno.

At the end of the third day the situation was critical. They were exhausted from the heat. They had barely enough water for another day of climbing, and the summit was two days away. The following morning the brilliant white globe of the sun returned, and by midafternoon a blank headwall

North America Wall, El Capitan.
The route goes up to the left of
the gray-colored "map" of the
continent, then through the two
shadowed overhangs in the
upper wall. *Tom Frost.*

blocked progress. They were approaching the end of their endurance, and for the first time they considered retreat. But even retreat meant another day in the oven. They doggedly carried on. Each in turn went up and laboriously worked on bolt placements until he was exhausted. Pratt and Chouinard were less experienced at bolting. Chouinard broke two drill bits, and between them they managed only to equal the three bolts Harding inserted alone. When Harding got back in the lead, he felt he must complete the job. Without placing another bolt he lassoed a stunted tree twenty feet above and prusiked up; the way to the top was open.

The North America Wall

By the mid-1960s Robbins had established himself as the preeminent Yosemite climber. He had made the first and second ascents of El Capitan's Salathé Wall, as well as the second ascents of the other three routes on El Cap. Although his partners on these climbs included either Frost or Pratt or both, it is fair to say that Robbins was the motivating force.

To be on top was fine, but to stay on top demanded a continual extension of the possible. Robbins needed a climb that would crown his achievements. El Capitan was the obvious cliff. The unclimbed southeast face was a wall markedly less promising than the previous El Cap climbs.

Royal Robbins, below, gazes at the route ahead while Chuck Pratt climbs, North America Wall. *Tom Frost.*

For the first time in the history of the sport, Americans lead the world. Royal Robbins, Chuck Pratt, Yvon Chouinard and Tom Frost after the North America Wall. *Tom Frost.*

Instead of clean granite broken by cracks and dihedrals, there is a massive intrusion of friable black diorite, which resembles a crude map of the North American continent, the North America Wall. Partnered by Glen Denny, Robbins made several probes in the fall of 1963. The following spring, together with Frost, they climbed the lower half of the wall. By now they felt sufficiently confident to dispense with fixed ropes on a new El Cap route, and they left no ropes after their reconnaissance.

The upper section of the North America Wall looked so questionable that Robbins and Frost wanted the strongest possible four-man team. Pratt was an obvious choice. When Denny appeared unlikely to make it, Chouinard was clearly the strongest contender, but he was as individualistic as Robbins. The two had seldom seen eye to

eye. However, for the North America Wall personal quirks were buried.

With the short October days and the 200 pounds of gear with which they started, they took most of three days to reach the previous high point. Their progress was the number one topic among valley climbers, and every day a small group gathered to watch. One day a sprightly man in his sixties hiked to the foot of the wall and gazed intently upward. He refused the binoculars that were offered, saying he could see quite clearly. At this stage they were entering a critical section where the route was in doubt; the various crack systems might not join up. However, John Salathé pointed out to the onlookers where he thought the climbers would have to go. He was exactly right.

Early on the afternoon of the ninth day the four

climbers coiled their ropes on top. They had accomplished the hardest big wall climb in North America (VI, 5.8 A5).

The Bolting Issue

On the North America Wall and elsewhere the leading Yosemite climbers made a major effort to avoid placing bolts. They would go into extreme A5 nailing and hang sky hooks from tiny flakes rather than drill a hole. They saw bolts as radically different from pitons. With bolts, climbers were free of the natural configuration of the rock and could go anywhere at will, provided, of course, they had the time and equipment. The unrestrained use of bolts opened up areas of rock where there were no natural lines and made success inevitable. These were the major objections to Harding's Leaning Tower route. However, the point at issue during the early 1960s was the use of bolts to avoid difficult nailing or to protect a free climb where better climbers would do without. Unskilled climbers were using bolts to overcome routes that were beyond them when using "traditional" means. The issue was hotly debated around campfires and in the pages of *Summit,* from Chouinard's "Are Bolts Being Placed by Too Many Unqualified Climbers?" through a whole spectrum of attack and counterattack. The purists wanted to keep climbing difficult. They despised the success-at-any-cost attitude of the bolting enthusiasts.

How Frank Smythe would have smiled to hear his arguments brought up to date!

In this debate the purists were partially successful. There have been outbreaks of bolting on established routes, but there is now nothing like the proliferation of earlier days. However, the issue of whether bolts should be used to connect up blank areas of rock, to create direct routes or "diretissimas," or even used at all was not then addressed. It has not been resolved to this day.

Due to his army service Chouinard had missed an attempt on El Cap's West Buttress, on which he had his eye. He was determined to make his own contribution on El Cap. After the four-man first ascent of the North America Wall the next step was obvious: a two-man push. His partner for the project was TM Herbert.

A then-essential item of a climber's equipment was a swami belt, a continuous length of nylon webbing wrapped several times around the waist, to which the climbing rope is attached. Herbert once mail-ordered a quantity of webbing. When it arrived, he cut off a suitable piece for a swami belt. As he did, he saw that the supplier had apparently marked the fifty-foot length with adhesive tape. Leading the crux pitch of the Mechanics Route at Tahquitz, he noticed that his swami belt was loose. When he reached the belay, he anxiously checked the webbing. The adhesive tape covered a makeshift join!

TM Herbert on the attempted second ascent of the Salathé Wall. *Tom Frost.*

Chouinard and Herbert reconnoitered their projected route, but while penduluming, they dropped the bolt kit and had to descend from about the level of Heart Ledge. On the fourth day of their all-out try, the rain began in earnest. That night sheets of water ran down the wall, and they huddled together to stay warm. By the sixth day they had placed all but nine of their thirty-one bolts. They were low on food and still had 1,000 feet to go. They considered retreat, but they were not sure how to do it. They had taken a diagonal line, and below them was 2,000 feet of unknown ground. Could they risk the descent with just nine bolts?

They carried on totally immersed in the vertical rock that was their whole existence. Days flowed together, and the pitches became indistinct in their minds. At nightfall on the ninth day they wearily pulled themselves on top of the Muir Wall.

The Muir Wall and the north face of Edith Cavell were perhaps Chouinard's finest achievements. Both epitomized much about his approach: a search for the ultimate experience. After the North America Wall he wrote that they could have carried on for another nine days. Two men had hauled while two had led; things were under control. On the Muir things were not under control. They had made the bold stroke, and they had pulled it off. Writing of the Muir Wall in 1968, Robbins characterized it as the "most adventurous ascent on rock ever accomplished by Americans."

The years that followed the ascent of the Muir Wall were a period of consolidation in Yosemite. The big guns of the early 1960s had made their mark and moved on. Their successors struggled in the hot California sun. The young Bay Area group spearheaded by Sacherer made remarkable advances on the shorter routes. They were obvious candidates for Grade VI. However, they were so much the inheritors of the Yosemite mantle, so overwhelmed by the big wall aura, that few of them could get themselves up for El Capitan. Indeed, when the Nose began to be repeated, the majority of the climbers were not Yosemite residents. Their lack of familiarity with Yosemite conditions was compensated by their freedom from the psychological millstone.

In 1966 a French rope and two home teams climbed the Nose, equaling the total number of ascents during the preceding eight years. The next year the trend continued. There were five ascents of the Nose and the third and fourth ascents, respectively, of the Dihedral and Salathé walls. Yet for every success there were several failures. Whatever reasons the unsuccessful parties gave, and they ranged from equipment failure to vitamin overdoses, the crux of the matter was that people were still scared of big walls. Nonetheless, the aura that surrounded the fabled Yosemite walls was receding. The super-climbs were within the reach of the newcomers.

The Yosemite Influence

In 1957 El Capitan lay untouched, and Yosemite was unknown. By 1967 a hardcore of dedicated individuals, totally committed to climbing, had pushed away the barriers and reached a new frontier.

Yosemite techniques and attitudes began to spread around the world. In the Chamonix Alps Americans made a direct start to the famed West Face of the Dru and solved the long-standing problem of the south face of the Fou. When John Harlin and Robbins made the direct west face of the Dru, it became apparent that *Les Américains* were ahead of the Europeans on granite walls. The locals were in awe of the technological wizardry, and American chrome-moly pitons commanded a high price in Chamonix. Before long Europeans adopted many of the Yosemite big wall innovations.

The Yosemite influence was not only one of pure technique. Ambitious Americans drew inspiration and confidence from the heady achievements in the valley. They felt that they were ahead of the world on big walls and adopted the Yosemite ideal of climbing without seige tactics. Successes on the Hummingbird Ridge of Mount Logan and South America's Chacraraju and FitzRoy owed much to Yosemite.

REFERENCES

Chouinard, Yvon. "Are Bolts Being Placed by Too Many Unqualified Climbers?" *Summit* 7(3) (March 1961): 11.

———. "Modern Yosemite Climbing." *AAJ* 13 (1963): 319.

———. "Muir Wall: El Capitan." *AAJ* 15 (1966): 46.

Cooper, Edward. "Squamish Chief: Climbed the Hard Way." *Summit* 7(10) (Oct. 1961): 10.

———. "The Squamish Chief." *AAJ* 13 (1962): 61.

———. "Direct Southwest Face of Yosemite Valley's El Capitan." *AAJ* 13 (1963): 337.

Dornan, Dave, and Chris Jones. "Yosemite: History." *Mountain,* no. 4 (July 1969), p. 10.

Kor, Layton. "El Capitan's West Buttress." *AAJ* 14 (1964): 79.

Pratt, Charles. "The South Face of Mount Watkins." *AAJ* 14 (1965): 339.

———. "Yosemite Climbing." *AAJ* 15 (1967): 355.

Robbins, Royal. "Half Dome: A Direct Ascent of the Northwest Face." *Summit* 10(3) (April 1964): 2.

———. "The North America Wall." *Summit* 11(4) (May-June 1965): 2.

———. "The North America Wall." *AAJ* 14 (1965): 331.

———. "Yosemite Climbing." *Summit* 12(6) (July-Aug. 1966): 22.

———. "Summary of Yosemite Climbing." *Summit* 13(2) (March 1967): 20.

———. "Happenings in the Valley." *Summit* 13(10) (Dec. 1967): 26.

———. "The West Face." *Ascent* 1(2) (1968): 2.

Roper, Steve. "Resume of Yosemite Valley Climbing: 1963." *SCB* 48 (Dec. 1963): 111.

Roper, Steve. *A Climber's Guide to Yosemite Valley.* San Francisco: Sierra Club, 1964.

———. "Overuse of Bolts." *Summit* 10(5) (June 1964): 25.

"Royal Robbins: Interview." *Mountain,* no. 18 (Nov. 1971), p. 27.

"Warren Harding: Interview." *Mountain,* no. 9 (May 1970), p. 15.

Weaver, C. M., and B. S. Traka. "Letters to the Editor." *Summit* 10(5) (June 1964): 30.

Wilts, Chuck. *A Climber's Guide to Tahquitz and Suicide Rocks.* New York: American Alpine Club, 1970.

Wilts, Chuck, and Gene Prater *et al.* "Letters to the Editor." *Summit* 7(4) (April 1961): 24.

Into the Seventies

A problem facing the historian is the imperceptible way in which history blends with current events. The latest achievements tend to overshadow earlier ones, and the hoped-for objective viewpoint may become hopelessly subjective. Today's "significant" climb may seem commonplace tomorrow. Conversely, climbs that we overlook may stand out as the key events of the era. Instead of forging ahead or cutting off the story at a safe distance in the past, we shall compromise. We shall focus more on the tide of events than the events themselves. We shall pick representative areas and performers rather than attempt to do justice to the gamut of present-day climbing. However, certain issues have evolved to a clear point since the late 1960s, and these will be treated much as earlier events.

The Big Wall Bogey

Yosemite Valley in the late 1960s was the most intense climbing scene in North America. The valley was *the* place for aspiring American climbers, and big wall climbing was their ideal. A glance at the list of new routes made on El Cap, however, would give quite the opposite impression. Whereas a new route was done each year from 1961 to 1965, the next four years saw only a new route on the less demanding 2,000-foot west face. Attention focused instead on the repetition of the earlier climbs.

By the spring of 1968 Robbins had made either the first or second ascent, and in the case of the Salathé Wall both the first and second ascents, of all seven major routes on El Capitan save the Muir Wall. Obviously this route, which still lacked a second ascent, was high on his list. In April he was on the Muir alone. It was a master stroke without precedent on El Cap. First, he led a pitch using a self-belaying system based on Jumars. Then he rappelled down and attached his haul bag to the rappel rope. As in a normal ascent, he jumared back up the fixed climbing rope while removing the pitons, hauled the bag, and was ready to tackle the next pitch. Small wonder that he averaged about 300 feet a day. On the tenth day he pulled over the top.

While Robbins upped the ante, his successors tried to get up as best they could. The majority who attempted El Cap lasted a couple of pitches before they were demoralized. Various unofficial counts put the failure to success ratio at eight or ten to one. Southern Californians Dennis Hennek and Don Lauria were consistently successful. They made the third ascent of the Dihedral Wall and in 1968 the prized second ascent of the North America Wall. The strongest influence in cutting Grade VI's down to size, however, were Northwestern-

Don Lauria and Dennis Hennek before the second ascent of the North America Wall. *Royal Robbins.*

ers Jim Madsen and Kim Schmitz. They were no sooner down from one big wall than they were up on another. Their two and a half day ascent of the Nose was a day faster than the previous best, and their similar time on the Dihedral halved Hennek and Lauria's time. Robbins commented, "Attitudes toward El Capitan will never be the same." Madsen was remarkably unconcerned on the walls. He would read a book while belaying, and listen to the transistor radio he brought along. In 1968 the cocksure Madsen climbed the Salathé in record time and repeated the Nose. In October he and several others hiked to the top of El Cap to check on Chuck Pratt and Chris Fredericks, who were weathering a storm on the Dihedral. Automatically taking the initiative, he rappelled down toward the climbers. It was a rappel from which he never returned.

In 1969 the new generation pressed home their advantage. The four ascents each of the Dihedral and the Salathé almost equaled the total number up to that time. Tom Bauman soloed the Nose, and two relative "unknowns," Scott Davis and Chuck Kroger, accounted for the third ascent of the North America Wall. Unlike the majority of those on the big walls, Davis and Kroger were not long-time valley climbers. They raced up from Stanford whenever they could.

In 1970 Davis and Kroger came to attempt a much discussed route lying to the right of the Nose, the Wall of the Early Morning Light, a name usually shortened to Dawn Wall. Several Yosemite "heavies" had turned back from the route disheartened by its apparently blank rock. Kroger and Davis were warned off by a rival team who had fixed ropes a short way up the climb. Not easily put off, the Stanford pair turned to the southwest face of El Cap and started up toward the Heart, a significant feature crossed by the Salathé and the Muir. Indicative of their relative innocence was the fact that they had never placed a bolt before. Nine days and twenty-seven bolts later they had completed the Heart Route.

The major deterrent to climbing the big walls was fear. Innumerable people talked about them. Many went through the ritual of gathering equipment. Some started up the walls, but only a few had the courage to go all the way and succeed. But the fear was going. It had been convincingly demonstrated that a first-rate climber could get up El Cap, and it was also apparent that you could be rescued. In 1970 three El Cap parties were helped to the top by climbers lowered from above. It is not clear when the rescue capability first existed, but by 1970 it was a proven fact. From their pedestal of terror in the early sixties, the big walls had become accessible to almost any first-rate climber. This was a development of great significance in American climbing.

Big Wall Ethics

During the sixties Americans established themselves as the preeminent climbers of big granite walls. It was not only their successes but their methods that put them ahead of the Europeans. Dolomite climbers had done remarkable "diretissimas" but had paid little attention to niceties of style. Repeated attempts, fixed ropes, and equipment hauled up from ground-support parties were almost routine tactics. In Yosemite the emphasis was on the self-contained climbing party and the single, all-out push. There was also a marked aversion to bolting whereas the Dolomites were the scene of all-bolt extravaganzas. However, as Yosemite approached the "saturation point" already achieved on the most appealing Dolomite walls, the new lines became less obvious and the number of bolts inexorably rose.

Robbins had established two routes on Half Dome's northwest face, and he worked to complete his "ownership" of the wall by climbing a much discussed route on the right side. After an abortive effort in 1968, he returned with Coloradan Don Peterson and finished Tis-sa-ack in eight hard days. They drilled some 110 bolt holes.

Harding was seldom in Yosemite during the late 1960s, but he still hankered after walls. His latest objective was the bald, almost featureless south face of Half Dome. As with the Leaning Tower he had no competition. Valley climbers dismissed the south face as too contrived. Harding never heeded valley pundits. He returned to Half Dome again and again with a succession of partners. In 1968 he and Galen Rowell were trapped high on the face during a late fall storm and were plucked off from above. It was Robbins who was lowered 1,000 feet to assist them. Harding and Rowell returned in 1970 to complete the route in six days. They had with them two Harding innovations: enclosed bivouac hammocks or "bat tents" and modified sky hooks that held in shallow drilled holes and thereby speeded the "bolting" process. In all, they placed thirty-nine bolts and drilled another 140 holes for "bat hooks."

Harding had bigger plans for 1970. He determined to climb El Cap's Dawn Wall, and he set out late in October with Dean Caldwell, who had made the first ascent of the Willis Wall's Central Rib on Mount Rainier. As well as the bat hooks they had another aid to speed up bolting, short aluminum dowels that were smashed into shallow holes.

They chose a different line from that taken on the earlier attempts. In part due to their 300 pounds of gear, they took twelve days to reach the level of the previous high point about halfway up the wall. There they were pinned down by a four-day storm and kept reasonably comfortable in their bat tents. When the storm passed, they climbed up an almost crackless dihedral, making some 100 feet a day. After twenty days 1,000 feet still remained.

No one had ever stuck on a Yosemite climb so long. Several climbers and Park Service officials were concerned about Harding and Caldwell's safety and even their continued good judgment. Inevitably, rescue plans were drawn up. Unfortunately, the Park Service's loudhailer was not working, and the two climbers were not asked how they were doing.

When the rescue team was helicoptered to the top of El Cap and contact established with the climbers, their feelings about the proposed rescue were emphatic, "A rescue is unwanted, unwarranted, and will not be accepted." Aided by the climbers' public relations man on the ground, the media were appraised of the unfolding drama and

Ensconced in his bat tent, Dean Caldwell weathers out the four-day storm on the Dawn Wall, El Capitan. *Warren Harding.*

converged on the valley. As the nation looked on, the Park Service had to explain away the strange events that led to the nonrescue.

Fortunately, the weather remained fair, and the climbers now had a good crack system to follow. On their twenty-seventh day they pulled over the rim to face a battery of television cameras.

The saga of the Dawn Wall was far from ended. The media hailed it as the greatest climb since Mount Everest, and the protagonists became instant folk heroes. Climbers were not so sure about the merits of the Dawn Wall. One aspect of the climb that could not be challenged was the guts that Harding and Caldwell had shown. While their tenacity was universally admired, their heavy reliance on drilled holes resurrected the bolting controversy once again.

Climbers hardly bothered to question the bolting on Half Dome's Tis-sa-ack and south face, the first probably because it was Robbins, the second because it was a route that few cared about. Why was the Dawn Wall different? It was a recognized problem on which others had tried and failed using "legitimate" means, that is, accepting a constraint on the number of bolts. The 300 drilled holes seemed outrageous, and then there was the incredible publicity.

Are bolts ever justified? A handful of first-class European climbers maintained they are not. If they are, what proportion of bolting is acceptable? The heart of the argument is that by the tedious but relatively simple expedient of bolting, any blank rock can be climbed, that bolting is not in the true spirit of mountaineering, that it threatens the foundations of the sport. It all comes back to Frank Smythe's thought, "It is knowing where to draw the line that counts in life."

While climbers up and down the country argued the merits of the Dawn Wall, Robbins decided to make the second ascent and "erase" the climb by chopping out the bolts. This was no easy deci-sion. In taking such an unprecedented step, he was laying his reputation on the line. He and Don Lauria spent the first day removing bolts. During the first bivouac doubts about their action assailed them. They continued to the top in another five days without removing any more bolts. Although the route was not erased, Robbins had made a strong statement.

The Dawn Wall become a symbol of the various schools of thought in climbing. Whatever the merits of the actions on the Dawn Wall, the purists' concern that bolting not get out of hand seems to have been realized. Subsequent routes on El Cap averaged around sixty bolts. Those outside the gut level of the sport may consider this concern over ethics far too heavy and serious. Does it really matter? The answer depends on your viewpoint. Does the sportsman take an automatic weapon to kill his tiger?

New Directions

While the Dawn Wall momentarily caught the attention of outsiders, the resident valley climbers were turning away from hauling and hammering on the big walls to concentrate on shorter climbs. Frank Sacherer's free-climbing standards were regularly equaled, and by the early 1970s Jim Bridwell, Mark Klemens, and others pushed on to the elusive 5.11.

At the same time it became apparent that the continual insertion and removal of pitons was destroying the rock. Even a single piton placement and removal may alter and scar the rock, and some classic routes are experiencing hundreds of ascents. Europeans never faced this problem because they have a tradition of leaving pitons in place. In the sixties British climbers started to wedge machine nuts into cracks. Later they developed special-purpose, wedge-shaped aluminum "nuts." Robbins advocated their use in 1967, though at that time more as a complement to pitons than a replacement. As climbers gained experience with nuts, they saw in them a way to preserve the rock. Moreover, dispensing with pitons was a new "game." The idea caught on fast. Today's beginning climber is unlikely even to own a piton hammer.

The concept of all-nut or "clean" ascents was also applied to the big walls, and in 1973 both the Nose and the northwest face of Half Dome were climbed on nuts plus hardware left in place by earlier parties. These were significant breakthroughs, but today pitonless ascents are becoming as routine as the pitoned climbs of the sixties. Indeed, nuts undoubtedly make many pitches easier.

In 1973 Sybille Hechtel and Beverly Johnson made the first all-female ascent of El Cap. Outstanding women climbers such as Mrs. Albert MacCarthy and Miriam O'Brien Underhill were rare in the past, but today they are increasingly in

Jim Bridwell on Butterfingers (5.11), Yosemite Valley. His hands are taped against abrasion and chalked to give extra grip. Note the nuts and chalk bag at his waist. *Keith Nannery.*

evidence. In 1965 Sue Swedlund and Irene Ortenburger climbed the North Face of the Grand Teton, probably the most arduous all-woman ascent then made in North America. Since then a women's team has climbed Mount McKinley, and Ellie Hawkins shared leads with her male partners on the North America Wall. Because of their lesser size, women are at a disadvantage where loads have to be backpacked or hauled. On shorter climbs they are on an equal footing with men, and several have reached a standard attained by only a handful of men in the sixties. In earlier times women tended to be camp followers; today they may outperform men.

Before the all-female ascent, Coloradan Jim Dunn made a solo first ascent on El Cap. A notable achievement that had eluded Robbins, it was emulated by others. Solo climbing was given a further boost by Peter Haan, whose ascents of the Crack of Despair and the Salathé Wall were impressive feats. Robbins and Klemens also made significant solos, but the boldest of all was Easterner Henry Barber's two and a half hour ascent of the Steck-Salathé. Barber's achievements on Sentinel and on the valley's hardest free climbs, including the coveted Butterballs (5.11), point up the skills of climbers trained outside the valley. Previously, it was the valley residents who picked off the prized free climbs. Now climbers from the East and Colorado vied with the locals.

The East

During the mid-1960s several good climbers came to the fore at the Shawangunks. Former junior, national, parallel bar medal winner Dick Williams made two contributions: He was the first person aggressively to seek out new routes after the pause in exploration that followed the publication of Gran's guidebook, and he introduced the concept of swinging for holds. Before he developed this technique, it was thought essential to keep three points of contact with the rock at all times and to move ahead with deliberation. In contrast, he made dynamic moves for out-of-reach holds.

Williams wanted badly to make the third ascent of the vaunted M.F. but never quite felt ready. One day he ran into John Hudson and saw his chance. Trying to appear casual, he brought up the subject of M.F.

"Wanna lead it?" he asked warily.

"Sure," replied Hudson.

He tied into the rope and led the crux in style. Hudson's regular partner was mathematician Rich Goldstone, who concentrated on climbing, gymnastics, and math to the virtual exclusion of all else. This forceful team made early ascents of many of the better Shawangunk routes.

Despite the achievements of the newcomers, Jim McCarthy remained a force to be reckoned with. Talented newcomers who arrived in the late sixties accepted the 5.10 standard as a given. Their goal was to climb to that standard and if possible surpass it. But when McCarthy had arrived in the early fifties, 5.7 was about the limit. In a major way he had been instrumental in the push from grade to grade, and at every advance he carried the psychological load.

During 1967 McCarthy and Goldstone forced their way up Try Again and Coexistence (5.10). The name of the first climb is apt; it highlights the method used to overcome the hardest routes. They were now like a set of interconnected boulder

Rich Goldstone on Matinée, Shawangunks.
Courtesy Royal Robbins.

moves, and it appeared impossible to lead them "on sight." Like Ament in Colorado the Shawangunk climbers worked on a new route over a period of days or weeks. A key move, a place for a piton, a resting position were each worked out; then they were connected up.

The concept of routes that demanded the virtuosity of bouldering was taken a step further by physicist John Stannard. He had been a regular at the Shawangunks for years without creating sparks. In the midsixties he had a change of heart. He decided to become a top climber and worked on the hardest routes until he mastered them. He then attempted to free-climb the roof on Foops, a project for which he had trouble recruiting belayers. It was bad enough to stand around holding the rope, but if Stannard got up, it would be even worse; the belayer would have to try to follow the pitch. After Stannard mastered Foops (5.11) in 1967, he took the bouldering approach a step further on Persistent, a single overhanging pitch on which he worked a reputed 160 days!

Interest in free-climbing accelerated with the 1972 publication of Williams's new guide to the Shawangunks. It listed thirty-eight routes that required aid. A year later all but five had been climbed free. The prime movers were Stannard, Henry Barber, who repeated Foops, Steve Wunsch, who made the second ascent of Persistent, and John Bragg, who freed Kansas City.

Coincident with the free-climbing boom came recognition of the piton problem. Stannard was

Henry Barber clips into a fixed piton on No Man's Land (5.10), Shawangunks. *Hether Hurlbut.*

principal spokesman for preserving the rock. Through his *Eastern Trade* newsletter he promoted the switch to nuts and fixed pitons. Climbers quickly saw the sense in this approach, and by 1973 they were donating their now redundant chrome-moly pitons to be left in place. The turn-about in attitude toward pitons came faster in the Shawangunks than in California. While valley climbers carried pitons "just in case," Easterners were totally committed to the cause.

Winter Climbing

While East Coast rock climbing surged ahead, winter ice climbing remained static. It was still carried out in much the same manner as in Hunt-ington Ravine in the 1930s: When the angle steep-ened, you cut footholds in the ice. It was a labor-ious, unglamorous affair and had little appeal to young rock tigers. In the late sixties Yvon Chouin-ard studied ice climbing technique and concluded that the French had the best method. They adopted a radical body position in order to place their crampons flat on the ice. It was effective on the relatively soft snow-ice of the Alps, but on hard ice it was hopeless. It was a blind alley, but it started Chouinard thinking. If the pick of the ice axe is sufficiently drooped, he discovered, it will give a secure hold in hard water-ice. Armed with such an axe in one hand, an ice hammer in the other, and sharp crampons, climbers can claw

their way up steep ice without step cutting. Favorite old routes were completed in a fraction of the usual time, and climbers turned to new challenges. Previously unthinkable routes are now under attack, from ice-covered rock climbs on Cannon Mountain to frozen waterfalls in Canada. Ice climbing gear had remained essentially the same for fifty years; it was left to Americans to rethink the tools and change the sport.

Colorado

Pat Ament and Larry Dalke continued to dominate Colorado rock climbing through the late sixties. Ament free-climbed the Northwest Corner of the Bastille (5.10) and soloed T2. Dalke freed XM (5.10) and soloed the second ascent of the Direct North Face of the Maiden (A5). By the seventies both had gone on to other interests. Jim Erickson and Ament's protégé Roger Briggs moved to the forefront. The impressive achievements of the new generation are underlined by Erickson and Duncan Ferguson's ascent of Naked Edge (5.11).

In the late sixties climbers employed gymnastic chalk to improve their grip on extreme boulder problems. Before long chalk was used on the crags, and climbers felt naked without chalk bags dangling from their waist. From chalk it was a

John Bouchard on the first ascent of Hands Across the Water, Mount Katahdin, Maine. In 1974 he soloed the north face of the Grands Charmoz, French Alps. *Rick Wilcox.*

Steve Wunsch on the first pitch of Guenese (5.10), Eldorado Canyon. *Dudley Chelton.*

short step to taping the hands against abrasion and using tincture of benzoin to toughen them. What portion of the claimed benefits is tangible and what portion psychological is hard to say, but the use of chalk does have a pronounced visual effect. There is hardly a popular rock climb on which the holds are not coated with chalk. The use of these aids raises the question of how climbers will react when an adhesive is devised for hands and feet. A few of the top rock climbers in Colorado have made their decision. They are climbing without chalk, tape, or tincture of benzoin.

By the late sixties the Diamond on Longs Peak had nine routes. The big wall fear had largely gone, and it was time for new challenges. The Diamond was climbed predominantly free; Bill Forrest soloed it in 1970; and Kris Walker duplicated that achievement twice in the following years. These two climbers combined in 1973 to solve a long-standing problem, the Painted Wall in the Black Canyon of the Gunnison (VI).

The Mountains

By the midseventies rock climbers had achieved mastery over their environment. The big walls had lost their luster, and climbers compensated by doing them predominantly free, with nuts, or for speed. Cragsmen concentrated on free climbing and nut protection where their forebears had struggled in aid slings.

In the mountains there was no such mastery of the environment. The hardest alpine routes retained their terrors. Where the issue was in doubt, there was little concern for niceties of style. In the already intensively explored Tetons, however, style was important. It is thus no surprise that winter alpinism developed faster there than elsewhere. Under winter conditions the best-known "trade route" may pose a major problem and turn back first-rate mountaineers. The preeminent Teton winter specialists have been George Lowe, his cousin Jeff Lowe, and others of their Utah companions. When they first tackled the winter Tetons, they did so in sizable parties, but as their confidence increased, they went in two-man ropes. Their winter ascents of the North Face and the combined Black Ice Couloir and west face of the Grand Teton were outstanding achievements.

The North Cascades are at a much different stage of development from the Tetons. There barriers of distance and weather still deter all but the most singleminded. As a consequence the range has yet to yield some of its finest secrets. Old warhorse Mount Rainier, however, has once more become the vehicle for advances. In 1970 Alex Bertulis and Jim Wickwire made a winter ascent of the Willis Wall.

A paucity of climbers is also apparent in the remote Canadian ranges, although accessible areas like the Bugaboos are now well developed. Major climbs of the sixties like the north faces of Robson and Edith Cavell are oft-repeated favorites, and

the search for difficulty has been carried onto some of the largest walls in the Rockies. As in the North Cascades, winter ascents of the big routes lie in the future.

Alaska and the Yukon

Whereas alpine climbing has continued in the directions laid down in the 1960s, a new trend is evident in the North. Throughout the sixties the norm of climbing on major Alaskan routes was the employment of fixed ropes and multiple camps, the "Alaska wave." This was similar to Himalayan and many, though by no means all, Andean climbs. (Except for McKinley, Alaskan peaks pose no real acclimatization problems.) Why this tactic was accepted in Alaska and the Yukon when it never was in the Alps or the rest of Canada is not clear, but it is probably due to a combination of circumstances. First, it became hallowed by tradition. Second, the weather is worse in Alaska, and climbers were reluctant to be caught away from a secure camp. Third, the bulk of Alaskan climbers were not first-rate alpinists and were unaware of the possibilities of climbing "alpine style."

Just as the big walls lost their aura and the North Face of the Grand Teton became an everyday route, so the North is less fearsome today. As climbers gain more confidence in the North, the distinction we drew in earlier chapters between "alpine" and "Alaskan" will be inappropriate. At present, routes are climbed in both styles: Alaskan on the north ridge of Mount Kennedy and the east ridge of Mount Huntington; alpine on the south face of Devils Thumb and the southeast face of Mount Dickey. In 1972 a six-man group repeated the west rib of McKinley's south face. Although they were pinned down by a storm for thirty-six hours, they completed the route in three and a half days, a convincing demonstration that alpine-style ascents are feasible on McKinley.

Reflections

In 1969 the Yosemite Park and Curry Company started a climbing school. In view of the long-standing antagonism toward climbers, this seemed faintly ridiculous. However, the action merely confirmed that climbing, hitherto the preserve of social misfits, had been assimilated into the mainstream. With the rise of the environmental movement in the late 1960s, there was a headlong rush to the outdoors. Backpacking blossomed, equipment stores multiplied, and every college student seemed to own a pair of hiking boots.

The increase in the number of climbers is the most far-reaching change of the past decade. It is not uncommon to have to queue up at the base of a popular climb, to see cracks scarred by repeated piton placements, and to find a proliferation of eroded trails at climbing areas. Heavy use has led to the "closing" of climbs and the imposition of head count limits in various areas. Climbers whose experience dates back to the early sixties recall the uncrowded crags of their youth and find it hard to accept the present-day climbing scene. "Ah, the good old days."

Against a certain amount of crowding and environmental damage must be set the newcomers' experience. It may not be the pioneering of earlier days, but it *is* equally valid. Each generation comes to the mountains anew and creates its own experience. Climbers are still intimidated by their first lead. There are still "last problems," still psychouts, still good times.

There are problems associated with the growth of the sport, but most of them will be solved. The rapid switch to nuts could not have been foreseen, yet it is now accomplished. Shawangunk climbers are working on trail maintenance, and others have been to McKinley specifically to remove trash.

Of all the issues that preoccupy climbers, this author believes there are two which pose a substantive threat, access and regulation. These issues were minor or nonexistent in the past, of course, because there were so few people in the outdoors. Today public agencies have begun to limit access to certain heavily used wilderness areas. The action may be desirable in areas of the Sierra Nevada set aside as bighorn sheep refuges but seems absurd on Mount Rainier. What damage can

climbers inflict on snow slopes? Climbers and conservationists were allies in the past; indeed, many conservation leaders are old-time climbers. However, they may not always agree in the future. Conservationists may support the concept of limited access; climbers may want to get to the mountains. The author believes that preventing foot travel on public lands is fundamentally wrong. It is reasonable, even desirable, to curtail horse packing and motorized sightseeing, but to lock out hikers is to lose sight of the purpose of our public lands. The federal authorities justify the restrictions by terms such as "carrying capacity" and "quality wilderness experience." Their present tactic is dispersion; spread the use to less frequented areas. This frustrates the visitor, who wanted to climb Rainier; it leads to the progressive deterioration of many areas rather than a few; and it certainly will not "save" Rainier. Further, why insist that all hikers want solitude; for most, their hiking is a social activity. Must we have a government-decreed quality wilderness experience?

Local rock climbing areas are more vulnerable to restrictions because access can easily be cut off. Some are threatened by quarrying, others by development, yet others by the owner's concern over property damage. Even more than the mountains, it is these local areas that will be the battlegrounds of the future. There is little that authorities can do to a Grand Teton; they could destroy an Eldorado Canyon. Climbers must be alert to these threats and work together to resolve them. When the president of the American Alpine Club leads a "climb-in" demonstration, we will have made a potent commitment to the future.

The hydra of regulation and control has been prompted by the rising number of accidents and rescue operations. Although volunteer rescue groups have done an excellent job, they are not generally permitted to operate inside United States national parks. There, complex rescues are carried out by rangers and climbers. These operations have cost tens of thousands of dollars, not least because the Park Service pays the climbers so that all parties are covered by insurance. Rescue pay has been a major source of income to a select few Yosemite climbers. When a public agency becomes responsible for our safety and pulls us off the crags, we must expect them to become increasingly concerned about what we climb. The precedents are clear. Either we bring our affairs into order by taking a greater responsibility for rescues, or the government will want to regulate us. We should never accept payment for rescue work, and we may well have to initiate a rescue fund or insurance scheme. It will be a small price to stay free of permits and certificates.

The old laissez-faire climbing of yesterday is dead and gone. The mountains and crags are no longer inexhaustible, and we must leave them in good condition for our successors. The sheer number of climbers will cause disruptions, but these can be handled. However, if our freedom to climb is seriously curtailed, the sport will have changed in a fundamental way.

The basic premise for this work is that certain persons and events shaped American climbing. The emphasis on performance is intentional but perhaps unfortunate. In our concern over who was first or best, we may have lost sight of the essence of the sport. The real value of climbing is not in categorization but in personal experience. The greatest benefit the author obtained in writing this book was in talking with fellow climbers and in particular those no longer active. It was a constant amazement how they recalled the climbs of their youth. Friends, triumphs, failures, whole conversations came clearly across the years. More than once tears came to their eyes as they relived the past. Clearly, their mountain experiences were among the most powerful they ever had and provided a reference point throughout their lives. Similar experiences are open to us today: sun-warmed rock, a valley draped in cloud, a high bivouac, the crunch of frozen snow. We have analyzed climbing long enough. I am going to throw a rope into my pack and head for the mountains. Care to join me?

REFERENCES

Allin, Phillip. "Letters to the Editor." *Summit* 18(1) (Jan. 1972): 42.

Almquist, Eric. "Letters to the Editor." *Summit* 18(5) (June 1972): 40.

Bridwell, Jim. "Brave New World." *Mountain,* no. 31 (Jan. 1974), p. 26.

Chouinard, Yvon. "Coonyard Mouths Off." *Ascent* 1(6) (1972): 50.

Creore, JoAnn. "Of People, Trees, and Environmental Extremists." *CAJ* 57 (1974): 49.

"Dawn Wall: Revisited." *Summit* 17(3) (April 1971): 38.

Forrest, Bill. "The Painted Wall, Black Canyon of the Gunnison." *AAJ* 18 (1973): 430.

Frost, Tom. "Preserving the Cracks." *AAJ* 18 (1972): 1.

Gruft, Andrew. "Editorial." *CAJ* 56 (1973): 49.

Harding, Warren. "Reflections of a Broken-Down Climber." *Ascent* 1(5) (July 1971): 32.

"Henry Barber: Interview." *Mountain,* no. 35 (May 1974), p. 34.

Horn, Rick. "Grand Teton North Face in Winter." *Climbing* 2(1) (Jan. 1971): 10.

Jones, Chris. "Yosemite Notes." *Mountain,* no. 7 (Jan. 1970), p. 5.

———. "The End of the Mountains." *Summit* 16(3) (April 1970): 28.

———. "Yosemite." *Mountain,* no. 13 (Jan. 1971), p. 8.

Jones, Chris, Galen Rowell, and Lito Tejada-Flores. "Letters to the Editor." *Mountain,* no. 16 (July 1971), p. 38.

Kroger, Chuck. "El Capitan Heart Route." *Climbing* 2(1) (Jan. 1971): 7.

Leeper, Ed. "Letters to the Editor." *Summit* 16(4) (May 1970): 41.

McCarthy, Jim. "The Last of the Mountain Men." *Summit* 17(9) (Nov. 1971): 8.

Messner, Reinhold. "The Murder of the Impossible." *Mountain,* no. 15 (May 1971), p. 27.

"Mountain Interview: Reinhold Messner." *Mountain* no. 15 (May 1971), p. 28.

Robbins, Royal. "Nuts to You!" *Summit* 13 (4) (May 1967): 2.

———. "Talus of Yosemite." *Summit* 14 (5) (June 1968): 33.

———. "Scree." *Summit* 14 (8) (Oct. 1968): 30.

———. "Incident on Half Dome." *Summit* 15 (1) (Jan. 1969): 2.

———. "Scree." *Summit* 15 (6) (July 1969): 33.

———. "Alone on the John Muir Wall, El Capitan." *AAJ* 16 (1969): 319.

———. "The El Capitan Climb." *Summit* 16 (10) (Dec. 1970): 30.

———. "Tis-sa-ack." *Ascent* 1 (4) (1970): 14.

———. "El Cap Commentary." *Mountain,* no. 25 (Jan. 1973), p. 22.

Rowell, Galen. "South Face of Half Dome." *AAJ* 17 (1971): 266.

"Royal Robbins: Interview." *Mountain,* no. 18 (Nov. 1971), p. 27.

Rubin, Al, and Paul Ross. "Vox for Vulgaria." *Mountain*, no. 21 (May 1972), p. 18.

Schenck, Jeb. "Mt. McKinley: Littered and Overcrowded Route." *Summit* 16(10) (Dec. 1970): 24.

Stannard, John. *The Eastern Trade.* Vols. 1–3 (April 1972-Oct. 1974).

Tejada-Flores, Lito. "Overpopulation and the Alpine Ego Trip." *Ascent* 1(6) (1972): 53.

———. "The Guidebook Problem." *Ascent* 2(2) (1974): 80.

Wickwire, James. "Mount Rainier's Willis Wall in Winter." *AAJ* 17 (1971): 288.

Wilson, Ken. "The Validity of the Bolt." *Mountain*, no. 15 (May 1971), p. 6.

"Yosemite Valley." *Mountain*, no. 19 (Jan. 1972), p. 10.

Williams, Richard C. *Shawangunk Rock Climbs.* New York: American Alpine Club, 1972.

Index

Abbot, Phillip: killed on Mount Lefroy, 37

Abruzzi, Duke of the, 53, 54, 178

Adams, Mount: east face, 306

Aemmer, Rudolf, 72, 91

Agathlan, 202

Aid climbing: attitude within R.C.S., 141; distinct from free, 297; introduced into Shawangunks, 214; 1950s, 236-237; tension eliminated, 201; vs. free climbing in 1930s, 134

Alaska: climbing conditions, 151; climbing style, 244, 378; European vs. home achievements, 331-332; Mountaineering in, compared to Yosemite, 155

Alaska Range: traverse by Vin Hoeman, 340

Alberta, Mount: first ascent, 42, 91-99, 319

Albright, Horace, 117, 118

Alexander, James, 103

Alippi, Luigi, 326

Allen, Samuel, 37

Alpenstock, 12n

Alpine Climbing: contrasted to rock climbing, 231-232; 1960s, summarized, 322

Alpine Club, 34, 37, 75; achievements in Canada, 50; founded, 33

Alpine Club of Canada, 75, 319; formed, 69; initiates Mount Logan attempt, 81

Alpine Journal: editorial on Logan, 86; interwar alpine climbing, 176

Alps: American climbers in 1960s, 330; early developments, 33; influence on Coloradans in 1950s, 227; Interwar developments, 175; preferred to Rocky Mountains, 111

Amedeo, Luigi. See Abruzzi, Duke of the

Ament, Pat, 297-298, 372, 374

American climbers: appraised by French, 1960s, 330

American Alpine Club, 238, 329; formed, 50

American Alpine Journal, 306, 347, 352

Amphitheater Lake, Tetons, 118

Anderson, Don, 306

Anderson, George, 27

Anderson, Lloyd, 150

Anderson, Pete, 59, 66

Annapurna, 219, 264

Appalachia: interwar alpine climbing, 177

Appalachian Mountain Club, 35, 46; achievements in Canada, 50; Alps, 111, 112; attempt on Mount Lefroy, 37; Canada, 49; Colorado in 1930s, 106; early skiing in New England, 116; Shawangunks in 1950s, 215-218

Appies, 287-288; vs. Vulgarians, 216

Arches Direct, 275

Argus, George, 257

Arnold, Jack, 140

Arrowhead Arête, 205

Arrowhead Chimney, Yosemite, 141

Assiniboine, Mount: first ascent, 43, 45; north face, 320

Athabasca, Mount, 41

Athabasca Pass, 4, 5, 7

Austin, Spencer, 190, 191

Ayres, Fred, 99, 124, 250, 264

Bacon, Paul, 336

Baker, Ken, 322

Baker, Mount: Coleman Glacier Headwall, 241; first ascent, 14

Baldwin, Jim, 200n, 347-349, 353

Barber, Henry, 371, 372

Baring, Mount, 241, 243

Barrill, Ed, 57

Bates, Bob, 154, 178, 265

Batkin, Jacques, 338

Bauer, Wolf, 145, 147, 148

Bauman, Tom, 366

Beck, Eric, 349-350, 353, 355

Beckey, Fred, 150, 234-235, 237, 292, 305; Canada, 316, 317-318; Devils Thumb, 232, 245; Mount Deborah, 258; North Cascades, 238-241, 306-307; Snowpatch Spire, 251-252; Tetons, 247; Waddington, 165-167

Beckey, Helmy, 150, 165-167

Bedayn, Raffi, 135, 140

Belay: deadman, in snow, 258; dynamic belay introduced, 129; first used in United States, 101; Outram's views on, 45, 47. See also Rope management

Bell, Charlie, 303, 305

Bell, George, 264-265

Berge, Richard, 241

Berques, Jacques, 143

Bernd, Ed, 332, 335

Bertulis, Alex, 306-307, 376

383